CONVERGENCE
Integrating Media, Information & Communication

Thomas F. Baldwin
D. Stevens Mc Voy
Charles Steinfield

SAGE Publications
International Educational and Professional Publisher
Thousand Oaks   London   New Delhi

For information address:

SAGE Publications, Inc.
2455 Teller Road
Thousand Oaks, California 91320
E-mail: order@sagepub.com

SAGE Publications Ltd.
6 Bonhill Street
London EC2A 4PU
United Kingdom

SAGE Publications India Pvt. Ltd.
M-32 Market
Greater Kailash I
New Delhi 110 048 India

Printed in the United States of America

Library of Congress Cataloging-in-Publication Data

Baldwin, Thomas F.
    Convergence: Integrating media, information, and communication /
Thomas F. Baldwin, D. Stevens McVoy, Charles Steinfeld
        p.   cm.
    Includes bibliographical references and index.
    ISBN 0-8039-5904-4 (hard: acid-free paper).—ISBN 0-8039-5905-2
(pbk.: acid-free paper)
    1. Communication. 2. Mass media. I. McVoy, D. Stevens.
II. Steinfeld, Charles. III. Title.
P90.B263 1995
302.2—dc20   95-37638

This book is printed on acid-free paper.

96 97 98 99 10 9 8 7 6 5 4 3 2 1

Sage Production Editor: Astrid Virding
Sage Typesetter: Andrea D. Swanson

CONVERGENCE

This book is to be returned on or b
the last date stamped belo
Fine 10c pe

For Jan, Susan, Andrea, George, Jessica, Haley;
Suzi, Paxton, Stefan, Robin;
Susan, Adam, William, Michael, Katherine

Brief Contents

Contents

Acknowledgments

The authors wish to thank the following people, who provided very substantial help in the writing and review of the manuscript, none of whom we can hold responsible for final product: John Abel, Richard Arron, David Childs, Steve Crane, Glenn Friedly, Wesley Heppler, Dennis Lewin, Barry Litman, Shelly Villareal, Harriett Wallach, Sug Min Youn.

The quotation from Ken Auletta in Chapter 11 is reprinted by permission; © 1995 Ken Auletta. Originally in *The New Yorker*.

1

Introduction

We now have a clear vision of an ideal broadband communication system that would integrate voice, video, and data with storage of huge libraries of material available on demand, with the option of interaction as appropriate. The telephone, cable, broadcast, and computer industries, relatively independent in the past, are converging to create these integrated broadband systems. Convergence is facilitated by federal policy in the United States, most dramatically by the Telecommunications Act of 1996 which opens all communications services to competition, creating a "digital free-for-all." The new legislation, according to its makers, provides a blueprint for the 21st century.

The convergence to integrated broadband systems requires a dynamic meld of technology—drawing upon the telephone, cable, and computer industries—and substance—drawing on television and information industries. In this chapter, an integrated broadband system is defined in simple terms. The history of the major events of the convergence is presented.

Much has already been said in media and in government about the information "superhighway." The participants in building the highway,

1

and many external observers, are prone to hyperbole. Some of the hyperbole results from genuine awe at the possibilities; much is competitive posturing. At the risk of understating the excitement that should rightfully be associated with the new communication services, we will be cautious not to feed the fire that is already somewhat out of control. A systematic, objective, and circumspect view of the current state of the art is vital to understanding the communication future.

Essentials of an Integrated Broadband System

This section briefly describes the essential characteristics of integrated communication systems. Chapters 2 and 5 will more fully describe the technology.

Information refers to any kind of communication: data, voice, visual, and audiovisual—that is, conversations, numbers and words, graphics, music, movies, and games. To accommodate all this, large bandwidth is important. Essentially, *bandwidth* represents the capacity of the communication system. The greater the bandwidth, the greater the capacity. Voice communication requires very little, but moving pictures a great deal. The speed of communication is also affected by bandwidth. If bandwidth is broad enough, large amounts of information move quickly.

Electronic communication is becoming *digital*. This means that information, even visual information, can be stored and manipulated by computers. It also permits transmission of messages—data, aural, and visual—in perfect fidelity to the original. Information and programs in digital storage can be accessed, transmitted, and used immediately or stored by another party.

Furthermore, with the necessary equipment, all information suppliers and communicators can be connected. One communicator can be switched to another or to a supplier of information. A communicator gets a direct, individual response from the supplier of information or another party; therefore, the system is *interactive*. Communication channels, including the processing equipment at each end, are referred to as *networks*. A network with the capabilities described here is what we have been referring to as an *integrated broadband system (IBS).* It may also be called an *integrated broadband network (IBN),* an *integrated broadband service, integrated broadband communications,* and a *full service network (FSN).* We use all of these phrases as there is no standardization and all are commonly used. When the term *integrated* is used, it helps to remind the reader that telephone, data, and video services are combined. When *full service* is used, the reader is reminded that a broad range of communication services and information (programming) access is included. An integrated broadband system is located in a particular place but interconnected to other systems (networks) elsewhere. A single company may operate full service networks in many different places. Or more than one company may operate full service networks in one city, each having only a part of the network or entirely duplicating each other. In any case, they will have access to each other's subscribers. Perhaps the most important characteristic of the integrated broadband system, in its most idealized conception, is convenience. All of it will be easily available to homes and offices. The product of an integrated broadband system may be the communication facility of the network itself, for example, a simple conversation between two people or, more elaborately, video conferencing. In each of these cases, the system has interconnected the parties to the communication. Or the product may be access to a body of information or program content, for example, a television program, an airline schedule, or one's own bank checking account. A person may interact with the information and change it, such as making a payment and reducing the check balance.

CONVERGENCE

The development of full service networks is dependent on information providers, designers and manufacturers of the equipment and software, the builders and operators of the networks, and the users. For the most part, information providers are film, television, and music producers; magazines, newspapers, and their distributors (including broadcast networks and syndicators); broadcasters; individual cable systems; game manufacturers; and online companies—but they could also be individuals because any subscriber can deposit information in the system. The designers and manufacturers of the technology are principally the computer software and hardware (data processing) industry, telephone and cable companies, and the manufacturers of their equipment. The process of creating integrated broadband systems closely allies elements of all these industries, hence the term *convergence*. These integrated systems are not likely to appear suddenly with all the bells and whistles, except in a few market trials. But advanced, integrated networks will inevitably grow toward the vision of the full service network. Some have held up the Internet as the model for an FSN. The Internet competes for attention and many types of services that telephone- and cable-based services will supply, but the Internet will need a broadband network for access to users. In all likelihood the major FSN providers will use the Internet as a transport mechanism to move products and services between providers and subscribers.

COMPETITION

The convergence of telephone and cable industry functions has been *accelerated* by the threat of competition in developing integrated broadband systems. The two industries poised to implement integrated broadband systems, cable and telephone, not only have an interesting opportunity to expand their product and markets but could be put in a desperate defensive situation under law designed to prevent the two industries from simply merging into a bigger communication monopoly. If the telephone company fails to rebuild and expand to a broadband network, it could be superseded by a cable industry that offers an integrated service including voice communication. If the cable industry does not anticipate the telephone industry conversion to broadband service, and stands pat with a one-way, video-only service, it could experience the same fate.

The Paths to Convergence

The industries now coming to a convergence of services have a history of independence in the United States. In fact, government policy sought to define them distinctly and keep them separate. Each industry, structured in part by government, took a different path to convergence.

TELEPHONY AS AN INDEPENDENT SERVICE

Telephone service, now 120 years old in the United States, began as a de facto monopoly service due to the awarding of an exclusive patent to Alexander Graham Bell for his telephonic device in 1876. For 17 years, the Bell Telephone Company exploited this monopoly and proceeded to develop telephone exchanges in the most lucrative markets in the United States. Competition came when the patent finally expired in the 1893. Multiple and competing telephone exchanges were built in many communities, and the previously ignored rural areas also saw the beginnings of telephone service offered by small independent telephone companies. Bell Telephone was a ruthless competitor, however, and soon reestablished dominance by refusing to interconnect competing exchanges to their own exchanges and to their monopoly long-distance network.[1]

The basic monopoly structure was frozen in the early part of the twentieth century, when AT&T agreed to be regulated in return for protection from competition. Over the years, AT&T withstood a number of attempts to break it up, but it was not until the 1960s that policy reform headed the telephone industry down the path of competition. Competitive entry into AT&T's business began with the infamous 1968 Carterphone decision, which permitted non-Bell devices to be attached to AT&T's network and progressed to the opening of the market for leased lines in 1975 and ultimately unrestricted competition in switched long-distance service in 1980.[2]

Policy makers never seemed to be fully comfortable with an unrestricted AT&T monopoly over telecommunication service. The outcome of one attempt at breaking up AT&T was the 1956 Consent Decree, in which AT&T agreed to confine its business to regulated telephone services. This ultimately limited telephone company activity in the emerging computer and information services markets, which were considered to be unregulated markets. Throughout the 1970s, many attempts were made to create a viable structure whereby AT&T could offer "enhanced services" (see Chapter 3) but their bottleneck control of the local exchange was always an obstacle for competitors. Other potential providers of information services felt that the Bell Operating Companies (BOCs) could easily undercut their prices by cross-subsidizing Bell-owned enhanced services. It was thus not surprising that when cable television began to take hold in the 1970s, telephone companies were restricted from owning any interest in cable television distribution in their own service areas.[3]

After 1980, AT&T found itself faced with competition in their core long-distance market, saddled with the costs of cross subsidies to their local Bell Operating Companies, and largely restricted from entering into new enhanced services such as electronic information and cable television services. More important, they also were confronted with the possibility that they would lose a 1974 antitrust case brought by the U.S. Department of Justice. Their solution was to seek a new consent decree, agreed to in 1982 and resulting in the 1984 breakup of the Bell system—often called the AT&T divestiture. The conditions of the breakup included the separation of the long-distance portion of AT&T from the local Bell Operating Companies, with AT&T largely freed to enter into new lines of business. The BOCs, however, faced a number of crucial line of business restrictions (see Chapter 3), including the continuation of the long-standing policy restricting them from providing information services (which by definition was thought to extend to video programming as a form of content).

We see below that telephone companies also had a short history in broadcasting and advertising. After following a different path for a time, it now appears that the divergence was only a brief interlude, historically speaking.

TELEPHONY AND BROADCASTING

AT&T acquired radio broadcasting rights through a key patent and was active in broadcasting in the 1920s. Cross-licensing agreements, resulting from an industry-government collaboration, allowed sharing of patents to make broadcasting possible for four companies—General Electric, Westinghouse, RCA, and AT&T. The agreements also apportioned rights in the communication industry: GE and Westinghouse as manufacturers, RCA for sales, and AT&T with exclusive rights in transmitters, which preserved its monopoly in wired and wireless telephony. AT&T used the cross-licensing agreement to assert an exclusive right to network stations, extending the WEAF signal from New York first to a station in Massachusetts and later to other stations interconnected with AT&T long-distance lines. The company maintained a *common carrier* attitude toward broadcasting, leasing time on its radio station, WEAF, to companies with a message. This concept came to be known as "toll" broadcasting and was a forerunner to broadcast advertising.

Complaints by the parties to the cross-licensing arrangements, which eventually led to a second cross-licensing agreement, left AT&T with exclusive rights to wired telephony, two-way wireless communication, and the terrestrial interconnection for broadcast networks and remote broadcasts. AT&T relinquished its ownership of all its broadcasting facilities and agreed not to come back into broadcasting.[4]

This separation of telephony and broadcasting has remained. But in recent years, the telephone industry has lobbied to be allowed to become programmers of their own video services. In the meantime, telephone companies have formed film and television production organizations.

BROADCASTING AND CABLE

A number of trade-offs to make broadcast television local, and to have a diversity of programming for the greatest number of people, left some households in the broad expanse of the United States without any television signal. As a result of a long debate in the 1940s, a table of assignments for frequencies was settled by the Federal Communications Commission (FCC) on the principle that as many locations as possible would have at least one television service. This principle, known as *localism*, was intended to provide opportunity for local selection and production of programming. A second principle, more related to the economics of television, would have as many people as possible with access to multiple stations, putting several frequencies in the most populated areas. The execution of these policies meant relatively low-power transmitters propagating signals over about a 75-mile radius. Because it had the most convenient propagation characteristics, the VHF band of frequencies was favored. After the table of assignments was settled in 1952, VHF commercial television stations were put on the air quickly on nearly every assigned frequency.

As a result of localism and the maximization of service to high-density populations, as well as the vast expanses with small populations, television did not reach some areas of the United States. These areas without any television signal were called *white areas*. Still other areas of modest population density had only one or two stations assigned, and topography denied the line-of-sight television signals to other places. Because television was so immensely and immediately popular, the people in the white areas and the limited-channel communities soon sensed their deprivation. Entrepreneurial owners of appliance stores and radio repair shops began to look for a way into the television market by building master antennae on high ground to bring in weak signals from a distance. Signals were also brought in by microwave relay—a line-of-sight, point-to-point transmission often requiring several relays to get to a remote community. The collected signals were transported to individual households by coaxial cable. The system was referred to as *community antenna television* (CATV).

From 1949, the number of CATV systems grew slowly but steadily. By 1961, there were 700 community antenna TV systems. Growth accelerated so that in 1971 there were 2,750 systems serving nearly 6 million homes.[5] During this period, CATV was first providing television to homes that were entirely out of rooftop antenna range of any television stations. Later, CATV came to be a business of filling out the complement of television services in communities that had less than the three commercial networks. Through much of this period, it was viewed as ancillary to the broadcast service, staying a community antenna or *retransmission* service.

In the 1970s, the concept of originating programs by CATV systems became established. Quite modest programming was fed directly into the cable from simple studios and fixed cameras on message bulletins and weather instruments, which grew to a studio and remote production capability. When satellites began to be used to distribute programs to CATV in the mid-1970s, such as WTBS superstation and HBO, the additional programming allowed CATV operators to begin serving large cities, supplementing broadcasting, which was already in relative abundance in cities.

Now no longer only a retransmission service, CATV became "cable" and was tapping what economists have called a *consumer underinvestment* in television. According to Noll, Peck, and McGowan:

The available evidence from both STV [pay television, via broadcasting] and cable experience suggests the existence of a considerable unfulfilled demand for television programming, both of the conventional type and a few categories not well represented in the present program logs.[6]

Because of the access to recent, uncut movies and more channels, cable television became popular enough to attract some of the broadcast station audience. This generated more advertising and subscription revenue for cable operators, who in turn plowed much of it back into programming, leading to still more audience (and advertising dollars) and more subscribers—an upward spiral in growth.

As a retransmission medium *and* an originator of television programming, with service in the big cities, cable was in fierce competition with television broadcasting. It was incumbent upon the operator to persuade people in the homes passed by cable that broadcast alone was not enough. To gain subscriber penetration, cable operators were required to spend more money for programming, sometimes bidding against broadcasters.

Federal regulation does not permit ownership of broadcast stations and cable systems in the same area, but broadcasters could operate cable systems elsewhere and many do so. Broadcasters were also brought into cable by the ironic result of legislation designed to allow them to share in cable subscription revenue. The *retransmission consent* provision of the Cable Television Consumer Protection and Competition Act of 1992 (or Cable Act of 1992)[7] permitted a broadcast station to opt for carriage by cable systems in its area or require permission of the cable operators to carry the signal. This implied that the cable operator and the broadcaster would negotiate compensation of some sort in return for the permission. Although many broadcasters at first expected to settle on a cash compensation per cable subscriber, cable operators resisted. A major alternative was to grant retransmission consent in return for cable operator agreement to carry a new network developed for cable by either broadcast networks or individual stations. This brought many more broadcasters squarely into the cable business.

The ownership of both broadcast stations and cable systems, the general similarity in many of the business practices and program sources, indeed the competition between broadcasting and cable for advertisers and audience, and then retransmission consent, have served to thoroughly cross-fertilize the cable and broadcast industries.

CABLE AND TELEPHONY

This background sets the stage for understanding some of the more important paths to convergence between telephone and cable television companies. Technological developments, and especially continued digitization of the telephone network, advances in video compression techniques, deployment of optical fiber, and new wireless technologies not only opened the door to new service possibilities for telephone companies, they also lowered the barriers to enter telephone service by other companies.

The initial government policy was to keep telephone and cable services entirely separate except in the case of rural areas, where it was only practical to combine the services. If the telephone company did provide video service in these remote areas, it did not build a broadband system to accommodate both video and voice telephone. It was a coaxial cable network built parallel to the telephone lines.

Telephone companies have always been somewhat uneasy about a second wire, coaxial cable, to the home for communication purposes. Where they owned the utility poles, they were reluctant to permit their use or to make any necessary adjustments ("make ready") for coaxial cable. In a few cases, the telephone companies built the cable system, then leased it to an operator (a "leaseback"). This was permitted by the FCC if the telephone company had no equity interest in the cable company. But a telephone company that owns the utility poles could not force a cable operator into a leaseback arrangement.

The Bell companies (80% of the local exchanges) were prohibited from entering nontelephone services by the aforementioned 1956 Consent Decree. FCC rules, and later the Cable Communications Policy Act of 1984 (Cable Act of 1984),[8] prohibited cable and all telephone company cross-ownership in the same service area. The federal ban on cross-ownership did not extend to telephone and cable cross-ownership *outside* the telephone service area for any company not a part of the original AT&T system. The prohibition of outside-the-region video services was subsequently waived by the Justice Department for the RBOCs as well.

The United States Independent Telephone Association had petitioned the FCC to drop the local cross-ownership rules in 1982. The Cable Act of 1984 preempted the petition, but the matter surfaced again during the preparation of the Cable Television Consumer Protection and Competition Act of 1992. It was argued that if competition in telecommunication services were a serious objective of the legislation, then telephone companies should be permitted to enter the field, a position supported by the Bush White House. But attempts to amend the proposed legislation were ultimately abandoned in the interest of passage of cable rate reregulation, which was supported by almost all members of Congress.

Recently, as noted earlier, there has been steady movement away from the constraints of the 1984 AT&T divestiture. In 1992, the FCC developed the *video dialtone* policy, which permits telephone companies to offer video distribution services on a common carrier basis to programmers, but without telephone company ownership of content.[9] In late 1992, Bell Atlantic brought suit on First Amendment grounds in federal court against the ban on ownership of content, and won in August 1993.[10] All of the other RBOCs, and some of the independent telephone companies, followed suit.

Telephone companies launched a few interactive video services for public schools to publicize their capabilities. In fact, there has been a relatively low-key, but costly, war of demonstration projects between the cable and telephone industries, each first seeking to claim the interactive video field for itself, and later, more defensively, not to abandon it to the other. Several of the major cable and telephone operating companies have technical and market tests in progress. The major telephone operating companies had a great many applications to the FCC for in-region video dialtone services pending or approved by 1995.

RBOCs began to purchase or invest in cable systems outside their operating region in the early 1990s. The first major telephone entry was in 1993 when Southwestern Bell (now SBC) purchased Hauser Communications with a quarter-million cable subscribers in suburban Washington, D.C. U S West invested $2.5 billion in Time Warner

Entertainment. The most dramatic alliance of cable and telephone was the announced $30 billion merger of Bell Atlantic and TCI (the largest cable operator and a major cable programmer). Another was the $5 billion partnership of Southwestern Bell and Cox Cable (cable systems and programming). But both the Bell Atlantic-TCI merger and the Southwestern Bell-Cox partnership failed because of an inability to agree on the valuation of the companies, partly attributed to the FCC rate regulation of cable, which was reducing and capping cable revenues.

The proposed Bell Atlantic-TCI merger brought a rush of interest in cable and telephone alliances. Other cable operators were afraid to be left alone as relatively small video service providers against the huge combinations. The telephone companies *without* any partners were concerned that cable-telephone combinations would invade their territories and that they would not be as well positioned to develop full service communication systems when federal rules or court decisions eventually permitted in-region combination services. The failure of the Bell Atlantic-TCI merger discouraged massive integration of the two industries. The result was to focus development internally and to attempt smaller scale partnerships.

Just as the rules banning telephone company entry into video distribution have eroded, so have the barriers to cable entry into telephone services. Rulings requiring greater access to local telephone company facilities so that competing companies can offer local leased and switched telephone service were established by the FCC in 1992 and 1993.[11] In 1994, with some success, the cable industry began to assault the laws in most states that prohibit or limit cable company operation of telephone services.

Although the RBOCs sought relief from the line of business restrictions, they had to progressively open up the local exchange market to others who sought access. Hence, new breeds of local telephone and data service providers, often called *competitive access providers (CAPs)*, came into service. Competitive access providers are supplying large business telephone users with private lines and interconnecting geographically dispersed units of the same business within a city. These business customers of the CAPs are also connecting to long-distance carriers, bypassing the local telephone network. The cable networks were conveniently located to make the local interconnections. Some CAPs were initiated as subsidiaries of cable companies; others formed partnerships with cable operators through negotiation for leased cable lines.

OTHER ENTRIES IN VIDEO, TELEPHONE, AND INFORMATION SERVICES

Cable television did not have a complete monopoly on multichannel television. The satellites used to distribute programming to cable systems were received in rural areas, where the large C-band receive dishes were practical. A single dish rotated from one satellite to another, depending on the channel the user wanted. In 1994, DirecTV and United States Satellite Broadcasting (USSB) began high-powered Ku-band, digital service to small, 18-inch, dishes. FCC policy also encouraged multichannel, multipoint distribution service (MMDS) by freeing up microwave frequencies. By facilitating these, and services provided through other technologies, the FCC hoped to encourage competition among both wired and wireless multichannel television services.

Wireless (radio-based) access to switched telephone service represents another means of competing with local telephone companies. RBOCs themselves are significant owners of cellular telephone service. Because of FCC policy, however, every market has had a second licensed cellular operator that is not owned by the local telephone company. Increasingly, various industry players are recognizing that cellular telephony does not have to be purely complementary to traditional wireline service but might in fact be a substitute service. AT&T's massive buyout of McCaw, the largest cellular company in the nation, signaled the beginning of this new orientation, and clearly represents a competitive reentry into local telephone service by the former monopoly.

Newer radio services are opening the door to telephone service provision by yet other players, including cable companies. New radio spectrum, auctioned off by the FCC, has been designated for *personal communication services* (PCS) (see Chapters 2 and 3). Many believe that PCS will be a competitor to local telephone service, offering a lower-cost, but untethered connection for residential subscribers who may not need a traditional wireline connection. How these new telephone service providers will ultimately fare in the new battle between cable companies and traditional telephone companies is not certain. They cannot provide the bandwidth necessary for video services but might be able to steal a significant portion of the voice services market from the other players. Other competition for the information services niche of emerging FSNs will arise from the online services industry and, of course, the Internet. A brief history of the development of these services appears in Chapter 3, pages 63-71.

Challenges to Integrated Broadband Systems: Book Organization

There are numerous obstacles to the realization of full service broadband systems. Some of the political hurdles have already been mentioned. In addition, there are daunting problems to be solved or resolved in services, programming, technology, and operations. The book is organized around these challenges.

TECHNICAL CHALLENGES

Chapters 2 and 5 lay the technical foundation for the development of full service broadband systems. The technologies used for wired and wireless communication networks for television, voice, and data, as they are deployed today, are described in Chapter 2. Then, in Chapter 5, we describe the technologies, or technical capabilities, that create integrated broadband systems. The greatest challenges are in the massive design and manufacturing tasks necessary to bring off full service, integrated networks: (a) telephony over fiber, (b) bidirectional signals in all modes, (c) switching control and billing software, (d) video storage and retrieval, and (e) the subscriber interface. There will be some false starts in the engineering. Moreover, efficient design requires correct anticipation of the market demand. Much energy can be put into good designs based on wrong guesses about the market.

The technical chapters are written for the nontechnical reader. The concepts presented are important to a full comprehension of the communication future presented in this book.

SERVICES AND PROGRAMMING

Chapters 3 and 4 are devoted to the base of services provided by wired and wireless television and telephone companies as they build toward integrated broadband systems.

Full service broadband networks need consumer products. The builders must invent communication services and programming that people will buy. We have already advanced to a telephone service that connects us cheaply anywhere else in the United States. We can also be interconnected with most of the rest of the world. The majority of people in the United States have more than 30 video channels with short-term prospects of 300 or more. Many ask, "What more can we want?" The challenge is to answer this question with meaningful services, as discussed in Chapter 6. Will these new services go beyond marginal enhancements of what already exists? Not all analysts answer in the affirmative.

OPERATIONS, CULTURES, AND CAPITALIZATION

Chapter 7 discusses operations, business cultures, and capitalization. Convergence of communication and media into single networks with interactive voice, video, and data services requires industry leaders to cooperate, and probably integrate. Major players, cable and local telephone, are monopolists in their own narrowly defined markets. Business cultures developed to operate in these independent modes may not easily shift to a codependent, competitive mode.

The networks make available the products of a diversity of information suppliers, facilitate interaction with these materials, and offer live and stored forms of communication services so that individuals can create their own communication environment. The chapter describes the complex coordination and operating systems that must be put in place so that a network functions simply and transparently for the user.

Another challenge is to acquire capital. The cable industry is highly *leveraged*; most of the capital is borrowed. The debt is covered by cash flow from operations in a hand-to-mouth way. The cable industry will have a difficult time finding capital for long-term development that does not immediately generate cash flow. Local service telephone companies have profits more or less guaranteed by the monopoly, but cannot accumulate these profits into tremendous cash funds because traditionally they must distribute the earnings to investors. The shareholders depend on quarterly income, not long-term growth. Therefore, two of the major builders of integrated broadband networks face problems in capitalization.

MARKETING

One of the great challenges of suppliers to and the owners of full service networks is to find products and markets that are sufficiently attractive to consumers to make the entire development economically feasible. Chapter 8 presents the data available on the services that will be a part of integrated broadband systems and discusses the process of market testing with examples now in progress.

ADVERTISING AND SHOPPING

Chapter 9 examines the process by which advertising and shopping services will be offered. Interactive media systems are expected to transform television advertising and create a powerful medium for direct marketing and shopping.

COMPETITION

The expectation of competition across the spectrum of media and communication services is central to planning. Chapter 10 discusses the theoretical and popular beliefs about competition, monopoly, duopoly, and oligopoly and how the formal and popular versions of these theories apply to the development of integrated broadband systems. Capital might be more easily acquired, and the process of building full service wired networks quite deliberate, if monopoly markets were allowed. But if public policy prohibits monopoly in service areas, then revenues from similar services must be shared by the competitors.

Consumer demand and government policy have encouraged entrepreneurs to seek alternative ways of supplying multichannel television and telephone service. Wireless networks will substitute for, or take a part of, the business of wired networks, making it that much more difficult to generate adequate revenue to cover capital and operating costs.

COMMUNICATION POLICY

With all the competing interests in the development of integrated broadband systems, making public policy is difficult. National policy makers have advocated many approaches to the building of the communication infrastructure—from government construction and control to getting the government entirely out of the process. States and cities have different roles in dealing with telephone and video services and have not yet experienced full development of broadband services in which the two are combined and offering entirely new types of service. Interesting jurisdictional questions must be creatively answered. The public policy questions and various solutions are presented in Chapter 11. The government has mainly been adaptive—adjusting policy incrementally in response to economic and technical reality. Communication law reform in 1996 allows more dramatic change in the future.

INTERNATIONAL DEVELOPMENT

Integrated broadband systems are in various stages of development throughout the world. Chapter 12 explains why rebuilding the global information infrastructure to new standards will be challenging and disruptive. Integrated broadband networks are likely to be the foundation of an efficient, postindustrial economy. Whether or not integrated broadband systems actually rise to this level of importance, they will be used as the *symbol* of a progressive economy. Many countries are vying for leadership in supplying network technology and operational skills. The United States, Great Britain, and a few other places may be the laboratory. Recovery of the capital investment could be dependent on worldwide development.

IMPACT

The evolution of integrated broadband systems would be much less interesting were it not for a number of profound questions for which there are no simple answers. Will potential suppliers to integrated broadband systems have open access? At the other end of the pipeline, will consumers have universal access? Will information inequities (gaps) among consumers arise from the pricing of information and geographic distribution of services? Does the capital-intensive development of full service networks force a significant redistribution of consumer income? Will consumption of the products of integrated broadband systems be rational? Will we destroy valued characteristics of the original services as we restructure the system? What is the risk to privacy? How do integrated broadband systems affect the sense of community, of reality? How does the expansion of international intercourse change societies? Do media theories, which have evolved over many years from a relative stable media structure, remain valid?

The final chapter assesses the impacts already felt in the prelude to integrated broadband systems and considers the future. We hope most of the issues are here. The positive social impacts must be exploited and the negative impacts addressed to actualize the full human potential of integrated telecommunication services.

A NOTE ABOUT ABBREVIATIONS

The cable and, particularly, the telephone industries are inclined to talk in abbreviated terms. We have attempted to limit their usage in this book, but some are so common to the industries that only the abbreviation is used. The reader should get used to these terms. Here are the most common:

ATM: asynchronous transfer mode—a method of digital switching

BOC: Bell Operating Company

CAP: competitive access provider—a company connecting major business telephone users to long-distance carriers

CD-ROM: compact disc-read-only memory—storage device for digital information to be used in computers

DBS: direct broadcast satellite—broadcasts from satellites to homes

EDTV/IDTV/HDTV/ATV: enhanced-, improved-, high-definition, advanced television—all terms used for better resolution, and shape, of television pictures

FCC: Federal Communications Commission—an independent federal agency carrying out the details of telecommunication regulation

GII: global information infrastructure

HFC: hybrid fiber coaxial—a broadband system architecture combining fiber optic and coaxial cable wirelines

ISDN: integrated services digital network

IXC/IEC: interexchange carriers—long-distance telephone companies

LAN: local area network—a private computer network contained within one building or group of nearby buildings

LATA: local access and transport areas—a geographic area of telephone service (161 in United States)

LEC: local exchange carrier—a local telephone company

MMDS: multichannel, multipoint distribution service—a wireless multichannel television system

MPEG 1 and 2: Motion Picture Experts Group—initial and advanced standards for digitizing video

MSO: multiple system operator—a cable company with more than one system

NII: national information infrastructure

NTSC: national television system committee—the standard established for television in the United States

NVOD: near video on demand—pay per view with major titles starting every 15 minutes or half hour

PCN: personal communication network—a wireless telephone system (sometimes PCS, personal communication service)

PPV: pay per view—television paid for by the program

RBOC: regional Bell Operating Company—one of seven independent multistate telephone companies that were created after the breakup of American Telephone and Telegraph (AT&T)

VDT: video dialtone—a common carrier video service

VOD: video on demand—television programs stored outside the home, available at any time

Notes

1. H. Shooshan, "The Bell Breakup: Putting It in Perspective," in *Disconnecting Bell: The Impact of the AT&T Divestiture*, ed. H. Shooshan (New York: Pergamon, 1984), 8-22.

2. Richard E. Wiley, "The End of Monopoly," in Shooshan, *Disconnecting Bell*, 23-46.

3. Leland L. Johnson, *Toward Competition in Cable Television* (Cambridge: MIT Press, 1994), 54-55.

4. For more detailed history, see Sydney W. Head, *Broadcasting in America* (Boston: Houghton Mifflin, 1956), 77-124.

5. Sloan Commission on Cable Communication, *On the Cable* (New York: McGraw-Hill, 1971), 31.

6. Roger G. Noll, Merton J. Peck, and John J. McGowan, *Economic Aspects of Television Regulation* (Washington, DC: Brookings Institution, 1973), 32.

7. 47 U.S.C. 533.

8. 47 U.S.C. 521.

9. 47 U.S.C. 56.

10. *Chesapeake & Potomac Telephone Company of Virginia v. United States*, 830 F. Supp. 909 (E.D. Va. 1993).

11. Johnson, *Toward Competition in Cable*, 36.

2

Existing Telephone, Cable TV, and Wireless Technologies

n this chapter, current telephone, cable television, and wireless transmission systems will be discussed, together with some of the fundamentals of telephone, broadcast, and television technology.

Fundamentals

FREQUENCY AND WAVELENGTH

It is important to have an understanding of the basic technology of audio, video, and data transmission to make sense of the many rapidly changing, multichannel technologies, both over the air and over wire or fiber. The technology influences the nature of the service—its quality, capacity, and cost.

Electronic media transmit information over the air or over wires and optical fibers. The information may be audio, video, or computer data.

Telephone service and radio and television broadcasting are made possible by electrons moving in a wire or by magnetic fields moving through space. Because these electrons and magnetic fields alternate, or change direction, they are called *alternating current (AC)*. This alternation has three characteristics: how many times per second a complete alternation takes place (its *frequency*), how strong its charge is (its *amplitude*), and where a signal is on its cycle compared with another (its *phase*). Frequency is measured in *hertz* (one hertz—Hz— is one alternation, or cycle, per second). One kilohertz (KHz) is 1,000 hertz, and one megahertz (MHz) is 1 million alternations per second.

Radio and television broadcasting is made possible through *electromagnetic waves*, which can travel through the atmosphere, space, and, in some cases, through buildings and even the earth itself. In addition to frequency, electromagnetic waves are defined by their *wavelength* (the distance from the peak of one wave to the peak of the next). Frequency and wavelength are inversely related; that is, the higher the frequency, the shorter the wavelength. Waves of different frequencies have differing characteristics, which affect the uses to which they can be put.

CONVERTING SOUND AND PICTURES TO ELECTRICAL ENERGY

Before aural and visual information can be transmitted over a wire or over the air, it must be converted to an electrical signal. Conversion of sound is done using a *microphone*, which generates a tiny electrical signal in direct proportion to the strength of the sound wave hitting it. Pictures are converted to electrical signals by a television camera, which generates electrical energy in proportion to the intensity of the light of the scene being televised. Because these electrical signals are analogous to their original sound or light intensity, they are called *analog* signals. These signals are also called *baseband*, meaning that they are the original signals. Baseband transmission is often used to send information over wires. Telephone systems, and some computer networks, use baseband transmission.

MODULATION

Electromagnetic waves are generated by *oscillators*, which produce a pure wave of electromagnetic radiation called a *carrier*. To make these waves useful, it is necessary to *modulate*, or modify, the carrier to convey information to the receiving site. There are many forms of modulation, including amplitude modulation (AM), frequency modulation (FM), and phase modulation (PM).

The simplest form of modulation is to turn the carrier on and off, using a code to represent letters and numbers. Early radio systems used this type of modulation with Morse code to transmit information from one location to another. This type of modulation is called *amplitude modulation*.

Later, a more sophisticated form of amplitude modulation was developed, in which the strength of the carrier is varied in proportion to the loudness of voice or music. The louder the audio, the higher the amplitude of the electromagnetic wave that is generated. At the receiver, the carrier is removed and the original audio is recovered. Amplitude modulation is used extensively in radio and television broadcasting. AM radio and the video portion of television are amplitude modulated.

A more recently developed form of modulation is *frequency modulation*. In this system, the carrier remains at a constant strength but is moved up and down in frequency as the amplitude of the modulating information changes. The receiver then converts the changing frequency back to the original modulated information. FM radio and the sound portion of television broadcasts are frequency modulated.

The phase of the electromagnetic wave can also be modulated. There are many types of *phase modulation* in use in wired and over-the-air broadcasting. The color information in the television picture is sent using phase modulation.

SIDEBANDS

All forms of modulation create *sidebands*, which are electromagnetic energy adjacent to the original carrier. The width of these sidebands depends on the amount of information modulated on the carrier and on the method of modulation. Generally, however, the more information that is transmitted, the wider the sidebands will be. Because of these sidebands, carriers must be well separated from each other in frequency.

AM broadcasting stations transmit relatively poor quality audio, covering the range of about 60 to 5,000 Hz (the human hearing range is about 50 to 15,000 Hz). The sidebands generated by modulating this audio information on a carrier extend about 5 KHz on each side of the carrier frequency. For this reason, AM radio stations are always separated by at least 10 KHz.

A television picture contains huge amounts of information and, as a result, the sidebands that occur from modulating a television picture on a carrier extend more than 3 MHz (3,000 KHz) from the carrier. A television channel must be 6-MHz wide to accommodate the carrier and its sidebands.

Digital Systems

The transmission systems used for the purposes described above are *analog*; that is, the carrier is modulated in proportion to the strength of the information to be transmitted. In AM transmission, the carrier can be modulated to an infinite number of strengths, corresponding to the modulating information. Analog systems are efficient and simple, and prior to the development of cheap and fast computer chips, almost all transmission was analog.

Digital transmission systems are an outgrowth of computer technology and are a regression to the simplest and earliest form of modulation, in which a carrier is turned off and on to convey information. The information to be transmitted is reduced to a code of on and off, or zero and one, information. For instance, the number "1" might be represented by OFF ON OFF OFF OFF; the letter "a" by OFF OFF OFF ON OFF. This is how information is processed in computers, and it is how computers talk to each other over telephone networks. Each "0" or "1" is called a *bit*.

To transmit audio, the strength of the electrical signal representing sound is measured thousands of times per second, and the measurements are converted to numbers (0 being the softest, 255 being the loudest, for example). The digital transmission system then sends the codes for the numbers representing the loudness. On the receiving end, the numbers are converted back to analog signals, and then to sound. Video can be transmitted in exactly the same way.

Digital systems have the advantage of high accuracy; that is, the received information will be an exact copy of what is transmitted.

This is why CD audio systems' sound quality is so good. Another advantage of digital transmission is that signals can be processed by computers to enhance and compress information (see the section "Bandwidth Compression" in Chapter 5).

Until very recently, digital transmission has been too expensive for most applications. As the cost of digital processing equipment has dropped, however, digital systems have become more economically attractive. Another limitation in the use of digital transmission had been the slow speed of computer chips, which made conversion of video from analog to digital impossible. Today, however, video digital transmission systems are being implemented for satellite and cable television networks and will soon be part of over-the-air broadcast systems.

Transmission Over Wires

Audio, video, or data signals can be transmitted over wires as well as over the air. Telephone networks use copper wires for transmission to and from individual homes. These wires are covered with plastic insulation to isolate the wires from each other, and then twisted together in pairs to obtain better transmission. The *twisted pairs* are then bundled together in cables containing from as few as six to as many as thousands of pairs. The larger cables can be several inches in diameter.

These cables have a very low *bandwidth*, or information carrying capacity. Originally, transmitting relatively poor quality voice (300 to 3,000 Hz) was all that was possible. Over time, new methods of modulation and digitization have increased the capacity of twisted pairs, and today it is possible to transmit video over twisted pairs for limited distances (see the section "ADSL" in Chapter 5). It is unlikely, however, that the existing telephone network will ever be capable of multichannel video transmission.

Cable television systems use coaxial cable, ½ to 1 inch in diameter. In coaxial cable, all of the signals are carried in the inner conductor, which is separated from the sheath (outer conductor) by plastic insulation material. The sheath's purpose is to keep signals from leaking out of or into the cable. Coaxial cable has a very large bandwidth capacity, in excess of 1,000 MHz. Cable television systems modulate information on carriers for transmission over the coaxial cable.

FIBER OPTIC SYSTEMS

Information can also be sent over optical fiber, which consists of a very fine glass strand, thinner than a hair. The fibers are bundled together, and a protective plastic jacket is placed around them. Even though the fibers are glass, they are flexible, and a fiber optic cable is extremely sturdy.

Optical fibers are so effective because, when light is put in one end, it can travel tremendous distances without significant *attenuation* (loss of signal strength). This means that information can travel over fiber optic cables for tens of miles without the need for amplification, as would be required for twisted pair or coaxial cable. In addition, optical fibers have very large bandwidth capacity, hundreds of times that of coaxial cables and thousands of times that of twisted pairs.

The light source used in fiber optic systems is the *laser*, a very powerful source of coherent light (all the rays of light from a laser are of the same phase). Fiber optic systems used in the telephone industry are digital; telephone conversations are digitized, and then used to modulate the laser. Modulation consists of turning the laser on and off corresponding to the 0 and 1 states of the digitized information. Fiber systems in use today have the capacity to carry hundreds of thousands of telephone conversations and hundreds of video channels. Fiber networks can also carry analog information (see the section "Fiber Optic Trunking and Backbone," below, in this chapter).

At the terminating end of the optical fiber, a *photodetector* is used to convert the light energy to electrical impulses for use by the receiving equipment.

Today's Telephone Networks

Telephone networks use a *star* architecture, with an individual cable pair (two wires are required to transmit the information) from a switching center called the *central office* to each subscriber (see

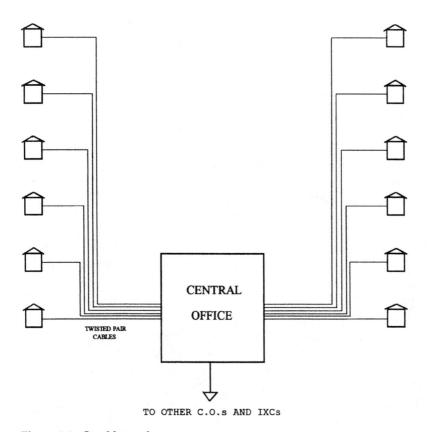

Figure 2.1. Star Network

Figure 2.1). These cable pairs, called *access lines* or *subscriber loops,* are bundled together into large cables containing hundreds of pairs and run along streets, either on utility poles or underground, to individual homes. If a subscriber has more than one phone line, a cable pair is required for each phone line. In the subscriber's home is the *terminal equipment,* or *customer premise equipment,* usually a telephone.

SWITCHING

The central office. The central office, or CO, contains the switching equipment to route calls to and from subscribers served from it, and to and from other central offices and long-distance carriers. Central offices are arranged by *exchange*, the prefix (first three digits) of the telephone number. Each exchange can have up to 10,000 lines (0000 to 9999). A central office may consist of one or more exchanges.

Originally, the switching function was done manually, with each phone line appearing on a panel in front of operators. To complete a connection, the operator would plug a cord into the panel to inter-connect the originating line to the terminating line (the line being called). Later, *step relays* were used to perform the switching function. These relays were controlled by pulses created by a rotary dial in the telephone. By using a series of step relays, one for each digit dialed, the call could be routed from the originating line to the terminating line.

Later, *crossbar relays* replaced the step relays, improving the reli-ability and speed of the switching process. In the 1970s, computers started to be introduced to central offices. Computers read the dial pulses or touch tones from phones and operate the relays to do the switching.

The latest generation of switching equipment is entirely *solid state*, that is, it contains no mechanical devices such as relays. With com-puterized switches, adding features, such as call waiting or call forwarding, can be done by changing only the software, or computer programming. This has revolutionized the speed with which the telephone network can be upgraded, and has greatly reduced the maintenance cost for telephone companies.

Calls destined for other cities (long-distance calls) must also be switched. Local exchange carriers and long-distance carriers have switching equipment to route these calls to the proper destination.

Packet switching. The telephone network was originally designed for voice communication. As the use of computers by business grew, more and more data were transmitted over the network. It soon became evident that the use of the public telephone network without enhancements was an inefficient means of carrying this type of traffic. One approach was for businesses to lease private, nonswitched lines from one location to another. These lines can be *conditioned*, or specially prepared to have less interference and somewhat higher bandwidth.

To more efficiently transmit data from one computer to another, *packet switched networks* were developed. Computer information is put into *packets* containing a *header* followed by the data to be transmitted. The header contains information about who sent the packet and where it is to go. Switches, interconnected by lines leased from telephone companies, route the packets to their proper destination.

TRANSMISSION

Trunks. Central offices are interconnected by *trunks*. A trunk is a circuit that can carry one or more telephone conversations between central offices. The number of trunks interconnecting central offices depends on the peak number of calls that normally takes place between the offices. If an insufficient number of trunks were installed between central offices, customers will frequently get a busy signal. Because trunks are expensive, installing too many trunks causes unwarranted costs for the telephone company. *Traffic engineering* is the method used to calculate the number of trunks required, based on gathering historical calling information and applying sophisticated statistical analysis.

Originally, trunks were cable pairs, each carrying one phone conversation, identical to those used for subscribers. Later, several calls were carried over the same lines. In the 1960s, methods were developed to digitize phone conversations at the central office and to send 24 calls over a single pair for short distances and over coaxial cable for longer distances. Later, these groups of 24 calls (called either T1 or DS1 circuits) were bundled together into DS3 circuits, containing 672 calls. DS3 circuits could only be sent over coaxial cable or over microwave radio systems.

Trunks also connect central offices to long-distance carriers. When a subscriber dials 0 or 1, the call is routed over a trunk to the long-distance carrier's *point of presence* (POP), the place where calls are switched and routed to distant locations.

Most of the new trunks being installed use optical fibers rather than cable pairs or coaxial cable, because calls can travel long distances without degradation and because thousands of calls can travel over a single fiber.

OUTSIDE DISTRIBUTION PLANT

Telephone cables are attached to utility poles, or buried underground, either in conduits or directly in the ground. Cables are limited to a few thousand feet in length, due to shipping and installation constraints, and must be *spliced*. An enclosure of some sort is used to contain the spliced wires. If the cable is large, a cabinet might be installed on the ground or on a pole. Smaller cables are spliced in housings located on the *strand* (a steel cable used to support the telephone cable) or in *pedestals* or *clotures* in the case of underground plant.

REMOTE TERMINALS

In the 1970s, when the cost of digitizing dropped, it became economically feasible to use *digital loop carrier* (DLC) systems to replace large cables. A single twisted pair, coaxial cable, or, later, optical fiber, carries many telephone calls, modulated on carriers from the central office to a *remote terminal* miles from the central office. At the remote terminal, the circuits are converted back to analog and connected to twisted pair cables for the last portion of the subscriber loop. Now, as new housing subdivisions are constructed, telephone companies often install DLC systems to serve them.

SUBSCRIBER TERMINAL EQUIPMENT

The telephone. The telephone consists of a microphone, an earphone, a bell or ringing device, and a dial or touch-tone keypad. In earlier phones, the microphone contained carbon granules located behind a metal diaphragm. When a person spoke into the microphone, the diaphragm vibrated as the sound waves hit it, compressing and expanding the carbon granules. An electric current (from the central office, over the twisted pair) was passed through the carbon granules. As the granules contracted and expanded, the electric current passing through was changed in amplitude.

This current then passed back up the pair, through the central office, and then to the other subscriber's phone. There, it went into the earphone, which consisted of an electromagnet located next to a metal diaphragm. As the electric current passed through the electro-magnet, it vibrated the diaphragm, which created a sound wave similar to the original sound.

Ringing was done by passing a strong alternating electric current down the phone line from the central office to the bell in the tele-phone. Most of today's phones use microphones that generate tiny electrical currents as sound enters them. Integrated circuits are used to amplify the signals, and electronic ringers are used rather than bells.

In phones with a rotary dial, the dial interrupts the electric current in the subscriber loop momentarily, one pulse for the number 1, two for 2, and so on. At the central office, the switching equipment counts the pulses to determine which number is dialed.

In touch-tone phones, the keypad generates two distinct audio tones for each number pushed. The tones were carefully chosen to avoid sounds that the human voice can create, so that the switching equipment could distinguish dialing information from speech.

Computers and modems. As soon as computers came into existence, telephone lines were used to interconnect them. Computers are digital, and the information to be transferred between them is digital. The telephone network is analog, so a way of transmitting digital data over phone lines was needed. The *modem* (a contraction of modulator-demodulator) is the device to do this. The modem takes the digital information from a computer and creates audio tones, one representing 0 (off) and one representing 1 (on). These tones are then put on the phone line. On the other end, the modem converts these tones back to 0s and 1s for the computer. Computers use the Ameri-can Standard Code for Information Interchange (ASCII) for alphanu-meric characters. With ASCII, each character is assigned a seven-bit code (plus one extra bit to detect errors).

The earliest modems could transmit at about 100 to 300 bits per second (each ASCII character requires about 10 bits to transmit, so 10 to 30 characters could be sent per second). Later, modems operat-ing at 1,200 or 2,400 bits per second became the standard. Now, modems operating at 9,600 or more bits per second are becoming commonplace. Fax machines have modems built into them, and typically operate at 9,600 bits per second. Even the fastest modems used over standard telephone lines (28 kilobits per second) transmit at very slow rates compared with what is desirable for computer users.

It is the bandwidth of the telephone networks (both twisted pair and switching equipment) that limits the speed at which modems can operate, and the current high-speed modems are pushing the theoretical limits for data transmission over phone lines. To get faster transmission of information, new telephone networks will have to be built.

ISDN

When the need for higher bandwidth for data transmission became evident, the telephone industry established a new standard, primarily for business lines, called *integrated services digital network* (ISDN). The standard telephone line is used to transmit two 64-kilobit voice or data channels. Much of the telephone industry's outside plant, especially in the primarily urban and suburban areas of business concentration, is capable of ISDN. Substantial changes are required in the switching systems, however, and ISDN has been slow to be offered in many areas. The development of high-speed modems for use over standard phone lines has reduced the advantages of ISDN, because a customer can send data at speeds approaching that of ISDN without the additional cost of an ISDN line.

Today's Cable Television Networks

THE TELEVISION PICTURE

The camera. A television camera works by converting the light energy from the scene to be televised to electrical energy. The light is focused on the surface of the camera tube. A very fine electron beam is focused initially at the top right corner of the surface, and a minute amount of electrical energy, proportional to the brightness of the light at that point, is released from the surface and captured. The electron beam then moves across the surface of the camera tube, creating electrical energy proportional to the light intensity as it moves. When the beam reaches the left edge of the surface, it moves quickly back to the right edge, but slightly below the top. This process continues until the beam has scanned 525 lines and has created a complete image, called a *frame*. Thirty frames are created a second. Many cameras today use Charge Coupled Devices (CCDs) in place of a camera tube.

The picture tube. In the receiver, the original image is re-created in the picture tube. An electron beam is aimed at the surface of the picture tube, which is coated with phosphorus. When the beam hits the surface, light is released proportional to the strength of the electron beam. The beam is scanned across the surface of the tube in exact synchronization with the beam in the camera (this synchronizing information is transmitted as part of the television signal), and the electron beam's strength is varied by the strength of the electrical energy generated by the camera.

The NTSC system. In the 1940s, the United States adopted a television system that is still in use today. The committee, the *National Television System Committee* (NTSC), that established this standard had to balance the quality of the picture with the amount of spectrum to be used for a channel. Better quality meant wider, and therefore fewer, channels. Six MHz was selected as the compromise bandwidth. Later, the *PAL* and *SECAM* standards were established in Europe, with somewhat superior picture quality.

Resolution. The sharpness of the TV image that is transmitted is called its *resolution*. In the NTSC system, the vertical resolution is 525 lines, the number of scanning lines used. This means that objects smaller than $\frac{1}{525}$ of the height of the TV picture will not show up. The horizontal resolution is about 300 lines, limited by the width of the sidebands that can be contained in a 6-MHz TV channel. To get increased resolution, more bandwidth would be required. PAL and SECAM systems have 625 horizontal lines and 25 frames per second.

Color images and quality. In the above, very simplified description, a black-and-white image is assumed. To get a color picture, the same process is used except that there are three camera tubes, one for each of the primary colors, and the picture tube has three different phosphorus areas, with three electron guns. When color was added to the NTSC system in the 1950s, it was necessary to find a way to put the additional information (now the light intensity information for three colors has to be transmitted—three times the information needed to transmit a black-and-white image) in the existing 6-MHz channel.

To make the color picture compatible with the old black-and-white receivers, severe compromises in color resolution were required. The result was a picture that has been adequate, especially on small screen TV sets. But, because the picture consists of only 525 lines, and because of the poor horizontal resolution, the picture is barely acceptable on large screens.

EDTV. One way of improving the quality of TV pictures is by finding ways of improving the NTSC system. Because technology has improved substantially since the 1940s, new ways have been found to transmit and recover more information within the existing NTSC format while retaining compatibility with existing TV sets. Such improved NTSC systems are called *enhanced definition television* (EDTV) or *improved definition television* (IDTV). These improvements take many forms; some require changes to the transmitter, some to the receiver. A major element in EDTV is the use of digital processing. *Within* the TV receiver, the analog video signal is digitized, then fed to a computer chip that modifies and enhances the image. The digital signal is then converted back to analog to be displayed on the picture tube.

EDTV systems are capable of improving resolution and color accuracy and increasing the number of lines in the picture displayed. They can also eliminate ghosts (double images). Today's best EDTV systems can produce pictures that are substantially better than standard NTSC pictures and, on smaller screens, are as good as *high-definition television* (HDTV) (see Chapter 5). A disadvantage of EDTV is that the TV screen is limited to a 4:3 *aspect ratio* (the ratio of the width of the picture to the height). EDTV, however, costs only a fraction of HDTV and is completely compatible with our current broadcast system. It is likely that EDTV will become a standard feature of TV broadcasting in the near future.

CABLE SYSTEM ARCHITECTURE

Today's cable television systems use a *tree and branch* architecture. A single cable originates from the *headend* (the cable system's equivalent of the central office). That cable, the system's *trunk*, is routed through each neighborhood. At various points, some of the signal is removed and fed to *distribution* cables, which go down each street to provide service to all the homes. The tree and branch system is a broadcast system; every household has the same signals available (see Figure 2.2).

The headend. The headend contains the equipment necessary to acquire, process, and combine all the channels carried by the cable system. A tower is located at the headend, with antennas to pick up the off-the-air channels. A *signal processor* then removes extraneous signals and levels the signal strength of the channel.

Most of the channels carried by cable systems are delivered by satellite (see the section "Direct Broadcast Satellites," below). Cable systems have several C-band (see below) dishes, 10 to 15 feet in diameter, to receive transponders from several satellites. Each channel requires a *receiver*, which captures the satellite signal and extracts baseband video and audio. A *modulator* then puts the video and audio on carriers.

Locally produced programming, such as replaying videotapes, local origination, or automated services (see Chapter 4) also use modulators to put the baseband video and audio on TV channels. The channels are then combined in a *combiner*, and fed to the distribution network.

The distribution network. Like the telephone network, the wires used in cable television systems are placed either on utility poles or underground. Underground cables, and aerial cables in coastal areas, have a protective plastic covering over the sheath.

Cable television systems use ¾- to 1-inch diameter coaxial cables for *trunks*. The purpose of the trunk is to carry signals from the headend to neighborhoods within the system. No subscribers are served directly off the trunk. As signals travel down coaxial cable, they lose strength and must be amplified. *Trunk amplifiers* are located

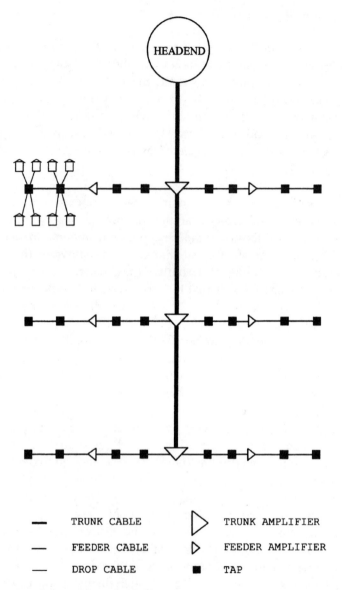

Figure 2.2. Tree and Branch (Cable TV) Network

about every 2,000 feet and are installed in small metal housings. Each trunk amplifier introduces electronic *noise* (which causes snow in TV pictures) and *distortion* (which causes lines and double images). As a result, cable systems must limit the number of amplifiers in a line, or in *cascade*, to 20 or 30 to keep picture quality good. Long cascades of amplifiers also cause poor reliability, because the failure of only one amplifier in the cascade causes all subscribers from there on to lose the signal.

At each trunk amplifier, a portion of the signal is tapped off and fed to the *feeder* or *distribution* network. The purpose of the distribution network is to deliver signals down each street to every house. Distribution cable is typically a half inch in diameter and is otherwise identical to trunk cable. In the aerial plant, devices called *taps* are installed at each utility pole where a house gets its electrical power service. These taps have one *port* for each house, which is passed by the cable system. In underground construction, the taps are located in pedestals. As in the trunk system, amplifiers are used to boost signals periodically, but no more than two are placed in cascade.

System bandwidth. Early cable systems carried signals from 54 to 108 MHz and from 174 to 216 MHz (i.e., broadcast TV channels 2-13 and the FM radio band; see "The Electromagnetic Spectrum," below). Later, systems were capable of carrying channels between 108 and 174 MHz (the *midband*, channels 14-22) and above 216 MHz (the *superband*, channels 23 and up). Cable system channel numbers are not the same as UHF broadcast channels. For instance, channel 14 on a cable system is from 120 to 126 Mhz, while UHF channel 14 is from 470 to 476 MHz.

Today, most systems carry 36 to 50 channels (54 to 300 or 400 MHz). New systems under construction can operate up to 750 MHz (110 channels), and in the near future, 1,000 MHz (150 channels) systems will be the standard.

The house drop. All of the above equipment is installed whether or not homes subscribe to cable service. The *house drop* is the cable and related equipment that connects an individual home to the system, and is installed only if a particular home desires cable service. The house drop cable is generally about a quarter inch in diameter and, unlike the trunk and feeder cable, is very flexible. The house drop cable is connected to a port on the tap. Splitters may be used to split the signal into one or more lines to serve multiple TV sets.

At the TV set, the drop cable is connected either directly to the TV or to a set-top *converter*. The converter can serve several purposes. First, it tunes all the channels on the cable system. This function is necessary when a subscribers's TV set is not *cable ready*, or capable of tuning all cable system channels. The converter can also control what services a customer receives. This is done either by programming the converter prior to installation with the channels it will receive, or, in the case of the *addressable converter*, signals from a controller at the headend turn off or on individual channels or groups of channels under the command of the operator's billing system. Addressable converters also make pay per view possible and are the predominant type of converter being installed today.

The converter can also contain a *descrambler*. When a cable system carries premium and pay-per-view channels, it usually scrambles the pictures at the headend to prevent unauthorized reception. The descrambler reconstructs the original, clear picture.

TWO-WAY SYSTEMS

Most cable systems today are one way, that is, they only carry signals from the headend to subscribers (*downstream*). It is possible, however, to carry signals *upstream*, or from the home to the headend. This is done by using the spectrum from 5 to 35 or 40 MHz and installing upstream amplifier modules and bandsplitting filters at each amplifier station. The coaxial cable itself is bidirectional; the standard amplifier routes signals from 54 MHz up downstream, while the upstream amplifier routes signals in the other direction, upstream.

Two-way systems are very difficult to maintain in today's cable systems, and reliability is always a problem. This is because strong over-the-air signals on the same frequencies as upstream signals can leak into the cable network (ingress) and cause interference. A large cable system can have hundreds or even thousands of miles of cable, and a single loose connector anywhere in the network can allow interference to enter and disrupt upstream communications. Incidentally, signals can also leak out of the cable (egress), which could cause trouble with over-the-air uses of the electromagnetic spectrum such as aircraft communication and navigation.

There are a few operating two-way systems today, but widespread installation of two-way will not occur until new fiber optic-based architectures are installed (see Chapter 5).

AUTOMATIC NUMBER IDENTIFICATION

As mentioned earlier, addressable converters make pay per view possible. Originally, customers would call the cable system business office and request a PPV event. A customer service representative would make an entry in the billing computer, which would send a command down the cable system to that customer's addressable converter, instructing it to activate the PPV channel. Later, automated order taking systems were installed. Both of these approaches required a large number of phone lines to handle peak ordering traffic before a major event, however, and often orders were lost because lines were busy.

The solution is *automatic number identification* (ANI). ANI is a feature of all modern telephone switching systems. When a customer places a long-distance call, the ANI equipment identifies the phone number of the calling party. To use ANI for PPV, a series of phone numbers are established, one for each PPV event. When a customer wishes to order an event, the appropriate phone number is dialed. A recorded message then thanks the customer for the order, and the ANI equipment forwards the calling phone number to the cable system over a dedicated data line. The cable system's billing computer locates the customer who has that phone number, bills the customer for the PPV, and activates the addressable converter. The telephone company, of course, bills the cable system a transaction fee. Most PPV today is done using ANI.

FIBER OPTIC TRUNKING AND BACKBONE

A major problem with cable television systems is the signal distortion and poor reliability resulting from long cascades of trunk amplifiers. As cable moved from rural areas to large cities, the systems became very large. In the 1970s, microwave was a common way of

reducing trunk cascades. Multiple *hubs*, or miniheadends, were located around the service area, and microwave radio was used to
deliver the TV signals from the main headend to the hubs. Later, fiber
optic lines were used. Television channels were digitized and sent to
hubs, where they were converted back to analog. Although the cost
of the optical fiber itself was acceptable, the cost of digitizing many
channels limited the usefulness of this approach.

In the 1980s, cable engineers began to experiment with analog modulation of lasers. The advantage of analog modulation, where the intensity of the laser's light is modulated, is that the entire cable TV spectrum
can be placed on an optical fiber with only one laser and no digitizing
equipment. Also, no equipment other than a photodetector is required
on the receiving end to reproduce the original spectrum.

Today, up to 80 channels can be sent up to 20 miles over optical
fibers, with the laser costing less than $10,000 and the photodetector
costing only $2,000. In the 1990s, cable operators have been installing
backbones of fiber optic cable. These cables parallel the existing trunk
line, delivering virtually undistorted signals to points way down the
trunk line, bypassing most of the trunk amplifiers, and greatly improving picture quality and reliability. This breakthrough in fiber
optic technology made engineers rethink cable system design, and
led ultimately to the architecture most likely to be used for integrated
broadband networks (see Chapter 5).

Today's Wireless Technologies

THE ELECTROMAGNETIC SPECTRUM

Different frequencies have very different characteristics and, therefore, different uses. The Federal Communications Commission *allo-
cates* communication services to blocks of frequencies according to
the characteristics and the demand for the services. Table 2.1 shows
the various frequency bands and their characteristics.

VHF. Very high frequencies (VHF) are from 30 to 300 MHz. These
frequencies require close to a *line-of-sight* path (line of sight means
that one could, in clear weather, actually see the transmitting tower

TABLE 2.1 The Electromagnetic Spectrum

	Frequencies	Common Uses	Characteristics
Low	30-300 kHz	–LORAN navigation –Communication with submarines	–Penetrates earth and water –Very low bandwidth –Travels long distances
Medium	300 kHz-3 MHz	–AM radio (550-1630 kHz)	–Travels long distances –Low bandwidth
High (Short Wave)	3 MHz-30 MHz	–International broadcasting	–Travels very long distances –Low bandwidth –Subject to interference from stations on same channel
Very High (VHF)	30 MHz-300 MHz	–TV ch. 2-13 (54-216 MHz) –FM radio (88-108 MHz) –Mobile communication	–Line of sight desirable for good reliability
Ultra High (UHF)	300 MHz-3 GHz	–TV ch. 14-70 (470-700 MHz) –Mobile communication –Cellular telephone (800 MHz) –PCS (2 GHz) –MMDS (2 GHz)	–Line of sight required for good reliability –Higher frequencies blocked by trees
Super High (SHF)	3 GHz-30 GHz	–Satellite communication C band (4 GHz) Ku band (12 GHz) –Microwave links for audio, data and video –Cellular TV (28 GHz)	–Absolute line of sight required –Higher frequencies blocked by rain

from the receiving location) for good reception. VHF waves will penetrate houses, trees, and other obstacles fairly well, making reception possible inside buildings. Broadcast television is the predominant use for VHF frequencies. Channels 2-6 are at 54 to 88 MHz (again, each channel occupies 6 MHz), and channels 7-13 are at 174 to 216 MHz. In between is FM radio broadcasting (88-108 MHz). Above FM radio, and above TV channel 13, are a variety of governmental and commercial point-to-point and mobile communication uses.

UHF. *Ultra high frequencies* (UHF) (300 to 3,000 MHz) are used for TV channels 14-70 and for a variety of commercial purposes, including cellular telephones. The frequencies used for UHF TV broadcasting (470-700 MHz) penetrate buildings much more poorly than VHF waves and, as a result, are less likely to result in good quality inside houses.

Microwaves. The frequencies above about 1,000 MHz (1 gigahertz, or GHz) are called *microwaves* because of the very small length of the waves. These frequencies require perfect line-of-sight conditions and are used for point-to-point relay of TV and audio information as well as for communication to and from communication satellites. Buildings, trees, and, in the case of frequencies above 10 GHz, even raindrops will block microwave signals. For this reason, these frequencies are not generally suitable for communication with moving vehicles or for terrestrial television or radio broadcasting.

Spectrum scarcity. From the above summary, it is evident that a very limited amount of spectrum is suitable for television broadcast (VHF and UHF). And, because this same spectrum is desirable for other services, such as cellular phones and mobile radio services, there is simply not enough spectrum to satisfy all users. This scarcity of spectrum is what brought about cable television.

CELLULAR TELEPHONES AND PCS

The original mobile telephone system had one tower located downtown, with only a few channels. All the users in a city had to share the limited number of channels, making the service expensive and subject to frequent busy signals. Cellular telephones use UHF frequencies and very low transmitter power, combined with a large number of towers (*cells*). The transmitter power is so low that two cells located relatively close together can use the same channel. As a user moves from one cell to another, a central computer monitors the signal strength coming from the phone and *hands off* (switches) the user to a cell where the signal is stronger. The computer also instructs the user's phone as to which of over 400 channels to tune to, without the user even being aware of the change. In this way, a very large number of users can be served with a relatively small amount of bandwidth. To increase the number of users, the size of the cells can be reduced. Cellular telephone systems operate in the 800-900 MHz region. Currently, most cellular systems use analog transmission, but digital systems are being introduced that will improve quality and increase the number of users that a cell can handle.

Personal communication systems (PCS) or *networks* (PCN) are nothing more than cellular systems with very low power and very small cells. In the cellular network, cells are located several miles apart. With PCS, cells might be located only 1,000 to 2,000 feet apart. PCS makes possible very inexpensive telephones (under $100) and could ultimately be competitive with the wired phone network for voice and data transmission. Because PCS licenses are just now being granted, the economics are yet to be proven. PCS systems will operate in the 1,900-MHz region.

OVER-THE-AIR TELEVISION BROADCASTING

TV broadcast stations. Television stations, as mentioned earlier, broadcast on VHF or UHF channels. They use very-high-power transmitters (100,000 to 5 million watts) and tall towers to serve a 60- to 100-mile radius with acceptable quality. TV channels can, to some extent, penetrate buildings, but especially with UHF channels, reception is often poor without an outside antenna.

Low-power TV. In the 1980s, to increase competition and diversity, the FCC allowed low-power (100 to 1,000 watts) TV stations (LPTV) to be built. Hundreds of these stations, which are inexpensive to build, are now on the air, but because of their low power, they have very small service areas. Most are not carried by cable systems, requiring that a cable subscriber install a switch and outside antenna to get them.

MMDS

Multichannel, multipoint distribution systems (MMDS), commonly called wireless cable, have been operating in the United States since the 1980s. They transmit 30 or so channels of television at around 2 GHz (2,000 MHz), using 100 watts or less of power. Because of the low power and relatively high frequency, MMDS systems require absolute line of sight to operate; even leaves on trees will block the signal. Typically, a tall (30- to 50-foot) receiving antenna is required, and in areas with hills or tall trees or buildings, homes cannot be served at all. Digital compression systems for cable systems will work with MMDS, and when they are available, MMDS will have a much larger number of channels to offer.

DIRECT BROADCAST SATELLITES

Communication satellites have been in operation since the 1970s, using *geosynchronous orbits*, 22,300 miles above the earth. At that altitude, satellites make exactly one revolution around the earth per day, and therefore appear to stand still relative to earth. Most video transmission today uses the *C band*, about 4,000 MHz for the *down-link*—or transmission from the satellite to the earth—and about 6,000 MHz for the *uplink*—or transmission from the earth to the satellite.

Each satellite has a number of *transponders*, devices that receive an uplink channel, convert it to a downlink frequency, and amplify it for the return trip to earth. Satellites are located about 2 degrees apart over the equator, and all use the same downlink frequencies. The receiving antennas, generally 8 to 10 feet in diameter, are able to focus on only the desired satellite.

The primary purpose of C-band satellites is to deliver television programming to cable systems and TV stations. Many people, mainly in rural areas lacking cable service, however, purchased satellite receiving equipment (these systems have motorized antennas, allowing them to be aimed at any of the satellites serving the United States). Originally, satellite programming was unscrambled. In the 1980s, however, the cable program suppliers found that they were losing significant revenue to purchasers of home dish systems, and scrambling was introduced. Today, most program services are scrambled; however, the technology used for scrambling is easy to defeat, and hundreds of thousands of users are receiving programming without paying for it. Modifications to the scrambling system have been made that, over time, will significantly reduce theft of service.

Ku-band satellites. In 1994, the first high-powered satellites de-signed specifically to deliver programming directly to homes were launched. These satellites operate in the *Ku band*, with an uplink frequency of about 14 GHz and a downlink frequency of about 12 GHz. The transponders are powerful enough to allow the use of receiving antennas that are only about 18 inches wide, making instal-lation much simpler than the C-band antennas. These satellites trans-mit digitally coded and compressed video, using techniques similar to those being used for cable television. Each satellite is capable of 80 or so channels of video. Digital compression equipment became available for satellite transmission earlier than for cable television because it is easier to compress signals on a satellite transponder, which is 36 MHz wide, than on a TV channel (6 MHz wide), and because DBS operators were willing to launch their services using a home terminal substantially more expensive than cable television home terminals.

Ku-band transmission suffers from rain attenuation, and during heavy rain, Ku-band users will experience outages of several minutes or more. The average outage time per year, however, is relatively low. Because of digital transmission, theft of service will be more difficult than with the current C-band systems, but not impossible.

3

Residential Telephone
and Information Services

The services provided by telephone companies have evolved since their inception in 1876 from the provision of simple voice connections between pairs of subscribers to a broad range of complex audio and information services. In this chapter, we examine the range of services, all of which will be essential components of future full service networks.

Common Carrier Origins

The early years of the telephone included much experimentation with potential applications. Many of these went far beyond the linking of subscribers for private voice conversations. Fascinating accounts of social experimentation included uses that today might be thought of as broadcasting, such as remotely attending concerts over the telephone.[1] Natural linkages to the telegraph (and, therefore, the association with postal service), however, soon froze telephony into a service conception that endured for the next 100 years. The telegraph connection was deeper than the similarity of the basic technology; many telephone company employees and managers were former telegraph men.[2] In fact, Fischer believes that the tendency to liken telephone service to telegraphy resulted in a deemphasis of the sociality function of telephonic communication, now long understood to be the principal driver of residential telephone use. Early marketing efforts stressed the use of the telephone for instrumental purposes—it was a tool for the business person or, at a minimum, for the business of running the household.

In addition to its connection with telegraphy and postal service, the very idea of basic telephone service is also rooted in our concepts of public transportation services. Before electronic communication, all "messages" were physically transported.[3] We, therefore, have always considered telephone service to be subject to the rules of common carriage, a concept derived from British common law.[4] *Common carriers* were businesses that provided a service to the general public. In return for the right to offer this service with limited liability for any failures, common carriers had to agree to all *reasonable* requests for service (e.g., if they had the capacity or provided a service to a particular place) at reasonable and *nondiscriminatory* rates. In the United States, the transportation common carriers (such as the railroads) were, in fact, regulated by the Interstate Commerce Commission in the late 1800s, which soon took over the regulation of telegraphy. Thus, like taxis, buses, railroads, the trucking industry, airlines, and the mail, electronic *communication* common carriers were providing a *transport* service, with little interest in the *content* of what was transported. These origins explain a great deal about the nature of telephone services and telephone company culture.

From Common Carriage to Universal Service

Although, in its earliest years, basic telephone service for the residential market was considered a luxury, Alexander Graham Bell himself envisioned a society where everyone had access to a telephone.[5] As early as 1910, Theodore Vail, president of the American Telephone and Telegraph Company (AT&T), espoused the view that universal telephone service would be best provided by a single, integrated monopoly, under the protection and oversight of government regulation.[6] Vail's vision proved to be convincing, as the government dropped what had been a serious threat of antitrust action against the Bell system in 1913. In return, AT&T agreed to restrain from certain "anticompetitive" practices, including refusing to interconnect with competing telephone companies. This agreement, known as the Kingsbury Commitment, determined the basic structure of the telephone industry for the next half century or more. In return for pursuing the goal of universal service, AT&T would be largely protected from competitive entry into their telephone service markets. Their virtual monopoly (80% of telephone subscribers and 100% of toll service), however, would be subject to rate regulation to prevent excess charges to the public, which had no alternative but to use AT&T.

To achieve universal service, AT&T employed a system of *cross subsidization*, whereby charges in excess of costs were applied to some services to be able to offer other services at prices below costs. Specifically, long-distance—or toll—calls were overpriced, and the excess revenue was used to keep the cost of residential connections lower. In addition, business rates were kept higher than residential rates, reflecting the notion that the *value of service* was greater for businesses than households. Finally, the cost of connecting a new subscriber was in large part a function of how far that subscriber lived from the nearest telephone exchange. Thus, rural subscribers were much more costly to connect than urban ones. Here, AT&T used a system of *rate averaging* to transfer revenue from the high-density urban areas to low-density rural ones. It is for these reasons that AT&T maintained for so long that universal service was only achievable in a regulated monopoly environment. They were aware that those charges in excess of costs would be targets of competitive entry, forcing a *rebalancing* of all tariffs to protect their market. This would limit opportunities for cross subsidization and, therefore, threaten universal service goals.

The Components of Basic Telephone Service

The brief background provided above gives us the essential character of basic telephone service, the main features of which have not changed for 100 years. Telephone companies provide for temporary, but dedicated connections between any two subscribers' telephones, regardless of where they each live or work. To do this requires a complex and interconnected infrastructure consisting of terminal equipment (i.e., telephones), local access lines, a local exchange or switching office, trunks to link local exchange offices to each other and to long-distance switches (the long-distance carrier's *point of presence*), and long-distance switches and trunks (see Chapter 2).

Basic telephone service—also referred to as *plain old telephone service* (POTS)—is therefore as dependent as cable television on a physical infrastructure of wires and terminating equipment. Here is where the similarity ends, however. Telephone lines must be bidirectional and connected to switches, and separate company facilities must be fully interconnected with all other networks. This is because telephone service is characterized by "network externalities" whereby the value is greater the more ubiquitous (that is, the more people who can be reached) the network.[7] Operations support and management systems are more complex. For example, the need to charge people based upon both usage and distance, and to effect proper settlements with other companies that may have carried some portion of a call, requires elaborate billing systems (this extends to calls that terminate on out-of-area carriers' networks). Thus, what appears to be a conceptually simple service—establishing a temporary voice connection between any pair of telephones—requires the nearly instantaneous control of an incredibly complex technological and management system.

The Structure of the Telephone Industry

Telephone service was for many years provided predominantly by a vertically integrated near monopoly—the American Telephone and Telegraph Company. AT&T arose from the original American Bell Telephone Company, the entity created to exploit Bell's patent on the telephone. The Bell system had a total monopoly due to this patent from 1876 to 1893. Upon its expiration, other companies rushed into the market, mostly focusing on the markets ignored by Bell, but in many cases building overlapping networks in areas served by Bell.

This was a period of rapid growth in telephone penetration, and by 1907, there were nearly as many phones supplied by the *independents* as by the Bell-affiliated companies.[8] AT&T fought back vigorously, helped by a new patent: the loading coil that made long-distance transmission practical. They refused to interconnect with any directly competing independents or other systems that they wished to acquire, driving down their value and then acquiring them at rock bottom prices. It was these practices that led to the threat of an antitrust suit by the government and the subsequent Kingsbury Commitment noted above. The United States was thus left with a large, privately held, near monopoly controlling long distance and the lion's share of local telephone service. Through their Western Electric subsidiary, they also had a monopoly on both network equipment and terminal equipment. There were, and still are, however, hundreds of smaller independent telephone companies. These companies were all interconnected and did not compete directly in any geographic area. Rather, they functioned much like cable franchises, with a monopoly in their particular area of service. The accepted wisdom was that local telephone service was a natural monopoly and could not sustain any form of head-to-head competition (see Chapter 10 for a discussion of basic economic and competition issues).

This organization of the country's telephone network held forth without serious challenge until the close of World War II.[9] Technology developments such as microwave transmission, which substantially lowered the costs of providing long distance, as well as a renewed effort by the Justice Department to divest AT&T from its equipment monopoly soon changed everything, however. AT&T fought hard to keep Western Electric, eventually settling an antitrust suit in a 1956 Consent Decree.[10] They agreed to refrain from entering into unregulated businesses, such as the newly emerging computer industry, and to make Bell Labs innovations freely available. Private use of microwave technology was authorized by the FCC in 1959 in an order known as the *Above 890* decision,[11] which, among other impacts, opened the door to an upstart firm called Microwave Communications Incorporated (MCI).

Thus began a long and persistent assault on the AT&T monopoly. A series of decisions by the courts and the FCC gradually removed the AT&T monopoly on equipment. The Carterphone decision in

1968 established the right of customers to attach non-Bell equipment to AT&T's network.[12] Seven years later, all restrictions and special arrangements in the equipment market were ended, and a flourishing new industry was born.[13] This new *interconnect* industry quickly became competitive, resulting in lower costs and greater choices and features for users.

The market-opening initiatives continued, with the FCC formally allowing competition for the provision of private, leased lines in 1971 due to MCI's successful challenges.[14] A year later, the FCC acted to ensure that the domestic satellite industry would be competitive, with their *Open Skies* policy.[15] Value-added services and the resale of telephone service were authorized in 1973 and 1976, respectively, and eventually switched long-distance service was opened to full competition in 1980.[16] The culmination of these actions was the 1982 modification of the 1956 Consent Decree (which was known as the Final Judgment, hence the name *Modification of Final Judgment*, or MFJ).[17] This settlement of a 1974 antitrust suit divested AT&T of its local operating companies (Bell Operating Companies, or BOCs— which were organized in seven *regions* and subsequently called regional Bell Operating Companies, or RBOCs) and ended restrictions on AT&T's entry into various types of businesses. It, however, precluded the RBOCs from entering into long-distance services, manufacturing, and information services.

Today, basic telephone services are primarily divided into local and long-distance segments, with the former still largely monopoly in structure and the latter competitively supplied. The BOCs, now often called *local exchange carriers* (LECs), are allowed to carry calls only within fixed areas (which do not exactly overlap with area codes) known as *local access and transport areas* (LATAs). Long-distance carriers such as AT&T, Sprint, and MCI (now known as interexchange carriers, or IECs/IXCs) carry calls across LATA boundaries (these are called interLATA calls, while LEC calls are intraLATA). Today, the local monopoly is increasingly under challenge, with cable companies and other competitive access providers (CAPs), many of which are owned by cable companies, active in various local telephone services primarily to businesses.

The telephone services market has evolved considerably beyond POTs and now includes custom calling features, mobile communication, data communication, and information services. The remainder of this chapter gives an overview of the evolution of telephone services into these areas. We first note, however, that as telephone service evolves, the question of which set of services are essential and, therefore, supplied universally must be addressed.

The Evolution of Universal Service

Universal service as a policy goal is rarely questioned. Yet its implementation is not easily solved. Despite the 60 years since the goal of affordable and universally accessible telephone service was articulated in the Communications Act of 1934, not everyone has telephone service. Some 6% of U.S. households (about 6 million) do not have a telephone; some for economic reasons, with a few more isolated homesteads remaining outside service areas. Moreover, exactly what set of capabilities is to be supplied universally is often a matter of some controversy. Mansell suggests that the set of *essential* services that should be supplied universally has, in fact, evolved from the provision of an access line for POTS, to include first automatic switching, then direct dialing for long distance, touch-tone (pushbutton) service, and finally equal access to all long-distance carriers.[18] In the current discussion of information superhighways, many believe that universal access to some set of interactive information services will be placed on the policy agenda. The dilemma, of course, is how to pay for any form of universal service in a competitive environment, given that traditional cross-subsidization strategies are no longer viable. Any service priced too high (to create a subsidy) would quickly become the target of a competitor sensing an opportunity to gain market share by undercutting the inflated price, eliminating the means of supporting universal service. One solution might be to establish a universal service fund to which telecommunication service providers contribute (see Chapter 11).

New Types of Telephone Services

Although the basic character of telephone service has not changed much from the residential subscriber's perspective, the capability of the network certainly has. In the search for greater efficiencies and new revenue streams, telephone companies have altered the way network services are controlled and administered. Essentially, networks are becoming more *intelligent*, permitting telephone companies to offer a variety of *custom calling services.*

An intelligent network is one where the various control messages necessary to actually accomplish a service are handled in a separate set of facilities from those that carry subscribers' conversations. An example of what happens when a call is placed between two cities can help clarify this notion. First, the subscriber picks up his or her telephone, which notifies the local exchange office of a request for service. The subscriber dials a number, which is registered in the local switch. In the old network structure, the local switch would select an outgoing trunk line and then forward the dialed number to the next switch over this trunk. Once the destination access line was rung and picked up, the subscriber's voice would be carried by this same trunk. If the destination telephone line were busy, the distant switch would send a busy signal back to the caller over the trunk. This was a rather inefficient use of trunks, which eventually led telephone companies to establish separate packet data circuits between switches just to carry *signaling* information. This process was known as common channel interoffice signaling. In the intelligent network, the control (or signaling) information travels over separate high-speed, packet switched circuits to a control switch known as a signal transfer point (or STP). The STP then chooses the best trunk to use to complete the call and, over the separate signaling circuits, instructs the originating and terminating switches to activate the trunk. All such signaling information is carried over a separate network from conversations, using a standard known as *Signaling System 7* (SS7). To add intelligence, the signal transfer points are linked to a database called a service control point (SCP) that contains information about the specific services that any subscriber has purchased. In this way, the network is intelligent enough to know that a particular subscriber's call should be handled in a certain way (e.g., forwarded to some other number or sent to a special answering service known as voice mail).

This type of design, which centralizes network control, is more efficient from two perspectives. First, the network facilities that carry user traffic are used more efficiently, because trunks are not actually activated (or *seized* in telephone company parlance) until conversation is ready to begin. Second, intelligent networks make it possible to quickly add new services to a network without reprogramming the many thousands of local telephone switches. Only the relatively few service control point databases need to be updated.

Based upon new capabilities of digital switches, common channel signaling, and intelligent networks, a number of new voice services have been introduced. These include the following:

- Call waiting: Perhaps the most popular new voice service, call waiting indicates the arrival of a new incoming call by a tone during an in-progress conversation. The person receiving the new incoming call can place the first party on hold and speak to the second.
- Call forwarding: Subscribers can have incoming calls temporarily forwarded to a designated number.
- Speed calling: Subscribers can use a shortened code to dial prespecified numbers.
- Voice mail: Unanswered calls can be forwarded to a service that stores messages for later replay by subscribers, similar to an answering machine.
- Three-way calling: A subscriber in an ongoing conversation can initiate a new connection to a third party, linking all three parties together.

In addition, because intelligent networks have the capability of passing the calling party number all the way on to the receiving party's station, a number of additional new services can be offered. These are collectively known as *custom local area signaling services* (CLASS) and include the following:

- *Caller ID* displays the telephone number of the calling party on a suitably equipped telephone prior to the receiver being picked up.
- *Call blocking* allows subscribers to block calls coming from prespecified numbers.
- *Automatic recall* allows subscribers to call the most recent unanswered call (e.g., if you missed a call while just arriving home).
- *Selective call forwarding* allows subscribers to have prespecified numbers temporarily forwarded to another number.
- *Distinctive ringing* distinguishes incoming calls from prespecified numbers by special ringing.
- *Call trace* allows subscribers to trace the most recent incoming call (useful for dealing with obscene, threatening, or harassing callers).

The CLASS services have been somewhat controversial and are considered by many as threats to individual privacy. Many states ban such services as caller ID or require telephone companies to offer at no charge the capability to callers to block the calling number delivery function. Particularly against caller ID services are those with unlisted numbers, hot line services, and telemarketing firms.

Another important voice service used by residential subscribers is "800" service. This is normally considered a business service, in that businesses typically purchase "800" numbers from local or long-distance telephone companies. It is often people at home, however, who benefit directly by free access to businesses that normally would need to be reached by a toll call. The number *800* is a *special access code*, which informs the local switch to pass the call over the SS7 network to a database, which routes the call and billing to the party owning the 800 number. Another special access code service—"900"" service—is discussed in the later section on information services. Today, 800 numbers are *portable*, in that a company that pays for a vanity number, like 1-800-car-rent, can use any long-distance service provider. The regional Bell Operating Companies manage a database of all "800" numbers, and deliver each call to the right interexchange carrier. AT&T reports that as many as one of every three calls on its network are "800" calls.[19] Today, this has become a hotly contested new market, with many new services that formerly required an operator, offered to home subscribers via "800" numbers (e.g., 1-800-COLLECT by MCI was a direct assault on AT&T's highly profitable operator-assisted collect calling service). A new residential phenomenon is the *personal 800* service, whereby subscribers can acquire their own "800" number, enabling those who know it to call them for free (e.g., their children away at college or their retired parents living across the country).

As competition gradually enters the local telephone market, we can expect even more innovation in features to supplement traditional voice services. Even greater competition for the residential telephone market is, however, emerging on another front: mobile telephony.

Mobile Telephone Services

Mobile telecommunication applications have been experiencing dramatic growth throughout the world in recent years, even in residential markets. Mobile services come in a wide variety of forms and are poised for significant growth in the United States due to the opening of additional radio spectrum, the introduction of greater competition, and the continuing advance of technology. All of these factors promise new product innovation and lower prices to an industry that formerly catered only to a niche, business market.

Home consumers first experienced the possibilities of untethered communications with the advent of cordless phones. The first generation of cordless phones permitted users to walk about their homes and to a limited extent their yards with a cordless handset that transmitted a low-power analog radio signal to a base station plugged into a standard telephone wall outlet. Frequencies allocated to cordless telephony were limited, however, and many users complained of interference and noise. In fact, all too often neighbors had a cordless phone operating on the same frequency, permitting eavesdropping and otherwise interfering with cordless phone operation.

In the United States, true mobile telephony (i.e., not homebound, cordless phones or the shared channel radio dispatch service) was first offered in a service known as Mobile Telephone Service (MTS). These services were offered by telephone companies using a single powerful transmitting and receiving antenna located in the center of urban areas. This was an analog service with very limited spectrum allocated, allowing a maximum of only 22 simultaneous conversations in any given market. The demand far outstripped the supply, and subscribers frequently had to wait considerable periods of time before finding an available frequency. Signals were not always clear, especially when vehicles attempted calls from near the outer reaches of the signal's coverage area. And there was no possibility for expansion of facilities, without new spectrum.

The answer to the problems of MTS came from research conducted at AT&T Bell Laboratories, where, in 1971, the original concept of *cellular* mobile telephone service was developed.[20] An attempt was made to create a competitive mobile telephone market by dividing the available spectrum between two licensed carriers in each identified market in the United States. The FCC created a market-by-market duopoly structure by licensing one *wireline* (i.e., a telephone company) and one *radio common carrier* in each market. As a result, a patchwork of cellular service areas prevented widespread *roaming* (i.e., using a mobile unit while traveling in another market served by a different cellular network operator) in the early years of the service, and the duopoly structure was not sufficient to bring service prices down. Fierce competition among equipment manufacturers, however, did significantly lower the cost of the mobile telephones. Innovations in manufacturing reduced the size and weight of mobile phones, further stimulating demand. Subscribers to cellular service have been increasing dramatically in the United States, growing from 1.2 million in 1987 to more than 20 million by the close of 1994.[21] Additionally, mergers and roaming agreements between cellular operators now permit subscribers to use their mobile units outside their normal area of service.

At the same time that the cellular telephone market was developing, a revolution in cordless telephony began in the United Kingdom, with the introduction of a new digital approach referred to as CT2 (or second-generation cordless telephone). An attempt was made to develop a new standard for the transmission from the handset to the base station, referred to as the Common Air Interface. These developments resulted in the creation of a new concept for cordless telephony, the *public* cordless telephone—a product quite distinct from traditional mobile telephone services. The United Kingdom was the home of the first *Telepoint* service, which permitted those who purchased the small, low-powered handsets to make calls from public base stations situated throughout London. A base station could accommodate up to eight simultaneous callers, and it was hoped that these would alleviate a public pay phone shortage in London. Users could not receive calls, however, and finding a base station from which to make a call was not as easy as it should have been. The only alternative for those wanting to receive calls was to link the service to a paging device, so that a user would know that someone wanted to reach them. The initial Telepoint service failed but spawned a number of copies in other countries, including the French *PointTel* service in Paris. It also planted the seeds for the next generation of *personal communication services*, to be discussed later (see Chapter 6).

Analog cellular telephone service is now in a transition phase, whereupon the major operators are beginning to introduce digital radio links. Once again, European carriers were able to move more quickly, with the help of the European Commission's endorsement of a European-wide digital standard. Termed *GSM* after the original technical body that worked on the new standard, Groupe Speciale Mobile, it was one of the first products of the newly formed European Telecommunications Standards Institute (ETSI). GSM services are now proliferating throughout the European Union and the European Free Trade Area (EFTA) countries. No such standard has been determined in the United States, however, and the existing cellular operators appear divided over the best technical approach to digitize their networks. Multiple, proprietary digital systems in the United States will, unfortunately, make it difficult for digital cellular subscribers to obtain seamless nationwide service and may even result in service areas where a subscriber is unable to use a particular type of digital mobile unit.

Cellular telephone service, both analog and digital, has traditionally been viewed as *ancillary to* rather than *competitive with* wire-based telephone service.[22] As primarily a vehicle-based service, it tied into the wireline network and originated or terminated traffic that would otherwise not have been generated. It was largely viewed as a service for professionals who spent large amounts of time dealing with clients over the phone and wanted to remain productive in their cars. Inroads into the residential market were limited to higher-income households, where cellular phones were purchased mainly for security reasons. That is, the cellular phone is often a safeguard for road emergencies and not a means of engaging in social conversation while on the road. The lower cost of terminal equipment coupled with the high usage fees contribute to this situation.

Technical developments and competitive pressures are now changing this view of cellular telephone service. In the technical area, emerging *personal communication services* (PCS) may stimulate the evolution of mobile telephone service into a competitor to today's local exchange service by allowing new entrants into the market (such as cable companies).[23] We focus on the next generation of mobile services in Chapter 5. In addition, the conclusion of AT&T's dramatic acquisition in 1994 of McCaw, the nation's largest operator of cellular telephone networks, signals the likely reentry of the former monopoly into local exchange service.

Basic Data Transmission Over Telephone Networks

Not long after computers began to proliferate in business, government, and institutional settings in the early 1960s, the need to transmit data over the public network emerged. In these early years, there
was no demand from the residential market for data communication
services. Business applications focused on giving computer users the
ability to connect remote terminals to large host computers for remote job entry and to interconnect mainframe computers. In this era
of large expensive mainframes, time-sharing services also emerged,
in which access to computer services was essentially rented to remotely located users. Geographically remote users connected to
time-sharing services over telephone networks for such applications
as database management or payroll processing. The continual trend
toward smaller, less expensive computers (minicomputers) resulted
in a rapid growth in the installed base and a movement from heavily
centralized to more distributed computing. This further increased
the demand for data communication services.

Residential Applications of Data Communication

Among households, the growth of data communication needs has
followed the adoption of home computers. Some estimates place the
penetration of home computers at over 35% of U.S. households.[24]
Although not all of these are equipped with modems, a sizable
number are, estimated at 40% of computer households in 1992.[25]
Home computers stimulate data communication traffic over networks for two broad reasons: (a) accessing bulletin boards, commercial online services, and the Internet for such purposes as downloading software, playing interactive games, sending electronic mail,
communicating in conferences and forums, shopping, and retrieving
information from online databases or other reference sources, and (b)
working from home and connecting to computing facilities and
networks located at work (or *telecommuting*). (See Chapter 6.)

Most data communications from home occur over normal dial-up
analog access lines, using modems. In early modems, data transmission

speeds were 300 or, at best, 1,200 or 2,400 bits per second. It generally took quite a few seconds at these rates to transfer a screen of text, making this type of data communication inappropriate for anything but basic text. Today, modems are far more sophisticated and use advanced techniques such as data compression to achieve higher bit rates. Home computers with modems capable of transmitting 9.6, 14.4, 19.2, and 28.8 kilobits per second are becoming increasingly commonplace. These higher speeds make it much more feasible to send graphic information, larger files, and facsimiles than in the past. But they are still too slow for any form of moving images, and very large files or complex graphics can take too long for the normal computer user's patience as well.

In addition to improved modems, the capability of the public network for carrying data to and from residential subscribers has been enhanced in two other ways. First, publicly accessible *packet switched* networks began as business-oriented services but now improve household access to a wide range of computer services at a lower cost and with greater reliability. The connection to these networks is still over the analog access lines via modems, however. Second, *integrated services digital networks* (ISDN), described in Chapter 2, now enable even the access line to be digitized, making it possible to have end-to-end digital connectivity over public networks. These two data communication services are described in more detail in the next two sections. Of course, many other highly sophisticated data communication services have been developed to meet the needs of the business community. Our focus here is strictly on those services with the most relevance for the residential market.

PUBLIC PACKET SWITCHED NETWORKS

As the needs for data communication for business grew, it soon became evident that the use of the public telephone network without enhancements was an inefficient means of carrying this type of traffic. Using modems and multiplexers (which allow multiple users on the same line), large companies could lease private lines and connect a number of terminals directly to a distant host computer for low-speed data transmission. These private lines could be conditioned, as well, so that they were less prone to interference and noise and, hence, could carry somewhat higher bit rates. If someone wished to connect her terminal to a number of possible host computers, however, she had to use a normal dial-up circuit and establish a voice-grade connection all the way to each host. This was not only expensive due to long-distance toll rates but also a poor use of telephone facilities. Data transmission based on a terminal connected to a host does not use a telephone circuit continuously as happens in a voice conversation. People type a few characters, then perhaps get a screen of data, ponder for some period, type a few more characters, get another screen, and so forth. The term *bursty* is often used to refer to this aspect of data communication. Moreover, due to the complexity of the procedures associated with establishing a connection (e.g., logging on and typing passwords), it was not uncommon for people to connect a terminal to a host computer and leave it connected for hours, even when not in use. Hence, the trunks used to complete the telephone circuit are occupied, but not very efficiently.

Based upon early research funded by the Advanced Research Projects Agency (ARPA), and now globally standardized by the International Telecommunication Union's CCITT, a new type of networking optimized for data communication among a set of inter-connected computers was developed.[26] *Packet switched* networks more efficiently use network resources by chunking transmissions into packets at the entry point to the network. The packet switches are connected by leased lines, but generally the access into the network is over a normal dial-up line. Networks designed in this way are often called *value-added networks* because they take a basic transmission capability and, by attaching computers, add functionality or value to users (e.g., error-free transmission, ability to send electronic mail, ability to store data and then forward it when networks are less busy). For reasons described in the section tracing U.S. policy regarding telephone company provision of such value-added networks, many competing packet switched networks emerged in the United States, built upon capacity leased from telephone companies.

ISDN

Beginning as early as the 1970s, the world's telephone monopolies began to cooperate on defining a standard for digitizing the access lines in the local loop portion of the network. Work done at the *International Telecommunication Union* (ITU) established the broad recommendations concerning the structure of an integrated services digital network.[27] As noted in Chapter 2, ISDN enables the basic access line to be converted into a digital line capable of carrying 144 kbps, organized into two B channels of 64 kbps and one D channel at 16 kbps. In terms of actual services, the B channels can each carry the equivalent of one digital voice conversation or fairly high-speed data. The D channel is generally used for signaling information for such purposes as call setup and termination but could also allow low-speed data transmission.

ISDN adoption rates have been relatively unimpressive up to the time of this writing. Two important problems have plagued ISDN deployment by the world's telephone companies. First, the original CCITT standards were not complete enough to avoid some incompatibilities among different vendors' ISDN switches and interface equipment. This resulted in the early implementation of ISDN "islands" in which users could not be assured of end-to-end ISDN connectivity with other ISDN subscribers. Bellcore, a research organization collectively owned by all seven RBOCs, has attempted to remedy this problem with their national ISDN recommendation, and as a result, equipment incompatibilities in the United States have been largely eliminated. A second, and perhaps more serious problem, however, is that after a decade of implementing local area networks (LANs) that routinely transport data at 10 Mbps (a common Ethernet LAN speed), the 64-kbps speed of ISDN B channels is not particularly exciting to business users. Other wide area network services such as frame relay or switched multimegabit data service (SMDS) provide much greater data rates and are finding favor among corporate users for interconnecting LANs.[28] Telephone companies now appear to be refocusing their ISDN efforts on small businesses and the residential market, where data communication requirements are much lower. In addition, the latest generation of digital compressed videoconferencing equipment is designed to work with basic rate ISDN. The ability to simply dial up another videoconferencing user over ISDN has proven to be attractive to the business community and is driving new demand for the service.

U.S. Policy in Data and Information Services

Packet switched networks, beginning with the government-sponsored ARPANET (out of which the Internet has evolved), began to appear to support data communication in the late 1960s and early 1970s. There was some controversy over the ability of AT&T to freely enter into this market, however, which took more than 20 years to resolve. This explains to some extent the reasons telephone companies have historically not played a very significant role in the provision of electronic information services in the United States as opposed to other countries where information services to the public are nearly always provided by the telephone monopoly. (See Chapter 11.) The following sections examine value-added information services delivered over telephone networks in the United States.

Electronic Information Services

Electronic information services are considered enhanced services, and as noted above, telephone companies have historically been prohibited from freely entering this market. The traditional fear was that through cross subsidization and discrimination (see note 14 at the end of this chapter), AT&T, with its bottleneck control of local access facilities, could unfairly compete against other information providers. The deep-seated U.S. belief in a plurality of information sources certainly favored restricting telephone companies from being information providers. Hence, their role has been one of traditional common carriage, providing the basic transmission capacity to independent online service providers. AT&T sought to enter into the electronic information services market but was not permitted to do so until it was divested of its local operating companies.[29] After the divestiture, the restriction on provision of information services remained for the RBOCs, although it has now been removed. In a series of court decisions, presided over by Harold Greene, the federal judge who oversaw the AT&T breakup, the RBOCs were first permitted to offer *gateway* services in 1988. Gateways provide intelligent access to other information service providers, but no content in and of themselves. RBOC gateway services fared miserably in the marketplace, and the RBOCs continued to lobby for further relief from the information services restrictions. Incidentally, this is similar to the more or less designed-to-fail video dialtone service (see Chapter 11). In 1991, after an appeals court questioned the validity of the information services restriction, Judge Greene finally lifted this prohibition. Many challenges continue to be made, both by other information service providers and by state public service commissions, making it still somewhat difficult for RBOCs to freely enter the information services marketplace. As a result, the major online services catering to the residential market are firms unaffiliated with traditional telephone companies.

Types of Online Services

Online services to the residential marketplace are a relatively small, but rapidly growing percentage of the overall electronic information services marketplace in the United States.[30] Often, consumer online services are referred to as *videotex* after the European national information service programs that began in the late 1970s. Videotex at the time differed from traditional online computer services because it included (a) an emphasis on graphical displays to increase attractiveness, (b) low-cost terminal devices, and (c) easy to use interfaces that did not require any user training.[31] Today, with graphical user interfaces now common on all personal computers, most of these differences are no longer relevant. In general, applications for home information services can be grouped into the following three broad categories:

Information retrieval. Access to government information, electronic encyclopedias, electronic news, and other sources of online information are all examples of information retrieval applications.

Transactions. In addition to the simple provision of information, online services enable subscribers to complete a wide range of transactions from home, including shopping in electronic "malls," electronic banking and bill paying, downloading files and software, and making reservations (e.g., for airlines or other travel-related services). Often, transactions require the participation of third parties such as credit card companies or other financial service firms.

Communication. Experience has shown that communication with other users is always among the most popular services offered by online service providers. Electronic mail (e-mail), enabling users to post simple text messages to one or more other users for subsequent reading and response, is perhaps the most frequently used online application. Other communication services are computer conferences, either real time or not; bulletin boards, in which users can post notices for public viewing; and "chat" services, where subscribers simply exchange text messages with whoever else happens to be connected at the same time.

History of Videotex

As early as 1974, visions of an interactive electronic information marketplace in the United States were stimulated by the emergence of techniques for linking communication networks to computers.[32] Even before the personal computer industry appeared and began targeting the residential market, various players from the broadcasting, cable, telecommunication, publishing, computer, and computer services industries flirted with the idea of delivering electronic information services to the mass market. Some players were heavily influenced by developments in Europe, where one Post, Telephone, and Telegraph (PTT) administration after another sought to establish national videotex and/or teletext services, mostly with little success.[33] Beginning with the first videotex system, Prestel in the United Kingdom, most European videotex systems used the TV set as the home terminal, included graphics as well as ASCII text, and provided national coverage. France's Teletel, which many consider to be the world's only successful videotex system, was the only service to vary from this theme, by using special purpose terminals (Minitels) distributed free to telephone subscribers. They also used a decentralized approach by having all third party information service providers maintain their own information on host computers connected to a nationwide packet switched network.

Early attempts to mimic European videotex in the United States were made primarily by large information publishers such as Knight Ridder and Times Mirror. Knight Ridder began test marketing a service called Viewtron in Coral Gables, Florida, in 1980, and offered it commercially in 1983. This system offered subscribers access to a range of information and transaction services, including home banking and shopping, news, sports, weather, stock market information, airline schedules, and movie reviews. They were convinced that home consumers needed graphics, and followed the Prestel philosophy of using the television set as a display terminal. A special decoder known as the Sceptre was developed for the trial by AT&T (which was searching for some role to play given their prohibition on offering their own information services). The Sceptre provided higher quality graphics than the Prestel graphics standard, but this increased the cost of the terminal device. After three years, Viewtron still had fewer than 5,000 customers, and in 1985, it shut down. A similar fate awaited Times Mirror with their Gateway service in Southern California. Gateway shut down within weeks of Viewtron, and both services resulted in losses of millions of dollars. These spectacular failures, and numerous smaller ones, convinced the publishing industry that they faced no threat from electronic text.[34] Many believe that the early emphasis on graphics and the home TV set as the terminal device were strategic errors.[35]

In contrast to these experiences, online services originating with computer manufacturers or computer service companies fared much better. We next examine the major online services in U.S. households today.

Major Consumer Online Services

In the United States, consumer online services depend on households equipped with home computers and modems. The three largest services are CompuServe, Prodigy, and America Online. CompuServe, a subsidiary of H&R Block, was a time-sharing firm offering remote computing services to companies that could not afford their own mainframe computers. They began experimenting with an online service to the home market as early as 1979 once it became clear that the demand for time-sharing services was diminishing. Online services were a natural alternative use of their installed base of mainframes and widespread packet switched network. They now maintain nodes in more than 100 countries and offer access to thousands of services. Globally, CompuServe subscribership now exceeds 2.45 million.[36] Prodigy originated as Trintex in the early 1980s, a joint venture between IBM, Sears, and CBS. CBS soon withdrew from the project and, after many delays, Prodigy commenced a national marketing campaign in 1990. The number of Prodigy subscribers has grown to over 1.2 million although they allow up to five users per subscription to encourage all family members to sign on.[37] This is to their advantage, because their revenue is in part based on advertising fees and commissions from sales of merchandise. America Online was formerly a number of separate online services targeted at specific brands of computers in partnership with manufacturers. The parent company was Quantum Computer Services, and they joined with such home computer vendors as Tandy and Commodore. A consolidation among these separate services catapulted America Online to be one of the industry leaders. Recently, they have experienced remarkable growth, with subscribership increasing from 1.5 million in December 1994 to over 2 million as of mid-February 1995.[38]

Structure of the Online Industry

For the most part, the commercial consumer online services have a similar structure. There are the actual *system operators*, such as CompuServe, who package a wide range of information services much like cable operators choose to include cable networks and other channels on their systems. System operators may or may not be *network operators*. Some contract with value-added network providers like Tymnet (now part of the BT-MCI alliance) or AT&T's Accunet to enable any subscriber to reach their service through a local call to the nearest packet switched network access point. Others, such as CompuServe, lease basic transmission capacity from local and long-distance telephone companies and offer their own value-added network. Currently, there are no full-fledged consumer online services offered by telephone companies (in which case the network and system operator would be one and the same) for reasons noted in Chapter 11. One possibility is for system operators to lease cable television channels for the downstream portion of their information service delivery, using telephone and packet networks for the upstream requests by subscribers. The actual content is generally supplied by third party *information service providers*. Often these are large information publishing companies such as Dow Jones or large newspaper chains, which then make their content available in many alternative formats.[39] Some information service providers are only accessible on one system under an exclusive arrangement. The largest services, such as the Dow Jones News Retrieval or the Official Airline Guide, however, connect to several online services to achieve a critical mass of users. Often these services can be accessed directly or through other system operators' gateways.

Revenue for online services comes from subscribers through subscription fees, connect time charges, and surcharges for accessing certain premium services; from third party information service providers through commissions on sales of merchandise; and from advertisers. Prodigy relies on the latter two, and therefore tries to encourage as many people to sign on as possible by having a relatively low monthly flat rate fee rather than connect time charges. The system enables highly targeted advertising because of the detailed information associated with each user ID. Prodigy's flat rate fees spurred other operators to do the same, with most now offering a basic package of services at a low monthly rate.

Information services are not just for information but also for communication. In fact, an often repeated story from the early days of Teletel tells of hackers setting up their own messaging service on one information service provider's host computer—hacking their way in for communication purposes. Rather than erecting barriers to such user initiatives, service providers recognized the opportunity and rapid growth of *messageries* where users could engage in online chats, and messaging followed.[40] The development of messageries also resulted in the growth of the so-called *Minitel Rose* (pink Minitel), the start of online pornography.

On CompuServe, the communication forums, which are much like bulletin boards organized by topic, are also highly popular and profitable. Electronic mail experienced a great boost when major service providers agreed to interconnect their mail systems, permitting intersystem message exchange. Thus, subscribers to the smaller systems could still benefit from the critical mass of potential recipients created across multiple systems.

The Internet

The online industry is a example of how home consumers might use the so-called information superhighway. For the most part, it is thriving with rather limited analog telephone line access to traditional packet switched networks. Most provide low-speed connections, rarely even getting as high as 14.4 kilobits per second. In the past, all were basically ASCII text systems, although Prodigy emphasized graphics as well. Prodigy attempted to minimize transmission delays by downloading graphic templates onto users' hard drives, so that as a session went on, the delays were shorter. In the past several years, graphical user interfaces have been incorporated into online service interfaces, functioning like the icons used in Macintosh and Windows-based computer operating systems. Today, however, many people use online services for downloading software and, increasingly, multimedia files (such as pictures, compressed digital movies, or sound). This can take a long time over existing networks.[41] It may be that multimedia applications of online services will drive the upgrading of the network infrastructure (see Chapter 6).

The most significant development in recent years for the online industry is the fantastic growth of the Internet. This network of networks began as a tool of the research community, and originally, as the Department of Defense-funded ARPANET, connected universities and research centers involved in defense-related research. Other networks connecting universities and research centers followed the ARPANET (with such names as BITNET and CSNET). In the 1980s, the National Science Foundation helped various regional networks grow to ensure that all university researchers had access to a relatively few supercomputers. They funded the development of a backbone network (that is, the main links to key institutions to which others connected) called NSFnet, to which all regional networks were connected. This set of interconnected networks now is known as the Internet, and its growth in recent years has been phenomenal. No one knows the exact number of users of the Internet, but estimates range from several million to 20 million users connected to millions of host computers worldwide. Moreover, analyses of the numbers of new hosts connecting to the Internet show it virtually doubling in size every year since 1988. At this rate, John Quartermann, a leading Internet analyst, has commented that the whole world could be connected by the year 2003![42]

In the past, the Internet was irrelevant to the home consumer market, with arcane commands needed to navigate among and use information from any of the computers connected to it. It was a tool only for the research community, mainly providing electronic mail transit and file transfers among all of the diverse participating networks connecting academics. Many attempts were made to simplify navigation on the Internet, including the widely used *Gopher* system. Gopher uses a menu structure to help set up information retrieval systems, and is widely used by institutions to make their information available to the Internet community. In recent years, the use of the Internet has been greatly facilitated by a new hypertext approach to linking disparate computers developed at CERN, the nuclear research center in Switzerland. Known as the *World Wide Web*, this hypertext protocol permits people to simply click on highlighted text to be connected to a computer file somewhere in the Web. Perhaps the most significant breakthrough was the release in late 1993 of *Mosaic*, a program that integrates a number of navigational aids, search tools, and multimedia browsing tools. Internet users can now point and click to retrieve text, see online images, hear sound files, and see brief MPEG digitized movies. Millions of free copies of Mosaic and other browser software have reportedly been distributed over the Internet, and it has attracted the interest of many companies who now view the Internet as an electronic marketing and shopping mecca (see Chapter 8).[43] Virtually all of the commercial online services have now created some form of Internet access, and schools, libraries, and other public institutions are all rushing to connect. A "gold rush" mentality is taking hold, and *Internet Access Providers* (including telephone companies, cable companies, and a number of new entrants) are now marketing Internet connections to the residential market. For many pundits, the Internet *is* the information super-highway! It must be noted, however, that the exponential growth in Internet in the past may not be a predictor of future growth and use. Currently, nearly all Internet usage is still free to end users, although their employers pay for interconnection. AT&T offers five hours of Internet use to its residential long-distance customers. Unlike telephone service, there is no access charge for data. Once there are usage-sensitive charging mechanisms, much of the current activity on the Internet may be curtailed. The current network is largely publicly funded. As use grows, at some point the government will no longer cover as much cost. These costs will be passed on to users. The indiscriminate use of the Internet may end as a result, just as indiscriminate use of television may decline when video on demand is available. (See Chapter 6.)

Audiotex

Often overlooked as a medium for the delivery of electronic information services, the simple telephone has a number of desirable qualities. Like the television, it is already in most households.[44] Unlike the television, it is connected to a two-way network already, and hence could be a medium for the delivery of audio information services, or *audiotex*. It has a simple, well-understood interface, and people become quite facile with using their telephone from early childhood on.

Given these qualities, it should be no surprise that in the past decade we have witnessed the emergence and rapid growth of a telephone-based information services industry. Since 1990, however, the pay-per-call version of this industry has fallen into a broad decline and may never recover from years of abuse by unscrupulous service providers.[45]

Audiotex encompasses several distinct types of services. First, it is important to distinguish between the vast amounts of audio information delivered free of charge to callers who call a place of business (often using "800" numbers so that there is not even a long-distance telephone call charge to the caller). This can be as simple as a passive, prerecorded announcement (e.g., calling a theater to hear a recording of the movie schedule) or more interactive, requiring callers to press numbers on their pushbutton telephone to make choices.

Of more interest for our discussion here are the *pay-per-call* services, which began to emerge in selected markets in the 1970s when AT&T adopted the special dialing prefix "976" for accessing information. In 1980, during the Reagan-Carter presidential debates, AT&T and ABC teamed up to offer viewers the opportunity to vote for the winner by telephone. Callers dialed a national *special access code*— "900"—and one number to vote for Carter and another to vote for Reagan. They were charged 50 cents for the call, all of which went to AT&T. Sometimes referred to as "Dial-It" services, the information service was purchased by AT&T for a flat fee, but then charged on a per call basis. The original providers of the information did not receive revenue based on the number of callers. The AT&T divestiture changed all of this, however, because RBOCs were only permitted to provide access to information but not to own the content. RBOCs began offering "976" services and long-distance carriers "900" services in which the telephone companies billed for each call and reimbursed information service providers based upon call volume. A related service is *Group Access Bridging* (often called chat lines) whereby callers dial a similar special access code to be connected on a sort of party line with other callers.

In 1987, an upstart long-distance carrier named Telesphere revolutionized the industry by offering *interactive* audiotex on a national basis. These services were built upon the technology of *interactive voice response*. Essentially, the tones generated by pushbutton telephones are used to select information that can be retrieved and read by callers through voice synthesis.[46] Other long-distance carriers introduced similar services by 1989, and the audiotex market began to take off.

Prior to 1989, local "976" services dominated the industry in terms of share of revenue. After 1989, the national "900" services accounted for the lion's share of audiotex revenue. Total revenues grew from an estimated $375 million in 1987 to nearly $1 billion by 1991.[47] IXCs and LECs offered billing and collection services, and *service bureaus* appeared to lease the necessary equipment and transmission lines, which they then rented out to information service providers.

Unfortunately, the ease of entering the market and the lure of fast money attracted many illegitimate service providers. Adult or "dial-a-porn" services flourished, preying on teenagers who rang up to huge telephone bills. Fraud was commonplace, with services promising cheap and easy credit cards that never appeared (often at the cost of a $50 call) or free gifts. Children became victims, with one notorious case involving a television commercial that instructed young viewers to get their telephone and hold it next to the TV if they wished to talk to Santa. The TV then played the tones necessary to dial a "900" number connecting children to "Santa" for a significant fee.

Eventually, public outcry forced the telephone industry to self-regulate and the FCC to impose stiff rules governing pay-per-call services. Telephone companies were required to offer subscribers the ability to block access to specific special access codes. They further began refusing to offer billing and collection services to certain classes of information service providers, such as those offering adult-oriented services and credit services. The FCC imposed a requirement that all services be preceded by a "kill message" that identifies the creator and nature of the service, and the exact cost, after which callers can disconnect with no cost.

Collectively, these actions, along with public distrust of the services, resulted in a plunge in revenues. Total revenues fell a reported 50% in 1992 and have continued to decline.[48] Of interest, the same pattern appears to be repeating itself in other countries that have introduced pay-per-call services.[49]

Conclusion

In this chapter, we have reviewed existing telephone and information services. We have seen how the vertically integrated telephone industry has been divided into a number of separate sectors, including equipment, long-distance, and local telephone services. Moreover, the industry has undergone a metamorphosis from monopoly provision of most services to competition in many areas. Because the only direction that market share can go is down when an industry changes from monopoly to competition, it is not surprising that the telephone companies have sought out new lines of business to make up for lost market share. Clearly, information and entertainment services offer such a possibility.

Technological developments have both facilitated telephone company movement into new areas and heightened the threat of competition in their core business. The former is illustrated by the growing digitization of the network, permitting integration of services (e.g., ISDN), while the latter is evident in the emergence of new mobile communication services.

Some of the basic advantages of telephone companies over others in the race to develop full service networks can be derived from our review as well. The increasing intelligence of the network makes it easier to create and offer new services on a wide scale without changing every local switch or expecting every user to buy new terminal equipment. The increasingly digital, inherently two-way, and totally interconnected network infrastructure provides the critical mass of potential users necessary to attract content and service providers. Our review of the French Teletel and audiotex services illustrates that even a limited-capability network can become a vehicle for information service delivery if such a critical mass is obtained. In part, this is due to popularity of person-to-person (horizontal) communication and the network externalities that characterize this type of service.

At the same time, the strongest asset of local telephone companies, a distribution plant that interconnects all households and businesses, is also their greatest barrier to becoming a full service network. The limited capacity of local access lines has even constrained the ability of online information service providers to offer multimedia information over the telephone network. The proliferation of CD-ROM-based multimedia as well as Internet browsing programs suggest that the residential market may be ready for such bandwidth-consuming services. Hence, the path to convergence for telephone companies lies in finding the means to upgrade the capacity of the local loop.

Notes

1. See Carolyn Marvin, *When Old Technologies Were New: Thinking About Electronic Communication in the Late Nineteenth Century* (New York: Oxford University Press, 1988).

2. Claude Fischer, *America Calling: A Social History of the Telephone to 1940* (Berkeley: University of California Press, 1992).

3. The link to mail and transportation is seen in the very language of the industry. The flow of telephone conversations over the network is called *traffic*, for example. And units of this traffic have historically been called *message units*. Long-distance calls are also known as *toll* calls, and this service was traditionally called *Message Toll Service*.

4. See Eli Noam, "Systems Integration and the Impending Doom of Common Carriage" (paper presented to the International Telecommunications Society, Gothensburg, Sweden, June 1993), for an interesting history of common carriage.

5. Ithiel de Sola Pool, *Forecasting the Telephone: A Retrospective Assessment* (Norwood, NJ: Ablex, 1983).

6. Harry Shooshan, "The Bell Breakup: Putting It in Perspective," in *Disconnecting Bell: The Impact of the AT&T Divestiture*, ed. H. Shooshan (New York: Pergamon, 1984), 8-22.

7. Economists refer to an *externality* as a benefit not captured in the price system. Thus, people who join a network only pay for their own connection but benefit from others who have joined. When a new subscriber is added, all existing subscribers benefit without paying for it.

8. Shooshan, *Disconnecting Bell*.

9. There were repeated rumblings inside the Justice Department about the need to do something about AT&T. Essentially, the concern was that AT&T was guaranteed a certain rate of return on all costs. Because of all of the rate averaging, cross subsidization, and common or joint use of the same facilities for multiple services, however, it was not at all clear how costs should be allocated. In particular, many felt that Western Electric was overcharging the Bell Operating Companies and AT&T Long Lines for equipment. The argument was that rate of return regulation actually encouraged inefficiency and inflation of costs, because there was no penalty to AT&T.

10. Shooshan, *Disconnecting Bell*.

11. Allocation of Frequencies in the Bands Above 890 Mc., 27 F.C.C. 359 (1959) recon., 29 F.C.C. 825 (1960). 890 refers to 890 MHz. Recall that in Chapter 2 we noted that, above 1 GHz, radio frequencies are called *microwaves*.

12. Carterphone, 13 F.C.C. 2d 420, recon. denied, 14 F.C.C. 2d 571 (1968).

13. See Richard Wiley, "The End of Monopoly," in Shooshan, *Disconnecting Bell*, 28.

14. This became known as the *Specialized Common Carrier Decision* (Wiley, "End of Monopoly," 33).

15. Wiley, "End of Monopoly," 34.

16. Wiley, "End of Monopoly," 35-37.

17. *United States v. AT&T*, 522 F. Supp. 131 (D.D.C. 1982), aff'd sub nom., *Maryland v. United States*, 460 U.S. 1001 (1983).

18. Robin Mansell, "Telecommunication Network Based Services: Policy Implications," ICCP OECD Report No. 18 (Paris: OECD, 1987).

19. A. M. Noll, *Introduction to Telephones and Telephone System*, 2d ed. (Norwood, Mass.: Artech House, 1991).

20. Of interest, the innovation took a full 10 years to reach the market, despite overwhelming demand and a proven technical concept.

21. This information is from Cellular Telephone Industry Association statistics, Washington, D.C.

22. There has been some discussion in the past of using cellular telephony *in place* of the fixed network to establish lower-cost service in rural areas. In developing countries, such as the emerging market economies of central and eastern Europe, cellular telephony has also been viewed as a quick way to establish an alternative infrastructure because the wireline networks, even in urban areas, were so underdeveloped. In fact, these are often built as *overlay* networks, with limited dependence on any existing wireline infrastructure.

23. These trends became widely popularized by Nicholas Negroponte, head of MIT's Media Lab, when he observed what has now come to be called the Negroponte switch. Services that formerly came over the air (broadcasting) would be delivered by wire (cable), while services that formerly came by wire (telephony) would be delivered over the air (cellular). Nicholas Negroponte, "Products and Services for Computer Networks," *Scientific American*, September 1991, 106-113.

24. "Home Computers," *Business Week*, November 1994, 89-96.

25. Michael Miller, "Contact High: Computer Networks Have Changed Campus Life—and the Changes Hint at What Lies Ahead for All of Us," *Wall Street Journal*, 15 November 1993, R4.

26. See Chapter 12 for more background on the ITU.

27. Once a network was all digital, it would be relatively indifferent to the various types of information carried on it. Voice, data, facsimile, and image were all types of services that could be carried in digital form, integrated on a common network. Hence, the new approach to the public network was called "integrated services digital network."

28. Frame relay is essentially a packet switched service that achieves faster data rates by eliminating much of the overhead associated with the early X.25 standard. It is one of a number of new *fast packet* services now commercially available to business. SMDS is another fast packet service that essentially transmits packets of data over a wide area in much the same way that a LAN does in a local area. Both of these new services potentially offer data rates up to 45 megabits per second.

29. They also faced a seven-year moratorium on entering the electronic information services business after the MFJ.

30. C. Steinfield, "U.S.: Videotex in a 'Hyper-Evolutionary' Market," in *Relaunching Videotex*, ed. H. Bouwman and M. Christoffersen (Amsterdam: Kluwer, 1992), 149-164.

31. J. Tydeman, H. Lipinski, R. Adler, M. Nyhan, and L. Zwimpfer, *Teletext and Videotex in the United States* (New York: McGraw-Hill, 1982).

32. W. Baer and M. Greenberger, "Consumer Electronic Publishing in the Competitive Environment," *Journal of Communication*, 38 (1987): 49-63.

33. See H. Bouwman, M. Christoffersen, and T. Ohlin, "Videotex: Is There Life After Death?" in Bouwman and Christoffersen, *Relaunching Videotex*, 7-13. In Europe, until only very recently, nearly all telecommunication services were provided by government-owned monopolies known as PTTs. Sometimes branches of government, sometimes government-owned companies, the PTTs saw the provision of electronic information over telephone networks as a means of increasing revenues derived from the residential market. Beginning with the Prestel (originally called Viewdata) service in the United Kingdom, most of these services offered alphanumeric information enhanced by crude graphics in a page-oriented format. Television sets equipped with modems and decoders were the display devices. Simple menu-driven control enabled people with no computer training to access the various services available. With the

exception of the French Teletel system, all of the European videotex trials failed to achieve significant market penetration.

34. Steinfield, "Videotex in a 'Hyper-Evolutionary' Market."

35. A. M. Noll, "Videotex: Anatomy of a Failure," *Information and Management*, 9 (1985): 99-109.

36. Interactive Services Association, Silver Spring, Md.

37. Interactive Services Association, Silver Spring, Md.

38. Interactive Services Association, Silver Spring, Md.

39. See P. Huber, M. Kellogg, and J. Thorne, *The Geodesic Network II: 1993 Report on Competition in the Telephone Industry* (Washington, DC: Geodesic Company, 1992), for an analysis of information service provider strategies.

40. G. Thomas, T. Vedel, and V. Scheider, "The United Kingdom, France, and Germany: Setting the Stage," Bouwman and Christoffersen, *Relaunching Videotex*, 15-30.

41. One report noted that thousands of fans spent more than an hour and a half online downloading the latest *Aerosmith* song that Geffen Records had made available to CompuServe (it is important to note that CompuServe did not charge a downloading fee for this!). Column in *New Media*, November 1994, 59.

42. These figures come from John Quartermann, editor, *The Matrix News* (online on the Internet), 4, no. 6 (June 1994), Austin, Tex. The *Matrix* is the term Quartermann uses for the larger set of interconnected networks that in some way link to the Internet but do not support the full set of Internet services. Thus, for example, including all online services, electronic mail services, enterprise networks, and so on would put the population of users reachable by electronic mail at figures as high as 80,000,000.

43. "The Internet Will Change the Way You Do Business," *Business Week* (November 1994): 80-88. The free distribution of browsing software, such as Mosaic, or the highly popular *Netscape Navigator*, parallels the French strategy of giving away Minitels to create a mass market.

44. Recent estimates place the telephone in some 90 million of the nation's 95 million households, for a penetration rate of about 94%.

45. See C. Steinfield and R. Kramer, "USA: Dialing for Diversity," in *Cash Lines: The Development and Regulation of Audiotex in Europe and the United States*, ed. Michael Latzer and Graham Thomas (Amsterdam: Het Spinhuis, 1994), 227-255.

46. For example, a caller to a sports service could select football scores from a list of sports and then choose a particular game that was played. The service would then look up the results in a database and read them to the caller.

47. These figures are from Strategic Telemedia, 1992.

48. Steinfield and Kramer, "USA: Dialing."

49. M. Latzer and G. Thomas, "Conclusions: Issues and Strategies for Audiotex," in Latzer and Thomas, *Cash Lines*, 257-295.

4

Entertainment and Information Television

Television has become the principal source of entertainment and information in the United States and elsewhere in the world. This chapter describes the evolution of television in recent years to the multichannel service now available in most homes. The focus is on how new distribution technologies have changed both the content and the structure of the television industry and brought us *almost* to on-demand television and audio entertainment, news, and public affairs. This is another part of the communication environment and infrastructure from which full service networks must emerge.

The Economics of Television Distribution

THEORIES OF ENTERTAINMENT PROGRAMMING IN A MULTICHANNEL CONTEXT

At one time, television was a medium with audience masses of incredible size. Television continues to aggregate audiences on this scale but now disaggregates these audiences as well. The contemporary situation is described by Gene Jankowski, former president of the CBS Broadcast Group:

> There are essentially two dynamics at work in communications. Let's call them audience aggregation and audience disaggregation. *Aggregation* brings forth mass audiences for those relatively few movies, television programs, books, records and so on whose great appeal cuts across boundaries of age, sex, income, education and taste. Its opposite, *disaggregation*, once confined largely to print, has now become an electronic process, thanks to the new technologies. It aims for smaller audiences of like-minded people who share specialized interests. These two dynamics serve two different human needs: the need to belong and the need to be individual. They are not competitive; they are complementary.[1]

Because there are only a few broadcast networks, substantial production resources may be invested in the programming made for the aggregated audiences. Broadcast networks and most stations are programmed for mass market advertisers for whom the large audiences are efficient. Until there are many networks, it is more profitable for any one to compete for a share of the mass audience. There is also room for a few cable networks, such as the USA Network and Turner Network Television (TNT), to attempt to get a share of the mass audience, particularly when they have subscription revenues in addition to advertising to help carry the programming cost. But there is a limit to the number of program networks that can succeed with mass appeal programming. At some point, it is more rational for the programmer to attempt to disaggregate the audience by creating a specialty service.[2] This type of cable programming is sometimes called *narrowcasting*, and the networks are called *niche* channels, such as the Golf Channel, TV Food Network, BET on Jazz, the History Channel, and Women's Sports Network. Niche programming is of value to cable systems because each additional channel brings the prospect of new subscribers and raises the probability of retention of existing subscribers.

BROADCASTING

Prior to discussion of program distribution, it is useful to describe current television outlets. *Broadcast* television stations may be either *network affiliates* or *independents*. The affiliates have exclusive rights to, or right of first refusal of, programs of one broadcast network (ABC, NBC, CBS, or Fox; with UPN—Paramount—or WB—Warner Brothers—also developing networks). Affiliated stations commit much of the broadcast day to the network programs. The stations are compensated for this broadcast time in two ways—through cash payments, network *comp*, and in *local advertising availabilities* within the network programs. The "local avails" are sold by the station at breaks in network programs (station breaks). The station retains all of this revenue after commissions. As broadcast networks struggled to maintain profitability in competition with multichannel television and independents, they reduced direct compensation to affiliates. Faced with lower compensation, affiliates have less loyalty to the network and have threatened or actually reduced carriage, *clearances*, of the networks' programs, substituting programs from other distribution sources. Recently, long-standing affiliations have shifted as stations and networks maneuver for economic advantage.

The independent stations, not affiliated with a broadcast network, buy rights to all of their television programs in the programming marketplace—the syndication market. They compete for the rights to available off-network programming with network affiliates, who have to fill nonnetwork time, and sometimes with cable networks or even local cable systems. The independent stations can sometimes improve their status in the market by buying *first run* syndication, not just reruns.

One broadcast station is permitted by the FCC to be programmed by another. Such an arrangement, designed for efficiency, is called a local marketing agreement (LMA). The licensee being programmed by another must retain financial and management control.

Cable: Broadcast Basic

A multichannel television service *packages* channels, grouping some channels under one price. There may be several *tiers* of these packages. The *basic* or *broadcast tier* includes all of the broadcast channels that the system carries as well as the public, education, and government (PEG) access channels (discussed later). The broadcast tier may also include some of the satellite-delivered cable networks, particularly those of a public affairs or religious orientation such as C-SPAN and Trinity, but excludes the most heavily watched cable channels. The broadcast tier is mandated by federal law.

SIGNAL CARRIAGE RULES

Cable programming must follow federal *signal carriage* rules. The cable system has to make room for broadcast stations, covering the cable system area, which ask to be carried under *must carry* rules. This is to protect broadcast stations from the loss of audience. After federal court rejection of two versions of FCC must carry rules as a violation of the First Amendment rights, the 1992 Cable Act created yet another must carry requirement.[3] By 1995, the issue was still in the federal courts. Cable operators are not permitted to change the broadcast stations they retransmit; therefore, they cannot insert their own commercials in place of the originals.

Under the *syndication exclusivity* ("syndex") rule, a cable system cannot carry a syndicated program from a distant station that has been licensed exclusively to a broadcaster in the community, even if the program is to run at a different time than the broadcast schedule. A cable system would have to black out the program on the imported station. Not all program rights are sold by the syndicators to broadcasters with an exclusive option. This allows broadcast stations that are distributed to cable systems by satellite, that is, superstations, to guarantee "syndex-free" programming. The superstations only purchase rights to programs that are not offered to broadcast stations on an exclusive basis.

Although there are some exceptions, a cable operator must follow the *network nonduplication* rule. Only the network programming of the *closest* broadcast affiliate of each network is to be carried.[4] The cable system can put on other affiliates of the same network during *nonnetwork* programming. This rule does not hurt the cable subscriber and helps the local advertiser buying spots at local station breaks in the network programming.

To protect the rights of sports franchises to control the television use of their games, cable cannot bring in a game from a broadcast station in a distant city if the local team has not licensed the game to a local broadcaster. This is called the *sports blackout* rule.

LOCAL ORIGINATION (LO)

Not all cable programming is networked. Cable systems also originate programming locally. Any programming that does not come from
outside the system is technically local origination. The term *local origination* (LO), however, is used to refer more specifically to programming
presented and controlled, editorially, by the cable operator. The other
system-originated programming is referred to as *access* programming.
The access programming, where it exists, is usually mandated by the
franchise agreement between the city and the cable operator and is *not*
controlled editorially by the operator except to prevent obscenity. Most
LO is news, public affairs, community affairs, community events, and
local sports. The access channels are generally separated into public,
education, government, and leased channels.

Local origination serves a number of purposes for the cable operator. It may be fulfilling a requirement written into the franchise
agreement. LO programming is good public relations. It gives the
local cable operation, which usually has an absentee owner, community roots. And LO programming can be profitable if local advertising is sold in the channels.

In programming LO and other channels where the cable company
has editorial control, the federal laws and regulations that apply to
broadcasting stations also apply to cable: political advertising, lotteries, wagering, obscenity, fraud, and sponsorship identification.[5]

A major component of local origination is local news presented in
several ways: (a) as 4½-minute to 6-minute inserts in CNN *Headline
News*, (b) 30-minute or 60-minute newscasts produced once a day
and repeated, (c) periodic *retransmission* of broadcast news, and (d)
24-hour local news on cable.[6]

The local news inserts in CNN *Headline News* are placed at 24
and/or 54 minutes past the hour, substituting for a styles and entertainment segment that is intended to be preempted for local news by
cable systems that desire to do so. The cable systems that preempt
the segment are obligated by the affiliation contract to present at least
4½ minutes of news in the 6-minute segment. The remainder may be
sold to local advertisers. The news items are repeated through the
day until updated. The news may be produced by the cable operator
or produced by a broadcast station.

The 30- and 60-minute local newscasts usually are produced for early evening presentation and then repeated on the hour or half hour throughout the evening on a local origination channel. Retransmissions of local broadcast news may be scheduled on cable concurrently and after the original broadcast to extend the possible audience for the news. Usually the news is not modified in any way for cable. But in Philadelphia, Pennsylvania, the NBC affiliate has experimented with transmitting via microwave a 5-minute *Citycast* to the two cable systems that service the city. This special edition of city-specific news replaces the last 5 minutes of the station's news in the cable systems' retransmission of that news. People living outside the city, and people inside the city who are not cable subscribers, see 5 minutes of more generic metropolitan news.

In 1986, 24-hour *local* news on cable was originated by Cablevision of Long Island in an effort to more thoroughly cover the news of Long Island for its 600,000 subscribers. They had been swallowed up in the metropolitan New York television market serving the city itself as well as the major population areas of Connecticut, New Jersey, Long Island, and upstate New York. This service was received with the same skepticism as CNN; the question then became whether or not there was *enough* news to fill 24 hours and whether there would be sufficient audience to generate advertiser support. Another 24-hour local news service was launched in 1989 by television station WWL in New Orleans in cooperation with the Cox Cable system there. Others include newspaper-owned *Orange County News* in Southern California on the fringe of the Los Angeles market; ALLNEWSCO Newschannel 8 serving the Washington, D.C., area; New York *News 1* with one-person-crew videojournalists; Pittsburgh; Sarasota, Florida; Chicago; New England (Boston); and the Northwest (Seattle). Local 24-hour news *coverage* on cable is of three types: (a) more locally focused than broadcast local news, (b) broad market coverage but with segments of more narrow geographic coverage, and (c) regional service.

Many in the cable industry foresee local cable news as a strength of cable against direct broadcast satellites (DBS), which would have a national "footprint" and no local service.[7] Broadcasters see a business in marketing news through cable, extending the value of their capital investment and expertise in local news. Furthermore, broadcaster-supplied local news on cable is a means of promoting the broadcast station. Being the first broadcaster on cable with local news probably preempts the other broadcasters in the market from doing the same and is a hedge against future decline in broadcast audiences.

PUBLIC ACCESS

In its 1972 rules, the FCC required larger cable systems to make available separate channels for public, education, and government (PEG) use. These channels are known collectively as the *access* channels or the *PEG access* channels. In 1979, the Supreme Court said the FCC had exceeded its authority in imposing the access rules.[8] But many cable franchise agreements and city ordinances still required public, education, and government channels separately or in combinations. The 1984 Cable Act sanctions these requirements: "A franchising authority may establish requirements in a franchise with respect to the designation or use of channel capacity for public, education, or government use." Under the act, all existing requirements for PEG access services—facilities, equipment, and financial support—may be spelled out in the request for proposal. Offers, beyond the requirement, made by the successful applicant may be built into the franchise agreement.

The public access channel is one of the most unique developments in cable television. In modern times, the concept of free expression for everybody is impractical. The population is too vast, printing is too expensive, and broadcast channels are scarce. Public access channels on cable were conceived as an opportunity to provide free expression in the television medium to any individual, and to counterbalance the monopoly of programming control given to the cable franchisee. Many of the public access channels went unused. But in some locations, the public access channel became a vital and diversified communication channel for the community.

Although its implementation may vary from community to community, generally the public access channel is available to any resident of the community on a first-come/first-served basis, without any constraints on the content except the personal responsibility of the access programmer for obscenity and libel. Minority ideas and tastes, as well as eccentric communication, have as much status in public access television as do communications from the mainstream of society. In fact, the public access channel may be one of the few places in which novel ideas may be introduced to the "marketplace of ideas."

EDUCATION ACCESS

Educational access channels are used mainly for external communication, that is, community relations—the essential communication between public school systems and citizens and taxpayers. School millage issues, new curriculum plans, and other general interest information may be on the channel. This could include school board meetings (live and/or taped for replay), school board informational programs, and community debate on issues (such as redrawing of school boundaries). More narrowly, the channel may serve the homes of students with instrumental information such as school menus and the calendars of events. Meetings of parents' associations are sometimes conducted by cable.

The education channels may be used for instruction, particularly for broad appeal topics.

GOVERNMENT ACCESS

Government access channels can serve purposes quite similar to those of the educational channels—communication between government and taxpayers, interconnection of geographically separated units (such as fire stations, police precincts, district courts), and training programs.

Many government channels are used as bulletin boards with such mundane but essential information as trash pickup schedules for holiday weeks, tax notices, city council agendas, street closings, city job listings, and availability of recreational facilities.

In the future, cable systems will be required to have an emergency notification system. The public safety director or police chief takes responsibility for its implementation. This service provides a one-line crawl message and/or an audio message on every single channel in case of an emergency (e.g., flood, hurricane, and tornado warning, gas leak). A visual message can be prepared on the same character generator that is used for the automated bulletin. An audio message is also an option.

LEASED ACCESS

Federal law requires cable systems with more than 36 activated channels to make channels available for "commercial use by persons unaffiliated with the operator." This kind of common carrier arrangement, where channels are available to anyone who can pay a fair price, has traditionally been referred to as *leased access*. Its object is to reduce the monopoly over programming held by the operator. Actually, it would be quite awkward for another business to operate, say, a premium channel, maintaining a separate, and costly, billing, marketing, and promotional structure. But one could imagine a sports franchise, or group of sports franchises, leasing a channel to market telecasts of their games. In this case, the sports franchises would be retaining their own telecasting rights. They would be able to maintain control of the marketing and not have to be dependent on the cable operator to set the price, develop the marketing plan, and carry it out effectively. Any other company with rights to program material or a service idea they think the cable operator is overlooking could lease a channel and try to make it work. Newspapers do lease cable channels to extend their news and classified advertising services. Others have leased channels for shopping services.

The FCC rules on candidates for public office, lotteries, and sponsorship identification *do not* apply to access channels.

Cable Programming Service: Expanded Basic

A second tier, formally identified by the FCC as Cable Programming Service, and variously named by cable systems as "satellite," "expanded basic," "extended basic," or some other name to suit marketing purposes, includes the more popular advertiser-supported cable networks delivered to the system by satellite. Under federal law, cable subscribers must take at least the broadcast tier to order any other additional program service, thereby protecting the broadcast stations from being bypassed by a cable subscriber. A few cable systems, instead of separating the broadcast tier and Cable Programming Service, combine them at one price. The industry name for the combination is "fat" basic.

BASIC NETWORKS, CABLE PROGRAMMING SERVICE

The cable network, often called the *programmer*, not only puts together the package of programming but gives the network a coherent *"look"* through the continuity—the network-originated identification and promotional material between and within programs. The look of a network, and the programming theme, give it a *brand* recognition that is of critical importance when 30 or more channels are offered, and will increase in importance as channels proliferate. The basic cable networks give their affiliates advertising time, usually two minutes per hour, to sell local advertising, paralleling the broadcast network system.

The superstations such as WTBS and WGN are broadcast stations that become cable networks by virtue of their national retransmission, by satellite, to cable systems. Local advertising is not inserted by cable operators in the superstations.

Some basic networks, such as CNN and Home and Garden Television Network, offer time periods for *local programming blocks*. Conceivably, many if not all of the niche channels could have complementary blocks of local programming, but these would have to be justified, in the value to subscribers and advertiser revenues, against the production and administrative costs. So far, very few operators have opted to take these time periods, and the networks cover with their own programming.

Basic networks either *acquire* or *originate* programming. Acquisition programming is generally the lowest cost, because it is obtained in the aftermarket, having already had a run in television or another medium. For example, the Discovery Channel, which launched in 1985, did not have an original program until 1989.[9] Networks with a small universe of affiliates and subscribers, and therefore a small potential audience, will have their license fees for acquisition programming scaled accordingly. Original studio programming in a talk format, important to many niche channels, is also inexpensive. Original programming for entertainment is quite costly regardless of the

size of the potential audience. It must be heavily promoted, run
several times, and anticipate an aftermarket.

PROPOSED BASIC CHANNELS

Despite programming structures now dictated by rate regulation
and cable system technical limits on channel capacity, which make it
difficult to add new channels, many new channels have recently been
launched or are now being planned in anticipation of bandwidth
compression. Some proposed channels are spin-offs of existing channels that are seeking new opportunities and hedging against dilution
of their audiences by the others. Many are new programmers seeking
to stake a claim in a particular program area before someone else. In
November 1994, there were about 100 channels in planning (which
are listed in the notes at the end of this chapter).[10] As an example of
the abundance of new channel development, in June 1994, there were
actually 12 health channels intending to launch in 1994 or 1995.[11] To
survive, it helps a new network to (a) be well capitalized (perhaps
about $75 million) to last through the early years of low penetration
and low audiences, (b) have an association with another programmer
for credibility and package deals to win affiliates or (c) be vertically
integrated with a large multiple system operator, and (d) be able to
break even with as few as 10 million subscribers.[12]

À la Carte and Pay Channels

Cable operators also offer some advertiser-supported channels à
la carte, meaning that once a subscriber has broadcast basic, he or she
can buy any à la carte channel by itself.

À LA CARTE

An à la carte channel may be packaged with other à la carte
channels to form a *minitier*, which is discounted from the total price
of the channels offered individually. Some new cable networks are
offered à la carte because it is felt that additional channels in the basic
tiers might be unwanted by many subscribers, and also because the

subscriber rates for à la carte channels were unregulated. A subscriber must deliberately choose an à la carte network. The network cannot acquire an audience over time by subscriber sampling of the channel as it is encountered through surfing a large package of channels. Therefore, the network must have a clear niche identity and be marketed rigorously.

PAY CHANNELS

The *pay* channels, such as HBO, Showtime, Cinemax, The Movie Channel, and Disney, have always been offered à la carte. The advertiser-supported à la carte channels are also pay channels but are not referred to as "pay" because they command a lesser price and carry advertising; the traditional pay channels are the "premium" services uninterrupted by advertising and, in the case of movies, unedited. The most distinguished programming spawned by multichannel television has originated with the pay channels. Once cable programming was admitted to the Emmy award competition, HBO was by far the major winner among cable networks. Although initially movie channels, the pay services have had to develop other programming to differentiate themselves and to justify the subscription price.

Other pay networks offer movies from specific periods or of particular genres. Some have relatively recent movies, such as Encore, including films from the 1960s, 1970s, and 1980s. This kind of channel is usually offered at a low price in combination with one of the pay channels with more current movies so that together the two represent such a good value the subscriber wishes to continue receiving the pay channel. For this reason, it is sometimes called a *value-added* channel, not to be confused with the value-added services of telephone companies discussed in Chapter 3. Still older movies, "classics" or "nostalgia," are marketed as low-priced pay channels or included in basic packages. A regional sports network may be offered as a pay channel.

Any channel may be *multiplexed*. In its simplest form, program multiplexing means that the same block of programming is run on different program schedules on two or more channels. This makes more program options available at any given time for the subscriber.

After the premium price for one of the channels has been paid, the multiplexed versions are offered free or at a much lower price as a convenience to the subscriber. Although, at first, multiplexing was wholly the time-shifting of programs, some multiplexed channels have now added new programs to make each somewhat different.

The curse of pay channels is *churn*, the turnover of subscribers:

$$\text{monthly churn} = \frac{\text{number of pay channel disconnects in the month}}{\text{average number of pay channel subscribers in the month}}$$

Churn is about 5% for each pay channel or, cumulatively, 60% a year. A number of problems cause pay churn. Primarily it is a dissatisfaction with the channel because of the limited number of hit movies. Hollywood releases only about 150 new films each year that earn their distributors more than $1,000,000 in theater rentals in the United States and Canada—about a dozen per month. Of this yearly output, about 30 are "hits" earning more than $20,000,000 at the box office.[13] This means only two or three hit movies in a month.

Pay subscriptions also suffer from the improvement of basic cable channels. The new channels, and better programming on the old channels of basic, at a price of about $20 for 30 or so channels, compares favorably with a single channel at $10. The incredible growth of home video stores has also hurt pay channels.

The pay suppliers use theater box office success as an index of which films to feature and how much to pay for cable rights. But sometimes a film that has failed at the theater box office will play well to pay cable homes. This may not be too surprising, given that the principal theater audience is about 12 to 24 years of age and the pay audience spans the whole demographic spectrum (still somewhat weighted at the younger end).

Both HBO and Showtime have experimented with *exclusive windows* for theatrical films. The practice comes in and out of favor depending on costs and competitive circumstances. At a high enough license fee, the networks can secure exclusive access to a major film for an early period of about a year while there is still consumer interest generated by publicity and word of mouth during the theatrical release. The practice of using exclusive films is condemned by some cable operators. It can stimulate churn, or *spin*, as subscribers switch from one pay channel to another in pursuit of the exclusive hits.

A subscriber to a single pay channel has a less satisfying service, and is a candidate for disconnect, because some of the best titles are licensed exclusively to another pay network and are thus not available.

Pay per View

Finally, multichannel services are marketed by the program—*pay per view*. A listing of the movies and events available is printed in a program guide and/or on a *barker* channel devoted to previewing the programming and presenting the schedule. The individual programs are ordered by telephone. Rather than self-book pay-per-view movies or events, cable operators are likely to receive the programming via satellite. Two major companies supply most of the movies and events to operators: Request TV and Viewers Choice. Other companies are more specialized. Spice and the Playboy channels offer sexually oriented product. The Action network programs action-adventure films. A few cable systems are *stand-alone* for pay per view, ordering movies directly from Hollywood distributors and events from promoters.[14]

CONVENTIONAL PAY PER VIEW

Cable systems usually offer one or multiple PPV channels. Because of the limited offerings at any given time, people must wait for movies they want to see to appear on the schedule. Although movies are repeated many times, this is still inconvenient.

PPV accounts for only a small percentage of cable revenue. This is *not* indicative of the importance of PPV, however. Most systems are giving substantial attention to its development for a number of reasons: (a) The cable industry wants to demonstrate that it is capable of PPV technology; (b) technical advances will soon permit near video on demand for cable and cable competitors (described later); (c) PPV rates are not regulated; (d) big video rental demand indicates a market that could be tapped by cable as a more convenient distribution mode; and (e) a DBS competitor, DirecTV, offers pay per view on a user-friendly schedule.

A few cable systems offer *impulse* PPV where the program orders are placed using the remote tuner and two-way technology. If subscribers watch a pay-per-view movie, they are automatically billed. Orders for PPV programs are greatest in an impulse system, but most systems will not have this technology until they become integrated broadband services. In the interim, addressable converters make PPV possible, without the impulse buying feature. Users phone the cable system to order each desired program, as described in Chapter 2.

PPV is constituted of two types of programming, events and movies. The PPV *event* is infrequent, often live, presented only one time, and special enough to be sold at high prices. Concerts and wrestling are about $20; major boxing events, $35 to $40. Cable subscribers are expected to plan in advance to watch and make it something of a household event, which means marketing begins three or four weeks in advance. *Movies* are the staple of PPV. The purchase of a movie is usually an impulsive buy, chosen over other content available on cable, when "nothing else is on" or when the movie is a much better option than anything else. Subscribers must have the PPV movie schedule continuously available, electronically on the system and in printed form, to include PPV movies in the viewing decision. In most years, events have accounted for a little more than half of the PPV cable revenues, movies the remainder.[15]

NEAR VIDEO ON DEMAND

A few cable systems have a large enough channel capacity as a result of 750-MHz and fiber technologies to permit an approximation of video on demand, where the program is always available at any time the subscriber wants to order. In *near video on demand*, several channels are devoted to PPV. On such a system, one movie of two-hour duration or less could be presented on channel 50 at 8:00 p.m., on channel 51 at 8:30 p.m., on channel 52 at 9:00 p.m., and channel 53 at 9:30 p.m. By 10:00, that movie finishes on channel 50 and is played again. On channel 51, it repeats at 10:30 p.m., and so on. The movie is available on a 24-hour basis across the four channels at 30-minute intervals. If 12 channels are used, three top current titles could be available, always on the half hour. This type of program service, whatever the start time intervals—15 minutes, 30 minutes, one hour—is near video on demand. The viewer who wants a break at any time during the movie may do so, picking it up at the next start time on another channel. The system is designed to accommodate the breaks without additional billings.

When digital bandwidth compression makes hundreds more channels available, very large blocks of channels will be used this way. For example, 40 channels would permit the top 10 titles to run continuously on the half hour; 80 channels could play 20 titles on the half hour or 10 titles at 15-minute start times.

Near video on demand could compete favorably with home video rental stores. In near video on demand, the top titles would always be available when wanted. The only difference, and some feel this is critical, is that the viewer does not have complete *control*. If there is a phone call or some other interruption, the near-video-on-demand viewer might have to wait 30 minutes to pick up the movie on another channel. The viewer could not personally control the viewing with pauses and replays, at will, as with a rental tape.

Programming Economics

PACKAGING

All of the cable networks, basic, pay per channel, and pay per view, have affiliation arrangements with the cable operators similar to the broadcast affiliate agreements except that the cable operators generally compensate the programmer for the service from the subscription revenue. There is no "comp" from the cable network to the cable affiliate.

Whether a system offers programs or channels in basic tiers, à la carte, as pay, or on pay per view is a programming and marketing decision. To understand the elements of the decision among these categories in present-day multichannel television, it is necessary to look at the economic factors inherent in the decision.

The cable operator pays from about 5 cents to 50 cents per subscriber each month for a channel on a satellite basic tier, depending on the cost of the programming and the amount of revenue it can generate. Presumably, each channel on this tier is valued by at least some of the subscribers so that it contributes to the price-value relationship for the basic package. Each channel can help retain subscribers to the tier and attract new ones. But the same channel could be offered à la carte for anywhere from a retail price of 50 cents a month to $12 or more depending on the system's estimate of subscriber perceived value. The operator retains about half of what is charged for an à la carte channel. The programmer needs to get more money for each subscriber to an à la carte channel because there are fewer subscribers to an à la carte channel than to a basic tier. Still another option is to offer programming on a pay-per-view basis and the operator splits the revenue with the distributor.

It is important to recognize that the traditional multichannel television programming schemes are quite flexible. Additional channels and digital technology will provide even more packaging options.

WINDOWS

Cable programming categories are often related to the *currency* of the programming, determining the *windows* by which the programs work their way through the television system. The distributor controls the window. Theatrical films are the principal substance of pay and pay-per-view channels. Films are exhibited in theaters and also by television through home video sales and rentals, pay-per-view cable, pay cable channels, value-added cable channels, broadcast networks, and syndication to broadcast stations and other cable networks. The period of time in any one is the *window*. New windows are added as new outlets and marketing strategies provide opportunities. In the 1950s and 1960s, a theatrical film would go from the theaters to the broadcast networks and then into syndication to individual broadcast stations. Later, pay cable was inserted between the theaters and broadcast networks, then home video between theaters and pay cable. Pay-per-view cable came into a window about a month to three months after the home video release date. Value-added networks get movies after the first broadcast network run. Sometimes the window is open ended; that is, the release date to a particular medium is the beginning of its window, but the window never closes. Home video and broadcast stations are cases in point; once the film is released to home video stores and broadcast stations, it remains in inventory as long as the store operator chooses or the broadcaster wishes to renew the license. The release date to the outlet is most important. A film proceeds through the windows in a sequence that the producer and distributor believe captures the maximum revenue. Each outlet vies for advantage in the release date. A film is heavily promoted before and during the theatrical window; a market and a word-of-mouth reputation, "buzz," begins. But the buzz does not survive for long. The demand for a film in the home video or television market, therefore, is bound to its recency. After a few months, it is much less interesting—it has been displaced by the newer films. It is this period, in the afterglow of the original theatrical release publicity, that is most valuable in the posttheatrical markets. As the relative dollars from each category change, the windows will change. For example, if pay per view could generate more money than the video store, its window would move ahead of the video store's.

CHANGES IN DISTRIBUTION

As noted in Chapter 1, broadcasting is the foundation for the television system in the United States. Almost all of the popular entertainment programs have two runs on broadcast television and then, having made a reputation on a broadcast network, continue in circulation in additional exhibition on individual broadcast stations and cable systems. There is a vestigial value in the programming; some people don't see the program in its first runs, some enjoy seeing a program again, and as time goes by, new generations of people are seeing the old programming for the first time.

The broadcast networks have had difficulty defining a new role in a multichannel world. Although cable may only supplement broadcasting for many people, audiences are diverted to cable and the overall broadcast network audience is reduced. One can imagine channels fragmenting indefinitely. Jonathan Alter lists 350 channels beyond the 150 already in existence. They include a Ken and Barbie Channel, Antiques TV, the Scholarly Association Network (peer-reviewed program topics), Skinhead TV, the Consumer Electronic Network, the Cowboy Network, the Indians Network, Jesse Jackson Television, the 1930s Nostalgia Channel, the 1940s Nostalgia Channel, and so on.[16]

The fragmentation of television audiences makes programming tougher for the broadcast networks; CNN can carry more news, Spice more sex, HBO more movies, and ESPN more sports than any broadcast network. Diversion of audiences makes it difficult for broadcasters to earn a return on big-budget programming costing millions of dollars per episode. When there were only three networks, programming promotion on the network was very effective. But it is no longer possible to reach the entire potential audience with only a few promotional spots on one's own network. Channel surfing and the plethora of new viewing options on multichannel television have disrupted audience flow. Ad hoc networks and *first run syndication*, using the less loyal broadcast network affiliates, independent stations, and cable, bypass the networks entirely and save the 30% overhead of the network. Some claim that first run syndication "puts more money on the screen." Nonetheless, as new networks form, such as the more recent additions—Fox, Warner Brothers, and Paramount—and the number of stations stays relatively constant, there are fewer broadcast slots for off-network programs.

Broadcast networks have lost ground in sports programming because regional cable sports networks can offer some home team games to fans in lieu of a national "game of the week" on a broadcast network. Cable networks bid along with the broadcast networks for sports, sharing NFL football, major league baseball, NBA basketball, World Cup Soccer, and other sports with broadcasting. The siphoning of games from broadcasting to cable, *sports migration*, has been a worry of broadcasters and fans but has not yet been a reality.

An overall concern about audience fragmentation is that the entire television system, across all distribution modes, is degraded. As critic Tom Shales has suggested, increasing the number of channels only thins out the available creative talent.[17]

MULTICHANNEL TELEVISION IN THE SYNDICATION MARKET

Many of the cable networks have been reliant on the syndication market for programming. Waterman and Grant, in a sample of programming from 22 nationally distributed cable networks, found 95% of the programming hours for dramatic shows originated on broadcast networks or in theaters. The *off-network* broadcast programs accounted for a substantial proportion of viewing hours as well.[18]

In the past, cable networks often picked up programs that were "resting" on the syndicators' *shelves* after exhaustive runs in broadcast syndication. But cable has also filled a unique place in the aftermarket. Half-hour programs work best in broadcasting in the early evening *strip* programming (across five weekdays at the same hour), apparently because in those hours many viewers are unable to commit a full hour to a program. As a result, cable networks were able to pick up some good one-hour programs that were not especially suitable for broadcast syndication, such as *Murder She Wrote* and *Miami Vice* on the USA Network and *Cagney and Lacey* on Lifetime. This was a modest breakthrough for the mass appeal cable networks.

A series from a broadcast network, which failed to produce enough episodes for profitable broadcast station syndication in a Monday-Friday strip, may go to cable networks, which can place them once a week in prime time, or in other *dayparts*. Cable networks do not require the audience levels of broadcast stations.

Cable networks have been considered for an early *window* in syndication, before broadcasting. Although cable networks do not produce anywhere near as much revenue for syndicators as the aggregate of broadcast stations, even when station clearance is not very high, an initial run in cable might generate revenue for the syndicator without cannibalizing the subsequent broadcast revenue because of the small audiences for cable networks.

Some syndicated programs are released simultaneously to cable networks and broadcast stations. As time wears on, it may be an economic necessity for syndicators to ply both distribution markets. Each program will have a value in its time slot whatever its distribution mode. There will be so many television channels available that exclusive syndication arrangements with any one television station will be impractical from the syndicator perspective and not especially meaningful to a station or other outlet.

Syndicators have also begun to distribute original cable programming in the classic mode of the broadcast system. Some of the Nickelodeon children's programs have been syndicated to broadcasters, over the protests of the cable system operators, who object to sharing the cable hits. HBO, Nickelodeon, the Discovery Channel, CNN, and the Family Channel have all placed programming in broadcast syndication.

A peculiar type of syndication agreement has taken place between cable networks and the studios. *Airwolf, The Days and Nights of Molly Dodd,* and *The Paper Chase* were all programs with a substantial following on broadcast networks but they did not generate audiences of the size needed. The off-network rights were purchased in a package while the series continued in the production of more episodes for the cable network. The arrangement represents the adaptive ingenuity of the television industry in devising new methods of program production and distribution.

A few individual cable systems and some interconnected regional cable systems have experimented with *"cable stations,"* imitating independent broadcast station in their programming and even giving themselves call letters comparable to broadcast stations (a practice that infuriated broadcasters). The cable station licenses syndicated product that is not currently in circulation in the market. A broadcaster in a television market, with exclusive access to the non-cable subscribers and all of the cable subscribers as well, can always outbid a cable station for syndicated programming in the typical *auction* situation. But in aggregate, in a television market, broadcasters do not have enough air time for all of the available programming. Thus, the cable station can select from a reasonably attractive supply of programs in syndication that were not taken by the broadcasters or are not currently under license to broadcasters.

It should be noted here that the Hollywood studios attempt to manipulate the television syndication windows to maximize the overall revenue from the product just as they do with movies. This process may benefit both the industry and the consumer by stimulating program production investment and extending the program availability to audiences.[19]

Other Programming

WIRELESS

Wireless video services—DBS, MMDS, and some experimental distribution technologies—are alternatives to cable. These are described in Chapter 10. They all rely on the same network programming but are without local origination or access programming, and in the case of DBS, do not carry the local broadcast stations.

TEXT

There are several cable channels that are basically text, with some graphic material (e.g., Associated Press Business Plus, AP News Cable, AP News Plus, Cable Sports Tracker, Electronic Program Guide, Reuters News View, Story Vision Network). Most of these channels are supplied by news-gathering organizations that transmit similar text information to newspapers, television, and radio stations. The product is reformatted for cable subscribers and can be transmitted by satellite subcarriers or telephone lines.

AUDIO

Cable FM radio services are offered by most systems. They are especially valuable in areas remote from large cities, where a limited number of radio formats are available. Distant signals are brought in by antenna and added to the local signals. Shortwave signals are also possible and are on some systems, such as the BBC and Radio Moscow. Some daytime AM stations have found a way to extend their service past sunset by leasing an FM channel on cable. The FCC has no signal carriage rules for cable audio.

Because each cable satellite transponder is capable of carrying at least six subcarrier channels, hundreds of audio signals could be provided to cable systems by satellite. Several are, including radio superstations WFMT, Chicago (a classical station), and KLON, Long Beach, California (a jazz station).

After others have failed over the years, two companies, Digital Music Express (DMX) and Digital Cable Radio (DCR), are now offering *satellite audio* packages. Each signal in the package is a distinct commercial-free format. For example, the DMX lineup is 30 channels: symphonic, chamber music, gospel, "lite" jazz, classic jazz, big band/swing, classic rock, fifties oldies, adult contemporary, folk rock, modern country, traditional country, ranchera/tejano, salsa, urban adult contemporary, Christian inspirational, dance, reggae, sixties oldies, love songs, great singers, beautiful instrumentals, new age, hottest hits, album rock, heavy metal, alternative rock, show tunes, rap, traditional blues. The "DJ" remote control displays the artist, song title, and sometimes writer of the music that is playing. A subscriber buys the whole package for a monthly fee. The two services are taking advantage of the interest in high-quality audio inspired by the compact disc technology. With an audio decoder supplied by the cable operator, the subscriber who has a good stereo system can receive CD-quality audio superior to FM broadcasts.

Cable operations have difficulty selling the FM service because so many cable subscribers connect themselves with a splitter from an electronics supply store. Premium audio services require a descrambler in the home and additional equipment at the headend. Commercial-free premium audio may have some appeal in the bigger cities, even in competition with broadcast radio, but operators have had difficulty breaking through a 3% penetration ceiling.

Summary

This chapter has described the transition now in progress in the television industry: the changes resulting from the technology that makes subscription television available and the programming innovations that have followed. On a much smaller scale, new audio services have come into being. The transition is not complete. It will lead us to full service communication systems, described in Chapter 6.

Notes

1. Gene Jankowski, speech published by the CBS Broadcast Group (undated).

2. For a thorough discussion of the economics of program choice, see Bruce M. Owen and Steven S. Wildman, *Video Economics* (Cambridge, Mass.: Harvard University Press, 1992).

3. 47 U.S.C. 614-615.

4. Older cable systems that carried distant network affiliates were "grandfathered"; that is, they were permitted to continue.

5. The rules on political candidates require that, if the cable system permits any legally qualified candidate for any public office to use the LO channels, then all other candidates for the same office must be afforded equal opportunities. This rule ex-

cludes newscasts, news interviews, news documentaries, and on-the-spot coverage of news. Cablecasts of advertisements of information concerning lotteries, gift enterprises, or similar schemes offering prizes, dependent in whole or in part upon chance, are prohibited. Advertisements, lists of prizes, and other information concerning a lottery conducted by a state, however, are exempted from this prohibition. For any commercial cablecast for which money, service, or other consideration is received, at the time of cablecast, an announcement must be made that the matter is sponsored, either in whole or part, and by whom. This rule applies to paid political cablecasts, and if the political cablecast is more than five minutes long, the announcement must be made at the beginning and at the end of the cablecast. According to the U.S. Criminal Code, whoever utters obscene, indecent, or profane language is subject to fine and imprisonment. Schemes using information transmitted by wire to defraud are also prohibited by the U.S. Criminal Code. Using wire communication for wagering or betting, except where legal under state law, is prohibited in the U.S. Code.

6. This categorization and the material below are based on a survey of local cable news providers. A summary of the study was presented in the paper by Thomas F. Baldwin, Marianne Barrett, and Tony Atwater, "The Maturation of Cable: Initiatives Portending a Comprehensive Local Service" (presented at the annual meeting of the Speech Communication Association, Chicago, Ill., November 1990).

7. Larry Wangberg, a cable executive, believes that one of the greatest strengths of cable against future competition is in local involvement, where cable operators become important community players. "Rx for Tough Times," *Cablevision*, 14 January 1991, 22.

8. *FCC v. Midwest Video Corp.* (*Midwest Video II*), 440 U.S. 689 (1979).

9. Richard Katz, "Acquired or Original," *Multichannel News*, 16 January 1995, Supplement, 8A.

10. Action America (audience participation); Adam & Eve (adult PPV); American Political Channel; America's Health Network; America's Talking (chat covering news and entertainment); Animal Planet; Applause (kids); Arts and Antiques Network; ATV, Advertising Television (5- to 10-minute commercials); the Auto Channel; BET—Home Shopping Network (aimed at African Americans); BET on Jazz: The Cable Jazz Network; Black Shopping Network; Booknet; Cable Health Club; Car and Driver Channel; Catalog 1 (higher-end shopping); Celtic Vision—The Irish Channel; Children's Cable Network; Christian Network; Classic Arts Showcase; Classic Music Channel; Classic Sports Network (sports events and heroes from the past); C/NET (computer news); CNN International; Collectors Channel (merchandise and memorabilia); Conservative Television; Consumer Resource Network (infomercials); C-SPAN 3, 4, 5 (public affairs); Cupid Network Television (shopping for adult novelty and romance products); Crime Channel (movies, specials, and documentaries about crime); DaVinci Time & Space (interactive children's games, education, online computer services); Eco (24-hour Spanish-language news); Ecology Channel (fiction and nonfiction related to the environment); Educational & Entertainment Network (owned by Michael Milken and Michael Jackson); Encore Language Networks; Encore Thematic Multiplex (love stories, westerns, mystery, action, true stories/drama, and youth all on separate channels); Enrichment Channel (social empowerment); ESPN3 (sports news); Fashion and Design Television/FAD; Filipino Channel; Fitness Interactive Television (FXTV); FXM: Movies from Fox; FYI (infomercials and ad industry coverage); Game Net; the Game Show Channel; Gaming and Entertainment Television (interactive bingo, horse racing, lottery jackpots); Global Village Network (international

business, people, culture); Golden American Network (50 years and older); Golf Channel; Gospel Network; Health Channel; Health & Fitness Network; Health Network; History Channel; Hobby Craft Network; Home & Garden Television Network; Horizons Cable Network (lectures, readings, symposiums—owned by PBS); Idea Channel (scholars discussing research in lay language); Independent Film Channel; Interactive Channel (electronic yellow pages); International Channel Multiplex (sports and entertainment in 21 languages); Jones Computer Network; La Cadena Deportiva Nacional (Spanish-language sports); Language Network (instruction, travel); Living (how to and cooking); LMT: Lincoln Mint Television (entertainment infomercials); Main Street (interactive information, entertainment, and education); Military Channel; MOR Music TV Multiples (middle-of-the-road music videos); MTV Latino; Much-Music; Music Video Service (by Time Warner); National Empowerment Television (conservative public affairs); National Health Network; New Culture Network (independent, foreign, and student films); NewSport (sports news); Network 1 (general entertainment, audience participation, direct marketing); Northstar (Canadian productions); Outdoor Life Channel; Ovation (visual and performing arts); Parenting Satellite Television Network; Parents Channel; PC Channel; Pet Television Network; Planet Central TV (environment); Popcorn Channel (preview channel for new films); Product Information Net (infomercials); Q2 (upscale shopping); Quark (science and technology); Real Estate Network; Recovery Network/The Wellness Channel (recovery from addictions); Ritmo Son (music videos for younger Spanish); Romance Classics (romantic movies and television programs); 'S' The Shopping Network (upscale shopping); Sega Channel (games); Sewing and Needle Arts Network; Shop at Home; Showtime Networks (five channels: En Espanol, Family, Action, Comedy, Film Festival); Singles Network (lifestyles, travel, dating); SOAPS (soap operas); Spice2 (adult); Sportscope Television Network (scores, news, standings, odds); Sports Recreation Net (lifestyle, sports, and information); Style TV (owned by Daniel Wolf and Diane Keaton); Talk Channel; TCI/Microsoft Channel (personal computing, multimedia); TCI Music Channel; Tele-Compras (Hispanic shopping); Telehit (Spanish-language music); Telenoticias (news in Spanish); Tele Novelas (Spanish-language drama); Television Shopping Mall; TFN: Telefashion Network (fashion, grooming, home shopping); Therapy Channel (mental health issues); Trax (motor sports); tv! (excerpts from several new channels); TV Macy's (home shopping); ViaTV Network (interactive home shopping); WEB (general entertainment, kids animation, off-network and original series); Western Channel (TV series and movies); WFIT/The Health and Fitness Network; Women's Sports Network; World African Network (movies and news about people of African American, Latin American, and Caribbean descent); World Interactive Network (shopping).

11. They are America's Health Network, Cable Health Club, the Enrichment Channel, Fitness Interactive Television, the Health Channel, WFIT/Health & Fitness Network, the Health Network, Kaleidoscope, National Health Network, Recovery Net, the Senior Channel, and the Therapy Channel.

12. Richard Katz, "Tough Road Ahead for New Cable Nets," *Multichannel News*, 17 October 1994, 3.

13. See the weekly *Variety* in January for the lists of films and the box office receipts.

14. One cable operator is experimenting with *local* PPV for its 220,000 subscribers. A jazz concert was offered; business seminars and "how-to" programs are planned.

15. Movies/events in millions of dollars: 1990, 112/131; 1991, 127/202; 1992, 140/186; 1993, 180/204; 1994 estimate, 212/201. Kim Mitchell, "A Mixed Year for PPV," *Cable World*, 14 November 1994, 68.

16. Jonathan Alter, "What's on TV?" *Media Studies Journal*, Winter 1994, 73-79.

17. Con West and John Eggerton, "A Fan's Notes (and Comment)," *Broadcasting & Cable*, 26 September 1994, 35.

18. David Waterman and August Grant, "Cable Television as an Aftermarket," *Journal of Broadcasting & Electronic Media* 35, no. 2 (1991): 179-188.

19. For a thorough description of the television syndication industry, including cable markets, see Sylvia Chan-Olmstead, "The Market Dynamics of the U.S. Television Syndication Industry: An Examination of Its Regulatory Environment and Market Competition, 1980-1990." Ph.D. diss., Michigan State University, 1991.

5

Technological Convergence

$\int$ ince the invention of fiber optic cable, the telephone industry has always assumed that, ultimately, the twisted pair network would be completely replaced by fiber. Until recently, it was assumed that the architecture for fiber networks would be identical to the twisted pair network: a star configuration with a discrete fiber going from the central office to the subscriber's home.

This approach has two problems. First, it is very costly, because it requires an optical receiver and digital-to-analog conversion equipment in each home. Second, the telephone network has always been independent of electric power in the subscriber's home; the phone works when the power is off. Because optical fibers cannot carry electric current to operate the telephone, this feature of the telephone network would be lost.

Developments in cable television technology provided solutions to both of these problems, and now the architecture originally designed for cable television is being adopted by the telephone industry. There are many variations on the basic architecture, and the final configuration of the integrated broadband network has not yet been determined. This chapter will describe bandwidth compression, the evolution of full service networks in the cable television industry, integrated broadband networks in the telephone industry, the many variations networks may take, and the possible role of wireless technologies in the networks of the future.

Bandwidth Compression

As the number of video programming choices increases, the capacity of cable networks must constantly be increased. Providing additional capacity by adding more bandwidth is very expensive. Another way of increasing the capacity of systems is by using bandwidth compression, which reduces the amount of information that must be transmitted, so that several analog NTSC programs can be transmitted on a single 6-MHz channel.

DIGITIZING ANALOG INFORMATION

Before a video channel can be compressed, it must first be digitized. The analog video, from a camera or videotape, is digitized (see Chapter 2) by a high-speed computer to produce a digital signal. That digital signal requires a very large bandwidth if transmitted directly. Compression, however, reduces the amount of bandwidth dramatically.

The most important feature of bandwidth compression is the removal of *redundancy* in television frames. Often, for example, a television scene will remain constant for a second or more. With an analog system, frame after frame would be transmitted, containing the same information. With a digital system, the frame can be transmitted once, followed by a digital message to the receiving system to indicate that the next frames are identical to the first. At the receiver, the original analog frames are re-created by displaying the first frame over and over. As the original picture changes, only the new information needs to be transmitted (the movement of a person is to be sent; the stationary background is not, for instance). Thus, the redundancy in the picture is not transmitted. The result is that only a small portion of the analog information needs to be sent over the transmission path, and much less bandwidth is required.

JPEG, MPEG-1, and MPEG-2

Bandwidth compression is now being incorporated into transmission systems, and several standards for compression of pictures and video have been adopted. The Joint Photographic Experts Group (JPEG) standards are for compressing still images, and the *Motion Picture Experts Group* (MPEG-1 and MPEG-2) standards have been adopted for bandwidth compression of video. MPEG-1 is an early standard, producing VCR-quality pictures, while MPEG-2 produces broadcast quality. In addition, General Instruments, a major cable television equipment manufacturer, has introduced its DigiCipher system, which, at present, is cheaper than the MPEG-2 standard. These bandwidth compression systems eliminate redundancy and incorporate other sophisticated ways of reducing information. The MPEG standards use *motion prediction*, for example, to reduce the amount of data to be transmitted.

There are two ways that compression can be used. First, a single 6-MHz TV channel could be used to transmit four to ten NTSC channels. This would greatly increase the channel capacity of cable, satellite, or broadcast systems. The other use would be to transmit a single *high-definition television* (HDTV) picture in one 6-MHz channel. The MPEG and DigiCipher technologies can accommodate both of these uses with the same hardware.

The limiting factor in the proliferation of digital bandwidth compression is cost. Currently, the receiving equipment costs hundreds of dollars. DBS operators are now using digital bandwidth compression, and manufacturers are promising set-top converters for cable and integrated broadband systems for about $300 by the end of 1995, and it is likely that the costs will continue to drop. Within a decade, digital compressed video transmission will probably be the predominant mode.

The Hybrid Fiber Coaxial Network

In Chapter 2, the use of fiber optic cables by cable television companies as "backbones" to improve picture quality and reliability was described. As the cost of fiber equipment dropped, and its capacity and performance improved, engineers began to explore the use of increasing amounts of fiber in the network. For new construction, fiber can be used to totally replace trunk lines in cable television networks. Fibers can be installed from the headend to *nodes* (locations where fiber terminates) in individual neighborhoods, where photodetectors can be installed to convert the light energy back to electrical energy for use in coaxial cable networks.

By the early 1990s, it was recognized that cable systems could be built with nodes of 500 to 2,000 homes, using from one to four amplifiers from the node to the most distant home, at less cost than an all-coaxial network.

There are several additional advantages of this type of architecture, commonly called a *hybrid fiber coaxial* (HFC) network (see Figure 5.1). Because the amplifier cascades are so short, higher bandwidth is possible; 750- or even 1,000-MHz systems become much easier to build.

Another advantage is that two-way communication becomes practical. As mentioned in Chapter 2, the main problem with upstream communication in all-coaxial networks is the leakage of over-the-air signals into the network. With small nodes, such leakage will disrupt only signals within the node where the leakage occurs, and can be located and corrected easily. Leakage of radio frequencies into optical fibers is impossible, because they carry light.

Perhaps the greatest advantage of HFC architecture is that each node can be programmed independently. Different programming can be sent over the same channel to different nodes, allowing video on demand (described later in this chapter). This architecture allows much more bandwidth per home, both up- and downstream, than a standard coaxial network.

CONVENTIONAL CABLE TELEVISION SERVICES OVER IBNs

Today's services can be offered over an integrated broadband network very easily. In a typical cable system, 40 or so channels are dedicated to basic and advanced tier services, with perhaps 10 channels for pay television and pay per view. These channels require a bandwidth of 50 to about 400 or 500 MHz. On the new networks, this bandwidth is transmitted down all fibers to all nodes in the standard analog mode. Cable-ready TV sets and today's relatively inexpensive addressable set-top converters can still be used.

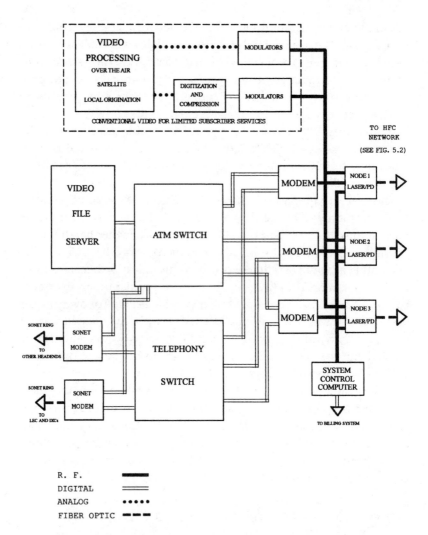

Figure 5.1. Integrated Broadband Network, Headend/Central Office

VIDEO ON DEMAND IN THE IBN

Integrated broadband networks will have bandwidth well above that required for current services, and some of these frequencies will be used for video on demand. Most likely, digital bandwidth compression will be used, but to illustrate how video on demand works, an analog transmission system will be described.

In this example, channels 2-60 (50 to 450 MHz) have been allocated for basic, tier, and pay TV services. Channels 61 to 120 (450 to 750 MHz) have been allocated for video on demand. When the first subscriber in a node orders a video-on-demand program, that program is modulated on channel 61 and routed down the fiber to that node. A command is sent to the subscriber's addressable converter to tune it to channel 61, and only that customer will receive that program. As additional subscribers order programs, their requests will be placed on the next available channels (62, then 63, and so on). Simultaneously, other subscribers in other nodes may order different programs. In this example, the first 60 users of video on demand will receive their requested programming. If the node has 500 homes, about 12% of the potential subscribers can watch video-on-demand programming at any one time before getting the equivalent of a busy signal. If this happens frequently, the node can be subdivided by adding another fiber, thereby sharing the 60 available channels among 250 homes.

DIGITAL TRANSMISSION ON BROADBAND NETWORKS

The above description is only to illustrate the concept of delivering different video programs to individual homes. When integrated broadband networks are built, they will use digital techniques to accomplish the same purpose.

Servers. After video programming is digitized and compressed, it will be stored in computers with hundreds of hard disk drives, called *servers.* Even when compressed, video requires huge amounts of storage capacity. A two-hour movie might require 600 to 1,000 megabytes (600 to 1,000 million bytes), or the entire capacity of a very large hard disk drive on a personal computer. Currently, video server technology is expensive but, over time, the cost will drop significantly. Large cable systems will have their own servers, used to store the most commonly ordered video programming. Regional, national, and even international servers will probably be used to store more specialized, or less frequently requested, programming (see the section "Regional Interconnection," below).

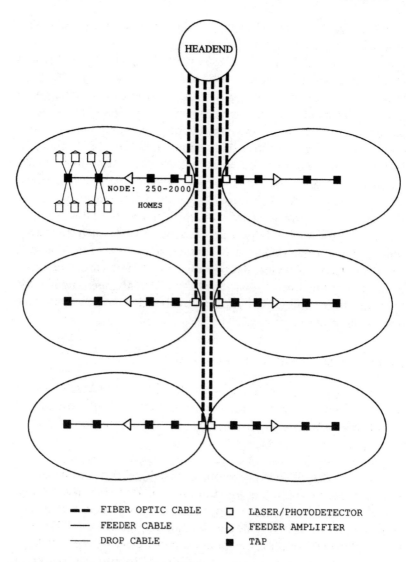

Figure 5.2. Hybrid Fiber/Coaxial Network

ATM switching. Routing the desired video programming from the servers to the subscriber requires switching technology. Although the function of the switching is similar to that required for routing telephone calls, telephone switches cannot handle video. The most likely technology for video switching in an integrated network is *asynchronous transfer mode* (ATM). When a subscriber orders a video-on-demand program, the ATM switch will access the server on which that program is stored. The server creates packets (see Chapter 2, "Packet Switching") containing small portions of the program and a header to indicate where the packets are to be sent. The ATM switch then takes each packet and routes it to the correct fiber node. At the home terminal, the packet is received and changed back to analog video for that customer.

Once a program is stored in a server, it can be accessed by many customers simultaneously, with the ATM switch routing different portions of the program to different subscribers sequentially, just as many users can access a single computer file in computer networks.

Because servers and ATM switches deal with digital data, the same process works for audio and computer data. For instance, a customer could order the music contained on an audio CD and have it delivered to a multimedia home computer, where it would be stored on the hard disk for playback. Computer software or databases from online services or the Internet could be transferred in the same way.

BANDWIDTH ALLOCATION

Integrated broadband network designs currently use 50 to 550, 750, or 1,000 MHz in the downstream direction. Analog transmission will likely be used for the lower frequencies of this range to allow basic cable services to be offered to standard set-top converters or to cable-ready TV sets. Digital compression will probably be used for the next higher frequencies for à la carte, tiers, premium, and some PPV channels. The upper bandwidth will be used for digital transmission of ATM packets for video, data, and audio-on-demand services. A typical frequency plan might look something like this:

Basic cable service	50 channels analog	50-400 MHz
Tiers, à la carte, pay	300 channels digital	400-600 MHz
Video on demand and telephony		600-750 MHz

There is, of course, nothing in the network that limits the spectrum to a particular use. Therefore, the allocation can be changed to accommodate different consumer demands and new technologies.

UPSTREAM TRANSMISSION OVER THE IBN

The problems of using coaxial cable for upstream transmission are described in Chapter 2. These problems are still present in the integrated networks but, because of the small amount of coaxial cable in each node, it is easier to locate and repair signal ingress. Also as noted, ingress will only affect upstream transmission from within one node, not the entire network as in a conventional cable system. Some designs for upstream transmission use *frequency agile* technology, where the frequency of the upstream signal is moved to avoid interfering ingress.

Many engineers are worried that reliability will be inadequate using the 5- to 40-MHz spectrum for upstream transmission. In addition, there is limited bandwidth in this area, and sometime in the future the upstream requirements from a node may exceed this capacity. An alternative method of upstream transmission uses the highest frequencies on the network. These frequencies are less susceptible to ingress, and much more bandwidth is available. The technology works like conventional upstream systems, except that upstream communication takes place at the highest frequencies. For instance, in a 1,000-MHz system, bandsplitting filters route the frequencies from 50 to 750 MHz downstream, and from 800 to 1,000 MHz upstream. Currently, engineers have not resolved the issue of whether to use the lower or upper frequencies for upstream transmission.

HOME TERMINALS

Today's cable television systems use relatively simple set-top converters to control and descramble TV pictures. The terminals required for full service networks will be much more complicated. These terminals, sometimes called *set-top boxes*, will perform the same channel selection, control, and descrambling functions that the current set-top converters perform. They will also contain digital processing circuitry to receive the MPEG compressed digital transmissions and generate analog signals for the subscriber's TV set. In addition, they may be able to receive ATM packets and reassemble them into digital data streams for conversion to video, audio, or use by a personal computer.

The home terminal will be able to format and transmit upstream data from the home. These data may come from a keyboard, a personal computer, a telephone, or other sources, such as home security systems or utility meters. It is not certain where the home terminal will be located. It may be on top of a television set or attached to the home computer. Its functions may be split into two or more units, with a common control unit located in some out-of-the-way place, such as a basement.

The home terminal will contain a powerful microprocessor, together with a number of special purpose integrated circuits for video decompression and other functions. One of the important features of the home terminal will be its *navigator* function. The navigator is the software that makes it possible for a subscriber to locate and access the services desired. Because the home terminal must be easy to use by customers, many of whom are not computer literate, the navigator will make extensive use of graphics and will be simple to use. Designing such a navigator is a major task and will require much field testing to determine what consumers will like.

This home terminal will be very expensive—$500 or more—and will have to provide services that will generate substantial new revenue. One of the advantages of HFC architecture is that it accommodates existing levels of cable service without new in-home hardware. Basic cable subscribers can still get broadcast and public access channels without a converter; expanded basic tier subscribers can get 50 or more channels of cable and premium services using a standard set-top converter; and subscribers with addressable converters can get pay per view. As digital compression terminals become available, they can be added to the integrated broadband networks to provide hundreds of additional channels. Full-scale home terminals as described here would be installed only in homes subscribing to advanced services. The subscribers who have a very limited video service will use a cable-ready television set and, therefore, will have no terminal. A variety of home terminals, from the simple set-top converter to the intelligent home terminal described above, will be used by other subscribers.

Interactive Services

Interactive services involve sending customer-specific informa-tion to individual homes and receiving data from these homes. Current interactive systems use the *polling* method. A computer at the headend, connected to a modulator, sends a customer's digital address over the cable system. In each home, an interactive home terminal contains a receiver and microcomputer, which look for the transmission of the digital address assigned to that home terminal. If the address transmitted from the headend computer matches that of the home terminal, information is transmitted back up the cable system to the headend polling computer. This information might be the channel to which the cable converter is tuned, a request for a pay-per-view or a video-on-demand movie, or data input from the subscriber's computer keyboard.

The headend computer then responds to the request for service it has received from the customer. For instance, if the customer has requested a PPV event, the computer activates the subscriber's ad-dressable converter. The headend computer also communicates with the cable operator's billing system if there is a charge associated with the customer's request.

In the polling system, each home is polled for information sequen-tially, in a cycle lasting from several seconds to several minutes. The polling system, therefore, is not capable of receiving even moderate data speeds from home terminals but is sufficient for many interac-tive services, such as pay per view, interactive games, opinion poll-ing, and home security systems.

The systems proposed for integrated broadband networks gener-ally use some sort of packet transmission (see Chapter 2). When the home terminal has information to be sent to the headend, a header identifying the originator of the packet (the home terminal's digital address) is placed on the data to be sent. The home terminal then waits for its turn to insert the packet into the stream of information going back to the headend. Similarly, the headend computer directs information to home terminals by adding headers specifying the destination of the packet.

Packet systems are capable of handling high transmission speeds to and from the headend but can be overloaded when a great number of home terminals want to send data to the headend at the same time. Traffic engineering (see Chapter 2) must be used to assign an adequate number of upstream and downstream channels to avoid overload.

Telephony and Broadband Networks

The telephone industry is in a different position than the cable industry in deploying integrated broadband networks. Although its architecture is a star configuration, ideal for point-to-point transmission, it has very limited bandwidth. The entire network must be rebuilt so as to offer video. Where remote terminals (see Chapter 2) are used in place of individual twisted pairs to serve areas, the fiber serving them can be upgraded to offer video, but, otherwise, all cables would have to be replaced. The cost of upgrading telephone networks to integrated broadband facilities is, therefore, much higher than the cost of upgrading cable networks.

Most of the regional Bell telephone companies have selected the HFC network described above for their IBN architectures. There is some disagreement about details of the networks as well as about whether to continue to operate the current twisted pair network for phone services or to put phone services on the IBN immediately. Much of this disagreement is because the technology of telephony over coaxial cable is still, at this time, under development, and the costs and capabilities are not yet fully understood (see the section "Unresolved Issues and Alternative Architectures," below).

TELEPHONY OVER THE IBN

One approach for carrying telephony over coaxial cable is to digitize the audio information and transmit it in ATM packets, just like video. This, however, would be expensive and would require complicated intelligent home terminals, designed for video on demand and other exotic services, in a home that might only want standard telephone service.

Another approach is to allocate a small amount of bandwidth for telephony service exclusively and to install devices at each home to interface the coaxial cable to the home's internal telephone wiring.

Each home would have a two-way channel to the central office/ headend over which telephone conversations could be transmitted. Some proposed systems use *frequency division multiplex*, allocating a specific frequency in both directions for each user. Others use *time division multiplex*, with many homes sharing time slots on a single, wider bandwidth. It is likely that a standard will be adopted by the cable and telephone industries for transmission of telephony over HFC networks (see "Standards," below).

HIGH-SPEED DATA/COMPUTER INTERCONNECTION

It is likely that most homes will have both television sets and personal computers connected to the broadband network. The television sets will be where entertainment functions will be performed, and the personal computer will be where transactional and information retrieval functions will be performed. Video games might be done at either location, as might home shopping.

Today, almost all computer interconnection is over telephone lines, at very limited speeds. To transmit complex graphics, such as is desirable for video games, high bandwidths are required. Some cable systems are now experimenting with modems that allow high-speed transmission from the headend to the customer over the cable system, and relatively low-speed transmission back over the telephone network. Because most of the demand for high bandwidth is to, rather than from, the subscriber, this approach may be a viable interim approach. Another interim technology that will allow higher-speed interconnection is ISDN (see Chapter 2).

The broadband network will allow high-speed transmission in both directions, using ATM packets to transmit the data in the same way as video. A personal computer will be connected to the network either by being attached to the intelligent home terminal or by having its own terminal connected directly to the HFC coaxial drop.

The integrated broadband networks will allow interconnection of personal computers to international data networks such as CompuServe, Prodigy, America Online, and the Internet. Currently, only institutional and commercial customers use expensive DS1 and DS3 lines on the telephone network to connect to the Internet. The broadband networks will allow home users to access digitized photographs and even full-motion video sequences, as well as text, from these networks.

The ability to transmit data at high speeds will make possible interactive video games, with players living in different parts of the network or even in other cities or countries. Similarly, video could be transmitted over the broadband network, making videophone service possible.

Unresolved Issues and Alternative Architectures

The network described above, called *fiber to the feeder* (FTTF), or *fiber to the serving area*, is the architecture that currently is the best compromise between capacity and cost. Much of the technology is experimental, and many questions remain. One of the most complex questions is how far into the network to build the fiber. There are several issues involved here: available bandwidth, upstream reliability, network powering, and cost.

The fiber to the feeder architecture adopted by most cable and telephone companies involves fiber to nodes of 500 to 2,000 homes, as described earlier. The larger the node, the cheaper the network; but reliability suffers because more electronic devices are used between the node and the home. There are potential problems with upstream reliability also, because transmission over coaxial cable can be for a mile or more. And bandwidth per home is limited, because 500 to 2,000 homes share a fiber. Most cable and telephone companies plan to install extra *dark* (unused) fibers to each node so that the node can be split into segments in the future, increasing bandwidth per home as the demand increases. Telephone companies, which already have near 100% penetration, must plan for smaller nodes initially if they want to put their voice service on the broadband network.

The deeper into the network fiber is built, the more bandwidth is available to each home. For instance, if fiber is built from the central office/headend directly to each home *fiber to the home* (FTTH), huge amounts of bandwidth would be available for each home. Reliability would be excellent, because there would be nothing but a piece of fiber between the central office/headend and the home. Upstream reliability would also be excellent, because the transmission from the home to the central office/headend would be entirely over fiber. But, because optical fiber cannot carry electrical current, the home terminal equipment would have to be powered from the subscriber's home and would not work during a power outage. In addition, the cost of this type of network is very high.

Another approach, called *fiber to the curb* (FTTC), or switched digital video (SDV), brings fiber to nodes of only 24 or so homes, where copper wire delivers phone service and coaxial cable delivers video the last few hundred feet to the home. This architecture is cheaper than FTTH but less reliable. By installing batteries at the curbside terminal, no power is required from the home, and the system works during a power outage. Some regional Bell companies are considering this approach, which also provides high bandwidth for each home (the bandwidth of one fiber is shared by 24 homes, which allows hundreds of MHz of bandwidth for each home). Upstream reliability is excellent, because transmission over coaxial cable is limited to a few hundred feet. FTTC technology costs substantially more than FTTF.

ADSL

In an attempt to find a way to offer video services over standard telephone lines, *asymmetrical digital subscriber line* (ADSL) technology has been developed. ADSL offers transmission speeds of up to 7 megabits per second from the central office to the subscriber, and up to 576 kilobits per second transmission speed from the home to the central office. This is enough to send two medium-quality video channels to a home. With a switched system, two, or perhaps three, video channels might be enough for each home (one is required for each TV set and VCR the customer wants to use simultaneously). ADSL, however, requires a perfectly maintained phone line, can be sent only over relatively short distances, requires substantial modification of outside plant for some subscribers, and requires very expensive encoding and decoding equipment on each end of the line.

ADSL allows telephone companies to upgrade their facilities for only those subscribers who want video services, but ADSL, a network with very limited bandwidth capacity, costs as much per home as building an HFC network. Although ADSL is being used in a limited way for telephone companies to experiment with video services, it is unlikely to be a viable large-scale or long-term way of offering video.

INTELLIGENCE AT THE NODE

At the current time, it is not clear at what point in the network the ATM packets will be reassembled into video. It may be at the central office/headend, at each node, or it may be within the home terminal. If ATM packets are reassembled at the node, much simpler home terminals are possible. If switching equipment is installed at the node, data generated within the node for transmission to another home within that node would not have to be sent all the way back up the fiber to the central office and then back down the same fiber for distribution to the receiving home. This issue will take years to resolve as consumer demand becomes known and technology evolves.

SECURITY

A major problem with today's cable television technology is theft of service. Analog scrambling systems, although better today than earlier versions, are relatively easy to defeat, and illegal descramblers, which receive all scrambled programming including premium channels and pay per view, can be purchased through mail-order sources that advertise in national magazines and local newspapers. Analog signals will be no different on integrated broadband networks, but digital transmission is much more secure. Although it will be possible to build bootleg digital decoders, it will be much more difficult and expensive. Equipment manufacturers have learned from the mistakes of their earlier technologies and will incorporate features in their digital systems that will make theft of service much less of a problem.

STANDARDS

A major problem in the development of the IBN is that of standards. Each manufacturer and operator has a different approach to the technology. The telephone industry has historically been very concerned with standards, because all telephone systems are interconnected, and information must flow from one system to another. Because customers can buy telephones, every phone system in the country must work with one standard for telephone instruments. The cable industry has paid less attention to standards because each cable system is a "network island." Different systems in different cities can and do use totally different technologies. Set-top converters are owned by the cable companies and need only work within a system. This, of course, changes with the upgrade to an integrated broadband network.

It is desirable for standards to be established for home terminals, so that large quantities of one basic design can be manufactured at low cost. Home terminal standards would also make possible sale of home terminals to subscribers as well as incorporation of portions or all of home terminal functions within TV sets or personal computers.

Broadband networks will be interconnected like telephone systems. Therefore, standards will have to be established for interconnection. Because most interconnection will be digital, many of the standards already adopted by the telephone industry can be used.

Standards will have to be established not only for interconnection but for *interoperability*. For instance, shop-at-home service providers will want all subscribers to use the same button on their home terminal remote control to order merchandise, so home terminal manufacturers must agree on what to call that button and how it functions.

The Alliance for Telecommunications Industry Solutions (ATIS) evolved from the Exchange Carriers Standards Association of the telephone industry but now includes members from any U.S. provider of telecommunication service with an investment in transport and/or switching equipment. The ATIS Standards Committee has developed standards for ATM switches, PCS, and SONET protocols. CableLabs, an industry research and development facilitator and coordinator and a member of ATIS, is working on national and international standards. The Motion Picture Experts Group, responsible for MPEG-1 and MPEG-2, is also a standard-setting association that has developed the video and audio coding syntax and transport stream/packetization for digital compression. The key function of these agencies is to find a solution to technical compatibility problems to assure interoperability at the optimum time, not to freeze development at a formative point or allow the early market successes to force the whole industry into a standard that is too far from the ideal, but at the same time not delaying progress unreasonably. Given the technical and economic complexities of full service networks, and the attempts at competitive positioning, the standards will be difficult to achieve. An underlying objective of these private agencies is to settle on standards internally without depending on government intervention.

OPERATING SYSTEM SOFTWARE

A major part of an integrated broadband network is the computer software that allows each element within the network to work with the others. Home terminals must be able to talk to servers; ATM packets must be routed from servers to the proper node and subscriber; channels must be switched at the central office/headend to the proper nodes; and information must be inserted on and retrieved from regional interconnection networks. The telephone industry has extensive experience with very complex software systems that control their switches, but the full service broadband network will be even more complex. Development of this software may delay some service on the new networks and will almost certainly have problems that will affect subscriber satisfaction with services as they are developed. These customer service issues are discussed further in Chapter 7.

Regional Interconnection

Integrated broadband networks have to be interconnected with each other, for a variety of reasons. Today, interconnection of cable systems occurs one way only, by satellite. Telephone systems, of course, are completely interconnected, but capacity is designed around low-bandwidth voice circuits. Regional satellite and fiber optic networks will have to be built or expanded to handle the huge bandwidth in the local networks. It will be necessary to interconnect networks with each other, for communication; with remote servers and other information providers; and with the long-distance telephone carriers.

An early type of interconnection is the *headend in the sky*, an approach pioneered by TCI, one of the largest cable television system operators and programmers. At a central location, 100 video channels are digitized and compressed onto 10 satellite transponders. These 10 transponders are received at each cable system and placed directly on 10 cable channels. The digitized channels then travel through the cable system to digital set-top converters in subscribers' homes, where they are decoded into 100 NTSC channels. This approach allows cable systems to offer many additional channels with very little investment in the headend. The system could be expanded to offer hundreds of channels.

Fiber interconnection of cable systems is already common. Most cable MSOs have installed fiber to tie together their nearby headends, and many interconnects have been built to distribute local advertising spots to cable systems owned by different operators in a metropolitan area. Because of the distances involved, analog fiber systems cannot be used for many interconnects. Transmission between integrated network central offices/headends will probably use digital transmission and a *ring* architecture (see Figure 5.3). Two fibers, following the same route, loop through each central office/headend in an area, forming a circle, or ring. The information from each location is sent on both fibers, around the ring in one direction on one fiber, and in the other direction over the second fiber. Therefore, each central office/headend will get signals from both directions over the ring. If the fiber is cut anywhere, the signals will still reach every point on the ring. Most likely, *synchronous optical network* (SONET), the worldwide standard for transmitting data over fiber optic cables, will be used over these rings. SONET rings are common in the telephone industry. SONET rings can be used to send data over vast distances. The ring serving one city can be interconnected with other rings and can be used to interconnect broadband networks in different cities and states. The major long-distance carriers are in the process of making their networks capable of carrying the large bandwidths necessary for video, and are adding SONET technology. The Internet will also serve as a way of delivering video and data to FSNs.

REGIONAL SERVERS

With regional interconnection, video servers can be located anywhere. It is likely that IBNs in major cities will have servers on which

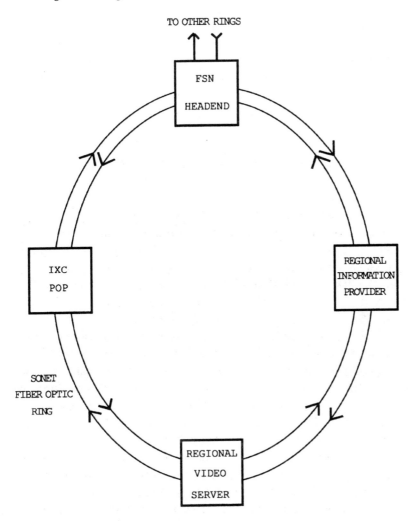

Figure 5.3. Regional Interconnection

the more popular movies are stored, and that nearby smaller IBNs will access these servers. Less frequently accessed movies and other video programming will be stored on regional, national, or international servers, which will be accessed by systems over fiber optic lines owned by long-distance carriers, telephone companies, or cable companies.

Satellites could also be used to access regional servers. Requests for programming that originate on a local network could be sent via telephone lines to the server, where the video programming is sent in a digital data stream on a transponder on a satellite to the requesting network. Integrated broadband networks could also install uplink capability to transmit data to distant servers.

High-Definition Television

As the quality of TV cameras, transmitters, and receivers has improved, the deficiencies of the NTSC system have become even more obvious. The popularity of large screen sets has also made the need for a better system more pressing. HDTV systems attempt to provide picture quality equal to the 35-millimeter film used in movie theaters. To accomplish this, somewhere around 1,100 lines of vertical and 700 lines of horizontal resolution are necessary. In addition, a screen that has an aspect ratio of 16:9 or 5:3, rather than the current 4:3, is desirable, because it is a better representation of the normal human field of view. HDTV will also have CD-quality sound.

It is not difficult to build cameras and receivers that have this resolution. Over 30 MHz of bandwidth is required to transmit the images, however. Given the scarcity of spectrum, it would be almost impossible to allocate such bandwidth for more than one or two over-the-air channels per city. And even on cable, bandwidth is limited. Adding one HDTV channel would require removing five NTSC channels (a 50-channel system would only have room for 10 HDTV channels). HDTV could be transmitted by satellites directly to homes, using microwave frequencies, but this approach would eliminate local broadcasters and cable systems as HDTV providers.

In the 1980s, Japan introduced its Muse HDTV technology. Muse produced high-quality pictures but was analog and required 8 MHz of bandwidth. In an attempt to develop a domestically designed system, the FCC in 1987 established the Advisory Committee on Advanced Television Service. Competing HDTV technologies were to be tested and one recommended for the U.S. standard. By 1992, it became clear that a digital system, using bandwidth compression, would be the best choice. Many of the competing systems joined forces, pooling the best features of each, to create a standard. By 1995, testing of the system, commonly called *advanced television* (ATV), had been completed.

COMPATIBILITY

Although ATV will fit in a 6-MHz channel, it is not compatible with standard TV sets, so cable systems will have to allocate bandwidth to transmit both formats for the foreseeable future. Over-the-air broadcasters face a more difficult problem, because they will need two channels to transmit their programming. The FCC has decided to allocate existing broadcasters an additional broadcast channel in the current UHF TV band to transmit both NTSC and HDTV pictures.

HDTV DISPLAY TECHNOLOGY

HDTV images are not noticeably better than NTSC unless viewed on large screens. Currently, large screen TV sets require a picture tube that is several feet deep, making the TV too large for most rooms. Projection systems, where the image is generated on a small picture tube and projected on a screen, are another option. Projection-type TV sets suffer from inferior contrast and must be viewed from directly in front of the screen. Both types are very expensive.

Development of flat TV screens, which would allow a large screen TV set on a wall, has progressed at a relatively slow pace. Color screens only 6 by 8 inches cost several hundred dollars and are currently used only on high-end laptop computers. Low-cost screens for TV use are no larger than 3 by 4 inches. For HDTV to reach a high proportion of homes, low-cost, relatively thin display systems will have to be developed.

Wireless Technology in the IBN

Wireless technology will have a role in the integrated networks. Personal communication networks (PCN) (see Chapter 2) are the most likely wireless technology to be part of the full service network. PCNs use UHF radio frequencies to provide voice and data service to subscribers, and require cells located only a few hundred or thousand feet apart. The IBN is an ideal network to interconnect these cells with switches and other networks. Cells would be located at nodes in the wired network, where a dedicated fiber (or bandwidth on a fiber used for other IBN services) would interconnect the cell with the central office/headend. PCN telephone service could, at some point, compete with twisted pair phone service.

CELLULAR VIDEO

Recently, cellular video (called *cellular* because many closely spaced transmitters, or cells, are used) has emerged as a possible multichannel delivery system. Cellular video systems use very short microwaves (28 GHz) in which the waves behave almost like light. Transmission is by absolute line of sight or by reflection off various objects between the transmitter and the receivers, making the location of the receiving antenna difficult. Cellular proponents claim that FM modulation and digital techniques, and careful location of the antennas, will result in excellent picture quality on 80 or more channels. Currently, only one prototype system exists, and the technology is experimental. Cellular television service of 28 GHz could be used to distribute multichannel TV or high-speed data to homes from cells interconnected by the integrated broadband network.

6

Convergence of
Voice/Video/Data Information

C hapters 3 and 4 have described contemporary communication, entertainment, and information systems at the threshold of integrated broadband service. The technology of the integrated broadband systems is explained in Chapter 5. Now we move to the communication services and content to which all this is leading. Most characteristic of the future, in the entertainment, news, and public affairs area, is the "on-demand" feature of full service networks. And a great challenge becomes the development of means of navigating on the sea of available material. The interactive feature in news and entertainment poses a different challenge, that of creating material sufficiently engaging to change people's use of television.

Full service broadband networks will technically enable a wide range of interactive services in addition to the various entertainment options such as video on demand. These networks will support the delivery of existing electronic information services including connection to online services and the Internet as well as many additional forms of home shopping, banking, and other types of home-based transactions. Moreover, as greater upstream bandwidth and broadband switching is implemented, broadband networks will be capable of supporting new forms of two-way communication.

Television

Having television entertainment available on demand in an interactive mode changes both its substance and its use. First, we will discuss these changes in relation to video on demand (VOD) and then, later, interaction.

It is important to recall, from Chapter 5, that once a switched broadband system is installed, it no longer has any limitations on channel or program capacity. The incremental cost of adding a program or channel is essentially zero. Regional, national, or even international servers can make available every minute of video ever produced. Remotely located distant video servers would aggregate small audiences from many locations to justify storage of the item.

PPV, VOD

Because movies are now made for theatrical exhibition, much of the content is skewed toward a young age group that accounts for the bulk of the box office and popcorn receipts. Topics unattractive to this group are generally not produced. It can be assumed that video on demand, that is, home viewing of movies on large screens, will open the medium to all demographic groups. Films can now be made on a greater range of subject matter, targeted for diverse audience groups. Success in the theatrical release may not be necessary given a VOD aftermarket. Some films will pass over the theatrical market, going directly to VOD. An example in this context is the movie *Finnegan Begin Again*, made for HBO, about an older couple, played by Mary Tyler Moore and Robert Preston, beginning again in love. This movie would never have been made for theatrical release but would play well to older audiences at home.

Buy rates for PPV support the hypotheses that the PPV and theater audiences are different. *People Under the Stairs*, a low-budget thriller that grossed a modest $22 million at the box office, did as well as

Thelma & Louise, which grossed $43 million, in Coaxial Communications' Columbus, Ohio, system. An animated cartoon, *Bebe's Kids*, which earned less than $10 million at the box office, outperformed many box office blockbusters in a number of cable systems. Although relatively unexplored at this point in the development of PPV, there may also be differences between the video store market and PPV buyers. Over time, the broader home market could have profound implications for Hollywood, permitting the making of films of much greater diversity, unleashing Hollywood's energies and creativity, and bringing in new talent.

It can also be expected that lower-budget specialty films, art films, and foreign films will find a better market in VOD than in theaters. Presumably, promoters will find a way to broaden expectations of television and broaden audience tastes.

EVENTS

Events will also change in response to the audience potential of VOD. To this point, promoters and the cable industry have had difficulty in creating events worthy of special consumer excitement. Professional boxing matches have worked, but not enough boxers have earned the national or international recognition necessary to justify a big PPV match. Wrestling extravaganzas worked well at first—*Wrestlemania I, II, III*—but as the novelty wore off, audiences decreased. There was the tasteless, shock jock Howard Stern's record-breaking 1994 New Year's Eve show. It relied on novelty, which probably could not be sustained, to break records for buy rates.[1] Rock concerts have had some success; however, the biggest stars have been unwilling to risk the damage to their reputations of a low buy rate. Promoters have not been able to come up with "spectaculars" that would make PPV more exciting. The event lineup has included such items as *Women's Wrestling*, a Garza-Rosario boxing match, *Thrillmania* (skiing), *Sisters in the Name of Rap*, Dwight Yoakam, *Bikini Open*, the Neville Brothers, Andrew Dice Clay, Jerry Herman, *Wrestlemania History & Heroes*, and the *Great American Motorcycle Rodeo*. These events were among many others that were purchased by less than 1% of the cable households to whom they were offered. In 1994, boxing accounted for half of the PPV event revenue; wrestling, one-third; music, 8%.[2] When the cable and telephone industries have completed the transition to a critical mass on full service broadband systems, and a majority of households have VOD, it is a certainty that promoters and impresarios will rise to the increased programming demand with more imagination and bigger name performers.

Some in the multichannel industry believe in a market for highly targeted PPV. For example, the *25th Gala at the Met* was offered to opera lovers in 1991. It was not expected to attract large numbers, and did not, but those who were interested paid about $35. In the future, with a large enough base of households, it will be feasible to program *niche VOD*. It should be noted, however, that niche pay per view has been in decline recently. Promoters of the smaller scale events have been discouraged by the high guarantees demanded by performing artists on the one hand and the unwillingness to promote the events locally by cable operators on the other.[3]

SPORTS

Regular sports contests are a special category of event. Recently, only three major league baseball teams, five National Basketball Association teams, and three National Hockey League teams offered any games on PPV. Currently, the number of games free on broadcast television and at a package price on regional sports networks have discouraged the development of pay-per-view sports. One possibility is to supply out-of-region sports on a pay-per-view basis. The ABC broadcast network and ESPN have combined to offer collegiate football games on PPV. ABC produces four or more games each Saturday, each broadcast in regions most appropriate to the game. Only one game is available in a region over the air. For example, on September 3, 1994, if you lived in California, you could have watched the USC-Washington football game on any ABC television station. But, for $9.95, you could also have chosen to watch, on PPV, Virginia versus Florida State, Boston College versus Michigan, Notre Dame versus Northwestern, or Tennessee versus UCLA. A similar out-of-region PPV system is contemplated for professional sports. Conceivably, one could watch any sports contest that is televised by broadcast or cablecast anywhere in the United States. So, if you were a Chicago Cubs fan living in Nevada, you could watch any of the Cubs baseball games that were telecast. Extending the audience for these sports is a logical function for multichannel full service networks and is already being done by DBS.[4]

Despite the problems with the 1992 Olympic Triplecast, the NBC attempt to combine broadcasting with PPV foreshadows the potential of VOD. Viewers could be presented an Olympic menu of live and recorded sports from which they choose events of interest and view the entire event rather than just a short segment. The menu would also include all of the human interest sidebars about the athletes and the sports venues.

An increase in television outlets and revenue for professional sports teams may increase the number of teams and leagues. It could improve the economic prospects for women's sports. Eventually, we will begin to see the effects of international coproduction in movies, events, and sports. Producers and promoters will design or create all three to maximize worldwide audiences. Movies will have international themes and stars from different cultures. Events may be concerts combining performers from different cultures, or set the star from one culture in the venue of another (e.g., Madonna in Tokyo). Television will work to develop international stars. Prototypes of international sports are World Cup Soccer and the Summer and Winter Olympics. More such events will be created for television such as the Goodwill Games.

AUDIO ON DEMAND

Full service networks will also provide audio entertainment on demand—pay per listen. Subscribers will be able to access any recording. A pricing system will develop to reflect the currency of the recording and its popularity. The user would be able to put together programs of high-quality digital recordings drawn on demand in sequence from remote record libraries. As in the television system, audio on demand would not supersede fixed schedule audio services for the listener who would prefer to select a particular channel and accept what is offered.

INTERACTIVE ENTERTAINMENT

At this juncture, most television entertainment is "passive." The notion of passivity in television viewing is misleading. Any entertain-

ment must engage the audience; the viewer is involved to the extent
of willingly suspending disbelief in fictional material, even when the
stimulus is a small flat television screen. It might be said that "escape" television should envelop the viewer to the degree she or he is
lost in the story. This may also be true of some news and public affairs
programming, where the viewer is not so much cognizant of the
currency of the information but is involved in the affective dimensions of the stories being told. To suggest a different kind of viewer
involvement might be at cross-purposes with the escape function.

But the viewer could be more actively engaged in some types of
television. Proponents of interactive television are experimenting
with formats that give viewers choices in plot and character and
allow them to compete with other viewers or at least be aware of
responses of others in the audience.

The CD-ROM previews interactive television entertainment. The
latest Indiana Jones episode, *Indiana Jones and the Fate of Atlantis,* by
George Lucas, is a CD-ROM in which the plot evolves dependent on
choices by the users. Carmen Sandiego, a television character on PBS,
has emerged from the Broderbund Software "Living Book Series" and
is poised to become interactive on television as well.[5] Note this description of a Voyager CD-ROM and imagine it as interactive television:

> "Freak Show"—put together by the Residents, a reclusive San Fran-
> cisco band that created some early music videos—takes you backstage
> at a down-at-the-heels carnival. Tex, the chain-smoking barker, intro-
> duces each act. There's Wanda the Worm Woman, Harry the Head,
> Herman the Human Mole, Jelly Jack the Boneless Boy and more. All
> have a story to convey, but you have to poke around in the trailers, read
> personal letters, listen to laments and look at photo albums to explore
> their sad yet oddly exhilarating lives.[6]

Computer books, where the reader makes decisions for the characters or selects plot options, preplanned by the writer, are also a
precursor of interactive television entertainment, and some television has been produced in this mode. The producer must assume that
the viewer *wants* to make such choices rather than leave it to the
producer's own best creative judgment.

Another possibility is to permit viewers to select camera angles. A
television program or film can be, and sometimes is, shot so that

every scene is covered with at least a close-up, medium, and long shot. The editor then chooses the shots to tell the story or create the mood desired. The viewer could have these options as well. A viewer may also have the option of three-dimensional navigation though the visual environment. In these applications, as in making plot or character choices, there is an assumption that the viewer would want this creative freedom.

Television game shows come almost immediately to mind as beneficiaries of the technologies for interaction. In the conventional one-way television game show, the viewer is presumed to be playing along. Why not make that participation real, where the viewer actually competes with guests and can earn prizes as well? Versions of *Jeopardy* and *Wheel of Fortune* already exist in this form. Conventional television game channels could be converted to interactive when enough full service networks are in place. Because many games are so extremely popular, it is no great leap of the imagination to expect them to work in the interactive mode for some people. The question is whether most people would like to mix it up with the carefully selected guests, or instead take vicarious pleasure in passively observing the games. Of course, new interactive game shows could be developed at various levels of difficulty to suit a variety of home players.

Text overlaying video holds the potential of enriching or backgrounding programs. Court TV is developing "BackChannel" to allow viewers to point the remote to icons on the screen, calling up text material. The "people" icon would produce biographical information on the attorneys, judge, witnesses, and other parties in the case. The "word" icon would bring to the screen definitions of legal terms. Incidentally, the information is already gathered for commentators and analysts. TV Food Network's "Recipes on Request," now being tested, would offer recipes via the vertical blanking interval of the television picture. The recipes have been prepared initially to answer mail requests.[7]

Andrew Curry sees television beginning "to provide the focus for a series of overlapping 'virtual' or 'electronic' communities brought together by a shared interest in the subject of a programme." He uses the example of a cooking program in which a viewer calls down a recipe, suggests modifications, and gets reactions and further modifications from others.[8]

Audiences have always interacted with television performers—talk show hosts, news anchors, and fictional characters—a phenomena called a *parasocial relationship*. Viewers sense an intimacy of fellowship with the television persona. Voice contact through an integrated broadband system will enhance intimacy. In digitally compressed systems, there will be many more programs (and channels) offering conversation with program hosts and guests, thus improving the probability of connecting.

Friedman sees interactive television evolving in three stages. The first, "pointcast," will be services such as video on demand, delivering a service to an individual household on order. The second stage, "passive interactive," moves into nonlinear entertainment as in games or plot direction. The third is "social interactivity," in which people talk to each other and participate in shared activities.[9]

Sports contests are also logical interactive events. To this point, programming has been developed to permit viewers to judge sports such as boxing, figure skating, and gymnastics. Viewers compare their own scores with the rest of the participating viewers and professional judges. Other formats include the calling of plays in football (e.g., run inside or outside, short or long pass, go for it, punt, or try a field goal). The viewer compares his or her choices with other viewers and, as the play unfolds, with the coach or quarterback. A basketball version allows viewers to select a subset of players. The viewer's fortunes are then tied to the performance, along several dimensions, of these players. Fantasy sports, such as rotisserie baseball in which game players select athletes and compete on the basis of the player statistics, could be enhanced by opportunities to interact and compete with other fantasy players, acquire data, and make player trades. There is also the possibility of real wagering on some sports such as betting on horse races in states where off-track betting is already available. Sports viewers could choose camera angles, as described for other entertainment television, ask to focus on a single player, or call for instant replays as desired.

Sega, the video game manufacturer, sees three levels of on-demand video games. The first is downloaded game play, where a small game is loaded into a set-top memory, which takes about 30 seconds. The customer pays by the month to access a catalog of games, or pays per play. The second is the server game play, in which case CD-ROM-type games are accessed from a server capable of "doing acrobatics to find new chunks of data every few seconds." This is a very demanding use of the server over extended periods. The third type is networked play in which two people play each other from different geographic locations, or there are online tournaments. The net-worked play works with either downloaded small games or the grander scale server play. Sega expects the most practical market is the small game, downloaded, with the networking feature.[10]

The Sega Channel, a game service owned by Sega, Time Warner, and TCI, began a market test in 12 cities in 1994 using 16-bit system technology (not waiting for upgrade to 32-bit or 64-bit platforms, which are in development). The channel offers about 50 video games monthly, with 75% of the games changing every month. Some of the games, called "test drives" (not yet in stores), allow a limited preview play. The subscribers are sold or leased an adapter that fits on their own Sega Genesis controller. The games are downloaded to the controller. The cartridge empties when the subscriber is through playing. Prices were tested at $11.95, $14.95, and $19.95 and appeared to be acceptable up to $14.95.[11] A special cartridge made for insertion in the Sega Genesis permits live, multiplayer competition over tele-phone lines on a pay-per-play basis with prizes scaled to the number of people playing. (Adult games for prizes, such as church bingo, take in $40 billion per year, compared with the $6 billion for video games.) At some point, Sega intends to include a violence control chip in the equipment so that certain games may be excluded from play. Another device makes possible real-time, two-way voice and data communication between players. Nintendo and Commodore/Amiga are also exploring electronic distribution of games. In the future, it will be important that games from different companies (e.g., Sega, Nintendo) can be sent over the same data stream to universal adapters that will interface with any type of game box.

In some CD-ROM games, "virtual actors" wear "waldos" that translate body and facial movement into animation. Games are drawing on theatrical movie themes and include digitized video from the films. Some games are made so that players confront and interact with the video characters or travel with characters, often major actors, through video scenes.[12] The virtual reality derivative and video games are expensive so it might not be practical to own the game; distribution via broadband networks on a pay-per-play basis could be more reasonable.

The cost of any interactive programming could be high for the consumer. It would include all of the costs of the conventional television, adding, as the case may be, more writing, camera shots, scenes, and graphics. Therefore, consumers could reject some forms of television interaction, not only on a negative assessment of the interactive mode for particular programming but because of the cost.

READING TELEVISION

An interesting aspect of interactive television is the integration of printed text and graphics with video. This may be small consolation to those lamenting the abandonment of the print media to television. Nonetheless, there will be many situations where users go freely between video and text because text will be the most efficient means of storage and display for specific purposes, such as background on a specific historical point related to a running video news story or the discography of a musical group on video. Further, supplementary printed material could be delivered to the home at low cost so that it is more conveniently accessible.

NEWS AND PUBLIC AFFAIRS

A full service network will provide news and public affairs on demand as well as entertainment programming. Menus will contain topics by headline, subject, and date. Users will be able to preprogram a set of topics of personal interest and, with a single command, call up all of the news on those topics during a prescribed period or since the last access. A headline service will assure users that they have not foreclosed on items of general interest that do not fall in the preprogrammed categories.

The viewer will have the option of taking a condensed version of a story, prepared by a professional journalist perhaps desiring the journalist's editorial judgment and style, or taking, instead, the raw material of the story without the intervention of the journalist. Here, too, the viewer may be able to select camera angles and will have the opportunity to draw on background material as necessary. Media now have "virtual newsrooms," where reporters in many different locations are interacting with editors and other reporters in cyberspace. Perhaps integrated broadband network subscribers could eavesdrop, or participate, in these virtual newsrooms. Journalists are worried about the libel problem with unedited news. A person in the news does not do much damage with a defamatory statement, and it is not libel, until it is "published."

Price Discrimination Model
of Television Distribution

The packaging and consumption of television programming in full service networks will change to a *hybrid* of several different distribution modes. These modes are already familiar: video on demand, à la carte, channel packages, broadcast basic, and broadcasting. Generally, customer classes can be separated by pricing across the modes of distribution and within the video-on-demand mode.[13] Programs in the video-on-demand mode will begin at a high price and be successively reduced as demand wanes. In much of popular entertainment, the relative value to consumers is based on the initial release date, or currency, as discussed in Chapter 4—the earlier the access to the program, the higher the price.[14] As demand becomes exhausted in the video-on-demand mode, programming may be released to the other modes of distribution. By making programs available at lower prices on VOD and then through à la carte and channel packages, each consumer who is interested in a program has access to that program at the price he or she is willing to pay. This maximizes consumer welfare, in the sense of facilitating the maximum diversity of program production. All consumers eventually have access to the programming although some consumers who have high interest in a program may have to wait until they can afford to view.

The hybrid modes of program distribution are necessary because the established consumer demand for television delivered in the traditional modes will not permit a radical change to video on demand. A significant market already subscribing to multichannel television services, which includes two-thirds of the U.S. population, is buying television programs by the channel and in packages of channels. Some people may prefer all of their television to be delivered in this manner. Others, who appreciate video on demand, may still choose to do some of their viewing with less specific choices—at times looking for a generic niche channel or surfing in a package of channels. Furthermore, as we discussed in Chapter 5, the relatively expensive home terminals necessary for video on demand need not be provided to every household. The investment can be spread over a number of years as the demand evolves. Even telephone company video providers have recognized the advisability of this transitional development; at least one company has placed a major order for analog converters.[15] A television service must offer a combination of options.

VIDEO ON DEMAND

With integrated broadband technology in place, video on demand will be the first priority or window—a menu offering the cream skimmed from the top titles and events, at a relatively high price, in the first television viewing opportunity. Once compressed bandwidth and addressability, or interactivity, are available in a critical mass of cable systems, almost all live programming such as sports contests and concerts will migrate to video on demand. Some specialized live news events will also be offered as VOD. In live events, the viewer gets *exclusive* access and the electricity of spontaneity. At high prices, successful event promoters have the potential of an enormous return, even at modest buy rates. It would take an audience of only about 2 million households to generate as much revenue as the Superbowl at about $30 per household.[16] There are political, public relations, and perhaps mass advertising goals that would prevent this from happening, but it illustrates the potential. (Please refer to the notes at the end of this chapter for a discussion of the principles of apportioning sports events across television outlets.[17])

Movies will have their first television window in video on demand. Some people will pay a premium to obtain recently released movies at the earliest date in the afterglow of the excitement generated by massive advertising and promotion activities, particularly when access is so convenient. Other programming, such as interactive games, personalized business information, and instruction, will be offered exclusively on demand. New generations of the top program series, of the type that now appear on broadcast television, may be shifted to the pay-per-view, video-on-demand menu. The producers of this programming have an opportunity to enhance their revenue by making some sales at an early date before release at progressively lower prices in other distribution modes—a "countdown strategy." Prices will accurately reflect demand because they are set in response to demand and can be adjusted quickly. Indeed, the prices could be determined automatically. (See Chapter 7.)

The on-demand menu can also include repeats of selected high-profile programs, and news programs, from other television distribution modes. The Discovery Channel is testing a service called "Your Choice TV" through which a subscriber may order episodes of broadcast network television programs that were missed during the first run. *ER* might be available at 59 cents, or a soap opera for 29 cents. Cooperation from the copyright holders of the programs and the broadcast networks is required. The rights holder and the full service network would split the retail price, with a small transaction fee going to "Your Choice TV." Such a service could become a library of current television programs, from channels with a *fixed schedule*, that would be now available continuously.

The two principal markets for movies—theaters and home video store rental—will at first relegate video-on-demand television to a second aftermarket—the first release to the theater, then video stores as the first aftermarket. Too early a release to video on demand could upset these principal markets. In the case of the theatrical market, according to Robert Klingensmith, president of Paramount's Video Division: "Every box-office dollar is an advertisement [for the studios]. It's a validation. That validation is very important to us. I don't see any reason to forsake that market."[18] To precede the theatrical release with VOD might risk the market value created by the simultaneous release of a film to theaters across the nation.

Because of the industry reluctance to test early PPV or VOD release of films, TCI, the large cable MSO, has forced the issue by investing in a small theatrical film production company, Carolco, in return for an agreement to release some films *before* or simultaneously with the theatrical opening. It is reasoned that, at $20 or $30 a showing the weekend before the release to theaters, good revenue could be obtained without jeopardizing the theater box office. In fact, an advance VOD showing could possibly stimulate box office sales.

Because home video rental and sales now produce more revenue than the theaters, the film industry is also reluctant to tamper with this outlet, even though the business of video on demand is actually quite attractive to Hollywood. The film studios and distributors prefer to share in each sale, as is the case with VOD, PPV, and theatrical rentals. They dislike the *first sale doctrine*, which only gives them revenue from the original sale of a tape to the video store operator and no share of the rental revenue. But for the moment, studios cannot put in jeopardy the huge home video store revenues.

One thing that could make VOD more palatable to the video stores and Hollywood is an anticopy device that can be built into home terminals preventing copying of VOD movies.[19] As long as VOD movies are relatively high priced, and not copied for underground circulation, the video rental business could remain viable. The experience of the computer software manufacturers with copy protection, however, might suggest that VOD television consumers will also reject it. Software manufacturers eventually eliminated copy protection in response to customer demand even though this made illegal use possible.

Once VOD is in place, studios are less dependent on syndicators or distributors for television exhibition. Multichannel operators will put on almost everything available. Thereafter, promotion plays a major role—a task that will fall to both the operator and the studio, with the main promotional burden perhaps with the studio. The studio will be reluctant to rely heavily on the operator because any given program is only an infinitesimal proportion of all the items on the operator's menu. This is similar to a grocery store. The store makes choices about what to put on the shelves and how to position the products, but basically carries all desirable products. The store then promotes some products itself, while the producers of the groceries do the majority of the advertising.

The price discrimination model of television distribution vastly expands the viewer's freedom of program choice. Programs of every imaginable type are available, on order. If television is used to fit one's mood, then many moods will be available. An evening of television may be constructed with modules of television purchased and placed in any sequence the viewer desires.

As noted above, it is possible for *all* television programming to be offered by the program, on demand. The most valuable programming would carry a high price tag, the least valuable perhaps only fractions of pennies. But many television viewers would be uncomfortable with a system in which a menu is used for every single program choice. There would be no opportunity for browsing through ongoing programming as a means of selection. Some viewers will want a program packager to help make the choices. Therefore, the hybrid system of television distribution adds à la carte channels and some packages of channels to VOD.

Video on demand could be available as an adjunct to each of the other modes of video service except broadcasting. Whether this is the case depends on the potential success of VOD across all types of subscription television users. It may not be feasible to supply all of the subscribers with the home terminals to receive video on demand. Such equipment could be wasted on light users. On the other hand, it may be difficult to market the concept of VOD to people who are not equipped to try it—the chicken and the egg problem.

À LA CARTE

À la carte distribution of television, permitting people to buy *categories* of programming by the channel, will be available for a great many channels at a wide range of prices. These will include some of the services now on basic cable broken out as à la carte channels so that only those people interested will have to pay. This was a trend stimulated by the Cable Act of 1992, which regulated prices for basic cable tiers, leaving à la carte channels unregulated. Full channels of movies would be available after pay per view and video stores, by genre, such as westerns, comedy, action-adventure.

Related à la carte channels may be put together and offered as a group at a lesser price than the total for the channels individually. Or people may be able to pick from a large group of à la carte channels. If they select six channels, there is a $2 discount from the à la carte price total; if they select 10 channels, a $4 discount; and so on.

Predictably, the à la carte channels will include high-profile television series after exhausting their value on VOD as well as lesser
quality entertainment series in the first run on à la carte. VOD and à
la carte channels can be expected to eventually include the entire
mass entertainment product once on broadcast network television.

But the number of channels could also shrink, in time, if subscribers accept and make heavy use of video-on-demand services. To
hedge against this scenario, the cable networks are now attempting
to acquire program rights in both pay-per-view and video channel
distribution so that they will play a role in distribution, whatever the
dominant mode.

In à la carte niche channels, the passive interactive devices (see
p. 134) might be popular. Presumably, the viewer is intimately involved with the content, sharing an affinity with the other viewers.
In this context, polling and displaying opinions would be of interest.
Because the viewer is so keenly interested in the subject, deeper text
information would be in demand.

Packaging programming into channels still has merit in full service
networks. In the microsegmentation of channels, the viewer may
know the channel but not specific programs. One may seek outdoor
life, on the Outdoor Life Channel, without wanting to make a discrimination between fishing and camping or between bass fishing
and trout fishing. A channel has a brand identity, image, and look
that a viewer can trust for programming of interest. The familiar
channels will be friendly refuges in the blizzard of programming on
high-capacity systems. This is why there are large numbers of start-
up channels, listed in the notes for Chapter 4, despite the imminent
availability of on-demand television.

BASIC PACKAGES

In the price discrimination model, some *bundles* of channels under
one price could survive for marketing purposes and for the convenience of consumers. It is difficult to break channels out of a package
if they have existed for many years as part of the package. Nor would
it be possible to compete in video service without offering large
packages of channels at a single price when others in the market are
doing so. The packages could have topical identity such as news,

including, for example, international and national channels, 24-hour local news, and specialty news channels such as business, weather, and consumer news.

Other packages could include movies, in still a later television window, and series, getting another run after video-on-demand and à la carte channels. Lesser quality entertainment programs and series (e.g., of the character of the current early evening syndicated programming), not quite up to the value of the entertainment programs in video on demand or on first run à la carte channels, would fit into these entertainment packages. Some new channels might be placed in this tier so that they could be sampled by viewers in the process of using other channels in the bundle. Pricing of the packages would be low, reflecting the value to advertisers of this most universal service for multichannel subscribers as well as the advanced age or lesser quality of the programming.

BROADCAST TIER

The basic "broadcast tier" includes broadcast channels and any channels that are free to the operator, such as religious networks and public, education, and government access channels. It is the most universal level of subscription television service. This tier of channels will be offered at a low price as a starter multichannel service and to accommodate federal signal carriage requirements. If current federal rules remain in effect, the integrated broadband system would be required to provide broadcast basic to all subscribers before they are eligible to access any other level of service.[20] Shopping channels would be included to maximize the potential customers.

BROADCASTING

Over-the-air television broadcasting will continue to be available without subscription to a multichannel television service. It will include national and local news, public affairs, and entertainment programming, most of it syndicated to broadcasting from earlier exhibition in the subscription services—broadband systems, DBS, MMDS, and SMATV. A few broadcast networks might remain, to avoid the high transaction costs of station-by-station syndication, but they would be a business convenience, not a necessity. Public broadcasting could be a significant element in this television service model, supplying programs to broadcast-only households to balance the commercial services offered by a reduced broadcasting system.

Advertising support for broadcast television will decline as budgets shift more money into targeted channels or programs. It will take time for the buyers of advertising to respond to the opportunities afforded by the finely differentiated programming of integrated broadband systems. Time is also needed to get the ordering, insertion, and billing systems developed to manage and automate the advertising purchase and placement process. (See Chapters 7 and 9.)

The price discrimination model of television distribution is actually a more natural schema for television product distribution in our economic system. The reason that access to television programming has been equal for all people, at no cost for programming, is because broadcast television had no means for directly charging viewers. With a limited number of broadcast channels, advertising was a sufficient source of revenue. In the near future when all integrated broadband systems will have the technology to charge by the program, or unit of time, and hundreds of channels are available to accommodate all sorts of programming at every price level, television programming will be placed on the market in the same way other goods and services are offered, approaching perfect price discrimination, with program suppliers capturing the marginal value of additional modes of distribution. The multi-level releases in this model would maximize revenues and draw more capital into program production. Leased channel users will have the opportunity to negotiate for any multichannel tier.

The emerging prioritization in the television distribution system suggests a massive siphoning, from broadcasting and perhaps from video stores, to multichannel television. Almost all top-quality programming would start in subscription television or VOD, except for politically protected programming (e.g., the World Series, Superbowl).

Many new program types will emerge as producers and promoters test demand. Consumers who express their demand through a willingness to pay high enough prices will certainly be satisfied. The people who can afford access to VOD and subscription television will become a new television elite who will decide, with the dollars they spend, the substance of program production.

The list below summarizes the hybrid price discrimination model:

Video on demand (all items pay per view)
- Live sports, concerts, and other events including some news
- Movies in first television window
- Very strong television series
- Programs (for time-shifting convenience) from all other modes of distribution

À la carte (purchased by the channel or in discounted groups)
- Niche channels (including news and some sports not in VOD)
- Channels of movies in the second television run
- Channels of mass appeal television series, not strong enough to be sold by the program in VOD, and reruns of those strong television series on VOD
- Leased channels

Basic packages—more than one channel, bundled (several packages, each package purchased separately)
- Packages of channels of movies in the third television window
- General package of channels with reruns from television series in VOD or à la carte including some channels of programming not of high enough interest value for first runs in VOD or in à la carte
- Some niche channels just being introduced
- Leased channels

Broadcast tier on subscription television (single low entry price for all channels in all categories)
- Local broadcast channels
- Some mass appeal cable networks seeking maximum exposure for advertising messages
- Public, education, government access channels
- Leased channels
- Shopping channels

Over-the-air broadcast ("free" over the air)
- Local broadcast transmissions (perhaps fewer stations than in the twentieth century; except for news and local programs, most other programs have already run on subscription television on one or more tiers)

The relative importance of these modes of television service will shift in time, with VOD and à la carte becoming more significant as *demand interacts with the structure being imposed by full service systems.*

Other Services of the Integrated Systems

EDUCATION

Instruction by television, or *distance learning*, has always intrigued educators. Until now, the missing element has been efficient interactive capability. Integrated broadband systems will accommodate full voice/video interaction between institutions and at least voice and digital interaction from the home. A principal benefit is in *aggregating* learners and resources.

Homework assignments could be administered over interactive television networks complemented by the Internet. Students would work on home assignments and receive immediate feedback, improving motivation. School systems are already developing private broadband networks. Integrated broadband networks will be able to interconnect these internal systems, and their libraries, with homes for instructional and administrative purposes.

HOME SHOPPING

Integrated broadband networks will become the venues for access to electronic shopping. Here we introduce some of the likely capabilities of future shopping services. As shopping and advertising represent such a fundamental component of interactive broadband networks, however, we provide more detail in Chapter 9.

Home shopping will extend far beyond the crude home shopping networks now seen on cable television. In the first place, these channels offer little opportunity for viewers to select product categories, and at best publish a schedule of when particular types of merchandise will be presented. Moreover, they do little to permit comparison shopping, on the basis of price, features, or any other criteria. Shopping services offered over a full service network will more likely parallel the types of services now common on commercial online services. Consumers will be able to use menus or key word searches to select product types, and can then use the intelligence of the service to find the particular item that most closely matches their needs in terms of price or features.[21] Because FSNs combine the interactive capability of telephone-based online shopping services

with broadband downstream transmission, however, these shopping services will provide much richer video and multimedia product information where it makes sense to do so. Multimedia product
presentations incorporating detailed photorealistic images of products, audio narrative with music, video clips, and even spread-
sheetlike comparisons on key features will be the new methods of
selling to home consumers. Product information like this is already
provided on disk or CD-ROM by some suppliers such as automobile
companies, and is now becoming commonplace on the Internet using
the World Wide Web. And, of course, companies offering telephone-
based home shopping have also long understood the value of integrating pictures and text in their catalogs, free telephone access, and
low-cost home delivery to attract the home shopper.

Electronic shopping services can be much more intelligent than
today's implementations, and this intelligence can add value to home
consumers. One way is to learn preferences and other buyer information from prior transactions. For example, a "smart" clothing store
might remember that a particular buyer prefers a certain style of blue
jean, and can suggest an appropriate product. A second way is to use
the information by-products created by transactions to add value to
customers. Purchase histories may be useful for home consumers in
preparing tax returns, managing budgets, or providing pre-filled-out
shopping lists (e.g., for groceries).

There appears to be some demand for the convenience of home
shopping, based upon the success of related services and extrapo-
lating from social research on residential communication needs.
First, the dramatic growth of catalog shopping transactions and the
revenues generated by cable shopping channels suggest a fundamental attractiveness of home-based shopping. In a recent study by
Bellcore, time pressures experienced by households (especially two-
career families, households with children, and households where
respondents reported working long hours) were significantly related to a range of dissatisfactions with residential communication
activities.[22] People with these types of time constraints felt more
rushed, were less able to keep in touch with family members, and
had a more difficult time pursuing entertainment options. This was
true even when households had VCRs, cable television, and other
telecommunication services, suggesting that adding convenience

and time-saving features to new services may find a responsive chord.

HOME BANKING

In addition to their role in electronic shopping financial settlement, banks will likely offer a range of financial services to people at home over an integrated broadband network. Banks have long pursued the electronic delivery of banking services to customers in an effort to reduce the "brick and mortar" expenses involved in maintaining branch offices. Automatic teller machines represent one step in this evolution, but bank-at-home services have also been a part of many electronic information service ventures. Today, many banks offer account holders the ability to query account status and transfer funds between accounts using a touch-tone telephone. In France, customers can use their Minitel terminals to check their bank accounts and perform simple banking transactions. The main limitation, of course, is the inability to withdraw hard cash from a home terminal. Possibilities here are digital cash developments or the use of smart cards to "withdraw" money for later use on a smart card reader. A chip on a card might store the amount withdrawn and then progressively debit it as the money is spent.

Full service network-provided electronic banking will extend beyond the simple capability of checking on account information or transferring funds between accounts. These services will also arrange electronic bill paying with banks and businesses, so that subscribers can pay utility bills and make mortgage or car payments. Loan applications are another likely service feature in this area.

TELECOMMUNICATION-BASED WORK FROM HOME

Integrated broadband networks will contribute to the growth of *telecommuting* and related telecommunication-based work from home. Exactly what constitutes telecommuting is subject to considerable debate, with home-based work for pay including (a) people who operate a business out of their home, (b) people who are employed by a firm that permits them to do some or all of the work at home, and (c) people who simply cannot finish their work at the office and bring it home for work in the evenings or on weekends.[23] Many economic and social trends suggest that whatever the definition used, more and more people will engage in work for pay at home. Downsizing by large firms has created a pool of highly skilled and technically literate people, many of whom set up small companies at home.[24] A study by Link Resources estimated that the number of telecommuters has grown at a consistent 15%-20% per year over the past decade and increased from 5.5 million people in 1991 to 8.8 million people in 1994.[25] Home computer penetration now exceeds 35% of households and is expected to soon outpace sales of personal computers to businesses.[26] Many economists have observed the growth in information-based work throughout this century.[27] Today, Bureau of Labor Statistics studies show that the number of jobs in software, data processing, and information retrieval exceeds those in the automobile industry.[28] Even clean air legislation now appearing in California, New York, and other states appears designed to encourage greater amounts of telecommuting.

There are several ways that full service networks will cater to the needs of these types of workers and offer more than is available over analog telephone networks of today. At the most basic level, newer broadband networks will allow people to link their home computers to office local area networks (LANs) at much greater speeds than obtainable by even the fastest telephone modems of today. FSNs will likely offer a "virtual" LAN service, whereby home computers act just as if they were physically connected to the LAN at work. Trials of remote LAN access using channels on a cable system are already taking place. Meanwhile, telephone companies have begun marketing ISDN for remotely accessing office LANs. As the computer world becomes more multimedia, the data speeds offered by broadband networks will be necessary to carry files of digitized voice, images, or compressed video.

We can expect the new broadband networks to support a range of integrated applications for the telecommuter. Multimedia personal computers will permit on-screen windows for videoconferencing (see the discussion of video telephony, under "Communication," below) while at the same time allowing subscribers to work collaboratively on documents or other computer applications. Enhanced telephone services (such as caller ID, call forwarding, and voice mail) will further permit home-based workers to convey an "officelike" image to incoming callers. For example, a person working at home might set her office telephone number to automatically forward to the home. She may, however, choose to send certain incoming calls to a voice mailbox so that the background noises at home (e.g., children playing) do not hinder attempts to create an aura of professionalism.

INFORMATION RETRIEVAL

With a computer, telephone, and modem, it is now possible to access many types of text and graphic information from home. Online services and the Internet provide access to nearly any type of information available. Even cable companies have attempted to participate in this market, such as with the X-PRESS service offered by TCI. X-PRESS provides access to a range of text-based information, which is downloaded to a subscribers' computer over a cable channel. Subscribers can set filters, so that only information in desired categories is selected.

Probably the most important, initial information service for full service networks will be electronic directory services. Experiences in France with the Teletel system have shown the utility of putting telephone directory information online, enabling national searches of residential and business/government telephone numbers. Savings accrue in the reduced costs associated with printed directories, which quickly go out of date, and the staff required to support operator-assisted directory services. Moreover, advertising in "yellow pages" can be greatly enhanced in a hypermedia (nonlinear) electronic environment.

FSNs will extend these existing capabilities, primarily by providing a higher-capacity downstream channel for the delivery of multimedia information resources. Hence, FSNs may become an alternative delivery system to CD-ROMs for multimedia software such as encyclopedias or "edutainment." Preliminary versions of what might become available can now be experienced on the World Wide Web over the Internet. Real estate information, for example, can now be found that allows users to select desired areas from an online map, see available listings, and then actually see digitized photos of selected homes. Prospective home buyers can examine floor plans and take virtual tours complete with pictures of each room, the yard, or even the neighborhood and schools. The hypermedia structure of these services will then permit buyers to link to agents or mortgage lenders for more information or even to schedule a personal visit with the homeowner.

Other information services would be similarly enhanced by the multimedia capability afforded by integrated networks. Travel and tourism services, for example, are also finding widespread application on electronic service networks. Air and train reservations are among the most heavily used services on the French Teletel system[29] and are a frequent component of the U.S.-based commercial online services. As images, sound, and video have been integrated with text on the Internet, however, a number of travel and tourism "home pages" have appeared. Virtual tours of European cities, famous golf courses, the Grand Canyon, and many other holiday destinations have appeared. Tour operators may find that networks help fill unsold seats, with steep discounts for last-minute sign-ons.

Health-related information services are another example of information that is greatly enhanced with visual and even sound capability. Imagine anxious parents who are worried about an infant's rash or a peculiar-sounding cough. They could access an online medical encyclopedia and see illustrations of measles or chicken pox, or hear an infant with croup or whooping cough. Such resources are also beginning to appear on the Internet, which is quickly turning into an experimental test bed for a wide range of innovative services.

These few examples only serve to highlight the possibilities. Multimedia information services will find use in many areas, from the delivery of government information and services (e.g., see the federal government's *Electronic Citizen's Handbook* on the Internet) to health, tourism, entertainment, and education.

COMMUNICATION

Full service networks blend the information and entertainment delivery functions of broadcasting, cable television, and print media with the horizontal communication associated with telecommunication common carriers and electronic mail service providers.[30] As noted in Chapter 3, the overall market for two-way telephone communication exceeds that for pay television, and there is no reason to believe that these services will not be a central and profitable component of FSNs. There will be many variations of horizontal communication on the networks, most of which can be broadly lumped into two categories: (a) real-time, or synchronous, communication and (b) message-based, or asynchronous, communication.

Real-time communication services will, of course, begin with standard voice telephony, enhanced with the various intelligent network features and calling services noted in Chapter 3. It also appears that many integrated broadband networks will include wireless *personal communication services* (PCS) either in place of, or as a complement to, fixed (wireline) telephone services. Current trends in mobile telephony suggest that people may be able to have their own personal telephone number, which would enable them to make or receive calls anywhere in the FSN service area using a handheld portable telephone. There would, in fact, be a unique number (or extension) for each member of a family, a need that highlights the importance of fair access to telephone numbers by all entrants into this market. This shows how PCS would free callers from the requirement of knowing *where* a desired call recipient is, only what their number is. It is not yet clear whether the next generation of PCS will support full *vehicle-based* mobile communications; they may require callers to remain within a single cell site for the duration of a call. And the ability to use their portable telephone outside the FSN service area will depend on whether FSNs can forge intercompany roaming agreements with competitors. Nonetheless, we anticipate that some form of mobile telephony will be a part of the FSN communication services portfolio. It is likely that FSNs will also offer paging, mobile electronic mail, and mobile faxing capabilities.

A distinct service possibility, given the two-way, switched broadband capability of FSNs, is video telephony. Although it may seem logical that people would like to add a visual channel to their telephone calls, the market for residential, two-way video communication is not well understood. To date, the limited evidence regarding demand for this service is quite mixed. Certainly, initial attempts by AT&T to introduce PicturePhones in the early to mid-1970s to the business market failed miserably, despite high expectations.[31] More recently, however, business use of video conferencing has grown dramatically, stimulated by a number of factors including (a) the emergence of a global compression standard for real-time video;[32] (b) decreasing equipment costs;[33] (c) corporate executive fear of terrorism during international travel, which peaked during the Gulf War; and (d) an explosion in transmission capacity, both domestic and international, which has lowered the cost of videoconferencing over ground-based, digital lines. The growth of telecommuting may further stimulate business use of video telephony once ISDN and desktop systems become inexpensive enough.

The recent success of videoconferencing in the business market, however, is not necessarily indicative of what will happen in the residential market, with the exception perhaps of telecommuters, once costs come down. Both AT&T and MCI have attempted to market a videophone that works over conventional analog telephone lines in the past several years, with disappointing results. High cost and low picture quality, however, do not make this the most ideal of market tests. Social research on possible needs for and interest in video telephony are also ambiguous. Dordick and LaRose found that only about a third of their sample of residential telephone subscribers showed any interest in subscribing to a video telephone service, far below other interactive services.[34] Dudley et al., using a combination of survey and ethnographic methods, focused on people's needs for richer communication with friends and families. They conclude that there may be some applications for video interaction in residential settings but suggest applications that go beyond simple video phone calls. They particularly highlight situations where private family communication needs to occur in quasi-public settings, such as allowing parents to view small children in day care during the day.

Studies of residential telephony historically show that most calls stay entirely within a local area, with the dominant function being social interaction.[35] Furthermore, recent Bellcore research shows that video telephony more often is used simply as a substitute for a regular telephone call rather than to replace a face-to-face meeting.[36] It may well be that, if successful, video telephone calls will more often occur between local family and friends (e.g., among teenagers!) than distant relatives.

More recent experimental work on desktop videoconferencing integrated with computing suggests other applications. Telecommuters participating in meetings with coworkers or clients may follow the growth in video meetings in business settings. And recent work on video telephony applications in schools may portend growth in home-based educational applications. A project at Northwestern University, using Bellcore's switched video system known as Cruiser, permits high school science students to call up specialists from the university to discuss their work.

Ultimately, we can expect FSN operators to experiment with a variety of real-time, two-way video applications, including simple point-to-point video phone calls, group meetings (showing only the person speaking, or all participants by dividing the screen), remote attendance of classes or talks, and video surveillance.

Message-based, multimedia communication services are also within the realm of possible integrated broadband network services. Both facsimile and electronic mail have achieved mass market status in business and educational settings, and their penetration in the home market is growing.[37] If the Internet is any indication of the directions that general residential use of electronic mail may go, we should expect the formerly text-based messages to incorporate images, sound, and even video. Some of the recent multimedia developments on the Internet that are precursors to commercial multimedia electronic mail services are as follows:

- *Hypertext markup language (HTML)* is the programming language that supports the easy integration of images, video clips, and sound clips with text, in a hypertext environment.
- *Multiple internet media extensions (MIME)* are an Internet standard for incorporating multimedia components into electronic messages, so that a person might include a picture, an executable file, sound, or a video clip inside the body of a message.
- *MultiCast backbone network (MBONE)* is an experimental Internet application that allows the broadcasting of digital video across the Internet.
- *Internet Talk Radio* allows the broadcast of audio over the Internet, for example, to enable people to listen to what was said at meetings.
- *CUSeeME* is low-cost software that permits people to capture a frame of video every few seconds and transmit it as packets of data to someone else across the Internet.

With the growth in penetration of camcorders, we might expect applications such as sending a video of baby's first steps to distant grandparents, posting brief video introductions to electronic dating services, and other new forms of asynchronous entertainment. It is not at all unrealistic to assume that pornography vendors will capitalize on these capabilities, just as they did with videotape rentals, videotex in France, audiotex nearly everywhere that it has been introduced, and are now doing on the Internet.

NAVIGATING THROUGH INTEGRATED
BROADBAND SERVICE OFFERINGS

There are several ways to approach navigation in the full service systems. The most familiar *menu* approach presents topics progressing from broad categories through successively narrow categories. This is conceptually very simple, but tedious to experienced users who would like shortcuts, and difficult when it is necessary to back up to explore a different path. The creator of the menu must know in advance the categories and logic the average user would most comfortably employ. The *key word* approach allows the user to type in the topic wanted. The creator of the file must know all of the words that would be used by people accessing the content. In the *hypertext* approach, users can obtain more information by selecting any highlighted word or phrase on the screen; background or further information is available for the major elements in the context of the information on the screen. For example, in a news story on the Oklahoma City terrorism case, the reader could click on "Michigan Militia" to obtain details on that topic. *Services that learn* rely on previous choices of the user as prompts. For example, in entering the movie category, the user might be reminded: "Recently you viewed 'Star Wars.' Do you want to see the science fiction titles?" *Intelligent agents*, sometimes called "knowbots," supply information after being provided criteria by the user, such as "the lowest priced lawn mower that bags clippings."

Multichannel television viewing opportunities and the hybrid programming types in a digitally compressed system complicate navigation. A viewer with a range of interests must study printed or electronic television guides and perhaps seek out program reviews and announcements to be fully alerted to the appropriate available programming. The technologies for informing people of the programming choices are only beginning to be developed. The full service network subscriber will be able to scroll through program listings accessed through a menu. Reviews and program audience rankings in previous runs may be obtained through hypertext techniques. Key word topics, stars, directors, writers, sports, a sports team, preschool children's programs, and so on could yield available titles fitting the key word and other information. Viewing preferences can be stored for each member of the household to permit retrieval of VOD titles and programs on a fixed schedule available at a particular time. When channel hopping, for any channel, the viewer can request text information such as the channel number, program title, and elapsed time since the start. The information would be superimposed on the screen briefly. People may block out some programs considered unsuitable for use in their households.

TELEVISION VERSUS COMPUTER

Computers and television receivers with intelligent home terminals will be in many households, all connected to the integrated broadband network. One will not replace the other. Television will no doubt retain its entertainment dominance, albeit with interactive features, and can also be used to access text. It is likely to have a compact, handheld, remote tuner and key input, with deliberately simple operation to accommodate people who are not computer literate. The computer, with a full keyboard, will have its place in a study or an isolated corner of another room for work, transactional services, e-mail, and other online services. Although the home computer also serves an entertainment function, it will be of a different character than the television entertainment in the living room, bedroom, or kitchen. Both computers and television receivers will be used for shopping.

Not all homes will have a computer. These households, if they subscribe to an integrated broadband service, will have access to many information and multimedia programs that heretofore have only been available in the home to computer owners. Although the device connected to the television receiver is not likely to be a full keyboard, limiting interaction, these services will be obtained at a much lesser starting cost—perhaps no initial consumer investment at all.

Analogous to the computer versus television debate, many argue whether the Internet or the cable/telco-provided FSN will be the information superhighway of the future. It is our contention that the FSN will emerge as a local high-speed connection to a wide array of information and entertainment services, some of which are provided by the FSN operator itself, and the rest coming from third party sources, including those on the Internet or any of the commercial online services. Thus, the question is not really the FSN versus the Internet. Both will compete on some types of information services, however, the FSN will remain as the local broadband access to a mix of service providers.

Notes

1. Matt Stump, "Shock Jock Stern Sets PPV Record," *Cable World*, 10 January 1994, 1.

2. Kim Mitchell, "A Mixed Year for PPV," *Cable World*, 14 November 1994, 68.

3. R. Thomas Umstead, "Niche-Event Distributors Climb out of PPV Ring," *Multichannel News*, 28 November 1994, 119.

4. For a discussion of PPV sports, see Thomas L. McPhail and Brenda M. McPhail, "The Effect of PPV," *Feedback*, Summer 1992, 2-6.

5. Kathleen K. Wiegner, "Everyone Can Be a Star," *Media Studies Journal* 8, no. 1 (1984): 101-108.

6. Quotation from Tom Redburn, "He's Finding the Fire, This Time in Interactive Media," *New York Times*, 17 July 1994, 8F. Copyright © 1994 by The New York Times Company. Reprinted by permission.

7. Kent Gibbons, "Interactivity 1995-Style," *Multichannel News*, 16 January 1995, Supplement, 32A-33A.

8. Andrew Curry, "Two-Way Traffic," *Spectrum*, Winter 1993, 3.

9. David Tobenkin, "The New Media 'Evolution'," *Broadcasting and Cable*, 30 January 1995, 36: Bear Sterns senior managing director Clifford H. Friedman.

10. Thomas Kalinske, "History Repeats Itself: Consumers, Technology and Entertainment," *CTAM Quarterly Journal* 2, no. 4 (1994): 15.

11. Interview with Sandy Weicher, General Manager, TCI Cablevision of Mid-Michigan, December 5, 1994.

12. Tony Reveaux, "Let the Games Begin," *New Media*, January 1994, 48-57.

13. This discussion is based on a paper presented on a panel: Thomas Baldwin and Barry Litman, "Maximizing Profits in a 400 Channel World: The Fate of Commercial Broadcasters" (paper presented at the annual meeting of the Broadcast Education Association, Las Vegas, Nev., April 1992).

14. For a discussion of price tiering in the home video market, see David Waterman, "Prerecorded Home Video and the Distribution of Theatrical Feature Films," in *Video Media Competition*, ed. Eli M. Noam (New York: Columbia University Press, 1985), 233-236.

15. Fred Dawson, "Ameritech Vendor Choices Spell Big Play in Analog," *Multichannel News*, 27 January 1995, 45.

16. Estimating 72 thirty-second spots at $900,000 each = $64,800,000/$30 per household = $2,160,000.

17. The television rights to sports events are controlled by the owner of the franchise and/or the league. Depending on the team and the sport, television rights

represent from about one-third to two-thirds of the franchise revenues. The sale of television rights can generate revenue beyond the cash received in licensing fees. Exposure creates interest in the team, which influences box office sales and, importantly, sales of team merchandise. But too much television exposure may satiate the market and negatively affect the gate. Licensing a heavy proportion of games to cable, at the expense of broadcast coverage, could affect the general interest in the team, and ultimately the gate, because of the much narrower audience for cable, particularly pay and pay-per-view cable, compared with the audience potential in broadcasting, which includes every television household. Distribution of national and local telecasts must be coordinated; too much of one may devalue the other. Each team, sometimes with league guidance, decides on how to apportion the home and away games to television—broadcasting and cable—according to its own theories about its best interests. In the case of cable, the team will attempt to influence the decision between basic and pay distribution. The team, of course, controls pay per view. The movement of some sports events from broadcasting to subscription television, *siphoning* or *migration*, is a public policy issue. Although there is no constitutional right to access to sports on television, sports contests are seen as a cultural product and an integrating force in society. The public, having experienced many years of free access to broadcast television, views televised sports as something of a universal right. Any restriction of access, such as having to subscribe to cable, or, as a cable subscriber, having to pay a premium for access, is disturbing. Sports events are a scarce economic resource. There are no satisfactory substitutes for the top teams. As a public good in the economic sense, the consumption (viewing) of a game by one person does not lessen its value to another person. Therefore, games should be made available to as many people as possible. Collette refers to the possibility of a "sports gap" between the media rich and the media poor; Representative Edward Markey is concerned about sports haves and have-nots. In response to political reality, sports teams and leagues have generally been careful to balance types of television coverage to avoid public relations problems and, in the case of major league baseball, jeopardy of a federally granted antitrust exemption. No less than three congressional hearings have addressed the issue of cable siphoning since 1988. In some cases, teams have licensed all of the games to cable, bringing on the wrath of fans and threats by the congressional delegation. The sale of the New York Yankees' baseball game rights to cable prompted Representative Charles Schumer to introduce a bill, not enacted, requiring major league teams licensing games to cable to reserve at least half the games for broadcasting. Although there has been a proliferation of sports on television as a result of cable, according to the professional leagues, broadcast coverage of professional football has not declined, and broadcast coverage of professional basketball and baseball has increased. The FCC was required to conduct a study of sports migration by the 1992 Cable Act. That report, released in mid-1994, found no "significant" migration of sports from broadcasting to subscription television. Among major television sports—professional football, basketball, hockey, baseball, and college football—the only area of concern was local broadcasting of college football. The FCC saw no need for regulation of migration, only continued monitoring. Broadcasters have helped preserve their carriage of professional sports and hedged costs against revenues, by entering "partnerships" with the professional sports leagues. Rights fees are relatively low for the broadcast networks in exchange for an agreement to share advertising revenue above a predetermined level with the sports league. See Larry Collette, Southern Illinois University, "Public Policy Issues Related to the Movement of Television Sports to Cable" (paper presented at the annual meeting of the Association for Education in Journalism and Mass Communication, Kansas City, Mo., August 1993).

18. Robert Klingensmith, PPV Panel, NCTA Convention, San Francisco, Calif., 14 June 1993.

19. In its digital terminals, Time Warner's full service network will use the Macrovision Corp. video copy protection technology.

20. 47 U.S.C. 533.

21. S. Wildman and M. Guerin-Calvert, "Electronic Services Networks: Functions, Structures, and Public Policy," in *Electronic Services Networks: A Business and Public Policy Challenge*, ed. M. Guerin-Calvert and S. Wildman (New York: Praeger, 1991), 3-21.

22. K. Dudley, C. Steinfield, R. Kraut, and J. Katz, "Rethinking Household Telecommunications Needs," Bellcore Technical Manuscript, Morristown, NJ: Bellcore, 1993.

23. Robert Kraut, "Telecommuting: The Tradeoffs of Home Work," *Journal of Communication* 39, no. 3 (1989): 19-29.

24. "The Information Revolution," *Business Week*, Special Report, 18 May 1994: 10-186.

25. *Information Week*, 13 June 1994.

26. "Home Computers: Sales Explode as New Uses Turn PCs into All-Purpose Information Appliances," *Business Week*, 28 November 1994, 89-94.

27. See F. Machlup, *The Production and Distribution of Knowledge in the United States* (Princeton, NJ: Princeton University Press, 1962); and M. Porat, *The Information Economy* (Washington, DC: Government Printing Office, 1977).

28. "The Information Revolution," *Business Week*, 18 May 1994, 30.

29. C. Steinfield, L. Caby, and P. Vialle, "Internationalization of the Firm and the Impacts of Videotex Networks," *Journal of Information Technology* 7 (1993): 213-222.

30. *Horizontal communication* refers to two-way, interpersonal communication between individuals. It may be synchronous (like a telephone conversation) or asynchronous (like voice or electronic mail). *Vertical communication*, on the other hand, refers to top-down, or one-way, communication, typically from a media organization to an audience.

31. The 1969 AT&T annual report predicted 1 million sets in use by 1980. Noll comments in his review of the failed service: "It seems very clear that AT&Ts PicturePhone service failed not because of . . . any . . . single technological factor, nor because of inadequate marketing efforts or price, but for the simple reason that most customers had no applications for it." A. M. Noll, "Anatomy of a Failure: Picturephone Revisited," *Telecommunications Policy* 16, no. 4 (1992): 315.

32. The ITU-T (formerly CCITT) has achieved consensus on a suite of standards known as H.320 to support digital, compressed videoconferencing. A specific subset of these are the H.261 standards, which enable the interconnection of different vendors' CODECs at varying transmission speeds in multiples of 64 kbps.

33. Fixed videoconferencing rooms have cost up to $500,000 per site. Today, roll-about videoconferencing systems can be purchased for $25,000 or less. And desktop systems using CODECs on internally installable cards are now appearing for under $5,000 per system.

34. H. Dordick and R. LaRose, "The Telephone in Daily Life: A Study of Personal Telephone Use," unpublished report, Michigan State University, 1992.

35. Claude Fischer, *America Calling* (Berkeley: University of California Press, 1993).

36. C. Pool, R. Fish, R. Kraut, and C. Lowery, "Iterative Design of Video Communications Systems," Bellcore Technical Manuscript, Morristown, NJ: Bellcore, 1993.

37. Through the more than 6 million subscribers to commercial online services, university and K-12 students and teachers provided electronic mail, and people who connect to electronic mail systems provided by their employers are able to work at home.

7

Management

The management, "end to end," of full service, integrated telecommunication systems includes several areas, which, although closely integrated, are identified as the topics of this chapter: (a) acquisition of the capital to construct the network and test its markets; (b) creating, acquiring, and organizing services; (c) distribution; (d) customer service functions; (e) collection and payment distribution; (f) and maintaining the technical infrastructure. We also discuss the special organizational challenges that will result from the evolution of the enterprise from the smaller scopes of the current telephone and cable industries and the necessary associations with other industries. Marketing functions are discussed in Chapter 8.

Acquisition of Capital

The initial, and ongoing, task of an integrated broadband network is the acquisition of capital. The cable industry is highly *leveraged*—most of the capital is borrowed. The average cable MSO debt costs are 22.6% of revenues compared with a 4% average for telephone companies.[1] Borrowing for the cable industry means going to banks or institutional lenders with business plans that suggest sufficient cash flow from new operations to cover new investment. Traditionally, many cable companies keep borrowing to their full capacity in something of a hand-to-mouth manner. Those who have made equity investments, the private investors or stockholders, understand that they are growing the asset value of their investment. Distributed earnings are not the goal; the average dividend on common and preferred stock is 0% of cash flow.[2] The difficulty here is that the cable operators will be venturing into new product categories where revenue projections are not supported by any experience. Institutional lenders will, therefore, be insecure in their judgments; the result is high interest rates.

Local telephone companies have relatively secure profits but cannot accumulate these profits into tremendous capital funds because they traditionally distribute the earnings to investors. The average LEC dividend on common and preferred stock is 24.9% of cash flow.[3] Stockholders have made their investment in this industry to generate income. Telephone companies must recast themselves as growth companies and reinvest a substantial part of their earnings—difficult if the stockholders are not compliant. For this reason some have slowed down deployment of FSNs or attempted to split off new technology units.

Manufacturers and software companies participating in building the full service networks are partners of the owners. Their products are custom engineered or designed for the network providers in the initial stages of development. Although they may take orders in advance for their products, they cannot recover the full cost of research and development or manufacture in the first orders. Their research and development investment consumes a significant amount of capital as well.

Probably only the biggest of the cable MSOs and telephone companies can access the financial resources to make the initial venture in full service networks. Smaller companies will have to wait for second and third generations of systems and hardware if they intend to be players at all.

Investment analysts have already sounded alarms about the short-term prospects of full service networks. Very few are negative about the long-run future, but they recognize the immediate capital costs and the uncertainty of the market for services. Today, financial markets have little tolerance for delayed gratification.

The high cost of capital for the risky venture into full service networks adds to the burden of making it work economically. The capital investment in FSNs probably requires significant recapitalization. The scale is dependent on the pace of development.

Creating, Acquiring, and Organizing Services

SELECTING SERVICES

A tremendous burden for the management of integrated broadband networks is the selection of services and information to be carried on the network. We tend to think of the "information superhighway" as limitless. Ideally, a full service network would be a huge pipeline from which the end user would be able to access any item in the world's entire store of information and entertainment—everything. Unfortunately, this is not to be the case. Every program, every bit of data, although digitized, will take space in storage and capacity in transmission. If video servers are not placed locally, but removed to a regional location, greater access costs are incurred. Every communication service requires complicated support services within the systems. Each new program, each new service, demands a specialized marketing focus.

There is also a limitation on the capacity of the subscriber household. Each piece of information and communication service in the system represents something of an opportunity cost for the integrated network. It may be consumed at the cost of time, which could otherwise be used in the consumption of something else that may provide more profit.

ON-DEMAND SERVICES

A great many types of television service, as described in Chapter 6, will be on the FSN. The FSN and its suppliers are keepers of many gates. A market system will fairly effectively facilitate the gatekeeping function for *on-demand* information in all forms. Almost all films will be included, even some low-budget projects that reached only a few theater screens. Titles that might attract only a few buyers can be included if those few consumers are willing to pay a high enough price, relative to the cost of production (and distribution). Some items can be offered to a mass audience at relatively low prices and stay on the menu at descending prices until the market is exhausted. The film owner will set, or negotiate with the FSN, a minimum price. The price above that minimum may vary according to such factors as estimates of demand, time of day of use, and time elapsed since the original release. The actual demand for the film can also factor into pricing: A success in video on demand would force up prices or lengthen the periods at the highest price levels; a poor buy rate would lower prices, either reflecting the true value of the film or the operator's attempt to get more viewer sampling in hopes of building demand.

But, although almost all films pass through the gate in this system, the more important threshold is into the more limited body of content destined to get promotional focus. The decision to promote, and how much, will be made by the FSN working with the studio. After the promotional effort to start a film on VOD, the continuing promotional effort will be responsive to demand. Interactive games and audio, accessed by subscribers on demand, will probably proceed through a similar selection and selective promotion process.

Once in the electronic catalog, films, games, and audio recordings will stay as long as there is demand. The simple buy rate (the percentage of subscribers who buy the item) is not the determining factor; the profit generated by the item is. Titles producing little profit could have a relatively sudden death in video on demand. We cannot expect that the VOD system will be too much better at nurturing and bringing to life deserving works than the current television system, or publishers and bookstores. To a significant degree, storage capacity, the cost of storage, and the cost of transmission will affect diversity and the allowable gestation period.

There will be a great temptation to, in effect, "rig" the market by forming partnerships between integrated broadband networks and producers of program material. To assure inclusion, promotion, and retention of programs, the producer may wish to share the profit potential with a large FSN. This, of course, has an unnatural effect on the market.

À LA CARTE CHANNELS

Even in a 500-channel environment, the role of full service networks in the selection of à la carte channels will be quite decisive. Hundreds of channels will confuse subscribers and cause administration problems for the operator, who is faced with the prospect of very high levels of churn—households remaking their lineup of channels every month. A huge number of channels also dilutes available advertising support. If advertising support is weak, the subscription price must be higher, making the à la carte channel difficult to sell. There is also the problem of channel and program promotion. Finally, there is the cost of marketing. Subscribers have no way of knowing an à la carte channel exists without marketing and promotion; they cannot discover it by channel surfing.

Therefore, the full service network will make a judgment about the marketability of the channel on the potential for both sales and retention, and how the channel might affect sales and audience for other program services. The sales potential will be based on the face validity of the channel concept. Will subscribers be attracted to the idea? The retention potential will be based on the quality of the programming. New networks have demonstration tapes and full program schedules before they are launched.

A proxy for test marketing of à la carte channels is possible. Some FSNs can wait for other FSNs to demonstrate the market. Or an FSN with multiple systems can offer the à la carte channel in one of the systems and observe the result. The defect in this kind of testing of the market for a channel is that the actual market *in a particular geographic location* is not being tested. The History Channel may succeed in Princeton, New Jersey, but not in Flint, Michigan.

Here again, an ownership interest in the à la carte channel, by the FSN operator, may influence the selection.

TELEVISION CHANNEL PACKAGES

A peculiar problem faced by multichannel television systems is that of determining the value of program networks that are bundled in a *basic* package. Because all of the channels in the package are offered at one price, it is difficult to assess the contribution of any one channel. To determine the relative value of a basic channel in a package, to decide whether or not a channel should continue in the package or be added if it is new, the operator either intuitively, or formally, applies the following equation:

$$\text{relative value} = \text{direct revenue} + \text{indirect revenue} - \text{cost}$$

Direct revenue can be estimated for a new channel or actually calculated for an existing channel. It is the *local* advertising revenue earned by a channel. Or, in the special case of a shopping channel, the *commission*, a percentage of sales developed by the channel.

Estimates of indirect revenue are much more complex. This is the portion of the subscription revenue for the tier that may be fairly allocated to the channel. But amount of viewing obtained by monitoring channel use is only one indication of a channel's value. For example, the Weather Channel may be referenced every morning, seven days a week, by a subscriber to help decide how to dress for the day's weather. It may take only a few minutes to acquire the desired information, not adding up to much viewing time over a week. The channel is very important to the subscriber, however. To value channels, reflecting this *intensity* of demand or satisfaction level, the operator can survey subscribers, asking something like the following: "If you were paying for the Weather Channel, all by itself, what would you be willing to pay . . . Would you pay $5? IF NO, $4? IF NO, $3? IF NO, $2? IF NO, $1?" If the same question were asked about a number of channels, a relative value could be established and the total subscription fee for the package apportioned accordingly.

The final term in the equation is cost. The monthly subscriber fee is subtracted from the sum of the two revenue estimates. The result gives a crude estimate of the relative value of each channel within the package of channels. It is important to be able to specify a relative value of a single channel in a package of channels, not only when selecting new channels for a package but in periodically negotiating the license fees for channels already carried.

FSN RELATIONSHIP WITH TELEVISION SUPPLIERS

There is a contractual relationship between the full service network and its suppliers of programming and also, in some cases, a close working relationship. Where the supplier has a product that generates substantial revenue for the network, both will work together to promote the product. The programmer, let's say a higher-cost, high-penetration à la carte channel, cannot afford to leave the marketing entirely to the system for fear that the channel could get neglected. Ideally, both invest in the promotion and both will have a unique role. It is most efficient for the programmer, rather than the operator, to make preview and promotional spots. The network can schedule these on a number of channels and in local media. In all cases, the relationship is formalized by a contract or agreement.

Although the television programmer is often called a network, the programmer and the affiliate *together* are the network. The programmer "wholesales" a program service to the cable operator to "retail." We know how affiliation arrangements will be made between integrated broadband networks and programmers, because this kind of relationship has been functioning for years between cable operators and cable networks. The same elements will be in place for full service networks, but some new elements may be introduced because of competition, the more critical role of promotion with the addition of video on demand, and a generally increased channel capacity.

Affiliation (or carriage) agreements specify the conditions of carriage, the contract period, and the monthly price per subscriber to be paid by the operator to the programmer. For video-on-demand programs and events, the price of the program is called the *split*; for a full channel, the *monthly program fee* or *license fee*. In only a few cases is programming available to the operators at no charge—mainly religious programming and shopping networks. Sometimes a new network is offered free for an initial period as an inducement for an operator to affiliate, but the agreement usually specifies a schedule of future license fees.

ON-DEMAND PROGRAMS

The split between the video service and the supplier of video-on-demand movies or events has two main determinants. The first is the presumed popularity of the program. For movies that have first been in theaters, the box office receipts are a guide. If made for television, the drawing power of the stars and the familiarity of the story may be used. The second determinant is the commitment to promote the program, often assured either by a contract specifying the promotional responsibilities of the operator or by a guarantee. In the case of a guarantee, the higher the guarantee, the better the split for the operator. To make the guarantee and the higher split, the system will have to promote using cross-channel spots, features on a barker channel, cross-merchandising, and newspaper and radio advertising. The promoter of the event is not willing to allow the multichannel system to simply run the event without promotion, therefore not risking anything itself and simply taking in cash derived from the national publicity and advertising. Even without a guarantee, the more resources committed to marketing by a full service network, the higher the split. Some individual programs, particularly events, may require an individual contract covering just one program.

The suppliers of VOD programs will receive reports of the buy rates and charges for their programs and have the right to audit an FSN operator's billing records for verification.

PROGRAM NETWORKS

The license fee charged by a programming network to the distribution network is negotiated. A number of factors enter into the negotiation. An operator is permitted a "volume" discount based on a count of all of the subscribers who have access to the network. For a big multichannel channel television operator, the subscribers with access to the network can be aggregated over all the systems owned by the company, earning a substantial discount. Volume discounts are based more on the bargaining power of the operator to demand the discount than any efficiencies inherent in high volume.

Especially at or before launch, a new program network is vulnerable to heavy-handed price negotiation by big, multiple system operators. If a big company with millions of subscribers is reluctant to carry the programming network, the network may have difficulty launching at all.

Large full service networks with multiple systems will be able to receive *equity* interests in return for affiliation, in which a percentage ownership in the network, scaled to the number of subscribers pledged, is given to major affiliates. If the broadband system has an equity interest in the programmer, then that network becomes a *corporate must carry*—the network is automatically carried by the system.

Once a program network is carried on a large integrated broadband facility, the balance of power in negotiating price at renewal may shift to the programmer. The only significant operator response to a price dispute is to drop the affiliation. Even the narrowest niche channel acquires a following among subscribers, who can become very vocal if the channel is withdrawn.[4] But a full service network will have bargaining power in the way the programming is promoted, packaged, and positioned.

Some other factors, aside from subscriber volume, affect the price of a program network. *Combination* affiliation agreements, where the distribution network agrees to affiliate with more than one of the networks owned by a single programmer, entitles the operator to a discount. For example, TBS (Turner Broadcasting Service) owns Superstation WTBS, TNT, CNN, CNN Headline, and the Cartoon Network; Viacom owns MTV, VH-1, Nickelodeon, Nick at Nite, Comedy Central, the Nashville Network, and Showtime. The number of program networks owned by one organization, such as Turner and Viacom, will probably increase in the future as channel capacity grows and new networks are created to meet the demand. The established programming companies have the credibility to win carriage.

Another effect on the program network price to an operator will be the tier on which it is placed. Programmers, depending heavily on advertising revenues, need to maximize the potential audience, which means being on the first tier of the television program service above the broadcast tier. If the advertiser-supported network is à la carte or on a minitier, some of that maximum audience potential is lost. To offset the loss in advertising revenues, and to claim some of the expanded tier additional subscription fee, the programmer will charge more to the integrated broadband network operator.

An affiliation agreement may be anywhere from one to ten years in duration, although three-year agreements are common. The programmer usually reserves the right to increase the license fee up to a stated percentage during the contract. A provision specifies the minimum *local* advertising time available for sale within the network and could include some conditions on the kinds of local commercial messages that may be inserted in the network programming (e.g., no habit-forming drugs, tobacco products, or distilled liquor; no misleading statements; no testimonials that cannot be authenticated). The program network wants to be sure the local commercial insertions are compatible with its character and image. Usually the network gives two minutes per hour for sale of local advertising spots, holding about ten minutes per hour to sell, itself, to national advertisers.

When a full service system launches a basic channel, it may be given five to ten cents a subscriber to promote the channel through bill stuffers; newspaper, television, and radio advertising; and so on. The operator would be expected to continue to promote awareness of the network and its programs with advice and promotional materials, and perhaps co-op funds from the network.

RETRANSMISSION CONSENT

Retransmission consent, discussed in Chapter 4, has been responsible for affiliation agreements stemming from negotiation between broadcasters and cable operators. These arrangements are likely to remain the obligation of full service networks originating as cable systems and may be imposed on FSNs not starting out as cable systems. The agreements are unique because they were not entirely voluntary on the part of cable operators and were negotiated individually between broadcast and cable companies. Nonetheless, they contain provisions similar to the other types of affiliation agreements already discussed. One clause, of note in some of the retransmission consent agreements, is that if the must carry rules, which are an integral part of the retransmission consent plan, are vacated by the federal courts, then the affiliation can be abandoned.

LOCAL SERVICE

While full service networks are global in their reach, they will include content that is local. This means that a large company with integrated broadband systems in several different cities must acquire, produce, format, and organize content at each location—news, schedules, sports, shopping, business, and civic data—on a smaller scale locally duplicating national and international networks and

integrating the local information. The system in each city will contract for some of the local information and programming from local
providers, such as with a broadcast station or newspaper, and produce some of the material in-house.

Information services could, in time, come to relate to full service
network affiliates in the same way as television programmers. Charges
would be made on a usage basis, in which case the operator would
split revenues according to a contractual arrangement with the information provider. Promotion of the availability of the information
would be shared by the provider and the full service network operator. Information services such as Prodigy, America Online, and
CompuServe would transfer their whole package of services, with
their unique navigation systems, to the broadband network. Charges
on a monthly or usage basis would probably be direct between the
subscriber and information provider with a percentage fee to the
distribution network.

If full service networks are, themselves, in the long-distance telephone business, they will still be required to offer access to other
long-distance carriers. The contracts between local system and other
long-distance providers are likely to be closely regulated so that no
outside provider is disadvantaged in competition with the full service network or pays access prices that are unreasonable. A part of the
agreement, also regulated, will be the billing arrangements, which
must be convenient to the subscribers to any service.

Distribution

The network management systems for full service, broadband
networks are now mainly theoretical, being developed in technical
trials and for market tests. In some cases, almost the entire control
system is being put in place and is, itself, a critical variable in the trial.
Postponements in start-ups and temporary discontinuation of some
services have sometimes been attributed to development delays and
malfunctions.

Because every integrated broadband network user is unique and
content is extensive, traffic on the system becomes so complex,
voluminous, and global that the development and operation of the

end-to-end management system is central to success. Traffic engineering, with its algorithms and models, is complex enough in the relatively simple telephone service.

A telecommunication network can be thought of as a vast collection of devices that are linked by transmission facilities to carry a variety of different kinds of traffic (such as voice, data, image, and video) resulting from the use of many different kinds of specific services by subscribers.[5] The processes required to operate complex networks are increasingly becoming automated and controlled by software.

Historically, telecommunication carriers' management systems were referred to as *operations, administration, maintenance,* and *provisioning* (OAM&P) systems.[6] The various types of operations to be managed by carriers (building up from the running of a technical infrastructure to the coordination of a large company) include the specific operation of the network and the elements that collectively constitute a network, the activities involved in managing services, and the business operations of the firm.

These various management functions are supported by built-in capabilities of various network elements (such as switches or other equipment) that communicate network management information, by operations support systems that can control and process information coming from network elements, and, of course, by the people who supervise the various types of activities. Prozeller notes that three major functional categories of operations support (OS) systems:

- *Administration* includes both network and service administration. The former involves keeping track of overall network performance, while the latter is concerned with customer billing and collections as well as diverse other activities.
- *Maintenance operations* focus on keeping the network running, in terms of both repairing faults and preventing malfunctions.
- *Provisioning* is the set of activities involved with meeting customer requests for service and deploying network resources in response to anticipated service demands.[7]

Telephone companies introduced large OS systems many years ago in the era of big mainframe computer systems. The various subtasks involved in network management were controlled by separate, nonintegrated systems. For example, one system was used for keeping track of the location and status of facilities (e.g., trunk lines), another system to record customer service requests, yet another system to collect billing data, and still other systems to inform personnel of a fault somewhere out there in the network. Because these systems were implemented on large mainframe computers and written in complex software codes such as machine or assembly language, making changes to them is costly and time-consuming. Armies of programmers working for months or longer might be necessary to update a telephone company's billing system to introduce a new service or even effect something as simple as a rate change.[8]

In today's competitive environment, relying on inflexible and nonintegrated OS systems like these turns what used to be a telephone company asset into a big liability. In a competitive, full service environment, companies need the flexibility to rapidly effect price changes, continuously introduce new services in response to market demands, ensure that adequate network resources exist for current and future traffic, instantly diagnose and automatically repair network faults, and immediately respond to individual customer requests. Hence, a great deal of effort by Bellcore and individual telephone company research and development centers has recently focused on the development of integrated OS systems that will provide the kinds of quick responses, and network and usage information, so crucial to their ability to compete.

One example of the direction that OS systems in integrated broadband networks must take is the ability to instantly provision a customer's request for a new service. Traditionally, many different parts of the organization, each with its own operations system, were involved in provisioning a single customer request. Customer service representatives took the orders, handed them off to a member of another organization to assign the appropriate network resources, who then passed the information on to others who effected the necessary changes to the central office switch providing the service. Other engineering and operations people, perhaps installers, might also get involved. With so many separate organizations and systems needed to respond to a service request, the potential for errors and delays is just too high. Kenny describes a new *on-line provisioning* system now being deployed at Nynex to address this problem.[9] It would allow customer service representatives to immediately provision a service request using a single system, often while the customer is still on the line. All the related functions, such as activating the service, updating the customer account record, and sending the necessary information to all affected network elements, are integrated into a common interface.

In the new competitive integrated broadband environment, all of the complexity of managing and provisioning video, telephone, custom calling, cellular, information, and long-distance services has to be handled by single systems that can be operated by customer service representatives.[10] Indeed, the OS systems will be the strategic weapon that permits some full service networks to adapt to changing market conditions more quickly than their competitors.

A telephone- or cable-originated integrated broadband network will outsource much of the system development. Manufacturers and providers of equipment and service have proprietary interests in elements of the full system. The most important thing for the FSN is that the elements interface and that the proprietors work together so that the system functions seamlessly. For example, if Microsoft manufactures a file server, General Instruments a digital box for the home, Northern Telecom a switch for telephone service, and IBM a system for processing transactions, each of these vendors will offer its product as capable of interfacing with all of the others. In the earliest market trials, the FSN operators had to coordinate the suppliers, but after a few such experiences, the various vendors should be able to accommodate each other to achieve the necessary integration.

THE SPECIAL PROBLEM OF ADVERTISING

A special problem is the insertion of advertising messages as scheduled. To illustrate the enormity of the task, Ross estimates that an operator selling time on 500 channels would schedule nearly 150,000 spots per week, retrieve and verify 50,000 spot records daily, accumulate 450,000 billable spots (excluding promotional announcements) monthly, print 12,000 pages of affidavits monthly, and process more than 4.5 million spots over a 13-week advance schedule.[11] The individual local FSN advertising billing system accommodates local advertisers billed by the FSN and national spot advertisers, and must account for advertising agency commissions where appropriate as well as national spot sales representative firm commissions and must attribute local sales to individual salespeople. Advertising availability inventories (spots unsold) must be kept current. Advertising spot prices may be adjusted automatically as a function of demand.

Customer Service Functions

In integrated broadband networks, customer service is a process that is at once an information resource collecting, organizing, marketing, and distributing information and answering customer needs promptly. In most cases, the locus of the service management system, along with the human beings who have occasional contact with users, is local. As more complex full service, integrated networks develop, this may shift to a geographically distant location. The distance, of course, is meaningless in the context of service management in the networks we are considering.

The people engaged in building full service networks are especially sensitive to the need to make the equipment and its usage simple and inviting. Although an order from a household for information may be processed from one network to another, and require some data transformation at one or more sites, thus requiring extensive geographic and system routing, all this is to be patched together *seamlessly* so that the process is *transparent*, not visible, to the end user.

Technological and cost factors will ultimately play the major role in determining the location of intelligence in the system. Customer premises equipment can be owned by the full service network or the customer. Equipment manufacturers prefer to build intelligence into the receivers, VCRs, and other devices, selling these to consumers. The full service network would like to own a peripheral box over which it has control and earns some revenues through lease to the customer, and also to have the flexibility to place some of the intelligence further back in the network. The location of the intelligence raises some of the same questions about customer cost and independence versus system integrity that came up at the time of the debate about consumers owning telephone equipment. If competing full service networks have exclusive content, some customers will want access to more than one network, suggesting that the home terminal (set-top box) be owned by the customer.

CURRENT CUSTOMER SERVICE STANDARDS

Federal, state, and local government policy specifies minimum customer service standards in telephone and cable services. The general areas covered will remain as we expand to full service networks. Rules about connection and disconnection charges, and the length of waiting time for each, help to assure consumers of efficiency and unbiased access. Complaint procedures are spelled out so that there is an impartial arbitrator between the customer and the provider, who is using city rights-of-way and has some type of government permission to do business, by legislation, franchise, or license. Other rules cover maintenance of office hours, minimum wait times for telephone calls, and minimum response time for repairs and orders. Customers must be notified of services offered, prices, and other policies. Bills have to be understandable and, incidentally, payable in person at a local office, because many people prefer to do so. As customer service will become a competitive strategy, some integrated broadband networks will want to have their own customer service standards, higher than the general requirements of government.

CUSTOMER SERVICE STANDARDS FOR FULL SERVICE NETWORKS

Where integrated broadband systems are competitive, government customer service standards might be entirely abandoned in favor of marketplace regulation. If standards remain for the very basic communication and information services, however, a reconciliation of differences between telephone and cable service standards would be required. Because telephone service standards are enforced by the state, and cable standards by cities, jurisdiction would have to be settled. Presuming that the services provided may take on more significance within the household—for work, management of house-hold records, or management of communication processes—service standards, whether government- or self-imposed, may need to be strengthened. Unfortunately, the changeover to an entirely digital system increases the risk of a serious system malfunction. With analog communication systems, a "roll off" of the signal serves as a warning of the need for maintenance. In the all-digital system, there is no gray area of function—it works or it doesn't. A tighter set of parameters and more redundancy are necessary. At this point, telephone companies have had more experience with digital signals, but both cable and telephone companies will need to make a large investment in the retraining of installation and maintenance personnel. If specialization is required, the dispatch of personnel is more difficult because of the need to match available specialties appropriately with problems.

Monitoring of most, if not all, of the standards will be designed into the network's service management system. For example, the system will average and report wait times and response times to repair calls. Although high standards are the ideal, and may be enforced by government authorities, there will be a long period, as new services are phased in, when service problems are inevitable. Where it exists, competition forces attention to service glitches, but there is a need for the standards to be forgiving at first.

Some new service standards are necessary to govern interconnection of communication services. The object of the standards would be to prevent discrimination in interconnection by an integrated broadband network and discourage the creation of deliberate disincentives to subscriber interconnection to more than one system.

A further difficulty in this system is that the billing and control systems function together with links to both the internal and the external networks.

Collection and Payment Distribution

Full service network revenues derive from subscription fees, user fees (from subscribers and providers), and advertising. The revenues will be collected and shared by several parties. The broadband network operator must collect the payments for some of these services and distribute them to all of the parties involved in the contracts to provide the services.

For those services that the distribution network does not bill, it will pass the usage information through to a third party.

BOOKKEEPING/ACCOUNTING

The distribution process must be tracked by a "bookkeeping" system that is doing several things in a single transaction. The user is billed. The provider of communication matter, such as the data, a television program, is credited with the proportion of the remittance due, varying by provider. An intermediary network may also be credited with a portion. Finally, the full service network itself is accorded a share. Advertising schedules are verified and the advertisers billed.

Most cable systems have contracted with outside suppliers for billing services—computer software on which the systems pay a royalty. The service is now completely integrated with the operational control system all the way to the addressable subscriber's home. It is anticipated that the same companies will continue to perform these functions although the billing process is so intimately integrated with the entire operation that some cable companies planning for future digital full service development are considering an entirely internal system. Even telephone companies have experimented with outsourcing the billing function. CableData, the largest billing service for the cable industry in the United States, has at least one RBOC client.[12] The company has integrated telephony-cable billing systems in service in the United Kingdom, Sweden, Norway, Argentina, Brazil, Australia, Taiwan, Portugal, Mexico, and Japan.[13] Where the FSN offers information, television programming, and communication services on a common carrier basis, it may be required to supply the billing service as well.

If current public policy continues, rates for some services will be regulated, others will not. To prevent cross subsidy of the unregulated services by the ratepayers for regulated services, it is necessary to make assessments in cost for the respective types of service. In a full service network, the distribution plant is shared by all of the services. To separate services, then, requires an allocation of capital and operating costs among all of the services. The allocation effort may also be valuable for business accounting purposes, to judge the profitability of a particular service, but the full service network will do it under government scrutiny according to government prescription, not necessarily in accordance with internal needs.

RECORDS FOR INTERNAL USE

The tracking system may also compile records of usage of services for internal scheduling and other tasks. For example, the record of consumer purchases of VOD movies could be used to trigger automatic scheduling of promotional announcements. The same data could be used to adjust prices to demand. The first use of a particular service may be discounted or free as part of the promotional plan. Promotional plans for other services may permit customers to accrue credits toward purchases on the full service network or with outside companies. Credit limits may have to be checked for pay-per-use services. Some of the local network services may be offered at a lower cost at certain times of the day as a consumer incentive to reduce peak traffic.

RECORDS FOR EXTERNAL USE

Records of consumption can be sold to parties external to the network. Reports of the viewing of programs and program networks may be purchased by program networks, advertising agencies, and advertisers for use in and of themselves or to be aggregated with reports from other integrated broadband networks for regional or national reports. The reports could include demographic, lifestyle, and purchasing behavior profiles of audiences. The practice would not violate any general privacy standards that might apply to full service networks if the audience information were to be presented in aggregate without identifying individual households or viewers.

Lists of individuals who order particular items from shopping services, or request information on products, or who are presumed to have been exposed to certain advertising messages can be sold to interested parties. Selling such information about individuals is a common practice among mail-order houses and is also done by some communication services,[14] although customers may avail themselves of protection mechanisms against it. The ethics of selling information collected from the subscribers of full service networks are of concern because one type of information about the household may be aggregated with other information about the household also held by the network provider, to create a well-rounded and intimate picture.

Customer response to the billing scheme is important. Operators may prefer to parse out the billing across several suppliers to consumers rather than have them receive a single bill for a very large sum. This has the effect of concealing the actual cost of services purchased through the network, and makes it easier to deal with credit problems. A subscriber could overspend and default on payment to one service while being able to maintain payments to another. Thus, the system does not lose all of the subscriber business as a result of one problem area.

Credit card use would be encouraged for those subscribers who have them. For a 2% or 3% charge to the distribution network, the credit card company assumes the risk and credit management problems. Pay per view has already amply demonstrated that people can get into trouble when there are no spending limits. Often, the people who can least afford it have the greatest difficulty with money management. It is likely that operators will set a limit applied to all customers by service category and then permit a higher level of spending for individuals who qualify by their credit record. This is less costly than doing a credit check on all subscribers. Full service networks have to be careful not to engage in discriminatory practices, or "redlining." Both consumers and the FSN providers will have to learn the most effective ways to cope with consumer payments for the FSN services. The attempts to control accounts receivable loss by the FSNs may become controversial, especially in an environment where there is already great concern about increasing the gap between the information rich and the information poor.

Maintaining the Technical Infrastructure

The maintenance of the technical infrastructure will require incorporating skills now present in the cable television, telephone, and computer industries. The complexity of the network will require a level of training and expertise not currently part of local telephone or cable operations.

NETWORK DESIGN

The first task of the technical staff of an integrated broadband network will be design. The headend/central office, the fiber optic and coaxial cables that distribute the signals, and the house drop that delivers the signals to the individual homes must be carefully engineered before construction begins. Although much local information must be supplied, the actual design is likely to be done by engineers located at corporate headquarters, where the high level of skill required for the task can be centralized. Often, full service network operators will rely on contractors or equipment manufacturers to design portions of the network. The operator, however, must take overall responsibility for system integration to make certain that all elements work together.

An important part of network design is its documentation, so that the maintenance staff knows exactly what equipment is in place and how it is installed. This is important to minimize the amount of downtime the system experiences when there is a failure.

CONSTRUCTION

Once the system is designed, construction can begin. Installation of headend/central office equipment may be by in-house personnel, contractors, or equipment manufacturers. Because cable companies have always relied on contractors to build outside plant, and telephone companies have just begun to do so to take advantage of less expensive nonunion workers, it is likely that integrated broadband systems will be built almost exclusively with contractors. Because telephone companies have to replace almost all of their outside plant, the complexity of their construction will be much greater than that of the cable companies, who only have to overlash, or place on top of existing coaxial cable, fiber optic lines through about 10% of their networks. The most difficult part of telephone company FSN construction will be in putting lines in existing subdivisions with underground utilities where landscaping, fences, and existing services must be avoided or restored to the original condition.

The final task in construction is the connection of customers. A house drop cable must be installed to the home, and the home terminal must be installed in those homes that subscribe to the digital services. When a customer is connected to telephone service (called *provisioning* in the industry), the appropriate changes must also be made in the headend/central office, such as connection of the subscriber's circuit to the proper place on the switching equipment.

MAINTENANCE

Monitoring. Integrated broadband networks will require extensive automated network monitoring to assure that all equipment is working properly. Such monitoring is an integral part of telephone networks, except in the local loop. Integrated networks will require 24-hour-a-day monitoring of vital functions. It is most likely that each FSN operator will have only one monitoring site, from which all of that operator's networks can be watched.

Headend/central office. The technicians who work within the headend/central office must diagnose satellite receiving and video processing equipment, telephone switching equipment for voice service, ATM switching equipment and servers for video service, and the terminal equipment for the fiber optic lines that serve the full service network and the rings to which it is connected. Because of the complexity of the equipment located in the headend/central office, highly trained engineers and technicians will have to be on 24-hour call to respond to outage alarms. Failure of one piece of equipment here can affect thousands or even hundreds of thousands of subscribers, so many items have *redundant* spares that automatically take over in case of failure. This feature is often referred to as *self healing*.

Outside plant. Much of the repair of outside plant requires a lower level of skill than headend/central office maintenance. Technicians must locate and cut and splice fiber optic and coaxial cables and locate and replace defective amplifiers and other devices in the coaxial plant. These technicians are referred to as *maintenance technicians*.

Technicians must also locate and splice house drops that have been cut, and diagnose and repair wiring within houses. Finally, they must replace defective subscriber equipment and home terminals. Technicians who perform these functions are called *service technicians*.

EXPERTISE

In the headend/central office, the expertise of telephone companies will be valuable in maintaining switching equipment for voice service and digital fiber optic terminal equipment. Cable company expertise will be called upon for maintenance of video and satellite systems and analog fiber optic terminal equipment. The experience of the computer industry will be needed to maintain servers and ATM switches.

Telephone companies have extensive experience with fiber optic installation and maintenance. Cable companies have less experience with fiber optic cables but extensive experience with coaxial cable distribution and house drops. Cable companies also have the expertise to diagnose and replace home terminal equipment.

For system monitoring, provisioning, and the extensive documentation required in integrated broadband networks, the expertise of the telephone industry will be vital.

SYSTEM SECURITY

The security of voice, data, and video communication on full service networks is a special concern because of the potential for *hacking, eavesdropping*, and *theft of service*. The operator must protect the integrity of the system at a reasonable cost. Holmes suggests that hacking is not as great a risk as in conventional telephone or wireless systems because access points are limited. Further, it is not easy for the hacker to remain anonymous because the transmission requires a source address. Nevertheless, the system should be designed so that a series of passwords and security codes are necessary to get through gateways in the network.

Holmes acknowledges that eavesdropping is a serious problem because a hybrid fiber coaxial system has "multiple points of shared access." He suggests, however, that the eavesdropper assumes considerable expense to "extract the RF carrier signal from the cable, demodulate the digital content and interpret the contents." Only business or financial information, not the other transactions of a household, would be at risk. Holmes recommends that subscribers be informed of the eavesdropping potential so they can circumscribe use as appropriate, that passwords be independent for each service use, that encryption methods be offered to subscribers who are interested, and that systems be configured so that several trunks are used for routing—all to complicate eavesdropping, increase its costs, and make it less rewarding. According to Holmes, theft of the service, that is, using a "rogue modem" for data transmission without paying, requires monitoring the traffic on the network to detect source addresses not assigned to an HFC operator using the "remote management capacity . . . to shut off the offending modem."[15]

Special Organizational Challenges

As noted earlier, several networks now exist in every metropolitan area: many cable systems, local exchange carriers, competitive access providers, and private networks. It would be possible to patch these networks together, keeping each independent. It is hardly likely that such a patchwork would be efficient enough to function at prices that would be tolerated by the market. Therefore, the expectation is that there will be consolidation in one or two wired networks representing areas coinciding with standard metropolitan trading areas or much wider regions coinciding with company operating territories. Wireless networks would stand alone and/or be interconnected with wired networks. In some cases, wired and wireless networks will vertically integrate content sources and distribution.

Most telephone companies are already organized into regional offices serving such areas, although they are not staffed, of course, to provide some of the local services suggested above. Cable companies generally do not serve broad metropolitan areas. Each metropolitan area has several cable companies, often 20 or more.

CLUSTERING

Through the 1970s and 1980s, cable systems acquired franchises where they could. Some of the larger cities were deliberately divided into cable districts so that at least side-by-side comparisons of the monopoly franchisees could substitute for competition. Cable was balkanized by awards of franchises at auctions where bidders, offering essentially the same thing, were more or less randomly or politically determined. In only a few areas are cable systems *clustered*, where all of the franchises in a meaningful geographic area are owned by a single operator. The exception occurred because a multiple system operator was an especially strong bidder for franchises in the area or aggressively acquired franchises by purchase or swapping to complete the cluster. Acquisition activity has now accelerated, in anticipation of the administrative and technical efficiencies required for full service networks to function in a competitive environment. This activity will continue until each metropolitan area has only a few, or perhaps only one, cable operator.

An interim solution to the problem of multiple system metropolitan markets is to form huge cooperatives that would centralize customer service and marketing and, eventually, eliminate multiple headends and separate system identities. Steps in this direction have been made in the San Francisco and Seattle areas.

TRANSFER

For cable, the acquisition of systems to build metropolitan clusters is somewhat cumbersome because the *transfer* of ownership must be approved by the franchising authority. This requires the same scrutiny of character, financial capability, and technical and legal competence as in the original franchise. Either the seller or the buyer pays the cost of the investigation, an *acceptance fee*, to each franchising authority.

CENTRALIZATION/DECENTRALIZATION

A key management strategy distinguishes cable and local exchange carrier telephone systems. The telephone company has *central* management with little strategic or operational discretion at the local branch level. Many cable companies functioned the same way in past years but have more recently become *decentralized* in operational decision-making autonomy for the purpose of fixing responsibility for system performance with the general manager. Part of this responsibility may be shared with regional offices that encompass several systems. The local programming and information on a full service network will require some local decision making, but the overall service will be so much more complex that staff support and operational decisions have to be more centralized, following the telephone company model.

PROBLEMS OF EXPANDING
BEYOND THE "CORE" BUSINESS

Full service networks will not grow from scratch. Each will emerge from a communication network and business organization developed to provide a much more limited service: the telephone and cable industries.

The cable industry has two distinct parts. The system operators are somewhat like the telephone companies in that they maintain and manage a network for subscribers. But the telephone companies until very recently have been *common carriers*—not supplying the communication content at all, just the network. The cable operator must buy programming, as described above, and create some in local origination. The cable operators market the programming to consumers and promote optimum use of the system by subscribers to ensure retention. Local operators are also television producers, originating news, public affairs, sports, and community events programming and helping PEG access users to produce television. Local production for almost all cable systems has been on a modest scale because cable operators have in the past been willing to cede most local television to broadcasters. Today broadcasters are already establishing themselves as local suppliers to cable systems. Full service networks will weigh the business benefits of producing their own local programming against using outside sources such as broadcasters. The principal local programming for broadcasters is news, which will eventually represent a major product of FSNs because of around-the-clock scheduling and on-demand retrieval capabilities.

Many of the cable operators, now active, founded their own companies. They are considered to be entrepreneurial and aggressive. Because cable operators themselves have a large ownership stake, they are cost conscious and quite "lean" as business operations. Cable operators are also small in comparison to the RBOCs and other major businesses. With only a few people at the top, they make and implement business decisions with agility.

By contrast, the local telephone operating companies are considered to be almost the opposite of the cable industry. The corporate executives do not have significant ownership interests. Because telephone rates have been regulated on a cost-plus-reasonable-profit basis, the industry is thought to have embedded high costs over the years so that the percentage permitted for profit yields larger numbers. Because plain old telephone service is essential to modern living, it has been suggested that the LECs lack marketing skills. The buying, production, and marketing of entertainment programming gives the cable industry an element of show business that is now absent from, even alien to, the telephone business. Speculative investment in high-risk new services by public utilities is at odds with a stockholder philosophy that values stability and earnings.

The description of the cable industry may seem to be a model of the all-American free enterprise system. But the same features have been used pejoratively to characterize the cable industry as greedy, consumer abusive, boorish, untrustworthy, and bullying. Much of the stereotypical characterization of the telephone operating industry arises from its maturity and history as a monopoly. The cable industry has also enjoyed a monopoly. A difference is that there has been no substitute for the product of the telephone company, telephone service, while the cable industry, at least through much of its existence, has faced relatively direct competition from broadcasting and video stores as well as indirect competition from a host of information services and leisure activities.

The character of the two groups, the hard-driving, entrepreneurial cable industry and the conservative, customer-service-oriented telephone industry, has been well suited to both in the recent past. But the broader function of full service networks needs people with the skills and business attitudes represented in both. Cable and telephone industries have been changing in recent years to defy the stereotypes. An obvious means of converging the two types of service within one is for both to raid each other's personnel. This is already occurring. But because the *corporate cultures* have developed and persevered over a long period, the crossbreeding of personnel will have a slowly evolving effect. Observers of both industries express concerns about the adaptability of either industry to the challenges of the future.

To a much greater degree than either telephone or cable companies have known in the past, the full service, broadband system is dependent on many external suppliers of equipment, management software, and content. Coordination of the independent, but intimately involved, partners will be a daunting new experience.

The builders of full service networks will risk their considerable assets as will all of the other businesses that originate in support of FSNs. For society as a whole, the efficiency of the transition and the effectiveness of the new networks is vital. Although not all of the products of the full service network are necessary to every household, the basic communication services are considered essential. The users of the networks will bear much of the original capital cost to build the networks *as they are being built*. (See Chapter 13.) Therefore, the management capability of full service networks has an intensely human dimension. Customers, interacting and supplying information, are integral to the network and have a large stake in its functionality.

Notes

1. "Facts and Figures," *Multichannel News*, 5 December 1994, 99. Source: Moody's Investor Service for 1993.

2. "Facts and Figures."

3. "Facts and Figures."

4. An example of the imbalance of power between an operator and a popular, established network is provided by the story of a cable operator in Massilon, Ohio, and ESPN, who were in a deadlocked negotiation over price and tiering. The operator had been carrying ESPN for several months without a contract during the negotiation. According to the operator, when negotiations broke down, the company was faxed a copy of the agreement and told service would be terminated in a half hour if it were not signed. The cable company signed. Kim Mitchell, *Multichannel News*, 1 February 1993, 8.

5. P. Prozeller, "Introduction to Operations and Management," in *The Froelich/Kent Encyclopedia of Telecommunications*, ed. F. Froelich, A. Kent, and C. Hall (New York: Marcel Dekker, 1995), 55-91.

6. Prozeller, "Introduction to Operations."

7. Prozeller, "Introduction to Operations."

8. V. McCarthy, "The Transformation of the Public Network," *Telephony*, 20 March 1995, 88-100.

9. J. Kenny, "Nynex Reinvents the Provisioning Process," *Telephony*, 10 April 1995, 28-30.

10. J. Bennett, "Putting Services on the Fast Track," *Telephony*, 10 April 1995, 24-27.

11. Michael Ross of CCMS, Inc., referenced by Steward Schley, "So Many Channels, So Little Software," *Cable Avails*, July 1994, 40.

12. CableData provides billing service for 33 million cable subscribers; Cable Service Group, for 16 million; ISD, for 4.5 million; EDS, for 2.5 million. "Cable Billing Services/Cable Subscribers Billed," *Cable World*, 28 November 1994, 173.

13. Carl Weinschenk, "CableData Debuts Intelecable," *Cable World*, 14 November 1994, 82.

14. Matt Stump, "Time Warner Cable Plans to Market Subscriber Database Lists," *Cable World*, 23 May 1994, 24.

15. Stephen Holmes, "Cable TV Data Network System Security," *Communications Engineering & Design*, December 1994, 60-64.

8

The Market

As full service networks are developed, new products and new ways of using old products must be offered to consumers. Because a huge investment is made in developing the capability, it will be necessary to find markets for the products quickly, putting considerable pressure on the marketing function. At first, the technical capability will exceed the immediate demand. The introduction of the concept of an integrated broadband network as a single location for extensive interactive communication resources, however user friendly, will require consumer education and the development of consumer skills. Although some of the services are simply small improvements on the familiar and can be routinely introduced following tested marketing procedures, others will be quite novel and require substantial consumer cultivation. As costs, services, and procedures change, there is also risk of alienating consumers. This chapter describes the current markets for communication services as the basis for the discussion of the issues to be faced in marketing integrated services.

The marketing task is not the sole province of the builders and suppliers of the integrated broadband networks and developers of other advanced communication services. Because they will be integral to the society's social and economic function, cultivation and expansion of the use of the services is not only a business necessity for the providers but *an educational priority for the society as a whole.*

While the systems are being built, it is natural that there be a preoccupation with the technical, financial, public policy, and organizational components of the enterprise. For consumer applications, MacDonald worries that the development "strategy has the scent of field-of-dreams thinking—build it and they will come."[1] And Jankowski and Fuchs call it the "supply-side concept" of providing a massive capacity independent of any attempt to understand the demand.[2] In the meantime, however, business users may have already funded much of the upgraded plant, reducing the burden on the residential side.

The advanced communication systems give consumers access to an information resource that includes the stored wisdom of the ages, all of the performing arts; instant data on every topic customized to meet particular needs; games and novel forms of entertainment, all of it continuously refreshed with new material; real-time events from anywhere in the world—along with an advanced communication capability that not only includes voice and custom calling services but integrated video and data. It might seem that the network providers would simply sit back and take orders for such a service from households most grateful to embrace the opportunities. But this probably will not happen.

People have already been consuming most of the information available through this new resource and communicating with each other in the established ways. Almost all of that consumption and use is ritualistic and pleasurable. Adoption of new services and regular use of the content involves rather fundamental changes in lifestyle that only the most innovative will welcome. Therefore, habit and lethargy are serious obstacles to marketing integrated broadband systems as described in Chapter 6. At home, we do not now expend much effort in finding information and entertainment. Once it is at hand, we do not invest much energy in using it. The search and interaction in using the full services of a broadband network may exceed comfortable levels for many people.

Most of us would not admit to a surplus of free time. Much of our information and entertainment is acquired on the run without preplanning. There is an upper limit of time that can be devoted to entertainment and information even if the time is shared with other activities. Many different services will appeal to different segments of the population for different reasons; *there will be no universal appeal for most services.* Industry dreams of a "killer application" have long ago faded. Because the new products are unfamiliar, marketing requires experimentation in their introduction in such areas as pricing, appeals, media, and demonstrations for reaching appropriate market segments. Getting a consumer trial is only a first step in marketing. For almost all of the new products, the *amount* of use will determine revenues. The consumer must be continuously reminded of the availability of the service and its value. If there is a base subscription fee, independent of usage, the frequency of use and satisfaction become vital to the consumer in the decision to *retain* the service, which must be made *anew* every month as the bill is paid. Finally, there is the *cost.* Ultimately the full service network will cause a redistribution of household income. This will be a hardship for some households, and even in the homes where the level of discretionary income more easily accommodates the shift, it may not be agreeable.

The full service networks will not be starting from scratch. Most of the builders are targeting existing markets: the $12 billion home video market, the $54 billion catalog shopping market, the $6 billion video games industry, the $28 billion telephone access-type business (for cable operators and the out-of-region telephone companies), the approximately $26 billion cable television market (for telephone companies),[3] and eventually the approximately $55 billion local telephone business, excluding access (for cable operators).[4] Telephone and cable industries participating in the building of the networks will be working from an existing *customer base.* Because these are the starting points, we will look at the dimensions and characteristics of each customer base and project its development as integrated broadband networks become available. And because there are other target markets prominent in the planning of all providers—shopping, video rental, video games, and Internet access—we will describe these markets in the context of their new potential in broadband systems.

The Television Market

There are about 94.3 million television households in the United States. Nearly all of them, about 91.6 million, are *passed* by cable (have cable available).[5] About two-thirds of the U.S. television households now have cable.[6] The growth in cable subscribers was quite steep in the 1980s but by the 1990s that growth, as a percentage of total U.S. television households, has slowed to about 1% or 2% per year.[7] The penetration of cable is quite different from one community to another. The difference is due mainly to the number of broadcast television signals available off air. Where only one or two signals could be received through set-top or roof antennae, cable penetration is nearly 100%. In urban areas where there are six or more broadcast channels, cable penetration can be as low as 40%. The subscription to a television service will probably be higher than current cable penetration if telephone and video services are packaged together at attractive prices. The average cable household spends about $32 monthly for the cable subscription.[8]

DEMOGRAPHIC FACTORS

The *demographic* composition of the cable-subscribing household no longer differs much from nonsubscribing households except for *higher income* in cable homes.[9] From a marketing perspective, it is necessary to address all demographic segments of the society. Because such a large proportion of the U.S. television households now subscribe to cable, there are hundreds of thousands in every age, income, and household composition category. As penetration increases, still more with integrated broadband systems, what will become most important are demographic distinctions between the users of the various types of services. These data, as soon as they are available, will inform the marketing process and help give it direction. Furthermore, advertisers will make good use of the household audience data.

VIEWING

Television viewing time for adults increased in the 1980s and early 1990s to about five hours per day for women and nearly four and a half hours for men.[10] Although there are more heavy television users among the "socially disadvantaged (by race, education and occupational prestige)," higher-income people are gaining on the others in time spent with television.[11] Cable households, aggregating the viewing of all members of the household, view television 58.2 hours weekly—a daily average of 8.3 hours—compared with non-cable-subscribing households (using only broadcasting), which view about 45.8 hours weekly—6.5 hours daily.[12]

In the 1993-1994 television season, 45% of the television viewing in cable households was of cable channels (37% basic, 8% pay).[13] The viewing shares for cable channels have been increasing steadily over recent years at the expense of broadcast stations. These stations (network affiliates, independents, and public), nonetheless, had a 55% share of viewing *in the cable households*, clearly demonstrating the importance of broadcasting to cable subscribers.

Because television in an integrated broadband network will be offered in all of the current forms—by the package of channels, by the individual channel, and by the program—the added value of a full service network is the greater diversity, a convenient navigation system, and programs on demand. The assumption is that people will gradually opt for more use of à la carte channels and programs on demand as program release dates and promotion favor those services. The first run of the best programming on video on demand, and the promotional efforts devoted to giving that early access a value—creating a "buzz" for VOD—should eventually shift more and more consumption to VOD and diminish the viewing of fixed-schedule channels. The existence of a great many à la carte channels, interactive games, and information services will reduce the viewing of general mass entertainment programming. The fans and audiences for sports teams can be expected to develop idiosyncratically, and not be quite as focused geographically as they are now, because the televised games will be distributed nationally or internationally. There may be a small audience for the Los Angeles Dodgers in New York and Tokyo.

Because cable subscribers do not use all the channels offered in large basic packages, cable operators use program tune-in advertising to broaden channel usage on the theory that greater use of cable channels will increase the perceived value of cable, reduce churn, and eventually increase advertising revenues. Tune-in promotion in full service networks will give first priority to on-demand pay per view because the results will most directly affect revenue. This may have a negative effect on the capability of a system with VOD to promote à la carte and packaged channels. A specialty channel, after promotion at its launch on a system, will probably have to be self-sustaining, more or less depending on word-of-mouth and its own direct mail and specialty magazine advertising for new subscribers.

An interesting approach to the marketing of à la carte channels is the TCI channel called *tv!* It is a composite of new channels that are available à la carte. In a given week, the viewer can sample 20 or so whole programs from 20 different channels or watch the whole day's programming from one channel, depending on how the channel is programmed for that day. It will help the system to get exposure for à la carte channels because they would not otherwise be available for nontakers.

GUIDES

Cable viewers have a variety of means of informing themselves about programming: newspaper guides, electronic cable guides, printed guides, online listings, channel hopping, memory, and others' recommendations. None is used exclusively. Cable subscribers are more likely to rely on printed guides than nonsubscribers; pay subscribers use the printed guides most often.[14]

The digital megachannel systems will be obligated to increase research into subscriber use of program guides of all types as channel capacities and programming increase, and as the new interactive guides develop. As Thomas Kalinske, president and CEO of Sega of America, suggests, "If channel surfing is no longer an option and if the TV guide starts looking like the phone book, consumers will be begging for landmarks and road signs."[15] Many of the à la carte channels will have their own printed guides, including material promoting individual programs, mailed directly from the programmer to the subscriber.

Television critics are important in calling attention to individual channels, programs, and series. They will be overwhelmed by the choices on the digital systems. The introduction of new programs and events on demand in pay per view justify critical attention because they will be the newest. The television viewers who most actively reference professional critical judgment are likely to be VOD users. A compendium of critical reviews of programs, proposed by some navigation systems, independent of the full service network that is selling the programming, may be necessary for the discriminating viewer. It benefits the system as well because it increases subscriber satisfaction.

STYLES OF VIEWING

Some multichannel television viewers have developed new *styles of viewing* with the aid of the *remote tuner*. Studies of multichannel television viewing have discovered a common television viewing style of "*surfing*" ("grazing," "channel hopping") across all channels, seldom settling for long on a single channel.[16] In fact, most people regularly use only a small portion of the channels and cannot name anywhere near all the channels available.[17] Even surfers, who tend to be young, male, and with high income, watch only a few separate channels a week.[18] One study indicates that after 30 channels, channel usage does not increase as the number of channels goes up; use peaks at about 12 channels for households with 30, 50, or 70 channels.[19] *Tuning duration*, the average length of time that a TV set is tuned to a network or station prior to someone switching channels, is lowest for cable networks: ABC, CBS, and NBC, 35 minutes; Fox, 26; Independents, 23; and cable networks CNN, ESPN, USA, Family Channel, and TBS average 15. The same study reports that the switching during the average half minute, that is, *viewer volatility*, is highest for the five-cable network average at 9.8%.[20] Except for video on demand, we can expect tuning duration to decrease and viewer volatility to increase with the greater channel capacity of digital television systems.

Changing channels to avoid commercials is called *zapping*. Zapping by television viewers with only broadcast channels available is frustrated by the practice of broadcast networks of placing commercials at exactly the same time, essentially *roadblocking* the viewer. Multichannel zappers can find alternative program material, other than commercials.

Audience flow theories that influence programming strategies are based on evidence that the audience for one popular program will passively stay with that channel for the next program, an *inheritance effect*.[21] The effect may be enhanced if the next program is of the same *genre*. These laws of audience flow are not likely to apply to a surfing cable viewer or a cable subscriber with higher viewer volatility.

Television may be called a *background* or *foreground* medium depending on the user's level of attention. In some households, a television receiver may be continuously providing "noise" in the background. Other activities or conversation take the foreground for much of the time and people are only occasionally fully attentive to television. Multichannel television lends itself to this kind of usage, for example, MTV and CNN *Headline News*. Movies and other entertainment programs may be in their second, third, and fourth runs *within a household*, playing in the background while people have an eye or ear attentive only to a memorable scene.

It is not clear how a megachannel full service network would affect viewing styles. Certainly, the wider variety of programming, some of it on demand, will increase the variability in subscriber patterns. For some people, surfing will be superseded by the more extensive menus and the convenience of the navigation systems where they can find a program and go directly to it. A new form of surfing could develop for the on-demand, pay-per-view programs. If these programs can be *previewed*, on demand, for promotional purposes, the opportunity for surfing is vastly expanded. The subscriber could theoretically run through the whole catalog or large parts of it. The system operator and program distributors may have to be careful not to give away too much in the previews—the most enticing scenes or action—lest the surfing of previews become a new form of television viewing, satisfying in itself, without buying.

Tuning duration and attention levels can be expected to increase in the full service network for the on-demand programs. Having made a selection and committed to the cost, the viewer will be attentive through the end. Tuning duration could decrease for the scheduled programming simply because there are so many more programs to check out.

Zapping of commercials could go up or down in the new television environment depending on the content. There will be more television without commercials, perhaps building resentment of commercial interruption and increasing zapping of advertiser-supported programming. On the other hand, commercials in the more narrowly targeted programming will be compatible with the programming, therefore holding the viewer's attention, such as advertisements for lenses on a photography channel.

The audience flow theories will be even less applicable with the coming digital megachannel systems. Television is enhanced as a background medium, in a multichannel digital television service, but at the same time can be more of a foreground medium with on-demand pay-per-view programming and programming more narrowly targeted to viewer interest.

When digital compression adds a large number of new channels, if individual viewer channel repertoire still plateaus at about 12 as the evidence suggests, it will be likely that all television viewers are spread more thinly across the channels. To support the infrastructure and programming cost of providing the extra channels, then, it is necessary for the channels as a whole to extract more revenue from each subscriber. This is possible if each individual's set of 12 channels becomes more relevant as a result of the expanded choices. The advertising is worth more to the advertiser; the channel subscription is worth more to the subscriber. But the marketing challenge is to lead each individual to the optimum set of channels and make sure the increased value of that individual set is recognized. And, of course, the channels must succeed in convincing the appropriate advertisers of the value of each channel as a means of targeting viewers.

INDIVIDUALIZATION

The multichannel television environment and VOD make it possible for a pattern of selections that is entirely unique for each viewer. The opportunity for individualization in multichannel television viewing is so great, it is possible that people in the same household might not come together at all for television viewing. The diversity makes it unlikely that at any given time a single program would be the most satisfactory choice for two or more people. Certainly, a frenetic surfer would drive others to another television receiver or another activity. The number of multiset homes in the United States rose from 35% in 1975 to 65% in 1991.[22] Because they tend to be higher than average income and interested in television, the multiset percentage for multichannel households is probably higher than the U.S. average.

If an integrated broadband system offers 100 à la carte channels, 30 channels in an expanded basic package, and 15 channels in broadcast basic, and the VOD menu includes 1,000 titles averaging one hour each, the total is 4,480 hours of television programming available daily. People have to be well enough informed to select the right à la carte channels and then be informed of the program choices across all of the channels to which they have access. The VOD options also require that the viewer have the information necessary to form price-value relationships. Providing the information will be a challenge to system management.

NEWS VIEWING ON CABLE

There are some unique marketing problems associated with news. Cable subscribers who are regular users of television news are more heavy users of broadcast news than cable news services. Nonetheless, these subscribers turn to CNN in a crisis.[23] The CNN and CNN *Headline News* audience hovers around a .7 rating.[24] Increases in the size of the CNN audience over the years have been a result of the increase in the number of cable subscribers rather than an increase in the usage of CNN among individual subscribers. The international prominence of CNN in major crises has not yet ratcheted up the daily audience levels.

Although the 24-hour *local* news services are claiming to attract substantial audiences, it is too early to judge their impact. The competition, local *broadcast* news, has large, loyal audiences. Although the growth of multichannel television, with its potential to divert audiences from broadcast news, has had a profound negative effect on the size of the national broadcast network evening news audiences, it has had little effect on the audience size of early and late evening local broadcast news.[25]

Full service network subscribers will be able to call up video modules of news on topics of interest, or a personal newscast will be composed and ready on demand from preselected topics. This will start with international and national items because of the broad market and perhaps eventually include local news. Watching news by appointment, at 7:00 a.m., 6:30 p.m., or 11 p.m., *at the convenience of the medium,* is expected to decline as viewers recognize the opportunity to time-shift news into their own schedules or watch news at random times. Also, specialty news will grow exponentially with digital television. But the current passive usage of television news and the seemingly obdurate habits of bracketing one's day with local news will be difficult to change.

CHILDREN AND CABLE

On the positive side, multichannel television offers much more programming for children; in total, cable has about 200 hours of kids' programming per week compared with about 60 hours weekly for broadcast television. Kids with cable available watch 5.2 hours weekly of commercial programs made for children compared with the 2.7 hours of commercial children's programming viewed weekly by children who have only broadcast channels.[26] The cable children are no longer forced to watch adult or family fare during the day. In prime time, while there is still very little programming specifically for children, there is an opportunity to view "family programming" on cable networks such as Nick at Nite, the Family Channel, the Discovery Channel, and Disney.

On the negative side, children in multichannel households may be overindulged in television. The cornucopia of television programming is seductive for youngsters. Because household viewing is heavier in cable homes, children's viewing is probably greater as well. Although cable children have access to more age- and child-specific programming, they also may be exposed to a wider variety of adult programming. Unless adult members of the household are vigilant, young kids could be seeing uncut R-rated movies and other television programming with more adult themes than in broadcast television. Cable operators report that few parents have made use of lockboxes and scrambling devices to deny access to channels with content that may be thought inappropriate for children.

Adults who might try to suggest prosocial viewing experiences for children are overwhelmed by the amount of programming. New interactive television guides could be helpful in this task if the creators of the guides and programs would identify and publish program characteristics. The adults would enter the program characteristics they desired for each child in the household in accordance with published codes. When the child used the interactive guide, these programs would be displayed. Indeed, the system could be programmed so that *only* the previously selected programs are available to children, giving parents much greater control.

Multichannel television presents other problems for households with children. Experts in child development and psychology believe that coviewing of adults and children is most healthy for the child.[27] The adult can reassure the child in frightening situations, teach that television entertainment is fiction, and explain content that is not comprehensible to children. Television viewing is one activity that adults can share with children. But as noted above, group viewing in multichannel households is *reduced*.

It can be expected that children will put some pressure on adults to acquire games and additional programming from full service systems. Furthermore, it is easiest for adults to justify the cost of new services for children, particularly if they perceive educational elements. We can expect a major emphasis on marketing integrated broadband services to children as well as the educational benefits of the services to adults.

CUSTOMER SATISFACTION WITH CABLE

Routinely, cable operators survey customers to determine perceptions of the service. Over recent years, the multichannel television industry has paid more attention to customer service with concomitant improvements in survey results; nonetheless, there has been some recent evidence of regression in perception of customer service, probably reflecting higher expectations as the price of service increases and the industry matures.[28]

LaRose and Atkin conclude that "subscribers' high level of TV use and continued patronage in the face of higher subscription costs present a picture of solid consumer dependence upon cable service— not unlike that which is displayed for telephone service."[29] One survey found that two-thirds of the cable subscribers approved of the job their cable operator was doing. For the same people, this compared with 82% approval for the local utility and 89% for the phone company.[30] Generally, comparisons of cable and telephone service find that consumers think the telephone companies provide a higher level of customer service.[31] Cable service is highly variable across the more than 11,000 systems. Customer service by telephone companies is more uniform because of the companywide standards of large regional operators and the extensive use of rate of return regulation, in the past, which rewarded spending for service. Under relatively recent price cap regulation, where savings in costs can go to the stockholders, service has declined in some telephone companies as personnel have been cut back.

Customer loyalty to the cable company is measured to serve as an index of customer satisfaction but also, importantly, because it indicates the degree of vulnerability to competition. A survey on this issue indicated that about one-quarter of the subscribers would switch to another cable company if it offered the same service at the same price and another half of the subscribers would switch for the same service at $2 less per month.[32]

There is evidence that, for some subscribers, cable is of marginal importance. Fewer than half of the subscribers in one study said that they would miss cable "a lot" and a majority admit that several times a week they cannot find anything to watch on television. Less than a majority agree that "these days, cable is a necessity." Duplication of programming is a problem for most people.[33] A Roper study found 55% thought cable a luxury.[34]

As cable prices increased, consumer groups, some franchise authorities, and other organizations began asking cable subscribers about the price-value relationship. Typical is a survey by the Conference Board, a nonprofit business group, which asked consumers to grade cable along with 50 other products. The question for all products was, "How do you rate the value you get for your money when you purchase each of the following items?" Cable in general ranked 44th, with pay cable last.[35]

Customer perceptions of service will play a major role in the marketing of integrated broadband networks. Both telephone and cable companies will be more attentive to customer service, making a greater effort through advertising, newsletters, and other devices to communicate a friendly and efficient image. The more established telephone companies have an edge. Nonetheless, subscribers who do sign up for new services on the new full service networks, whether offered by an incumbent telephone company or a cable company, are likely to do so somewhat tentatively. Glitches in service could lose the customer quickly, poisoning the well for return marketing efforts.

Consumer difficulties in comprehending television, in its new forms represented now by cable and DBS, will be exacerbated by the comparative complexity of a full service network. It will be years before most consumers are fully cognizant of all of the dimensions of the services. This problem will be made worse by experimentation in the structure of the service, and the products (programs) them-selves, necessitated by the uncertainties of marketing in new areas.

THEORIES OF MEDIA CONSUMPTION

A number of studies of media consumption over long periods of time have led to the *principle of relative constancy* indicating that media expenditures are consistent with the overall economy and that, al-though *intermedia variations* in spending may take place, expenditures for media remain a constant proportion. The proportional constancy of media expenditures has persisted with increases in income—the *income share constancy* hypothesis. Later studies have found that dramatic innovations in consumer electronics in the United States resulted in some spending increases—deviations from constancy having been dis-covered as a result of products such as television and VCRs. Dupagne found similar results for the United Kingdom.[36]

Consumer expenditures for cable television in the United States, however, have steadily increased beyond the inflation factor. Over time, the product has improved—better programming and more channels. Recently, there has been some evidence from market stud-ies of a relative constancy principle operating within video-on-demand and near-VOD services. These early results indicated that people were buying VOD programming but were trading off expenditures on other cable services so that there was little net increase in con-sumer expenditures.[37]

From a marketing and investment perspective, intermedia vari-ability could favor full service networks if, as a new mode of communication, they were to divert spending from other media. But these dollars are probably not enough. And it would be a business disaster if the new networks would simply cannibalize their own established products with the new services. The innovation represented by the integrated broadband system may produce the uptick in household expenditures related to the introduction of major new consumer electronics products, as observed in some media constancy studies. Furthermore, the integrated media and communication services may invalidate the previously determined consumer perceptions of an *appropriate* level of media expenditure because the system, the services, and the packaging have changed so dramatically. Furthermore, even though there is a 24-hour ceiling on daily media consumption, Demers argues that both time spent with media and available free time have increased over recent decades and, further, that media use at work has also increased.[38]

The Market for Telephony

TELEPHONE SERVICES

The early years of telephone service provide an interesting example of how an entirely new means of communicating is marketed to the general public. *A recurring theme is that people use new communication technologies in ways that are unanticipated by the original designers of systems and services.* Fischer, in a comprehensive historical analysis of the AT&T's advertising in the early 1900s, concluded that telephone marketing to residential subscribers overemphasized *instrumental* uses of the telephone, showing it as a tool for making calls to doctors and businesses, mainly by men.[39] A number of studies of early telephone use have found that the primary reasons for calls were, in fact, for social conversation with friends and family members, often by women, who were more likely to manage the social needs of households.[40] Fischer suggests the reason was that the primarily male managers of AT&T came out of the telegraph business, which was not a residential service at all and mainly served business communication needs. They brought the experience of the telegraph industry, with its emphasis on efficiency, where social conversation was largely absent and generally discouraged. In fact, early popular and trade press articles about the telegraph contain a number of humorous anecdotes describing women who engaged in lengthy chitchat via telegrams, often to the chagrin of men receiving and/or paying for the expensive transmissions.[41]

The telephone was different. With low local rates and no intermediary who had to key in messages, it quickly became a medium for social conversation. This was especially true in rural America, where farm wives, isolated from neighbors and family by large distances, sought out conversation over the telephone. Many of these conversations occurred without anyone actually completing a call, using party lines to talk with others on the same circuit.[42]

With greater telephone penetration and more experience with usage patterns and desires, AT&T adjusted their marketing techniques. The emphasis switched from getting people to sign up for service—this was largely taken for granted—to increasing toll calling. Who can forget AT&T's campaign to "reach out and touch someone"?

Local telephone companies arguably never developed much experience in the marketing function. For those who can afford it, telephone subscription is taken for granted, and 94% of U.S. households have at least one telephone line. With no competitors in any region for local telephone service, and with virtually no charges beyond monthly subscription for local telephone use, in the past there was little to gain from extensive advertising campaigns.

If there are any lessons to be learned from the breakup of AT&T and the intense competition that has occurred in the long-distance market, however, we can expect the LECs to fiercely defend their core business. High-profile advertising, price cuts, innovations in the packaging of calling services, telemarketing campaigns, credit and calling cards, and joint marketing efforts with banks, airlines, and other types of businesses quickly became features of the competitive landscape in the long-distance market after the AT&T divestiture. These strategies will also be used by the RBOCs to defend their turf.

A survey by Opinion Research Corporation, sponsored by a cable marketing association, found that about one-third of the cable subscribers and one-quarter of the nonsubscribers would be willing to try a cable operator's phone service. Price would be a major issue.[43]

The same research organization, however, in another survey sponsored by Bell Atlantic, found that nearly two-thirds would try a telephone company video service.[44]

ADVANCED TELEPHONE SERVICES

The RBOCs did receive a taste of the difficulties in launching new services with the advent of custom calling services and the newer CLASS services (see Chapter 3). Many of these new services were not promoted very heavily, and potential customers only learned of options at the time of initial sign-up (e.g., after moving into a new home or apartment). Customer service representatives were the sales agents, who were instructed to suggest new options that were available, such as call waiting, call forwarding, three-way calling, voice mail, and caller ID. Take-up rates for these services have not been overwhelming, suggesting that RBOCs still have a lot to learn about the promotion of new types of calling services to the residential market. Other examples of LEC difficulties in marketing new services are their failed attempts to enter the electronic information service business, first through the now defunct gateways to the online services and then through the disastrous "976" audiotex services.[45]

In addition to broadening the range of channels through which customers may learn of new services, RBOCs appear to be exploring alternative usage options as well. In the past, people had to subscribe to a service on a monthly basis, with fees attached to signing up and discontinuing a service. Today, some of these products can be explored on a per use basis, with no sign-up fee at all. For example, one service first sold on a monthly basis was automatic call return. This service allowed someone who arrived home too late to answer a ringing telephone to press a code and have this last caller called back. It seems that many people could not justify paying for this capability ahead of time on a monthly basis but might be induced to use it for a usage fee on those infrequent occasions when a call is just missed.

Today, the slow penetration of the integrated services digital network (ISDN) is yet another indicator of how difficult it is to market a new telecommunication service. The challenge posed by a service like ISDN is even greater than for other types of calling services, however, because it is not in itself an application, but simply a better channel. Until a host of actual end-user applications become available that take advantage of the extra bandwidth offered by ISDN, it will be very difficult to promote to the residential market in any meaningful way. For example, online service providers might package membership in their services with an ISDN subscription, offering the necessary software and rental of interface equipment to make it simple and effective to use. Until these types of end-user applications are prevalent and combined with ISDN, it is unlikely to experience any surge in demand.

Recent research conducted at Bellcore highlights a different, more user-centered approach to the design and marketing of new telecommunication services.[46] The study investigated how changes in the structure of modern American families have created new needs for telecommunication. Based on a national survey of nearly 2,000 households, and complemented with a set of 25 in-depth interviews, four basic residential communication problems were explored, including problems of staying in touch, coordinating activities, obtaining information and entertainment, and getting things done efficiently. The analysis examined the extent to which various demographic factors and social variables related to the experience of the four problem areas. To find out how these new needs might be addressed by telecommunication, the use of a variety of telecommunication services and technologies was also examined.

The findings shed light on who uses certain technologies and services. *Greater use of household services* (call waiting, caller ID, touch-tone service, answering machines, pay phones) was associated with being younger, being sociable, having a higher income, doing work at home, spending more time working (and commuting to work), and being nonwhite. *Use of business-related services at home* (cellular phone, fax, pager, voice mail, the number of separate lines in the home) was best predicted by income, working at home, sociability, being employed, and having teenagers. Greater *consumption of video media* (cable TV, VCR, camcorder, video game) was reported by younger families with children and teens, and higher incomes. They also tended to be more sociable, have more leisure time, and have a child who does not live in the household. *Home computer use* (personal computer, modem, online service) was primarily related to the amount of work done at home and income. Other factors are being male, being young, having parents living at a distance, having teen-agers, and not spending time on chores or child care.

One of the most important findings was a strong association between having relatively inflexible and constrained time schedules, and the experience of having problems of keeping in touch, coordination, information and entertainment access, and getting things done efficiently.

A surprising finding was the lack of an association between the communication problems people report and their use of current services. Regression analyses illustrated that product usage was best predicted by social factors, not the magnitude of reported problems.

One conclusion by Dudley et al. was that current services may not be well tailored to the diverse needs of today's households, and therefore do not adequately address the kinds of communication problems examined. One area in which this diversity was evident was in the way households structured their use of time. Younger families with child care responsibilities and the demand for two incomes are experiencing the time pressures in ways that singles and the elderly are not. As more women enter the workforce, there is a greater need to maintain communication with dependent care institutions. Longer workdays and commutes, as well as the expansion of work into the home, further constrain the amount of leisure time people have. This decline in leisure time negatively influences people's consumption of telecommunication for non-work-related purposes. Therefore, Dudley et al. recommend developing "time transcending" technologies that would help people make the best use of their limited time.

Additionally, although people depend on telecommunication—especially basic telephone service—the distinctive nature of residential communication may also limit the usefulness of existing telephone services. People appeared to have difficulty applying telecommunication to solve social and familial communication problems, particularly when these problems occur in the public domains of work and other institutions. Meeting the needs of the household market requires a careful balance between satisfying people's instrumental needs for *efficiency* and their social needs for *emotion-rich* communication. Therefore, in addition to the time transcending technologies recommended above, Dudley et al. suggest that services that exploit the full range of multimedia capabilities to support interpersonal communication may indeed find a receptive market in modern American households.

WIRELESS COMMUNICATION

In the past, cellular telephony had an image of being a tool mainly for the professional business community: doctors, lawyers, salespeople. It was considered too expensive for the consumer market. Decreasing terminal equipment costs, however, have opened the door to the marketing of cellular telephony to the home market.

In the early years of cellular telephony, the cost of the terminal equipment, along with the costs of installation necessary to put transmitters and antennae in vehicles, limited its appeal for the residential market. As devices became smaller, cheaper, and more portable, however, an opportunity for creatively packaging the service for the residential user was created. Social research on telephone use identified an important cluster of uses best labeled "security."[47]
✦ That is, people make calls simply to ease the concern of others, letting them know they arrived somewhere safely, or warning spouses that they will be home late. If cellular telephone service were affordable, it would play right into this desire for security. To do this, cellular service providers offer a variety of pricing packages, tailored to the type of user. For professionals who anticipate making a larger number of calls, lower per minute charges can be balanced with a higher minimum monthly fee. For residential users desiring a cellular phone for the infrequent times when it might be used for security reasons (e.g., a car breaks down or they need to warn someone they will be late but do not wish to stop to find a pay phone), then packages with higher per minute charges but lower monthly fees are available. Coupled with the lower costs of equipment, including sets that easily fit in a purse or briefcase, the demand for service has soared.

Strategies for marketing the emerging personal communication services to the home will build on these trends to some extent. It is likely, however, that these services will also be marketed as a replacement for traditional wireline service to the home. Although we can only speculate at this time about the types of appeals PCS providers are likely to use, an appeal based upon customer convenience seems likely. PCS phones will be small enough that they will fit in a pocket. They can be carried around the home and yard with ease, ensuring that people no longer miss calls or have to run to answer the phone when doing yard work, walking the dog, or are otherwise in a part of their residence away from their phones.

PCS providers will clearly seek to package their service with long-distance carriage, making the substitution for traditional telephone service more likely. Given the high profile of Sprint and AT&T in the PCS bidding, and, in Sprint's case (see pp. 274-275), the alliance with the cable industry, such joint marketing of PCS and long distance is all the more likely.

Home Video Rental Market

Video on demand aims to capture some of the video store rental market and expand on that market by providing more convenient access. Research demonstrates that this is a substantially different market than traditional television.

About 80% of U.S. homes own a VCR. Of these homes, half rent a tape once a week to twice a month. Users recognize a value in control over both selection and scheduling. There is a shopping function involved that often includes two or more people in the decision making. Viewing is a social event involving preparation and more people per screen than traditional television viewing. Because there is a direct cost along with shopping and preparation for viewing, people are more attentive to VCR tape rentals than other television; there is less sharing of television viewing with other activities. According to Krugman and Johnson, these things have "changed television as a social object."[48]

A major economic factor in video store rentals is the tendency of customers to rent a lesser title along with a hit title or as a substitute for a hit that is sold out. If pay per view or video on demand skim the cream on the hit titles, the video stores could lose the secondary business in the less desirable titles on inventory.

Video on demand is something like VCR tape rental—and different. The convenience of VOD probably reduces the shopping and preparation for viewing, although the long menu and cost of the programs will keep a vestige of these activities. It is not entirely clear that the convenience of video on demand is desired. The shopping event associated with viewing may be quite important to some people. Veronis Suhler & Associates, an investment banking firm, point out that while VOD will be successful for recent hit titles, at a $3 price point, scrolling through older or less familiar titles may be less satisfactory to the consumer than shopping for these titles in the store. Further, most households are not likely to abandon their VCR equipment.[49]

VOD menus and preview (barker) channels must be designed to simulate the VCR tape shopping experience. The consumer attempt to maximize the benefit from the expenditure for VOD will refocus television as a family and social activity, as does VCR tape rental. Appeals to the possibilities in VOD for social viewing will be an important marketing approach, playing on the genuine enjoyment of group viewing and family guilt about solo viewing. Yet, if video on demand is to be the cornerstone of full service networks, and the VCR tape rental market a prime target, it should be sobering to the planners that, of the approximately 51 hours of weekly household television viewing, only 5 go to VCR tape viewing.[50]

Video Games Market

The video games market is mainly young boys playing in video arcades or on millions of private units although the industry claims that young girls and adult men and women are also beginning to play.[51] A combined effort by game designers and marketing specialists will be necessary if the games are to significantly broaden the market demographic characteristics. To allay concerns about violence in the games, interactive systems intend to supply a security device to block games at parental discretion based on general and age-appropriate ratings.

CD-ROM games will further stimulate the market. Interactive video games, on integrated broadband networks, will be the next step up in the technology. This will permit playing against people in other households at various skill levels, adding interest. Game players could make a meaningful contribution to an advanced system's gross revenues.

Home Shopping Market

Despite several years of operation, video shopping networks have demonstrated only a narrow market when one considers the potential. Almost all of the current users are women and a significant proportion of their purchases are of jewelry.[52] A survey of cable subscribers determined, however, that 53% had made purchases through direct marketing in a six-month period: 37% from a mail catalog, 19% from a mail offer, 12% from an "800" number, 8% from a home shopping channel, and 4% from telemarketing.[53] Shopping services are now expanding to a much greater diversity of products and retailers and gaining experience in online services. Most retailers plan to test interactive media in the next 10 years, although it is currently too new and too expensive for most.[54] Full service networks will be required to market themselves to merchants, in competition with other direct marketing media, and at the same time to market the interactive television shopping concept to consumers.

Truly interactive television, where the viewer can select shopping categories and particular items for information and purchase, will be a better test of the home shopping market. A broader range of users should be drawn into television shopping when it is possible to go directly to categories or items of interest. The challenge is to generalize the acceptance of printed catalog shopping to the relatively more active seeking of products by calling up information on television. On the other hand, the automated interactive television ordering process will be much less cumbersome than mail or telephone ordering because the billing and shipping addresses, credit card numbers, and other customer identification information are already stored in the billing computer and can be transferred automatically with the order.

A broader view of home shopping as one form of the direct marketing services of an integrated broadband system is provided in Chapter 9.

Online Services and Data Markets

CD-ROMs and educational programs have helped to revive home personal computer sales. This market will be the first target of broadband online services, particularly the 45% of PC homes that have children.[55] The popularity of computer-based online services has closely paralleled the growth in penetration of home computers. In the early years, when home computer penetration was low, most online services were marketed to the business customer.[56] All attempts to create a home electronic information services market using television sets as terminal devices were dramatic failures (see Chapter 3). Decreasing prices of home computers and modems have now created a significant home market for online services.

Some of the marketing strategies now used by online services include the following:

Offering access to a subset of services for a low monthly fee on a flat rate basis. This removes the disincentives for trying out services that usage-sensitive charges (e.g., connect time fees) create. This can be especially critical for new users, who will obviously be less efficient in finding desired information and services.

Offering free trials of the service to new users, packaged with disks containing easy-to-use software that automatically launches the application to dial up and log on to the online service. Often these disks with free trial offers are given out with computer or modem purchases and are sometimes prepackaged with computer magazines.

Online services have certainly benefited from the remarkable publicity surrounding cyberspace and the Internet. At the time of this writing, most have either announced or implemented access to the Internet. In many ways, this move is similar to their earlier need to interconnect with popular electronic information services such as Dow Jones or the Official Airline Guide. The popularity of the Internet, however, raises important questions for online service providers such as America Online, Prodigy, and CompuServe. They will still need to maintain some exclusive services to differentiate themselves from their competitors and to add value over generic Internet access providers who provide none of their own content.

Finally, the global experience with videotex and audiotex has taught us the essential role of advertising in making customers aware of particular information services. When an online company provides access to thousands of services, it is easy for any individual service provider to get lost in the mass of alternatives. Part of what draws information service providers to affiliate with any network provider is the likelihood of attracting new customers. Yet, if customers are not aware of a service, they will be unlikely to wind up connecting to it by chance. Many new strategies are being tried to figure out how to make people aware of new "home pages" on the Internet. Just as the French Minitel service providers and the "900" service providers learned, however, there is no substitute for advertising. In fact, marketing costs may easily exceed the costs of generating information and creating the service in the first place.

During a technical test by Prodigy and Cox Cable Communications in San Diego, California, a Prodigy executive claimed he would switch to cable from phone lines because "speed translates into a quality product."[57] The initial cost of the cable modem for the Prodigy test was over $500 but is expected to drop to about $100. A problem with cable from a consumer perspective is the possibility of outages that could disturb "lifeline" services such as e-mail. From the cable operator perspective, crashes caused by the home computer and software could be wrongly attributed to the cable service.

The noncomputer home may also be a market for information retrieval through the home terminal (set-top box) to the television set. This market will be more difficult to cultivate, as the potential consumers would be less familiar with the concept and benefits.

Market Research

Most companies interested in operating full service networks believe it is essential to do market research. Preliminary focus groups and market surveys have been useful in bringing out consumer foreknowledge, interests, and very crude estimates of demand. In one study, cable subscribers said they would pay for video on demand (44%) and online information services (23%); choose their own camera angles (22%); use interactive program guides (21%), pay-per-view rebroadcasts (20%), interactive video games (18%), and interactive shopping (13%); and participate in game shows (12%). People ranked online information in order of usefulness: weather, news, consumer reports, movie listings, encyclopedia resources, sports scores, theater listings, airline information, restaurant listings, book reviews, traffic reports, and hotel/car information.[58] Bell Atlantic estimates people would be willing to pay for video phones ($16.50 per month), distance learning ($12/month), database access ($6.50/ month), movies on demand ($6/month), medical services ($5.50/ month), home shopping ($4.75/month), video banking ($4/month), and games on demand ($3.50/month).[59] Chilton Research found one in five consumers "very" or "extremely" interested in interactive services. These people were likely to be male, have incomes of over $50,000, have at least some college, and be members of Generation X (18 to 34). These "convergers" used a variety of custom calling telephone services and almost all of the high-tech consumer electronics equipment.[60]

But survey techniques at this stage of development of integrated full service networks cannot provide much dimension to understanding the market. Integrated broadband network services are varied and relatively unfamiliar. It will take months, perhaps years, of regular use for consumers to understand the products, judge their value, and establish a pattern of use. The provider of the network system needs the long-term opportunity to experiment with format, marketing techniques, price, packaging, and services.

Several types of trials and market tests of full service networks are in progress now. They include tests variously called technical, internal, or limited field trials, which do not involve customers or serve only company employees ("friendly homes"). Market tests range from attempts to assess the demand for a narrow aspect of service all the way to studying a fully operational integrated broadband network with all of the telecommunication, management software, and customer premises equipment in place, simultaneously doing a technical trial and market test. In response to competition, at least one telephone company plans to bypass the trial stage entirely for what they term *full development*, bringing a minimal integrated network to an entire community with upgrades in response to demand, much as a cable operator would do. This strategy is partly based on the theory that time is lost in waiting for market trial results when competition will force the changeover to switched broadband networks anyway. Rollout to other communities will be determined by the experience in the initial markets.

In this segment, several of the projects are briefly described.

Littleton, Colorado: VCTV (AT&T, TCI, and U S WEST)

A pioneering effort to assess the market for video on demand, called Viewer-Controlled Cable Television (VCTV), began in 1992 under the sponsorship of three companies: AT&T, TCI, and U S WEST. The study did not attempt to evaluate the technology for VOD, but its usage and features of the service. Enough channels were available to supply near-video-on-demand movies to 150 homes (first at 30- and then at 15-minute intervals) at $2.99 per movie, and enough VCRs (located at the headend) to supply a second group of 150 homes with video on demand at $3.99. After the first year of the research, in phase two, all 300 homes were given both NVOD and VOD. Phase two officially ended for the partners in June 1994, with the conclusion that buy rates had reached a "steady state" at 2.5 movies per month per household; 70% of the trial participants made monthly use of the service; there were no difficulties in ordering through the remote control unit; and 20% of the homes used personal identification numbers to limit the access of children to certain programming.

As of this writing, the VCTV project has not reported any differences between NVOD and VOD usage, an issue in the study, although two of the companies conducting the study have been reported to have interpreted the results differently—one supporting VOD and the other NVOD.[61] This is a particularly important issue in the development strategy for both cable- and telephone-based providers of digital television services. It would not be necessary to make an immediate investment in VOD technology if, through expanded channel capacity provided by digital compression, near video on demand were satisfactory to consumers. NVOD may be the most bandwidth-efficient means of movie distribution.

Orlando, Florida: Time Warner

As one of the largest cable operators and a major media company with a substantial investment from U S West, the regional Bell Operating Company in the northwest, Time Warner, after a few delays, initiated a full service network in suburban Orlando, Florida, in December 1994. When fully deployed, Time Warner expects 4,000 or more subscribers to participate in the test. In December 1994, the company was offering (a) 36 movie titles with fast-forward and rewind functions; (b) interactive shopping including Spiegel, Williams-Sonoma, Sharper Image, the Nature Company, Crate & Barrel, the U.S. Postal Service, Warner Brothers, Studio One Store, and Chrysler; (c) 13 downloadable Atari Jaguar games featuring 64-bit speed, 3-D graphics, and digital sound as well as real-time, cross-network games including gin, PODS, and Klondike; and (d) an interactive preview guide with seven-day listing scroll and point and tune.[62] The network also intends to provide concierge services (e.g., restaurant reservations), music on demand, financial services, classified advertising, interactive games, news on demand, educational services, videophone, personal communication services, and GOtv, an entertainment information service.

Advertisers will be able to try out interactive advertising for 18 months if they pay a fee. Participating subscribers will also have an electronic post office in which they can buy stamps to be delivered within 24 hours, use express mail, and order packages picked up within two hours.

The news-on-demand service, the News Exchange, includes content from two local broadcast stations, the *Orlando Sentinel* newspaper, ABC *World News Tonight*, NBC *Dateline*, CNN, and magazines owned by Time Warner—*Time, Fortune, People, Sports Illustrated,* and *Entertainment Weekly*. The development of the News Exchange will progress sequentially through four levels. Level 1 will be time-shifted newscasts and programs, such as the 6 p.m. news at any later time. Level 2 permits news access from a menu of special topics, such as background on a current tax proposal. Level 3 will allow the user to go deeper into news items. Level 4 delivers text to printers.[63]

Illustrating the complexity of the system and the need for *partnering*, the Time Warner FSN "teaming partners" engineering the system hardware include AT&T for the ATM (asynchronous transfer mode) switch, Silicone Graphics Computer Systems for the servers and digital hardware (MIPS chip for the set-top box), Scientific-Atlanta/Toshiba for the home communication terminal with Silicon Graphics, Hitachi for the demultiplexer, and Hewlett Packard for the color home printer. The software partners are Silicon Graphics for the operating system for the server and set top box and the subscriber navigation system; Warner Brothers for an alternative subscriber navigation system; Time Warner Interactive for applications development; AND Communications for work on the navigation system; Ikonic Interactive for the News Exchange; Medior, Inc., for the navigation system; Objective Systems Integrators for the network operational support system; and Andersen Consulting for systems integration.

Although the set-top/home communication terminals for the market trial are said to have cost $3,000 each, the company expects that to drop to $300. As one of the participants says, "Don't sell people today's technology tomorrow; sell them tomorrow's technology today."[64]

West Hartford, Connecticut:
Southern New England Telephone (SNET)

An independent telephone company (not one of the seven Bell Operating Companies) serving much of Connecticut has moved aggressively to become a full service, digital broadband network. Southern New England Telephone (SNET) is faced with competition for intrastate long-distance service from AT&T, MCI, and others. SNET is expecting to lose the monopoly on local calling as well. The company has elected to build a hybrid fiber coaxial transport system hoping to provide "one-stop shopping" for local calling, long-distance calling, and television.[65]

The first phase of the market test was similar in concept to the VCTV project. Video on demand, "Command Performance," relied on manual insertion in a bank of VCRs feeding 60 channels. The full library of about 1,000 titles was listed in the monthly guide, which even included movie quality ratings: *, **, ***, ****. In addition to theatrical movies, special interest categories were education-information (e.g., art instruction, biography, computers, home improvement, personal development, wine), sports-recreation, musical-performing arts, and children. SNET relied on a number of suppliers for classic movies and special interest programs. Prices varied. In August 1994, *Philadelphia* was $3.95 in VOD or NVOD; *Wayne's World 2* was $2.99; *Boating Basics*, $2.29; *Rand McNally Australia*, $1.95; and *Connecticut News on Demand* (the most recent weekday newscast from the Connecticut NBC affiliate), $.50.

Near video on demand, "Reel One," was available with 30-minute start times on 18 channels. The other video channels were typical of a cable system with the exclusion of LO and PEG channels. Participation was encouraged by a free three-month trial in which users were given four coupons for free viewings each month. Three months into the trial, households were buying three to four movies a month[66] and, according to SNET reports, taking business from the cable operator.[67] About 60% of the VOD movie buys were drama, about 24% comedy, 9% horror/suspense, and 7% action-adventure.[68]

The VOD service was dropped after a few months. SNET claimed that the demand was good but the company was waiting for the delivery of a video file server to replace the manual insertion of playback tapes.[69]

Northern Virginia: Bell Atlantic

Bell Atlantic Video Services is a unit of Bell Atlantic that will develop and market video and information services nationally, becoming a video information provider in its own locations in the middle Atlantic states and an affiliate of cable operators and other video services out of region. Bell Atlantic Video Services will begin with a market trial in Northern Virginia focusing on VOD movies, starting with about 180 titles, to help consumers make the transition to transaction services. The other initial emphases are to be children's and learning programming, and shopping. Some programming will be original, evolving from a video production association with Pacific Bell and NYNEX. As home terminals develop in capacity, the business plan calls for the company to go further into video and information services. The video service will also include a package of broadcast and access channels, another tier of the popular cable networks, and many à la carte channels. Shopping (including Lands' End, J. C. Penney, and Nordstrom) starts with "800" number ordering but shifts to on screen soon afterward.[70]

Other Projects

Frontier Communications (formerly RochesterTel), a large independent telephone company with operations in the Northeast, Midwest, and South, attempted video on demand in Rochester, New

York, where it faces competition from Time Warner. The two have agreed to interconnect each other's customers and offer common directory assistance for telephone service. Frontier offered VOD in a stand-alone test in 52 homes. The trial was canceled after the company concluded that video on demand was not sufficient as a stand-alone application.[71]

Your Choice TV is an on-demand replay service for earlier run, scheduled programs (from ABC, HBO, NBC, PBS, BBC, CNN, C-SPAN, and others; mostly programs owned by the networks because of the reluctance of the Hollywood studios to participate). A market test used 20,000 test homes from nine cable systems. For these homes, the average monthly bill of $4.40 came from programming priced at $.49 to $1.49 with over 815 programs. This indicates a consumer value for the time-shifting function.

Omaha, Nebraska, is unique in that both the cable operator, Cox Cable, and the telephone company, U S West, will conduct separate market tests there. U S West plans 77 analog and 800 digital video channels in its 50,000-home one-year video dialtone test, which began in late 1995.[72] An independent company leased U S West channels and lined up the programming. U S West marketed the service. At the same time as U S West began service, Cox started offering *free* 21-channel basic which included broadcast network affiliates, public affairs, educational, local sports, and entertainment channels. A similar U S West basic tier is $5.95. The Cox FSN market test seeks to include 2,000 homes.[73] These market trials offer a new dimension in that they are taking place in a competitive environment where two providers may react to each other.

Interactive distance learning, in point-to-point, point-to-multipoint, and multipoint-to-multipoint modes, is being explored in several locations by a number of organizations, including the AT&T Center for Excellence in Distance Learning, TCI's J. C. Sparkman Center for Educational Technology, the Elkins Interactive Training Network (Elkins Institute and EDS), and at the National Model Technology Demonstration School in Chula Vista, California, through a joint project of Cox Cable and San Diego State University.

Several cable systems are testing access to online information services, using high-speed cable modems, which work over existing one-way cable systems, as well as low-speed telephone modems.

Because downstream is where the speed is needed, these tests might lead to early revenue streams.

Other major trials in progress or announced include the following:

- Ameritech in Chicago, Columbus, Cleveland, Detroit, and Indianapolis
- Bell Atlantic in Dover Township, New Jersey, Pittsburgh, Philadelphia, Baltimore, Washington, D.C., and Hampton Roads, Virginia
- BellSouth in Chamblee, Georgia
- GTE in St. Petersburg and Clearwater, Florida, Ventura County, California, and Honolulu
- Nynex in Warwick, Rhode Island, and Manhattan
- Pacific Bell in Los Angeles, San Diego, and Orange County
- SBC in Richardson, Texas
- TCI in Arlington Heights, Illinois, San Jose, California, Seattle, and Denver
- U S West in Denver, Minneapolis/St. Paul, Portland, Salt Lake City, and Boise, Idaho

Several interactive systems are operational through broadcasting and/or cable using data embedded in television pictures, FM broadcasts, and phone lines for the interactive components. Most of these adapt existing programming to permit subscribers to play along, predict sports plays, acquire "more information," select camera angles, do trivia quizzes, participate in educational programs, shop, select plots, access program guides and statistics, respond to polls, and participate in instructional programs. These early efforts are producing significant experience in creating interactive materials and obtaining consumer reaction.

ANALYSIS OF MARKET TEST RESULTS

The analysis of market test results must be cautious. The test area is often chosen to give the full service network its best chance, such as affluent, well-educated consumers in cable or telephone markets where consumers have shown an interest in new services. The projection of these results to broader markets is risky. Furthermore, people in the test market have to agree to close tracking of their usage and the survey of more general household characteristics. This narrows the test group, again affecting generalizability. Often the inducements to use the various services reduce the consumer costs. Thus the services are sampled, which is important, but the cost to the subscriber is unrealistic and, therefore, not a test of revenue potential.

There is always the danger of the "Hawthorne effect." The participants know that they are among the first on the "information superhighway." In the recruiting to participate, they have been told their cooperation is very important. And they have heard about the specific test and the new communication technologies in the local and national media. Giving the participants this attention, that is, creating a sense of importance in the novelty of their situation, may affect their behavior.

Marketing Administration of Full Service Networks

Although it takes imagination to form a marketing strategy and execute it creatively, the proof of a marketing system may be in the administration.

ORGANIZATION

Full service, integrated broadband network marketing will parallel but expand upon the marketing administration in cable. The entire *universe* of homes passed by the service must be identified, then a record kept of each home. Some in the universe will be *nonsubscribers*. They will be subdivided into *nevers*, who have not ever subscribed, and *formers*, who have disconnected. In a competitive situation, the formers may be further divided into "ours" and "theirs." The *subscribers* will fit into several categories based on the different communication services customers, such as POTS, the various custom calling services, and video phone; and classes of information service users and television subscribers by their types of usage, online services, basic packages, à la carte channels, NVOD and VOD, and audio. They are further qualified by extent of usage in either dollars or units of consumption, such as the number of movies purchased per month. The account history in each of these categories is vital to the marketing plan. Each of the compound categories of subscribers will be marketed differently because they have different needs and backgrounds. Marketing personnel will be organized both by service and by function, thus permitting specialization.

MARKETING TASKS

There are three basic marketing tasks: acquisition, retention, and consumption. *Acquisition marketing* refers to bringing in new subscribers, either from among nonsubscribers or by *upgrading* existing subscribers, for example, getting a regular telephone customer to go to a video phone or a broadcast basic cable subscriber to take an à la carte channel. *Retention marketing* is the process of keeping customers. It is a process because it involves an extensive set of continuing activities including friendly and efficient customer service, efforts to get subscribers to make better use of the services and products, and last-ditch attempts to prevent a loss of a subscriber to a lesser level of service or a competitor.

But for the full service system, acquisition and retention marketing is only a beginning for products sold by the unit of consumption. The *consumption marketing* approach is similar to the sales of long-distance telephone service and pay-per-view television in which the marketing success hinges on usage. Video-on-demand events will require a three- or four-week marketing period with publicity, newspaper, radio and television advertising, direct mail to previous event buyers, and promotional tie-ins with relevant advertisers, for example, a beer distributor with a boxing match. Because VOD movies are likely to be impulse buys, that is, the decision to view will be made at the last minute after a review of other viewing options, schedules have to be conveniently available in print and through a barker or preview channel—an entire channel devoted to promotion of the scheduled movies. VOD movie marketing will also require *previews on demand* as well as listings of movies available by category, for example, the 20 newest titles, current action-adventure films, videos on carpentry.

Cross-channel promotion, where a promotional spot on one television channel is used to promote a program on another, will be critical for selling major VOD titles and à la carte channels. A significant proportion of the local advertising availabilities on advertiser-supported channels would be dedicated to cross-channel promotion. The advertising spots used to promote VOD may be more profitable for the integrated broadband system than the sale of the time to external advertisers.

Direct mail, or direct electronic communication, where it is possible to design messages for narrow market segments, will play an important role for full service networks; for example, the immediate prospects for video games are boys eight to 14, and for shopping networks, adult females.[74] They require specific communications to specific targets.

It should be noted that the inital marketing hurdle for advanced digital broadband services is in marketing the terminal itself. The customer may resist the perceived complexity or the high price of the equipment. Before video on demand, high-speed information retrieval, interactive guides, and other services can begin to produce any revenue, the marketer must get the box in the house.

MARKETING STRATEGIES

The most basic strategy in marketing is to establish priorities. (a) A major priority is to identify high-demand products that bring in the greatest number of people at the earliest time. The industry is generally agreed that video on demand, video games, high-speed Internet access, and shopping fit this criterion. (b) Another priority is revenue and operating income. Shopping services may have high revenue potential for FSNs because they will be targeting a typical 100% retail markup. (c) Priority will also be given to prosocial utility such as education. The availability of such services has been used to lower regulatory barriers to the development of full service networks, so there is now some obligation to follow up. And, as noted, the utility of integrated broadband services for young people may motivate adults to subscribe. (d) System ownership interest in the product will factor into the priority scheme—a result of the synergies that most participants in full service network development are seeking.

An integrated broadband system, with ownership of "anchor services" in both video and telephone, will *cross market* at relatively low cost. An example is the use of cross-promotional television spots in local advertising availabilities to promote subscription to a companion telephone service. There are also cross-marketing opportunities in direct mail to customers, newsletters, bill stuffers, and *transaction marketing*, in which, during a transaction related to one service, another is offered. Perhaps a major potential for full service networks in marketing is their intimacy with the consumer afforded by the regularity of these various contacts. Certainly *customer loyalty programs*, in which the customer is rewarded for continued use of a service (or the full scope of services) of an integrated system, will be employed. The "frequent flyer" programs of the airlines are an example. A customer loyalty plan for a full service, integrated network might allow consumers to earn credits for consumption of VOD programs or for accumulated consumption across all services—telephone, information retrieval, games, and shopping as well as VOD. These credits make it difficult for the consumer to switch to another company.

Much attention and experimentation will be devoted to the pricing and structuring of services. Initial prices are experimental until a demand is established. Price may also determine usage of the service, so low entry prices can lead consumers to the service, thereby exposing them to within-system promotion and sampling of other services. To be sure, the highest-demand products will be somewhat overpriced, permitting introductory pricing of the new products, and within the FSN, the development of an intricate system of cross subsidy of products. Market research and trials in various communities will be necessary to determine the optimum packaging of services within the limits imposed by regulation. One of the difficulties of this necessary trial-and-error method of structuring services is the *consumer reeducation* required at each change.

In this context, it should be noted that the prices for basic video service channel packages, broadcasting, and the most popular cable networks are inelastic. Demand is not affected much by the price level. This is probably even more true of plain telephone service, but the issue is complicated by the subsidies telephone companies claim they make to residential service. Since services consequently may be overpriced, there is room for price competition. Higher level services such as pay channels and custom calling are price elastic and may already be priced appropriately with little opportunity for reduction.

As discussed in an earlier chapter, the navigation systems in full service networks are being designed to be consumer friendly, *not* suggestive of computer technology. A primary objective of most of the market tests is to explore ways of conquering the fear of technology—to present the services as high-tech wonders but as low tech in the consumer interface.

Full service network providers must paint themselves with a much broader brush; they are no longer just one-way cable or plain old telephone service companies. Without jeopardizing the utilitarian image, the telephone-based FSN must also represent fun and games. The cable-based FSN needs to project a more serious side, capable of reliable lifeline communication services. Both cable and telephone companies have recently worked hard at this kind of generic promotion, heightening awareness of the communication future and thus softening the market, at least for innovative consumers.

A critical marketing need is to help break through consumer-perceived ceilings, "relative constancy," on media and telecommunication expenditures. More value must be created for these intangibles. This could be a difficult challenge in a society where material goods have been a sign of well-being—a home, an automobile, a stereo, and good sneakers.

It will become a marketing responsibility to match consumers with the product, that is, to be sure that people are using the integrated network products that will bring them the greatest satisfaction at an affordable price. Only the buyer with full knowledge of all the broadband system products makes such choices. Because the buyer is likely to be only partially informed, long-term marketing goals work *toward* improving the consumer's ability to search the system for suitable products. Marketers, of course, may have to find a balance between pushing the user toward the most expensive or profitable products—to lift the ceiling described above—while still keeping consumers happy. An example is provided by the quality ratings offered by SNET in marketing its movie library. A one-star (*) rating is in effect saying that this film is not very good, an unusual admission for a company trying to sell films. But the ratings, for those who use them, will be a helpful guide to a library that cannot be entirely consumed anyway. Customer satisfaction is a key to further consumption and retention.

The coordination of marketing initiatives coming from many of the independent program and service providers in the integrated networks will also fall to the operator. Producers of the individual elements—television programs, movies, events, television channels, online services, shopping services—will market nationally and offer support to local marketing efforts. The system itself must balance the supplier marketing programs with its own marketing priorities.

Much of the sales effort in full service broadband systems may be the type in which classic rules and decorum are discarded in favor of hard-hitting negative appeals and other techniques in reaction to quickly changing circumstances. This is often called guerilla marketing. It does not dwell on analysis but on rapid-fire trial-and-error thrusts. Guerilla marketing is well suited to the competitive introduction of new products.

REGULATION

Some constraints on marketing are placed by federal and state regulation. If regulated and unregulated services exist within one company, it will not be possible to market them together without making an allocation of the expenses. This may be somewhat difficult, especially in generic promotional efforts.

The Communications Act prohibits negative option marketing by cable operators.[75] The *negative option* is an offer of service made to the customer, who must then affirmatively decline or the service is taken to be accepted and billing begins. Also, cable subscribers must be given at least a 30-day notice of any free trial of a "premium" channel, carrying movies rated by the Motion Picture Association of America (MMPA) as X, NC-17, or R. The operator has to block that channel at the subscriber request so that subscribers are not surprised by channels they do not wish to receive.[76]

The cable subscriber cannot be required to *buy through* any service other than broadcast basic to get access to still further services.[77] That is, once the cable subscriber buys broadcast basic, he or she can then buy any à la carte channel or service. The operator cannot require the purchase of broadcast basic, and an enhanced basic tier, to order HBO, or require ordering HBO before getting Showtime. And, the consumer would be able to buy VOD services if properly equipped, without taking anything else but broadcast basic.

Societal Participation

Although we may look at the development and marketing of fully switched broadband networks in the United States as the function of private enterprise and private investment, the character of the communication infrastructure is important to individuals, the national and international economy, and society. Educational institutions will bear some responsibility for creating an awareness of the immensity of the interactive media and information resources accessed through full service networks and for cultivating effective and discriminating use in homes and public institutions.[78] Agencies of the government must connect to the system, making public resources available to citizens. Some community media centers, often evolving from public access channels, have taken leadership in informing people of the options in new media.

Notes

1. Richard J. MacDonald, "The Vision Thing," *Media Studies Journal*, Winter 1994, 95-99.

2. Eugene Jankowski and David Fuchs, *Television Today and Tomorrow* (New York: Oxford University Press, 1995), 161.

3. "Q & A," Time Warner Cable Full Service Network (Orlando, Fl.: Time Warner Corporation, May 1994); "Cable Television Developments" (Washington, DC: National Cable Television Association [NCTA], Fall 1994), 8A-9A (combines about $23 billion in subscriber revenue including local advertising with $2.7 billion in national cable network advertising revenue).

4. Leland L. Johnson, *Toward Competition in Cable Television* (Cambridge: MIT Press, 1994), 50.

5. "1995 Cable TV Facts" (New York: Cabletelevision Advertising Bureau, 1995), 7.

6. "Cable Television Developments," NCTA, 1-A. Sources: Nielsen Media Research and Paul Kagan Associates.

7. "1995 Cable TV Facts," Cabletelevision Advertising Bureau, 7.

8. Sources: Veronis, Suhler & Associates; Wilkofsky Gruen Associates; NCTA— quoted in "Facts and Figures," *Multichannel News*, 31 August 1992, 42; and "Cable Television Developments," NCTA, June 1993, 2A.

9. Rod Granger, "CTAM Study: Demo Difference Much More Subtle," *Multichannel News*, 7 November 1994, 40.

10. "Nielsen Report on Television, 1992-1993" (Northbrook, Ill.: Nielsen Media Research, 1993), 9.

11. Hao Xiaoming, "Television Viewing Among American Adults in the 1990s," *Journal of Broadcasting & Electronic Media* 38, no. 3 (1994): 353-360.

12. "1994 Cable TV Facts," Cabletelevision Advertising Bureau.

13. "1994 Cable TV Facts," Cabletelevision Advertising Bureau, 13. Viewing reported is for all cable households, those subscribing to pay channels and those who do not. The viewing levels to cable programming in just those households who subscribe to one or more pay channels are higher, at 50%, and higher in each daypart.

14. Bradley S. Greenberg, Roger Srigley, Thomas F. Baldwin, and Carrie Heeter, "Free System-Specific Cable Guides as an Incentive," in *Cableviewing*, ed. Carrie Heeter and Bradley S. Greenberg (Norwood, NJ: Ablex, 1988), 264-288.

15. Thomas Kalinske, "History Repeats Itself: Consumers, Technology and Entertainment," *CTAM Quarterly Journal* 2, no. 4 (1994): 14.

16. For discussions of viewing styles, see Robert P. Hawkins, Nancy Reynolds, and Suzanne Pingree, "In Search of Viewing Styles," *Journal of Broadcasting and Electronic Media* 35, no. 3 (1991): 375-383; Carrie Heeter and Bradley S. Greenberg, eds., sections 2, 3, and 4, *Cableviewing* (Norwood, NJ: Ablex, 1988), 67-203.

17. Carrie Heeter, "Program Selection With Abundance of Choice: A Process Model," *Human Communication Research* 12, no. 4 (1985): 126-152.

18. Rod Granger, "CTAM's 'Pulse' Report is Surfin' Safari," *Multichannel News*, 25 July 1994, 82-86.

19. Thomas Kalinske, "History Repeats Itself: Consumers, Technology and Entertainment," *CTAM Quarterly Journal* 2, no. 4 (1994): 12.

20. "Switching Channels," *Multichannel News*, 18 November 1991, 49.

21. James G. Webster and Jacob Wakshlag, "A Theory of Television Program Choice," *Communication Research* 10 (1983): 430-446.

22. "Nielsen TV Information, Fall 1991," *Multichannel News*, February 3, 1992, 17.

23. Thomas F. Baldwin, Marianne Barrett, and Benjamin Bates, "Uses and Values for News on Cable Television," *Journal of Broadcasting and Electronic Media* 37, no. 2 (1992): 225-233.

24. CNN research, 1993.

25. Thomas F. Baldwin, Marianne Barrett, and Benjamin Bates, "Influence of Cable on Television News Audiences," *Journalism Quarterly* 69, no. 3 (1992): 651-658.

26. "1994 Cable TV Facts," Cabletelevision Advertising Bureau, 51.

27. Evelyn Kaye, *The Family Guide to Children's Television* (New York: Pantheon, 1974).

28. Peggy Ziegler, "Cable's Biggest Problem," *Cable World*, 4 May 1992, 84.

29. Robert LaRose and David Atkin, "Understanding Cable Subscribership as Telecommunications Behavior," *Telematics and Infomatics* 5, no. 4 (1989): 387.

30. Peggy Ziegler, "Cable's Biggest Problem?" *Cable World*, 4 May 1992, 78.

31. Linda Moss, "Roper Survey: Cable Gets Good, Not Great Marks," *Multichannel News*, 26 July 1992, 30.

32. Peggy Ziegler, "Cable's Biggest Problem," *Cable World*, 4 May 1992, 82.

33. ASI Market Research/CTAM Research Committee, "Attitudes and Usage of Cable Television: Wave II" (Washington, DC: ASI/CTAM, 1 June 1992).

34. Moss, "Roper Survey: Cable," 30.

35. John M. Higgins, "Customers in Survey Rate Cable as a Lousy Value," *Multichannel News*, 22 February 1993, 44.

36. Michel Dupagne, "Testing the Relative Constancy of Mass Media Expenditures in the United Kingdom," *Journal of Media Economics* 7, no. 3 (1994): 1-14.

37. For a current review of the literature of the "relative constancy hypothesis," see David Pearce Demers, "Relative Constancy Hypothesis, Structural Pluralism, and National Advertising Expenditures," *Journal of Media Economics* 7, no. 4 (1994): 31-48.

38. Demers, "Relative Constancy," 36.

39. C. Fischer, *America Calling: A Social History of the Telephone to 1940* (Berkeley: University of California Press, 1992).

40. Fischer, *America Calling*. For modern studies finding similar patterns of use, see H. Dordick and R. LaRose, "The Uses of the Telephone," unpublished report to Bell Atlantic (East Lansing: Michigan State University, 1992); J. Dimmick et al., "The Uses and Gratifications of the Telephone" (paper presented to the annual meeting of the International Communication Association, Washington, D.C., May 1993).

41. C. Marvin, *When Old Technologies Were New: Thinking About Electronic Communication in the Late Nineteenth Century* (New York: Oxford University Press, 1988).

42. Marvin, *When Old Technologies*, and Fischer, *America Calling*.

43. Kent Gibbons, "Survey: Public Open to Cable Telephony," *Multichannel News*, 12 September 1994, 55.

44. Kent Gibbons, "Bell Survey: Many Subs Would Drop Cable," *Multichannel News*, 24 October 1994, 45.

45. C. Steinfield, "U.S.: Videotex in a Hyper-Evolutionary Market," in *Relaunching Videotex*, ed. H. Bouwman and M. Christoffersen (Amsterdam: Kluwer, 1992), 149-164; C. Steinfield and R. Kramer, "U.S.: Dialing for Diversity," in *Cash Lines: Audiotex in Europe and the United States*, ed. M. Latzer and G. Thomas (Amsterdam: Het Spinhuis, 1994).

46. K. Dudley, C. Steinfield, R. Kraut, and J. Katz, "Rethinking Residential Services," Bellcore Technical Manuscript, Morristown, N.J., July 1993.

47. Dimmick et al., "Uses and Gratifications."

48. Dean M. Krugman and Keith F. Johnson, "Differences in Consumption of Traditional Broadcast and VCR Movie Rentals," *Journal of Broadcasting and Electronic Media* 35, no. 2 (1991): 213-232.

49. Tom Kerver, "VOD: Yes, No or Maybe?" *Cablevision*, 19 September 1994, 24.

50. Gene DeRose, "The Customer Is Always in the Right Lane," *Convergence '93*, Winter 1993, 28.

51. "What Do You Get When Millions of People Stop Just Watching TV?" Sega Channel brochure, 1994.

52. Christopher Stern, "Home Shopping: Who's Buying?" *Broadcasting & Cable*, 4 October 1993, 63.

53. Kim Mitchell, "Cable's 'Best' Customers?" *Cable World*, 6 March 1995, 18.

54. Matt Stump, "Vos, Gruppo Study Shopping," *On Demand*, June/July 1994, 36.

55. DeRose, "The Customer Is Always," 26.

56. Over 80% of the revenues for the electronic information services industry in 1990 were in the area of financial information services. C. Steinfield, "Videotex in a Hyper-Evolutionary Market."

57. Kent Gibbons, "Cox Prodigy Trial in San Diego Enticing Viewers," *Multichannel News*, 5 December 1994, 37.

58. "New Yardstick for Interactive TV," *Broadcasting & Cable*, 23 May 1994, 6 (probability sample of 1,000 cable households).

59. "How Much Is Monthly Service Worth to Consumers?" *Cable World*, 25 July 1994, 4.

60. Nancy Reed, "If You Build It, They Will Come . . . Maybe," *Convergence '94*, November 1994, 38-39.

61. Kent Gibbons, "U S West Fleshes Out Omaha Menu," *Multichannel News*, 27 February 1995, 1.

62. Peter Lambert, "FSN-2: The Two-Year Challenge," *On Demand*, February 1995, 8.

63. Peter Lambert, "All the News That's Fit to Digitize," *On Demand*, December 1994/January 1995, 44.

64. Lambert, "All the News," 6, quoting Ed McCracken, chairman and CEO, Silicon Graphics Inc.

65. Kent Gibbons, "SNET Moving Fast in Self-Defense," *Multichannel News*, 25 April 1994, 51.

66. Paul Donnelly, "Putting Interactivity to the Test," *Convergence '94*, September 1994, 31.

67. Mark Berniker, "SNET Claims 40% Market Share in West Hartford," *Broadcasting & Cable*, 10 October 1994, 92-93.

68. R. Thomas Umstead, "SNET Pulls Back on VOD Push in Conn.," *Multichannel News*, 23 January 1995, 3.

69. Umstead, "SNET Pulls Back."

70. Stuart C. Johnson and Robert Townsend, "BVS Video Vision," interview in *On Demand*, December 1994/January 1995, 6.

71. Russ Shipley, project director quoted in "Stand-Alone VOD Falls in Rochester," *Broadcasting & Cable*, 23 January 1995, 10.

72. Kent Gibbons, "U S West Fleshes Out Omaha Menu," *Multichannel News*, 27 February 1995, 1.

73. Kent Gibbons, Ted Hearn and Linda Haugstead, "War on the Plains: Cox, U S West Face Off," *Multichannel News*, 4 September 1995, 1.

74. DeRose, "The Customer Is Always," 26.

75. 47 U.S.C. 623.

76. 47 U.S.C. 544d.

77. 47 U.S.C. 623.

78. The purpose of the National Model Technology Demonstration School project by Cox Cable and San Diego State University is to cultivate interactive media skills among students and teachers.

9

Advertising and Shopping

dvertising will play a role in subsidizing much of the service on the new communication networks in its traditional ways and develop into several new forms. Shopping services, as an extension of advertising, and on their own, are also expected to contribute substantially to full service, broadband system development. This chapter examines the forms of advertising and shopping and the business and consumer opportunities in this area of integrated broadband network services.

Advertising in the Multichannel Environment

PRODUCT AWARENESS

Advertising will be of three main types in the full service network. The first is traditional *product awareness* advertising, which serves the complex functions of product introduction, brand image development, and reminder, usually represented in television by the 30-second spot participation in programming. The audience is relatively passive;

the message intrudes briefly on the consciousness of people who are not intending to receive that particular message. A brand image, established in part by advertising, requires maintenance by continuous advertising.

INFORMATION OFFER

A second type of advertising in a full service network is an *information offer*. In this case, the television advertising spot encourages people to seek additional information. One viewer option is to key in the request on the home terminal. The information is then printed in the viewer's home for reference or is stored in video or text in the viewer's system while he or she continues with the program. Or the viewer is diverted from the program long enough to see the information before returning. Contrary to traditional advertising, the message is "invited" into the home. Coupons can be printed on the conventional computer printer or a simple dedicated printer. The offer of information may be incorporated in the program itself, "embedded advertising." For example, the viewer could be offered information about the apparel worn by the star or any prop that is featured in the program.

The advertiser would have to anticipate the kind of information consumers would seek so as to have that information packaged and ready, although in some cases a consumer could also have the option of live interaction with a person. Where the viewer requests the information to be stored while he or she continues watching a program, the advertiser takes the risk that the printed or recorded *reference information* may subsequently be ignored by the viewer.

In research conducted by Videoway in Quebec, four times as many viewers were able to recall interactive advertising than normal advertising. In one of the Videoway projects, viewers could even choose the language (French or English), which could be significant in bilingual areas.[1]

Most of the FSNs in market tests seek partnerships with advertisers who are interested in exploring the creative and business components of interactivity. Generally, the participants are paying much more than the advertising to such small audiences would be worth. They are mainly large companies, such as Chrysler, spending a very small part of their huge advertising budgets in underwriting a part of the FSN development in exchange for an early experience with format and consumer response.

DIRECT SELLING

The third type of advertising function is *direct selling*, or *direct response television* (DRTV). This could be a single 30-second spot, an infomercial, or a program-length commercial where a product can be purchased by telephone or entering the order on a remote keypad. Or the advertising may be an extension of an information offer, where there is an attempt to consummate the inquiry in a sale.

Infomercials, longer form commercials, two minutes or so, will have interactive options with the viewer able to branch to more specific or detailed information as appropriate to individual needs and usually urged to buy now. A number of the early interactive commercials included brief games in the attempt to involve the viewer.

Program-length commercials have become a direct selling trend in television that will develop further with the larger channel capacity of digitally compressed systems. The programs are hybrids of entertainment and direct marketing, merging the dual American interest in television and consumption. In the talk programs, each guest has something to sell—a book, a gadget, a vacation, sports merchandise. More than one full channel dedicated to infomercials and program-length commercials is in planning for megachannel systems.

Per inquiry advertising, transaction-based compensation. In some advertising involving interaction, information offers, and direct selling, the FSN may not necessarily sell the advertising time. Instead, the transaction may be *per inquiry* advertising, in which the system takes a fee based on the inquiry (which could provide a sales lead) or a commission on the sale—*transaction-based compensation*.

AUDIOTEX AND ONLINE ADVERTISING

Audiotex information may carry advertising as a means of increasing revenues and reducing costs to users. This is also true of online services, which can embed advertising messages in the text or use the borders of the screen. In both cases, the advertiser takes advantage of the known interest of the user to focus the message.

TARGETING

The targeting of subscribers is an essential advantage of advertising in multichannel systems. Ideally, the advertiser would be able to aim at demographic, psychographic (lifestyle) interests, geographic targets, or, even more specifically, people with intention to buy a particular product. Conventionally, advertisers were interested in gender, age, and income demographic characteristics. As minorities have grown in numbers, ethnicity—or racial categories—have also become important. For many products or services, the purchase decision is made by people who fit fairly neatly into demographic categories, such as for disposable diapers by women 18-34. Full service networks will be able to supply such information about most of their subscribers. Generally, the more narrow the niche of a TV program, the more focused its target audience.

Advertisers also have an interest in the geographic location of the subscribers—the market described physically. Companies with national distribution may advertise their products in geographic phases. Antifreeze and winter clothing would be offered first in the north, then in the middle latitudes, and finally in the southern areas. Retailers define their trading area specifically in terms of their merchandise or service. In a small city, it might be the entire city and an area of about 20 miles from the city center, made irregular by trading areas for retailers in other nearby cities. The 20-mile area might be much greater for a merchant with a highly specialized product. In larger cities, the trading area for a retailer may be defined by only a small part of the city.

A broadcast television "market" is not defined by a general retail market or trading area but instead by television signal strength— roughly a 70-mile radius from the center of the city. The market is further defined by audience usage. If people in a particular county spend more than half of their time viewing television stations from one city, they are put in that "market."[2] Neither the "total survey area" nor the less extensive "metro area" reported by Nielsen Media Research suits all retailers. Some, serving much smaller trading areas, are either precluded from broadcast television advertising or pay for audience that is outside their specific market.

Cable television audiences can be more specifically defined geographically because a great many headends serve each area. It is more likely that subscribers served by one headend, or two or three, will fit the geographic market of a particular retailer quite well. That retailer, while not able to buy broadcast television advertising because of the waste, is a potential client for cable advertising.

GEODEMOGRAPHIC TARGETING

The following illustrates the very significant impact of these differences between broadcast and cable television advertising. We will assume a broadcast television market with 2 million households. Within that broadcast television market is a cable system in a suburb of the city that has 70,000 subscribers among 100,000 households passed. A record store with only one outlet is located in the suburb. The store considers its market to be defined by the suburb's city limits. Very few record buyers from outside would come into the suburb to buy records. If a broadcast station in the television market sells 30-second spots for $600 per spot and the average household rating for that station is 7%, the average audience is 140,000 households. In cost per thousand households (CPM), a figure used in the industry for comparisons, each 1,000 households cost $4.29 (.07 × 2,000,000 = 140,000/1,000, $600/140 = $4.29). If the cable network on which the cable company inserts local ads has an average rating of .8% and the system charges $10 per 30-second spot, its cost per thousand is $17.86 (.008 × 70,000 = 560/1,000, $10/.560 = $17.86). The cable spot costs four times as much as the broadcast spot on a cost per thousand basis.

But, if we *exclude* the broadcast area that is outside the suburb, which the record store says is not its trading area, the picture is much different. The cost for the broadcast station time stays the same, whatever the audience in which the advertiser is interested. Therefore, the cost per thousand, *in the suburb*, for the broadcast spot is $85.71 (.07 × 100,000 = 7,000/1,000, $600/7 = $85.71). Looking *only at the market the record store wants*, the broadcast spot is nearly five times the cost per thousand as in the cable system.

Now, suppose that the record store does almost all of its business with people 14 to 24 years of age. If the record store buys a spot on MTV, almost the entire audience is 14 to 24. If it buys time on the broadcast station, let's say only one-third of the audience is 14 to 24. The cost per thousand people 14 to 24 in the broadcast audience is \$257.40 (.07 × 100,000 × .333 = 2,331/1,000; \$600/2.331 = \$257.40), more than 14 times the cost of the time on MTV. Under these conditions, if the record store has a television budget of \$3,000, it would buy 300 spots on MTV instead of 5 spots on the broadcast station. The store must realize, of course, that only 70% of its market is reached by cable.

If we introduced a psychographic, or lifestyle, variable, it might look even better for cable. If the 14- to 24-year-olds in the suburb all had expensive stereos and sat around listening to CDs in their spare time, they might buy twice as many CDs as the youth in the television market as a whole.[3]

IMPROVING ON TARGETING

Cable systems as they now exist are still not ideal in the opportunity they provide to target markets. The franchise fits political boundaries, not retail market boundaries. In a large integrated broadband network covering a metropolitan trading area, the geographic market can be defined any way the advertiser wants by selecting the appropriate nodes. A neighborhood convenience store might only want four nodes, each with only 250 households. With this flexibility, the Metropolitan Chevrolet Dealers Association, a citywide chain of gas stations, the Eastside theater complex, a florist on the southeast side of town, a neighborhood auto mechanic, and an independent dry cleaner could all use television advertising, each ordering only the appropriate *geographic* area.

Given the range of *interests* represented in programs and channels offered by an integrated broadband network, a vintage wine merchant, an interior designer, an art dealer, a custom auto supply store, and a tatoo parlor can also find a place on television. At the extreme, the demographic characteristics of the audience could be preselected. The advertiser could say, "I want only households with females 14 to 24." The advertising message would then be addressed only to those households.

Advertising announcements pertinent to the subscribing household background and interests could be inserted in programming on cue at the times reserved for advertising. Or there may be an *intelligent tag* placed at the end of an advertising spot that would personalize the message, such as a person's name; for example, "Imagine [fill in the name—Jane Smith] in this dress. Talk to Cindy in the Chandler Store sportswear department."

Any service that is on demand, where customers tacitly or directly permit it, can insert video or text advertising blocks designed to fit the interest of a person who would then request that specific information or video. This is the ultimate advertising targeting by interest level.

Interactive television advertising may actually narrow the audience down to people who are actively in the market for the advertiser's product. As an example of this benefit, we might look at the automobile industry, which is one of the largest buyers of television advertising time, mostly broadcasting. The industry knows that about 10% of adults are actually in the market for a car in a given time period. Until interactive advertising, the only way to reach that 10% by television was to buy the whole audience. If a short interactive advertising announcement offers information about an automobile, the people who respond are likely to be among the 10% who are in the market. So the interactive announcement serves to screen the audience to more interested individuals. The money invested thereafter in talking to just these people is well spent.

CLASSIFIEDS

Classified advertising is now available on many cable systems with increasingly attractive graphics or video components. Categories appear on schedule, for example, real estate on the hour, employment at :15, autos at :30, merchandise at :45. Interactive capability adds immeasurably to the convenience of classified advertising by allowing the user to call up categories in a variety of ways based on key characteristics, for example, "used automobiles," then, "Chevrolet," then "midsize," then "1990." Or the user requests "used automobiles," then "$1,000 to $1,500." The major concern is that the menus be simple; the user must be able to get to the items of interest as directly as possible.

SUBSIDIZING MEDIA

Media in the United States are subsidized by advertising. In broadcasting, the entire cost of providing the programming is borne by the advertisers. In multichannel television, subscription fees and advertising contribute to the revenues of most channels. Advertising revenue varies from a small proportion to as high as two-thirds or more of the total.

As we have seen, all but the most recent cable networks ferociously guard their position as *basic* channels. Several lawsuits are now pending over the rights of cable operators, under their affiliation agreements, to move programmers to a higher tier or to à la carte. In these suits, programmers are attempting to maximize their potential audience by maintaining status as a basic channel.

Full service networks also offer consumers the option of programming without advertising. The consumer will be trading off the irritation of the commercials with the cost of the programming— fewer commercials, higher cost. There is evidence that advertiser-supported channels may have to curtail the amount of advertising time to compete with pay channels.[4] A safe assumption, however, is that lighter television entertainment will continue to carry advertising. Audiences are quite accustomed to the commercial interruptions, even count on the interruptions for necessities, snacks, conversation, and so on. And, of course, they are entertained by the commercials. Surveys of television audiences generally conclude that people believe the commercial interruptions are a fair price to pay for "free" programming. If the heaviest users of advertiser-supported television are the lower-income households that cannot afford much video on demand, then the trade-off will be more compelling. Thus, we have another kind of "gap" between the affluent and the poor. The poor will be exposed to more commercial television.

Eventually, consumers and operators will come to an agreement on which programming will carry advertising, and how much, and which will not. But it will be difficult for both provider and consumer to come to an optimum amount of time. Most à la carte programmers will be reluctant to offer a channel at a high price to permit lower levels of advertising for fear the price will turn away potential subscribers. Instead, there will be a tendency to insert as much advertising as the consumer will tolerate, that is, until the consumer cancels the subscription. Where the advertising and the program content are closely allied as we would expect in most à la carte niche channels, the viewer may be sufficiently interested in the advertising to accept high levels. The programmer only knows by in-depth questioning of subscribers.

VOD ADVERTISING

VOD movies, events, games, and data could also come to carry some advertising if the consumer would accept it or could be convinced that the price of the desired content is less as a result. The provider of this programming or information might take advantage of natural breaks or create intermissions or pauses for advertising.

There is also the possibility that the viewer could suit her- or himself by choosing video or data either with or without advertising. An advertiser may offer discounts on VOD programming if the viewer accepts commercial messages. Those accepting advertising could also agree to supply household demographic information for the record. Most advertisers might prefer to buy into programming where all viewers would be captive to the message, particularly those who could afford *not* to watch it. Nonetheless, in this new environment, advertisers may have to take what they can get. In this case, they would know the demographic characteristics, in aggregate, of the audience that chose the commercial programs.

There is a possibility that the audience for advertising will be eroded by high-capacity digital television systems. When substantial libraries of VOD or NVOD programming are available to subscribers, plus games and information services, without advertising, people will be diverted from advertiser-supported television. At the same time, some analysts believe that advertisers will "pay the way" for many of the interactive services of digital networks.[5]

À LA CARTE CHANNEL ADVERTISING

As long as subscribers to a television video service perceive themselves to be at a ceiling price in buying "packages" of channels, new networks will be added à la carte. On à la carte channels, advertising of mass market products remains a possibility. Golfers subscribing to the Golf Channel and gardeners subscribing to the Home and Garden channel also buy soap and breakfast food. To reach a mass market through à la carte channels means the purchase of time on many, many channels to aggregate a meaningfully large audience across all of them. This may be necessary as continued fragmentation of the television audience means *underdelivery* of audience, even in a massive schedule of spots on any one channel.

The best advertiser prospect for an à la carte channel, however, is the supplier of a product or service that precisely fits the channel, a "pure play" for advertisers. The match of audience to channel may be of two types: interest, where the advertiser presents fishing tackle on a fishing channel, or demographic, where the advertiser presents a Mercedes Benz automobile on a financial markets channel. In the first example, the fishing channel will have plenty of data available that will tell the advertiser that the subscriber to the channel buys something like 20 times more fishing tackle than the average consumer. In the second example, the financial markets channel will have data that says the subscribers to the channel have an average income of $122,000 per year and are 5.6 times more likely to buy a luxury car than the average consumer.

There are several problems in dependence on advertising as one means of supporting the development of FSNs. Megachannel television is in a sense its own worst enemy. As more advertiser-supported channels, and advertiser-supported programming, come on line, incredibly large inventories of advertising time go on the market. As these supplies of time increase, prices are kept low. Advertising budgets must be spread across many vehicles; the advertising announcements may need to be customized for each vehicle, and perhaps each consumer. This greatly raises the transaction, or administrative, costs per advertising exposure.

Advertising Administration

NETWORK

Buying time in national networks is a convenient, low-transaction-cost means of advertising for companies with national distribution.

The spots are sold in advance of the season at a discount, the *up-front market*; the remainder sold during the season are the *scatter market*. In the television world of digital compression, there will be more networks. The specialized networks will create many more national television advertisers, whereas just a few years ago mainly mass marketers used national television. Because some of the niche channels will have limited audiences, it will not be practical for the network itself to sell the advertising time as in the bigger networks. Some of these networks use *representative firms* ("reps") who will sell several different networks generally not competing for the same advertising dollars. Some of the program networks may be sold in a package to a single advertiser desiring to *roadblock* the audience by putting the spot on all the channels at the same time to make the advertising more or less unavoidable for viewers in the time period.

Video-on-demand programs that carry advertising may be produced on the *barter* plan, in which the advertiser invests in the program up front in exchange for commercial time within the program, or buys into the program through the producer or distributor after it has been produced. All of the commercial time may be acquired by national advertisers, but in some cases a portion of the time may be reserved for local sales as a means of encouraging a full service network to put the program on the menu and promote it.

NATIONAL SPOT

Programming networks sell and retain revenues from about ten minutes of commercial time in each hour. Usually two minutes in each hour are given to the local system to sell. The spots the system has to sell are called *local availabilities*, or simply *avails*. Advertising spots, delivered by satellite or obtained locally, will be stored in a computer and inserted into the programming at the proper place on cue. This replaces a computer-driven series of VCRs holding analog spots. The digital spots can be changed quickly for advertisers such as supermarkets, department stores, electronics retailers, and movie distributors who need to make rapid adjustments in their messages.

The local availabilities are sold nationally, regionally, or locally. National and regional sales are called *national spot*. In national spot, the advertiser selectively buys local avails within cable networks and spots in local origination. If the idea of national spot is to place advertising at the appropriate time in the appropriate geographic areas, a full service network will refine that concept to its limits. National spot buyers will be able to select their precise markets, geographically, or their consumers under standardized parameters: demographic, psychographic, or household purchasing histories.

The *"rep firm"* will represent enough systems to justify placing salespeople in all of the major cities. A rep firm cannot be very efficient in serving small broadband systems. Therefore, the systems must *interconnect* for spot sales or acquire ownership in a cluster of systems making a meaningful market in a population or geographic trading area for national advertisers. At the same time, the spot buyer may specify submarkets within the broader interconnection or cluster. An interconnect or large cable cluster could offer specific zip codes to national spot buyers. In integrated broadband systems, markets defined by the geographic logic of advertising time sales may contribute to the configuration of clusters or service areas. It will probably be inefficient for a system to be smaller than the general trading area for the largest metropolitan advertisers.

National spot advertising in multichannel television is the fastest growing segment of the advertising industry. Practically nonexistent at the turn of this decade because of the logistic difficulties of buying time across multiple cable systems, national spot buyers were not spending anywhere near what the audiences would justify. This deficiency is slowly coming into balance as the mechanisms for advertising sales of this type are developing. Multichannel television revenues would be much greater if it were to get its fair share of national spot revenues. National spot television spending is now about $15 billion. Cable gets about $500 million.[6] But, because cable ad-supported channels have about 23% of all of the television viewing, the figure should be at least $3.45 billion.[7] We might estimate that there would be another $1 billion from advertisers who can now buy national spot on television because of the specialized networks.

LOCAL ADVERTISING SALES

The improved storage and insertion capability of digital television will greatly increase the number of channels on which local advertising time is sold—now varying considerably across cable systems but averaging about 13 channels.[8] A local staff makes these sales. In the case of an interconnect, the interconnect staff may sell all of the local avails for all of the systems participating, in which case the individual systems do not have advertising sales staff. Sometimes, however, the bigger systems in an interconnect reserve some of the spots for sale by an internal staff.

In addition to the two minutes or so of advertising availabilities hourly in the program networks, FSNs will have all of the advertising time on local origination channels to sell locally or in the national spot market. Cable systems or interconnects sell this time now using the rep firms for national spot, as described above, and their own sales staffs for local advertising buyers.

In a few cases, broadcasters have emerged as the sales agents for cable systems within their markets. Broadcasters sell advertising time on a much larger scale than cable systems. It is a logical role for a broadcaster in the cable market, particularly as long as individual cable systems are relatively small and cable advertising a minor factor in system revenue. But, if integrated broadband networks develop to encompass larger geographic areas and more subscribers, the advertising sales would probably be kept in-house.

TRAFFIC MANAGEMENT

FSN advertising sales will require the management of a huge inventory of "avails." The traffic system must manage the insertion of spots, according to the time or program or channel ordered (*fixed placement*) or inserted throughout the schedule (*run of schedule*, or *ROS*) so that the spots are distributed across the schedule according to the contract parameters, which will include "zones" or natural "trading areas" within the overall market covered by the local network. If spots are sold in upward of 100 channels, and in some program titles, information is ordered on demand and then customized to the individual household, the FSN has a big task in administering the traffic. The software that manages this traffic monitors the advertising inventory, that is, the status of all the advertising spots in all of the channels and programs. It could also adjust the going prices of the spots to reflect demand, which is *yield management pricing.* Software is now under development for use on a more limited scale by cable operators. Work is also in progress on a system for inserting national spot advertising from a central point, so that the local FSN is not even responsible for placing the spots.

Not everything described here for full service network advertisers, or everything envisioned by advertisers, will be practical. The sheer magnitude of the possibilities may overwhelm the ability to design and manage the system. In some cases, the value of the advertising time may be less than the cost to place the advertising.

ADVERTISING AGENCIES

Advertising agencies have not always looked with favor on the opportunities provided by multimedia television technology. Cable has not provided the mass audiences, nationally or locally, that the traditional agencies are accustomed to having. The local cable system may not even be able to tell the agency the size of the audience reached because ratings are not provided for local programming for all systems.

A further problem for the agencies is the compensation system customary in the field. The agency usually works for a 15% commission on media purchased. The medium buys $1 million worth of television time, pays the television medium $850,000, and bills the client $1 million. When the agency is buying time on cable networks and, worse, on local cable systems, the cost of the time is so small in relation to the work of preparing the commercials and buying the time, the agency gets very little compensation for its efforts. For decades, the advertising industry has realized that the commission system should be replaced by a more professional fee-for-service structure. The problems of using multichannel digital television systems may finally bring about the fee structure.

If the advertising agency becomes the provider of the information to be accessed by subscribers, the role is expanded. If, however, the advertiser supplies the information, instead of the agency, because it may be so technical and so specific to individual inquiries that using a third party is awkward, the role of the advertising agency is diminished. Also, some product information will be provided by organizations not under the control of the advertiser, such as by those reporting for consumers.

Evaluation

Where products and services are sold directly through a full service network, to evaluate the effectiveness of the services of the FSN the advertiser simply examines the costs against the sales volume. The evaluation is more difficult when the consumer seeks information and does not buy direct. The advertiser may never know whether the consumer bought the product. But, at the least, the advertiser can have information provided by the broadband network on whether or not the consumer acts on the information. The system may store direct television purchasing behaviors of the consumer and then relate this information to advertising exposure and information requests. The only limits on such a tracking system are the cost of the tracking against the value to the users of the system, and the issue of privacy.

It would be most valuable to the advertiser if the identification of the person making the inquiry or having been exposed to advertising can be retrieved, along with information about the person—not only the previous purchasing but demographic and lifestyle characteristics. Persons might identify themselves by asking for customized information to be later addressed to them or giving electronic consent to supply specified background information to obtain additional information, a discount, or a premium.

Retailers are now collecting and storing information about customers that could be matched with full service network usage. For example, the Incredible Universe stores owned by Tandy require the buyers to use a membership card to make purchases, and thus have considerable data on the members. Grocery stores have cards that are used to obtain "bonus points." They could obtain aggregate data on television advertising exposure to integrated broadband network subscribers who qualified for the bonus points.

NATIONAL NETWORK RATINGS

The measure of effectiveness of traditional product awareness advertising is the audience rating. Nielsen Media Research syndicates national ratings for cable networks based on a national sample of television households. The size of the sample is building up to

5,000 households. A network is covered in the survey when it accesses a certain threshold of homes. Now about 30 networks have national Nielsen ratings.

The multichannel network ratings are different than the broadcast network ratings. The broadcast rating is the percentage of all U.S. television households viewing. The cable rating is generally presented as the percentage of households viewing within the *universe* of subscribers who have access to a network. So the rating for ESPN, which has about 58 million subscribers, represents the percentage of those 58 million households that viewed ESPN. A rating for CNBC, which has about 46 million subscribers, is the percentage of those 46 million households that viewed CNBC. The actual number of households represented by the rating are also reported so that the user will know how many households are viewing. In the examples above, a cable universe rating of 1.0% for ESPN would be 580,000 viewing households; a 1.0% rating for CNBC would mean 460,000 viewing households. Only recently has Nielsen Media Research been also reporting the national cable ratings as a percentage of all U.S. television households, whether or not the households have access to the cable network.

Cable network ratings even within their own subscriber universes are low compared with broadcast networks. The big cable network (e.g., USA, TBS, ESPN) ratings have remained nearly constant in recent years. Increases in the absolute multichannel audience numbers have come as a result of the growth in new networks and the increase in the number of multichannel subscribers.[9]

The top-rated cable nonsports programs, usually made-for-cable movies or major syndicated series, get ratings of about 3% in the cable universe. At best for cable, an NFL football game or NBA playoff game may go as high as 8% and a major news event, 15%.[10] Most of the cable programming household audiences are much lower. Table 9.1 presents a typical set of ratings for some cable networks. It will be noted that most of the "prime-time" and almost all of the "total day" ratings are below 1%. Also note that some of the ratings are only small fractions of 1% and some of these are for networks with relatively few subscribers, meaning that the household numbers are *very* low.

Households participating in the Nielsen sample (panel) are monitored by a *peoplemeter*. Individuals must manually log in and out of

TABLE 9.1 Typical Ratings and Numbers[a] of Households Viewing Cable Networks

Network	Prime Time Rating*	Prime Time Households (000)	Total Day Rating**	Total Day Households (000)
USA	2.4	1,500	1.1	650
TBS	2.3	1,400	1.3	800
TNT	2.0	1,200	1.0	650
ESPN	1.5	940	0.8	480
Nick	1.6	1000	1.5	900
Lifetime	1.5	950	0.8	370
Discovery	1.0	600	0.5	300
Family	1.0	590	0.4	230
TNN	1.0	580	0.5	280
A&E	1.0	570	0.7	430
CNN	0.9	550	0.7	500
MTV	0.6	370	0.5	280
WGN	1.0	360	0.6	210
Headline	0.3	170	0.3	150
CNBC	0.6	380	0.4	200
VH-1	0.3	145	0.2	95
Cartoon	1.4	140	0.9	90
Learning Channel	0.5	130	0.3	90
Prevue	0.4	120	0.2	70
Comedy	0.4	110	0.3	90
Sci-Fi	0.5	90	0.4	60
E! Entertainment	0.5	170	0.2	60
Country Music TV	0.3	70	0.3	60

a. These are fictional numbers very close to the average for the networks over several quarters.
* 8-11 p.m., with some variation in networks.
** Some variation by individual networks, eliminating very early morning hours.

the viewing audience, which causes the programmers to worry about the reliability of the device, particularly for children. The ideal is a *passive* meter that does not require the viewer to make any effort to record presence in the audience. The passive meter would automatically recognize different household members by some means, none of which is perfected.

A network that has not reached the qualifying threshold for Nielsen must contract with Nielsen or other research companies for custom surveys. The cost is high. Once there is a critical mass of television households subscribing to broadband systems, research companies could contract with the systems to supply data on usage.

The syndicated researcher would select the systems, then specify which subscribers are desired and set standards for data collection. This would not be a measure of all television viewing but an important subset of viewers.

LOCAL RATINGS

Thus far, we have discussed national ratings for networks. National spot buyers and local advertisers need data on local audiences. Sometimes the national rating for a network is simply projected to the local system. For example, if the network has a national household rating of 1.5%, and a local cable system has 100,000 subscribers, the audience projection for the cable system is 1,500 households. This, of course, makes some very large assumptions about the comparability of the relatively homogeneous local cable system with the national sample.

Many cable systems have not purchased local audience data because of the cost in relation to their advertising revenues. Nielsen reports audiences for the major cable networks in the local market ratings, but the figures might not be reliable for any particular cable system within the market. Another Nielsen report will provide an audience share comparison for each of the broadcast stations and the combined basic cable networks on which a cable system sells local advertising by various dayparts. For example, the report might indicate that in City A, between 6 a.m. and 9 a.m., Monday-Friday, the aggregate share for 14 cable channels is 19%; the CBS affiliate, 23%; the NBC affiliate, 32%; the ABC affiliate, 6%; the Fox affiliate, 4%; and others, 16%.

There is some research evidence to support the cable operators' fears that the diary method used by Nielsen for some markets, which depends on recall to make the proper entries in the viewing diary, understates the cable audience. Cable subscribers do not remember or do not accurately report viewing of their relatively large repertoire of channels. A new service, named ADcom, which has investment interest by Arbitron, GE Capital, and Veronis, Suhler & Associates (an investment banking firm with a specialty in media), claims to have developed an inexpensive passive meter for local cable ratings. Integrated broadband systems will be able to monitor viewing and aggregate the results for advertisers, but only for the households with home terminals.

Full service networks will remake the advertising industry, at least the television advertising business, changing the function and message, opening new doors to consumers ("micromarketing"), and helping to support many of the system services. The expectations for shopping services are similar.

Shopping

In about 20 years, printed catalog shopping has emerged to $60 billion in annual revenue. Electronic shopping services could capture a significant part of the catalog business and also some of the huge business from retail stores. Full service networks offer both interactive television shopping and high-speed online shopping services.

ENTERTAINMENT-SHOPPING HYBRIDS

QVC (Quality, Value, Convenience) and HSN (Home Shopping Network) attempt to be entertaining and informative. The networks recognize the "bias" created by the relatively narrow-appeal merchandise and the format.[11] But because they each do over $1 billion in gross sales annually,[12] they are reluctant to risk that market with programming changes. Both have new networks that are designed to broaden the television shopping market. Other companies intend to cater to high-end buyers.

Traditional cable channels are experimenting with direct sales programs. MTV Networks, which include MTV, VH-1, Nick at Nite, and Comedy Central, are contemplating content-related shopping blocks offering video games, concert tickets, music paraphernalia, music videos, albums, clothes, and other items. TCI and the Bertelsmann Music Group (BMG) are planning a new "cutting edge" music channel to appeal to Generation X. They will sell music-related merchandise, CD packages, T-shirts, and tickets.[13]

Designed for full service integrated broadband networks, the U S West shopping entry, U S Avenue, is dividing programming into categories: retailers, manufacturers, catalogers, advertisers, and professionals.

Broadband networks will seek to enhance revenues through commissions on purchases, much as now occurs with online and cable shopping services or by owning one or more of the shopping services themselves. They will package their own set of products and suppliers into an electronic mall while at the same time providing gateways to other shopping services. All commercial online services, offering their own shopping services, will be reachable via the full service networks, and the Internet will also be a vehicle for accessing many different shopping services. In this case, several *electronic malls* will compete on an FSN. The most attractive electronic mall will be the one that contains that set of *stores* most desired by consumers. For any particular FSN, this may mean providing electronic access to the largest number of local commercial enterprises, which will be recognizable to subscribers and with which subscribers may already have an established relationship (such as an account or a product under warranty) as well as providing gateways to the largest number of distant product and service suppliers. Hence, a part of the competition is between the mall operators as each seeks to make its mall more attractive to store owners than competitors' malls. Early stages in this competition are already under way, with companies like MCI aggressively marketing their electronic shopping services to companies that want to have an electronic presence. They offer assistance in creating electronic catalogs (such as a *home page* on the World Wide Web), secure data transmission to customers, and a financial institution (Bank of America) that will perform such tasks as credit approvals and funds transfers. Many telephone, computer service, cable, and other types of companies will compete in this arena.

PC shopping services are being developed as a precursor to interactive television, affording merchants and consumers valuable experience. CompuServe's electronic mall has 130 stores; Prodigy's 70. CompuServe charges the merchant $20,000 per year plus 2% of sales for a 100-product store. The fun and functionality of the PC malls will be enhanced by broadband communication systems with speed and multimedia capability. But CD-ROMs are also a good shopping medium. CompuServe sells the shopping CD-ROM at a nominal charge. When using the disc, orders can be placed automatically through CompuServe.[14]

CUC International, scheduled to participate in FSN trials in Orlando, Florida, has had a pricing and buying service on Prodigy,

CompuServe, and America Online. Shoppers can browse or go directly to specific items that are described by a digitized audio narrative. Dating services have also been established.

An interesting online shopping service, "Peapod," is a grocery shopping service, now partly owned by Ameritech and tied in with the grocery chains Jewel, in Chicago, and Safeway, in San Francisco. In 1994, there were 7,000 customers ("members") spending $100 on average of 2.5 times per month. The members are mostly women from dual-income families with children, although disabled people and people without convenient transportation also use the service.[15] An interactive television version was to debut in 1995.

The advantages of a computer-based shopping service, accessed through interactive television or online services connected to cable or telephone lines, over printed or CD-ROM catalogs, is that the service may be less expensive, in the long run, and can be continuously updated, such as by eliminating sold-out items or introducing sale merchandise. Many of the companies developing interactive shopping services are exploring multiple platforms that could include CD-ROM and online services over conventional telephone lines or broadband systems.

The electronic shopping services must first attract attention to the merchandise among those who are not specifically seeking it out. Direct marketers are less enthusiastic about electronic retailing than the full service network developers. For example, the direct marketers predict a $28 billion business in electronic shopping by the year 2004; the telecommunication operators, $110 billion.[16] However skeptical of the electronic shopping services, the existing catalog outlets must follow the electronic shopping developments closely, as do all retailers, lest they be left out of the loop.

INTELLIGENT AGENTS AND SMART SERVICES

Most of the new networks have *smart agent* software that will help find products for household members (e.g., a birthday gift for a 45-year-old women interested in gourmet cooking) and to alert them to needs (change the oil, restock laundry detergent, select an anniversary present) according to stored information about the household, its characteristics, and previous behaviors.

Smart services, or services that learn (see Chapter 6), are based on a more general trend called *database marketing* in which merchants use data collected about consumers to model the purchaser of specific products. The information is supplied by the consumer in response to warranty registration, automobile registration, surveys, responses to offers of discounts and coupons, applications for credit cards, and other sources. The most valuable information that can be collected about consumers is actual purchasing behavior, which is highly predictive of future purchases. Direct marketers, including shopping channels, therefore, are collecting extremely valuable information about their users.

Interactive broadband shopping services and consumer information services can be both a provider of data for general database marketing efforts and a user of the data in directing the attention of their users to information and customized buying opportunities.

It should be noted in this context that FSN advertising can profit by information on television viewing, collected by the FSN, plugged into advertisers' models of product consumers. Presumably, in the most refined models, viewing of niche channels and patterns of viewing of video on demand would surface, suggesting specific advertising buys.

CONSUMER INFORMATION

Full service networks will make electronic directories—electronic yellow pages—of local, national, and international businesses. The directories can carry as much information as the business is willing to pay for.

Traditional advertising supplies information. Although the information is seldom rational and objective, consumers, even very young people, discount the puffery. But what if we had a system where people could access an exhaustive array of information about any product: nutritional information about food items, performance data about stereos, safety reports on utility vehicles, consumer reports on refrigerators, prices on eyeglasses, and so on? The consumer could do almost everything but try on clothing, and eventually that will be possible in three-dimensional virtual reality.

A subscriber to an FSN buying a boat could enter the menu for boats; ask for 17- to 19-foot motorboats; find all of the manufacturers of motorboats that size; obtain descriptions of the performance, technical specifications, and design features of the boats as well as the lifesaving equipment necessary to operate the boat legally; watch videos of the boats in the water; compare the boats according to consumer reports; obtain maintenance cost records; learn the color and interior options; study boat financing plans; get suggested retail prices and even bottom line discount prices; and, finally, after having selected a boat, find out if it is in stock at the chosen dealer. This is far more information than would ordinarily be acquired by a boat buyer from traditional advertising, over the telephone, by visiting dealers, or even by attending a boat show.

The information might in part be (a) a biased presentation of the sellers, taking their best shot (features, video of the boat in water) at no cost to the consumer, and partly (b) objective information provided by neutral reporting services for a fee to the user (e.g., evaluations, prices). The information acquisition may not be entirely automated. It would be possible to talk to salespeople or experts at any point, through e-mail or in person, to ask questions not addressed by the general information. In becoming better informed, the buyer is free to express idiosyncracies of individual taste. For example, the buyer may eliminate all red boats even though the best-priced boats happen to be red. Nonetheless, there is the opportunity to be fully prepared to enter the market.

CREDIT

To consummate a purchase, customers have to initiate payment, either via credit card or through some form of direct electronic funds transfer. Currently, home catalog shoppers and cable television home shopping network users are accustomed to telling agents their credit card numbers. The agents record the number and subsequently use a separate network service to perform the credit authorization. Future electronic shopping services will seek to simplify this process by automating these various aspects of transactions. Shoppers will use service features to identify and select products. The operator's billing system will have payment authorization information stored on the user (either credit card or direct electronic funds transfer authorization from prespecified bank accounts). Selection and payment preference will be automatically captured by the electronic "store," and payment or credit authorization will then be automatically verified. Note that this will require the integration of financial service providers such as credit card companies and banking institutions into FSNs. It further implies that such transactions will be secure, or no one will trust entering their credit card or bank account information into the network. Such security problems are now the major stumbling block to the full commercialization of the Internet. Many so-called Internet shopping malls offer product information but still direct users to call a toll-free number for purchase.

Much attention is now focused on establishing secure transactions and electronic payment options. In fact, some have proposed using *digital cash* as a form of network-based payment. Digital cash is essentially a packet of data that represents a payment authorization from a bank. Whoever *holds* the packet would be entitled to have funds transferred into his or her bank account. Network users could exchange these payment authorizations as a means of making electronic purchases. Digital cash is not identical to an electronic check, however, because each receiver could in turn send it as payment to anyone else. Hence, it is more like hard currency than a personal check. An encryption system with chains of digital signatures is used to prevent forgery or attempts by the same person to reuse the same digital cash packet.

Digital cash and credit card use, with a billing system entirely separate from the broadband carrier, remove the network service from having to process network disconnects for nonpayment of shopping bills.

FULFILLMENT

An industry has developed to provide the "back-end" functions of direct marketing, called *fulfillment*: order taking, credit checking, warehousing, shipping, and returns. Only in recent years, as fulfillment has become very efficient, has direct marketing been successful. Most orders are filled within three days. For staples such as groceries, delivery is quicker. Fulfillment is usually contracted out to a subsidiary or independent company.

Problems

Direct sales through linear or interactive television or broadband online services can present some problems for the consumer.

HYPERCOMMERCIAL TELEVISION

As channel space expands, it is increasingly filled with infomercials and program-length commercials. If channel capacity is essentially unlimited, as we can expect in a broadband system, there is no opportunity cost to the subscriber. That is, the hypercommercial programming will not be taking the place of less commercial programming. But in the entertainment-direct marketing hybrids, the consumer may have some difficulty distinguishing the direct marketing from less directly commercial entertainment and information. The viewer is always free to switch to another channel, but it sometimes takes several minutes to discover the true nature of the programming. To provide a compelling reason for viewing, long form advertising often becomes a strident, breathless, intimate persuasion that overstates the value of the product. Even wary viewers may be induced to give up time that could be better spent with other television.

As shopping channels proliferate, the numbers of merchants will increase. Most will be leasing channel space on integrated broadband networks. The network will have some constraints on its ability to exclude businesses to prevent antitrust violations that might, for example, favor merchants who have given the FSN equity interests.

DECEPTION AND PRIVACY

There are multiple opportunities to mislead the consumer. The product could be inadequately, or fraudulently, described; the terms (warranty, credit, cancellation, return) may be unstated or misstated. There may be unreasonable substitution, shipping damage, failure to deliver, or delay in refund. Products such as jewelry are almost impossible to evaluate in either quality or price through television. Handling costs, when included, may make the price less attractive.

The privacy of the transactions themselves, and the information about the consumer specifically gathered for a particular transaction, should be protected in the interest of the consumer against the commercial and "technocratic disregard"[17] for privacy. The use of such information as consumer background (e.g., as it functions in the "smart agent" system) may sometimes be in the interest of the consumer, but the consumer must be willing to have it used on a continuing basis and remember that the permission has been granted. The U.S. Office of Consumer Affairs has a set of recommendations for "electronic communications service providers," which are presented in abbreviated form in the notes at the end of the chapter.[18]

Opportunities

Concerns about the problems of efficiency and privacy of electronic consumer transactions should not distract from the potential value of electronic shopping. For competition to work in creating markets, ideally the consumer is *perfectly informed* about price, product features, and conditions of purchase. Only then does consumer behavior weed out the inefficient and sustain the efficient.

Current mechanisms for consumer information are crude. The consumer acquires snatches of information from advertising, direct mail, catalogs and product literature, telephone and telephone directories, friends, and shopping. Advertising exposure by the consumer may be quite deliberate in some cases—for example, grocery store newspaper ads and specialty magazine ads—but much is random and it is often difficult to find information at the time a particular item is needed. To shop systematically, comparing prices and features across all the available possibilities, takes too much time and travel. And only some of the information gathered in this way is objective.

Electronic shopping can give consumers the opportunity to be more fully informed. If the system evolves to having complete listings of products with seller-provided descriptions, as well as objective evaluations and current prices from all possible sources, the consumer can make purchases directly based on the information thus acquired, or use it as background for going out to make a final decision, by touching, trying out, smelling, tasting, and so on. In electronic shopping services, the time invested, in relation to the information gained, is minimal (although the consumer is free to linger over the information as desired).

Furthermore, marketing and distribution costs could be much lower. Display space in convenient, expensive locations is not needed. Delivery may be accomplished by one truck making 100 stops in a neighborhood rather than 100 cars from the neighborhood traveling to several scattered locations to make purchases. Much of the transaction is handled electronically. Traditional retail markups could be reduced.

The efficiency of the system, for consumers, is dependent on the *depth* and *breadth* of the information. Product listings in a category must be complete. Because the provision of the objective evaluation must be funded, the consumer has to be willing to pay for it.

Finally, the broadband network service provider must value the integrity of the system, and subscriber satisfaction, over the immediate opportunity to make money from the sale of merchandise. There is some evidence that the commercial opportunity for the FSN may take precedence over the development of a broad consumer information service. There were early shopping service plans in which cable and telephone companies had an equity interest, for example, the Time Warner interest in Catalog 1, TCI and Comcast in QVC, and U S West with U S Avenue. If the greatest development effort goes into these services, with these particular products, to the exclusion or neglect of others, the ideal consumer information system fails.

Notes

1. Adam Snyder, "Videoway Pioneers: Testing Ground for Interactive Ads," *Multichannel News*, 11 April 1994, 32A.

2. Nielsen Media Research labels the "market" the DMA (designated market area).

3. In some cable markets, broadcasters have created "zones" by having cable systems insert spots in the broadcasts. The noncable households would get one message but specific messages would go to each cable operator to broadcast.

4. Steven S. Wildman and Bruce M. Owen, "Programme Competition, Diversity, and Multichannel Bundling in the New Video Industry," in *Video Media Competition: Regulation, Economics, and Technology*, ed. Eli M. Noam (New York: Columbia University Press, 1985), 244-273.

5. Snyder, "Videoway Pioneers," 33A.

6. Total cable advertising revenues in 1994 were $4.4 billion. "1994 Cable TV Facts" (New York: Cabletelevision Advertising Bureau, 1994).

7. According to 1994 Nielsen estimates, there are 59 million basic cable homes and 94 million television homes. The Cabletelevision Advertising Bureau estimates that 37% of the viewing in cable homes is of basic channels. "1995 Cable TV Facts" (New York: Cabletelevision Advertising Bureau, 1995). This assumes television is viewed equally in cable and noncable homes. Actually, viewing in cable homes is higher, so the figure is conservative.

8. Alan Breznick, "Local Advertising Begins to Come of Age," *Cable World*, 5 December 1994, 38.

9. Toula Vlahou, "Broadcast Networks Suffer Losing Season," *Cable World*, 26 April 1993, 6.

10. "Cable's Top 15," *Multichannel News*, 27 June 1994, 18.

11. Barry Diller in "QVC Annual Report," 1993, 2, Westchester, PA.

12. "Databank, Home Shopping," *Cable World*, November 22, 1993, 56.

13. Spice sells lingerie during the breaks and both Spice and Playboy advertise "900" number sex lines. The shopping services of cable channels could become permanent features or eventually spin off as separate channels. Lifetime, Sci-Fi, Americana, and ESPN2 have also offered home shopping. Black Entertainment Television (BET) is planning a shopping network, BET Shop, for African Americans, using a 13-week test on BET with 80% mainstream and 20% Afrocentric product. BET Direct already sells two product lines: BET Music features music played on BET as well as Color Code, which sells feminine skin care products. HSN, which is working with BET, is considering a Hispanic shopping service.

14. Seth Tapper, "Online Shopping: Interactive TV's First Test Ground," *On Demand*, October/November 1994, 50.

15. Peter Lambert, "Diving into the Direct Marketing Pool," *Cable World*, 25 July 1994, 21; "Ameritech's Peapod Play," *On Demand*, December 1994/January 1995, 42.

16. Van Wallach, "Direct Marketers Eye Interactive Options Cautiously," *Response TV*, May 1994, 22.

17. Eli Noam quoted in "New Home Shopping Technologies" (Paris: Organisation for Economic Co-operation and Development, 1992), Annex III, quoting U.S. Office of Consumer Affairs.

18. "New Home Shopping," Annex III (quoting U.S. Office of Consumer Affairs):

   a. An assessment of privacy implication of the product or service should be part of the development process. Such assessment could include evaluation by focus groups, consumer advisory panels, telecommunications complaint handling entities at the state or federal levels, qualitative research and feedback from external stake holders.

   b. Service providers should establish internal standards to protect customers from being assessed by or distributed to those not authorized by management.

   c. Personally identifiable information concerning specific communication services to which the consumer is a part should not be transferred to a third party without the consent of the consumer.

   d. Service providers should tell consumers, in language they can easily understand, what information they accumulate about consumers and how that information is used.

   e. Service providers should advise consumers periodically of the option to have their names removed from marketing lists generated by service providers.

f. Service providers shall not let the fact that a consumer has removed his or her name from marketing lists adversely affect any other service provided.

g. If a service provider agrees to keep a number from being divulged in both directory assistance and the published directory, that number should not be transferred to third parties except for basic provision of service.

10

Competition

B

ecause of an inherent cultural bias against monopoly providers of communication services, the real and assumed benefits of competition, the technical and economic pressures on the telephone and cable industries to expand across traditional service types, and the industry lobbying to do so, public policy has increasingly favored competition over the last several years. This has culminated in the Telecommunications Act of 1996 which removes almost all the barriers to competition. This chapter will discuss the prospects for competition in the development of both the communication infrastructure and the services themselves. Competition will be considered from the strategic perspectives of the developing industry and the service and price perspectives of the consumer.

Video Business Basics and Competition

In this section, we describe the cable business and other competitive wired and wireless video providers as well as the telephone business and competitors in voice service.

CABLE BUSINESS

Revenue to cable operators comes from subscription fees (96% including ancillary service charges such as printed guides, installation, remote tuners, converters, additional outlets, and home wiring maintenance), local and national spot advertising sales (4%), and commissions on purchases from shopping channels (less than 1%). Most of the subscription revenue is for basic services, although pay channels make a substantial contribution. Pay per view, at this point, is a minor revenue source, about 2% of the 96%.[1] Major expenses are programming, technical operations, customer service/billing, and marketing.

The cable industry is considered capital intensive. About $700 is invested per subscriber in building a system, but if an operating system is purchased, the price is about $2,000 per subscriber. This difference, incidentally, is an indication of the monopoly value of the cable franchise. To become a full service network, the cable operator will make additional investments of from $30 to $300 per subscriber in the distribution plant, depending on its state; spend up to $400 per subscriber, mainly in the home terminal; and spend as much as $500 per subscriber for the server system.[2] Some cable operators are selling out or concentrating on smaller markets, where competition is less imminent, rather than face these costs.

The cable industry is *vertically integrated*. Large multiple system operators have investments in program networks, often shared with other MSOs. Some cable operators own television and film production subsidiaries as well, completing the vertical integration—that is, retailer (system operator), distributor (program network), and producer (film or television studio). The industry is *concentrated horizontally*; that is, a few multiple system operators serve a majority of the cable subscribers.

A cable system has universal service obligations to the extent that some local franchising authorities require cabling of the entire community as a condition of the franchise and prohibit discrimination among subscribers. Where population densities are uneven within a community, there is usually a parameter set to determine the obligation to provide service, such as when housing density reaches 30 units per mile of cable.

COMPETITION IN VIDEO

Current competition for cable, as a television distribution service, in urban areas, is now principally from broadcasting. If the cable service is not satisfying, subscribers may disconnect and use the broadcast signals available in the area. Home video rentals take some of the pay channel and PPV business. DBS, MMDS, and SMATV are now encroaching on the cable multichannel business. DBS channel capacity and picture quality are hastening technical upgrades by cable systems. Under these conditions of competition, cable systems are less willing than in the past to provide free community services and facilities.

For the most part, through its relatively short history, the cable industry, to avoid regulation, has denied that it is a natural monopoly. While enjoying de facto exclusive franchises, the industry defined its *relevant market* broadly to include substitutes inside and outside the home such as broadcasting, movies, home video rentals, multichannel multipoint distribution service (MMDS), satellite master antenna systems (SMATV), and direct broadcast satellites (DBS). The cities granting the franchises labeled them *nonexclusive* but awarded each franchise as if it were exclusive, taking applications and then accepting a single bidder in an *auction* system. If another company were to emerge later, the city would decline to accept the application or would deny the second franchise. The city granted an exclusive franchise, or a de facto exclusive franchise, under home rule privileges granted by a state. The exclusive franchise did not violate antitrust law, if the state required enforcement of franchise rules. The treatment of cable as a monopoly has been challenged on economic and constitutional grounds.

Hazlett, arguing for competition in the cable business, says:

> The notion that cable suppliers should be protected by public agencies [through exclusive franchises] from giving away their fortunes to consumers in the form of over investment—and the resultant low prices—is uncompelling. Normatively, it is bad consumer policy. Positively, it lacks credibility. The argument that public officials realize such economic realities more finely than self-interested economic agents is not persuasive.[3]

A challenge to exclusive franchises in the case of *Preferred v. Los Angeles* established cable as a *First Amendment speaker.*[4] This meant that rejecting a franchise application was a violation of the First Amendment rights of the applicant unless there were some compelling public interest in denial, such as a physical limit on the number of wires that could be hung on utility poles to maintain safe clearances, or an applicant who was unfit by reason of character or financial resources. Subsequently, the Cable Act of 1992 (the Cable Consumer Protection and Competition Act), specifically stated that a franchise authority may not grant an exclusive franchise or unreasonably refuse an additional competitive franchise.[5]

Assuming that a competing video service can get a franchise, or the franchise is not necessary, as is the case for MMDS, DBS, and SMATV and may be the case for telephone companies, the video service still needs programming. The cable programming networks have purchased rights to syndicated, off-broadcast network programs, all of the Hollywood movie product, instructional materials, videos of the performing arts, music videos, sports, and almost anything else anyone would watch. Furthermore, this video material is packaged into networks that have brand recognition, such as MTV, ESPN, and HBO. Without these networks, a competing video service could offer only a few leftover niche channels and movies not licensed exclusively. And a new operator would have difficulty aggregating enough viewers to do much original programming. Therefore, to assure competing video services a source of programming, the federal law prohibits exclusivity arrangements on the part of vertically integrated programmers and cable operators.

OVERBUILDS

Despite the removal of these barriers, there has been no rush by multiple system cable operators, or other cable firms, to *overbuild* incumbent cable systems. The number of subscribers in communities where there is a choice between cable companies is very small. Most situations with choice have occurred where a cable company has extended into an adjacent new construction area and overlapped on a few streets with another operator building out from a different direction. In a very few places, where cable has *high penetration*, two companies have passed all of the homes in a community and each settled for a comfortable share. In some of these towns, the municipality owns the second company, competing directly with a privately-owned operator.

The idea of municipal cable systems has been examined periodically in several places. Some municipal systems were built before private investors showed interest, and remain in operation. Where municipalities have overbuilt the cable franchisee, it is often the result of a rancorous dispute between the city and the cable operator.[6] In retaliation or desperation, the city builds its own system. City ownership of a system, in competition with a franchisee it regulates, has been termed unfair by the cable industry, but the Cable Act of 1992 expressly accepts the concept.[7]

Municipal ownership of full service networks may come into play in the future in relatively small cities where neither an incumbent cable nor a telephone company is willing to build a broadband network and no other business responds to a request for proposal. In this case, the city might buy one or both, or overbuild the two incumbents with an entirely new network. Because private companies do not come forward, there is an implication that the city would subsidize its integrated network through tax dollars, tax exemptions, and municipal bonds (with some advantages over commercial loans) so as to provide the general economic and consumer benefits of a modern communication service.

If an overbuilder assumes *there will eventually be two providers of video services* in a community, it could have an advantage over the incumbent that has recently purchased the system for around $2,000. The overbuilder's construction cost would be about $700 per subscriber,[8] and it would cost the new system, at most, another $100 to acquire a subscriber. Why, then, have we not seen more overbuilding?

The answer may lie in the structure of the cable industry. Almost every system is part of a company owning many other systems. An overbuild in one system could be met by price competition subsidized by all of the other systems in the multiple system operation. The large MSOs in the industry are relatively loyal to each other and have usually respected each other's territory. At any rate, growth has been through acquisition at the fairly high prices, with an assumption of no competition, rather than through overbuilding, which creates competition. Furthermore, in places where there is a cable penetration of about 70% of homes and relatively low density, the number of subscribers may be too small to support the capital investment and operating costs of two operators. Now, of course, the overbuilder would have to think in terms of building a full service integrated system, which would demand a larger investment than a conventional cable system.

Nonetheless, the FCC used prices in areas where there are competing cable services as the basis for establishing its benchmark rate regulation scheme in 1994. The price differential between cable systems with no competition and places where there is competition was 28%, according to the FCC study.[9] This study, however, was subject to criticism. Some of the competing systems in the survey were municipal systems subsidized by taxes or special financing. In other cases, one or both of the competing systems were losing money.

A full service digital broadband fiber network may provide one-stop shopping for electronic communication services, but subsets of the integrated services will be available from others. A number of these partial competitors will have established a solid foothold before FSNs are widespread. Most are wireless. Consumers who find the service adequate may be out of the immediate market for some of the full service network products; therefore, they pose an impediment to development and profitability as well as a check on market power. The wireless services may first seek their customers from uncabled areas, now estimated to be only 3 million homes,[10] but their business plans are dependent on expanding beyond into the cable franchises. To the extent that any of these services succeed, the integrated broadband system is handicapped in recouping its heavy capital investment.

DIRECT BROADCAST SATELLITES

Direct broadcast satellites have been available for several years to the rural household that has a large TVRO ("dish"). DBS homes have access to all of the cable networks, although the most desirable are encrypted. A monthly or annual fee is paid directly to the networks or a third party to unscramble the signals. The dish size, 9 to 10 feet, and cost, about $2,000, have been a deterrent to broad usage.

Three other DBS services, now sometimes called digital satellite service (DSS) and direct to home (DTH), became available in 1994. DirecTV, a subsidiary of General Motors Hughes Electronics, and United States Satellite Broadcasting (USSB), a subsidiary of Hubbard Broadcasting, Inc., are on the same high-power satellite. The consumer buys the 18-inch antenna from an authorized retailer for about $700 and installs it, or pays another $150 to $200 for professional installation. Adding a second television set brings the total cost to nearly $2,000. A monthly fee is paid for various levels of programming. Primestar, a third service using a medium-power satellite, owned by some of the cable MSOs, installs a 30- or 36-inch antenna, including its lease price in the monthly programming service charge.

Although some of the rural market for DBS has already been claimed by the C-band dishes, many of these are not active. The uncabled locations will be an immediate market. But DBS operator business plans anticipate head-to-head competition with cable in existing franchised areas.[11] Because the converts to DBS are likely to be pay channel subscribers and pay-per-view users, the *best* cable customers, this could represent a big loss in cable system revenue.

Under the law, DBS has access to almost all of the programming available to an integrated broadband network. The law also gives the FCC authority to oversee affiliation agreements so that there is no discrimination against these secondary affiliates. Of course, DBS has no local franchise and, therefore, is exempt from franchise obligations. This is another advantage over the wired multichannel systems.

Because of the national distribution of DBS, the major programming difference is in local service. DBS leaves broadcast stations to over-the-air reception or subscription to broadcast basic on cable. Except in remote areas outside the reach of broadcast stations, the broadcast networks are unwilling to supply national feeds to DBS subscribers because they do not include the local commercials. By offering the national feeds, the networks would be undermining their affiliated stations. The households in rural areas will have broadcast antennas and can switch back and forth between DBS and broadcasts, but in urban areas many cable subscribers have removed their antennae.

The national distribution also prevents DBS from local origination. Full service broadband systems will probably make greater investments in 24-hour local news; however, 24-hour local news channels are expensive. They have to be of sufficient quality to compete with broadcast television news, which means expensive equipment and personnel (with expensive hair). The annual operating budgets are $10 million or more.[12] Multichannel television system operators creating or buying this programming must be patient, waiting for audiences to break the strong habits of local broadcast news viewing before it will have any affect on FSN-DBS competition.[13]

NFL football was a success on DBS in the 1994-1995 season and DirecTV now has a huge optional sports package and over 40 channels dedicated to pay per view, permitting near video on demand. USSB multiplexes several of the cable premium movie channels (five HBO channels and three each of Showtime, the Movie Channel, Cinemax, and Flix). Because USSB and DirecTV have exclusive programming, to get the programming equivalent of a high-capacity cable system, a DBS subscriber would have to take both, making DBS very expensive in programming fees. If competing broadband networks also become differentiated in programming, however, the same problem would lead to subscription to two FSNs, also expensive.

The limited differences between full service, broadband networks and DBS in programming place great emphasis on price competition. DBS is underpricing cable in many markets and attempting to establish pay per view at $2.99, about $1.50 to $2.00 below cable prices. Because the movie distributors are licensing the films at about $1.50 to $1.95 per buy, the viability of DirecTV prices will depend on high volume. There is some early market test evidence that the $2.99 price is about the limit for many consumers, perhaps having been conditioned by home video store pricing. The broadband system may have to meet these prices.

The up-front antenna cost for DBS is a hurdle for DirecTV or USSB marketing against a wired system with equipment costs built into the monthly service charges. The wired systems will exploit this initial cost difference. A threat to cable is the prospect of new manufacturers of antennae, entering after RCA-Phillips have sold 1 million, competing in price and bringing the consumer investment down. Or DBS programmers may decide to subsidize the antenna; for example, the dish costs $49.95 if the subscriber signs up for two years of program service. This plan could be supported by national advertising, which is not as practical for cable.

DBS competition to the wired multichannel television systems requires higher broadband marketing budgets in self-defense to retain subscribers, differentiate the services, and acquire nonsubscribers. The consumers who go to DBS are lost for some time, having made a minimum investment of $700 in the antenna and reception equipment.

Because of DBS, the integrated wired networks must also face limited future growth in unwired areas. Where new construction for wired service in the past was a routine capital investment decision based on population density, the presence of two or more DBS services will change the model. The projection of just one of the DBS operators is to reach 30% to 40% penetration in the unfranchised areas by the end of 1998.[14] If this happens, much higher densities would then be necessary before a wired system could expand into the area. Therefore, DBS customers in uncabled areas represent a containment of business development for a full service network.

After one or two years of operation, when there is a significant subscriber base, DBS companies expect to explore advertising sales. The initial affiliation agreements with some of the major cable networks did not permit insertion in the spots set aside for local cable availabilities, but USSB and DirecTV could sell time on the others and between movies.

The DBS companies are not weak competitors for integrated networks. DirecTV is owned by the Hughes Electronics division of General Motors. USSB is a subsidiary of Hubbard Broadcasting, Inc., and has a number of other major investors. GM Hughes will put at least $600 million into DirecTV.[15] AT&T has made an investment in DirecTV with an option to increase the proportion of ownership. This gives AT&T an immediate interest in a video service scaled to the whole nation, commensurate with its long distance service. AT&T will offer to combine its bills for long distance and DirecTV subscribers and lend its marketing support to the satellite service. AT&T's competitor in the long distance business, MCI, with media conglomerate News Corp., was the successful bidder on the remaining direct-to-home satellite orbital slot. These powerful corporations may stimulate further development of satellite direct video and other communications services.

Because DBS cannot offer VOD, and additional channel cost is high, 'DBS may be only an interim technology while integrated, full service networks are building. Nonetheless, because of the initial attraction and the customer investment in equipment, DBS could have a significant short-term impact on broadband service economics.

MMDS

Multichannel multipoint distribution services (MMDS) compete directly with cable in a few places and winning some customers in unwired areas. Along with DBS, MMDS could foreclose expansion of integrated networks into those areas. MMDS carries the major "cable" networks, again, with the blessing of the Cable Act of 1992.

By leasing spectrum allocated to instructional television fixed service (ITFS) and other channels specifically available for MDS use, the *wireless cable* operators can accumulate as many as 33 channels. Their lineup includes the most popular cable networks and the local broadcast stations. The initial capital investment in the transmission equipment is relatively low, $750,000 to $1.1 million.[16] The wireless system obviously has low maintenance cost compared with cable because there is no plant to maintain, but this is partly offset by the distance between residential installations, which makes service calls expensive. Weather is also hazardous to the rooftop antenna installation. In 1994, there were 500,000 MMDS subscribers. This is less than 1% of total wired cable subscribers, but the number has been predicted to reach 3.5 million by 2001 with revenues increasing from $26 per household per month to $40. Homes "seen" by MMDS transmitters, if the predictions are accurate, will have increased from 24.8 million in 1993 to 37.6 million by 2002.[17] Funding for digitization and expansion is a problem, but recently the industry, which was once characterized by disreputable firms seeking "get-rich-quick-in-television" money from small-change investors, has been acquiring capital through major stock and bond issues.

Telephone companies Bell Atlantic and Pacific Telesis have been investing in MMDS. This will give them firsthand experience in video at very low cost, while permitting development of broadband networks to go more slowly.

The first priority for MMDS systems are the homes that are not passed by cable within the service range, about 25 miles from the transmitter. The system may also seek customers in commercial areas where cable is not available, including bars, restaurants, and hotels. Finally, the MMDS operator goes after price-sensitive cable subscribers offering fewer channels but at a comparatively low price. As a result, some of the MMDS subscribers are nonpay disconnects from cable who may eventually be nonpay MMDS disconnects as well.

In one of the most successful MMDS systems, Cross Country in Riverside, California, most of the customers have switched from cable service. The company claims that about 70% are attracted by the price. Cross Country's chief operating officer says that the MMDS competition in Riverside has lowered cable cash flow margins from percentages in the 40s to percentages in the 30s, raised cable marketing costs, brought about free installations, lowered prices, increased churn, and improved service. These competitive conditions have been verified by a competing cable operator.[18] This is exactly the outcome proponents of competition in video services desire. If the cable operator is not satisfying customers, or is charging too high a price, MMDS is an option.

But Cross Country also notes that its customers who go back to cable do so for more programming. A channel limitation is placed on an MMDS system by its ability to license or lease television frequencies. Although the maximum is 33 channels, many systems have not reached that limit because they are waiting for the FCC to license some of them, or they cannot obtain some channels because a competitor has locked them up, or educators are making use of the channels. The channel limitation problem could be resolved by digital compression. Digital compression boxes designed for cable will work for MMDS with minimal changes. Digital availability is dependent on new FCC rules changing the microwave technology to accommodate digital transmission, the amount of investment in equipment that is necessary, and access to digitized signals. Although cable systems, and eventually full service networks, may be able to provide 300 or more channels, MMDS systems with 100 or more channels might serve most needs, cherry-picking the best channels as they do now. Although cable digital technology can be adapted for MMDS, it will be costly. The required investment in digital could wipe out the MMDS cost advantage over cable. The present MMDS industry is small and underfunded. Telephone company investment in MMDS may change that.

MMDS could compete with wired systems for local advertising dollars. Even if penetration is only 10%, MMDS could not be ignored by advertisers because local advertising would otherwise be "underdelivered" in MMDS households.

Because the individual subscribing household is addressed by the microwave MMDS signals, MMDS can provide pay-per-view channels. One system in Dayton, Ohio, has installed the Videoway interactive system developed in Montreal for cable.

An important difference between cable, or an integrated broadband system, and wireless cable is that the former has to make the large capital investment to wire an *entire* area where only a portion of the homes actually become subscribers, perhaps less than half where there are two wires. The MMDS service makes its major investment ($320 to $535 for the antenna and receiver) only when the subscriber is installed.[19]

CELLULAR TELEVISION

Local multipoint distribution service (LMDS) is a television distribution service using frequencies in the 27.7- to 29.5-GHz range, as described in Chapter 5. CellularVision of New York, backed by Bell Atlantic, Philips Electronics North America Corporation, and others delivers 49 channels in Brooklyn, New York. Technically, LMDS requires a clear path to the antenna, which could be obstructed by new construction. The cell size must be very small, so LMDS is only practical in the most densely populated areas. The economic viability of the service is further dependent on whether it can share the frequencies with other proposed users for the same spectrum. This issue may take some time to resolve because the FCC has formed a large advisory committee of interested potential users. The FCC may permit cable and telephone companies to license LMDS.

SMATV

Satellite master antenna television systems (SMATV) take another small part of the video business—nearly a million residences.[20] SMATV is confined to relatively large multiple-dwelling units because it is not franchised to use public rights of way and must install an expensive headend at each location. SMATV operators could obtain franchises to expand beyond these limits, but to do so would no doubt mean the payment of a 5% franchise fee, in addition to about a 5% royalty paid to building owners and the assumption of the burdens of public, education, and government access channels. Because the franchise fee and programming requirements are not now a cost for SMATV operators, expansion outward may not be practical.

Large companies are, however, investing in SMATV, planning to use 18-GHz microwave or fiber to interconnect apartments across a city, offer telephone service, and carry more than 50 television channels. These systems could be FSNs in the future.

IVDS

Interactive video and data services (IVDS) are another type of wireless service that permits interaction with broadcast, cable, wireless cable, and DBS television programs. Distance learning, taking multiple choice tests with instructional programs, on-demand catalog shopping, multiplayer games, home banking, and responding to polls will be possible with systems under development. One such system, from the EON company, uses over-the-air spectrum for the interactive information. The FCC assigned two positions in the spectrum to each local service area and auctioned the licenses. The bidding was furious, generating millions in revenue for the government in 1994. Since that time, some of the bidders have defaulted on their payments to the FCC.

BROADCASTING

Broadcasters are recognizing that they must find new roles in the changing communication environment. The broadcast television networks have expanded information and entertainment programming production in-house, after the financial interest in programming rules were relaxed. The ban on broadcast network prime time access and first run syndication expired in 1995 permitting further expansion. Each of the networks is the leading supplier of its own programs. With the prime-time access rule (PTAR) being eliminated, a half hour that the networks could program is added to prime time, creating further incentive to develop programming.

Hollywood studios are merging with broadcast networks. Disney owns ABC; News Corp. (20th Century) owns Fox; Time Warner and Paramount have started broadcast networks. The economic value of such an arrangement is fairly clear. The studio is assured of national distribution. The broadcast network gains television production capacity and expands into theatrical film. With a broadcast network also permitted to enter the domestic syndication market, it enters as a major player. A studio-broadcast network combination establishes a market force in mass entertainment that precludes displacement as the industry moves in new directions. Additional combinations of broadcast television networks and Hollywood studios can be expected. The intended merger of Time Warner with Turner Broadcasting System would combine Hollywood studios with several cable networks, a broadcast network and cable systems. Such a merger could expand advertising exposure and perhaps permit the control of release windows for maximum revenue.

The full service network, then, is faced with powerful entertainment giants as the suppliers of news and entertainment attractions. These companies may have the ability to dictate the terms of carriage and even consumer prices. Nevertheless, the full service network does have the capacity to accommodate independent producers, if those producers can find the financial backing for both production and promotion. Individual broadcasters, apart from their networks, will attempt to supply programming to full service networks. Inviting programming from broadcasters, the chief executive officer of Bell Atlantic quipped, "There are not enough New Jersey Bell safety films to fill up the fiber optic pipeline."[21] Although the retransmission consent policy did not result in broadcasters' sharing cable television subscription revenue, many broadcasters negotiated the right to become program suppliers on cable channels in return for retransmission consent. The most likely broadcaster-supplied programming is local news. A survey of broadcasters determined that 40% are planning to be or are now actually in business with another media outlet (generally cable) for news distribution.[22] Where there are two broadband networks, to be competitive, it will be necessary for each to have a 24-hour local news service. One or both could be programmed by broadcasters. Broadcast audience loss to cable has seemed to slow in recent years. If broadcasters continue to offer strong programming, they will check the market power of broadband systems with broadcast television service still a satisfactory substitute if prices get too high.

Once broadcasters convert to transmission of digital signals, they can use conventional radio and television frequency bandwidth and the HDTV bandwidth to broadcast multichannel television, as well as to distribute data streams for transactional services, interactive advertising, and other purposes. The *wireless* broadcast medium can communicate with pagers, fax machines, appliances for utility load management, personal digital assistants, audio receivers, and other devices for many of the applications discussed in this book. Real- and non-real-time messages with traffic, weather, medical, educational, and other information may be transmitted to portable and permanently located equipment. Interaction is possible over the air with technology under development, or by telephone.[23] To provide these services, broadcasters have received federal approval for *flexible use* from the Telecommunications Act of 1996. Flexible use could include reducing the bandwidth used for HDTV to include additional television signals (multichannel broadcast) or other digital services, but the government will assess a spectrum use fee.

The availability of broadcast data services may duplicate or substitute for services of a wired system, perhaps at lower cost to the consumer. Because broadcasting has universal reach, it starts with the broadest possible market.

OTHER INDUSTRIES

Potential competitors, or partners, in developing integrated networks are the long-distance telephone carriers. An objective is to avoid the *access charges*, payments for use of the local connection assessed by the local carriers. These are around $30 billion annually.[24] Both MCI and AT&T have asked permission to enter the *local* telephone business. AT&T, which owns NCR, a computer company, McCaw, a cellular telephone company, and Western Electric, a telecommunication equipment manufacturer, has all the pieces, in-house, to create integrated networks. The company is participating in several of the integrated broadband network market tests. Sprint has aligned with TCI and others for PCS.

Another major element in the development of integrated networks is the computer industry. The companies in the industry, software and hardware, are reluctant to enter alliances with telecommunication services in the secondary role of a supplier bidding for contracts but see themselves as equity partners expanding the computer industry into telecommunication.

Electric utilities are also considering broadband telecommunication services. The first interest is for internal uses such as power load management and time of day rate differentials. Excess capacity, however, could be leased to telecommunication companies or operated by the utility itself as a full service network.

Many programmers and information providers would be competitors to the integrated broadband network that decided to provide program material of its own. Industries that are potential content sources for full service networks are developing program and information services so that they are not preempted by full service network creation of similar products. The newspaper industry is a good example. In the face of shrinking circulation, publishers are trying to redefine themselves as information resources instead of a print medium. In the broader role, they would be capitalizing on their near monopoly, in most cities, on local information. The first step is to use the information gathering organization to offer newspaper editorial content and classified advertising, already digitized, over online computer networks or the Internet. Broadcasters also have local news-gathering resources and some are planning to go online. When the local news services can be delivered by broadband networks to home computers, these news organizations will be ready. Newspapers would also like to use their association with local advertisers to take a part of the directory advertising (yellow pages) business, now highly profitable and largely uncontested. Cable-based full service networks might contract this function to newspapers but not telephone-based services.

The Internet is already a prodigious information provider and a network. In the future the Internet will use integratred broadband networks to reach the home. The Internet will be a serious competitor to any information services owned by the integrated broadband network.

Organizations owning magazines have been leveraging these resources into online, Internet and video services. Times Mirror's Outdoor Life Channel draws on *Outdoor Life, Field & Stream, Salt Water Sportsman, Ski Magazine, Skiing Magazine, Golf Magazine,* and *Yachting.* If programming and information services by content specialists of long standing are up and running, taking advantage of synergy with other services, at reasonable prices, it would be difficult for the broadband system to create a similar service for itself. The full service network would not have the credibility, the resources, and the time to start from scratch.

TELEPHONE BUSINESS

Local telephone companies derive revenues from many sources, including but not limited to residential subscription fees for basic telephone service, monthly and sometimes per use fees for certain advanced services such as voice mail and caller ID, monthly flat rate and usage-based fees to business subscribers, toll charges on intraLATA long-distance calls, installation and monthly fees for "special access" circuits used by high-volume subscribers, and "access fees" paid by interexchange and other carriers who deliver terminating traffic to the local loop. Special access circuits are basically high-capacity trunks that are typically leased by companies who have their own switches (e.g., PBXs). Access fees most commonly are charged on the basis of the number of minutes of traffic delivered to the local exchange carrier for completion. Subscribers also pay a small amount on each monthly bill as an access fee. Other sources of revenue include advertising income from yellow pages as well as service maintenance contracts.

Local distribution networks and local switching nodes are the core of a local exchange carrier's business. Like the cable industry, the telephone industry is capital intensive, with extremely large sunk costs. This is especially true in the residential arena, where expensive facilities (wires, telephone poles, line termination, and so on) may need to be deployed even to serve a single remote customer. Because of the need for dedicated facilities for individual residences, many economists and regulators have traditionally considered the local distribution network a natural monopoly that could not sustain competitive entry.

A recent treatment of the economics of local telephone networks can be found in a text by Baumol and Sidak.[25] One interesting contrast with cable is the traditionally higher capital cost per subscriber among local exchange carriers. In part, this may be due to the higher demands on service reliability for telephone service. Typically, public telephone networks are engineered to offer a $p = .01$ *grade of service*, which implies that subscribers will experience a busy circuit one in every hundred attempts during peak usage.

Related to this is the traditional distinction in local telephony between traffic-sensitive and non-traffic-sensitive costs. Some parts of the local distribution plant are fixed costs (e.g., the wire pair to the subscriber's home) that do not vary regardless of how often or for how long a subscriber uses the facilities. Other parts of the network (e.g., switch and trunk capacity) are dependent on the degree of traffic generated. Relatively little in the cable television plant is "traffic sensitive."

Another key difference in the economic structure stems from the fact that telephone service is characterized by network externalities, which are benefits that subscribers get that are not captured in the traditional pricing system. For example, when a new subscriber is added to the system, other subscribers benefit from this addition but do not pay any additional price. In general, the value to users of a telephone network is greatest when the network is interconnected with all other networks, and the United States has pursued a policy of ensuring interconnected telephone carriers since the Kingsbury Commitment in 1912. This suggests that important revenue sources for a local exchange carrier with a monopoly in some area are the fees paid by other companies for interconnection privileges and for access to local subscribers.

As noted earlier in Chapter 3, the U.S. telephone industry has pursued a policy of universal service, which is conceptually supported by the logic of externalities noted above. One problem with the provision of universal service, however, is that the actual costs of providing service are not equivalent for all subscribers. In general, costs per access line are higher for rural subscribers than for those in urban areas. To ensure rural subscriber access, telephone companies traditionally used various forms of rate subsidization, including rate averaging between rural and urban areas, higher charges for business than residential lines, and some subsidy from toll revenues. Now that local and long-distance carriers are separated, the toll to local subsidy has reappeared in the form of access fees.

Complicating this issue is the difficulty of actually allocating costs to specific services because facilities are used for multiple purposes. How much of the local subscriber line or local switch should be allocated to long-distance service access?

COMPETITION IN TELEPHONY

Local telephone companies face competition in a number of areas, although relatively little direct competition in the residential market exists to date. Primary competition is now or will soon come from five sources, with each targeting specific areas of the LEC's business: wireless (e.g., cellular telephone) companies, long-distance carriers, other local exchange carriers, competitive access providers, and cable television firms.

Wireless telephone companies traditionally have been considered ancillary to the local exchange carrier wireline business, and not direct competitors. They do directly compete for the cellular telephone market, as many LECs are also in this business. They all currently interconnect with the LEC network, rather than bypass it, and arguably are delivering or originating traffic that otherwise would not be carried at all by the LEC. In the future, however, this may not be the case as PCNs may make it feasible to substitute wireless access for a traditional telephone line. Additionally, wireless firms that align themselves with long-distance carriers (e.g., AT&T and McCaw) that deploy local switching nodes can conceivably bypass LECs for a substantial portion of their telephone traffic (i.e., all traffic not destined for other LEC subscribers).

Long-distance carriers now compete for the very lucrative intraLATA toll market wherever not prohibited by state regulatory commissions. Conceivably, long-distance carriers might in the future align themselves with wireless firms and/or cable companies to offer local/long-distance package deals. Some long-distance companies even control certain local network assets that could provide a point of entry into local service provision. Long-distance carriers also compete for some of the "special access" business. That is, they may also provide high-capacity trunks, such as DS1 or DS3 circuits to large businesses, directly connecting them to their point-of-presence in the LATA, and hence bypassing the LEC for all long-distance traffic. There is an incentive for them to do this, because they then avoid paying the per minute access fees to the LEC. In general, long-distance company moves into various segments of the local loop represent one of the most significant threats to LEC revenues.

There is relatively little direct competition from other local exchange carriers at this point in time. Several RBOCs have encroached on the telephone directory/yellow pages business of other RBOCs. Some direct competition may ensue from control of wireless licenses, and there is a threat of direct competition through alliances with cable MSOs who have overlapping network infrastructures in an LEC's region.

Competitive access providers (CAPs) such as Teleport and Metropolitan Fiber Systems (MFS) compete for business traffic, particularly in urban areas. They provide alternative special access (DS1 or DS3) to long-distance carriers, bypassing LECs, and can also offer competitive switched services. To date, they have not entered the residential market for local switched service. Conventional wisdom in the local telephone industry is that 80% of revenues come from 20% of the customers. Baumol and Sidak note that the bulk of the high-volume, and high-revenue, business is now in areas subject to competition, particularly by CAPs and long-distance carriers.[26] The various forms of rate subsidization used by LECs to maintain universal service (or forced upon them by state regulators anxious to keep residential telephone affordable) place LECs at a competitive disadvantage in the lucrative high-volume business market. This is because they have traditionally overcharged urban and business telephone subscribers so as to lower the costs for rural residential service. Moreover, the access fees charged to long-distance carriers are passed on in the form of higher rates to business customers. When these business customers use a CAP or long-distance company to bypass the LEC, they receive additional savings on long-distance rates.

Finally, cable television companies offer the greatest probability of direct competition in the residential market. They alone (except for electric utilities, who may also be a competitive threat in the future) have a network that reaches into the residential market. Modest investments in new technologies such as cable telephony modems (see Chapter 5) could permit this existing plant to be upgraded for telephone service. In the meantime, cable operators do compete with LECs for special access services, mainly by their ownership interests in competitive access providers.

One form of competition not mentioned above originates from business users themselves. Certain large business users own their own facilities, often terrestrial microwave or satellite up- and down-links but in some instances, wire, cable, or optical fiber links. Microwave and satellite use requires a license from the FCC. In addition to providing connection to a long-distance carrier, microwave links are often used to interconnect several company locations within a metropolitan area, and hence bypass the LEC for all internal calls. They also permit video and data transmission. Private satellite networks, and especially VSAT networks, are usually more for data and/or video connections outside the local area. They mainly bypass the LECs' leased line services that would interconnect a company to a long-distance carrier. Private cable or fiber networks owned by the users themselves require obtaining rights-of-way from cities and, therefore, are a rather uncommon form of private networking. Certain types of companies, such as gas, water, and electric utilities, however, often do have extensive cable and/or fiber networks for their own internal use in local telephone company territory. Hence, privately owned networks are a type of competition for local telephone companies.

Competition Policy

COMPETITION AMONG DISTRIBUTION NETWORKS

In the ideal competitive model for telecommunication, there would be available innumerable full service, broadband networks, in addition to wireless systems. Users could weigh the service and content of each, selecting one network that is most suitable. Or consumers could subscribe to several or all networks and then make choices among those networks for services and content in addition to the option of wireless services. The consumer is freed from a situation where a monopolist exercises market power over distribution network access and price. In the conventional wisdom, the competition model is appealing for a number of reasons. First is the element of choice. Consumers want the security of options; if service from one supplier is unsatisfactory, another can take its place. Second, competition assures a supply of products and services equal to the demand. Third, it is expected that prices will be efficient—no more than necessary to keep a supplier in business. The prices are set naturally by the market at an optimum level, not arbitrarily at the highest feasible levels. Government intervention is not necessary. Fourth, competing companies will maintain a high level of customer service; the customer will always be right. Finally, competing companies will continuously upgrade technology to gain an advantage or prevent a rival from gaining an advantage.

Theoretically, a sustainable monopoly has no incentive to provide efficient prices, provide good service, and innovate. Therefore, the monopolist must be regulated by some government entity, at least in the pricing and customer service areas, perhaps with a stipulation that the monopolist maintain the "state of the art" in technology. Many people think governments are not capable of effective regulation, particularly of prices. *If price regulation is based on cost of service, there is an incentive to inflate cost. If prices are capped, then there is an incentive to reduce costs with the possibility of a reduction in the quality of service.*

Although there are problems in coping with communication monopolies, by virtue of their exclusive status, they are vested with public service obligations. In a competitive environment, the exclusive service area and dedication of the property to public use is lost. The justification for regulation becomes less clear. Competition suggests an ability to choose among parties to be served and the right to refuse to serve others for business reasons. A business may not be compelled to use its property in a particular way. Competition and some aspects of public service could become antagonistic under private property concepts.

In addition to having competition among integrated network infrastructure providers for individual customers, the ideal system requires that consumers have the opportunity to access the broadest range of content possible. The overarching goals are to permit the free marketplace of ideas and to take diversity to its limits. Competition could stimulate the output of programming as integrated broadband systems attempt to attract subscribers by developing an enticing library of materials.

IDEALIST VERSUS STRATEGIC MODEL

In discussing competition policy, with multiple wire and wireless providers, each with a multitude of information and programming suppliers, we have presented an ideal. Comparison of the ideal competitive model of development in telecommunication to practical economic and political reality is described by Mansell.[27] She is discussing intelligent networks mainly in reference to global development of telecommunication and computerized databases, but Mansell's two models of development also fit full service, broadband networks in a residential service context. The *idealist* model is based on the interaction of competition and technological change that serves the collective interests of policy makers, suppliers, and users. In the idealist model as described by Mansell, intelligent networks integrate information and communication services, eliminate boundaries between public and private networks, converge competencies across telecommunication, computing, and audiovisual sectors, provide universal service because of declining costs and the response to customer requirements expressed interactively, and transform telecommunication from a supply-led to a demand-led industry. In Mansell's terms, demand leadership will take the industry to flexible, high-quality services at lower costs. The new entrants in the industry will reduce the market power of the incumbents and limit the domination of a few players. New forms of collaboration and competition will be stimulated by the supply-demand balance. Competition in telecommunication supply from equipment as well as local, national, regional, and global service supply will assure long-run ubiquitous access. During a transitional phase, specialized telecommunication regulatory institutions will assure that the efficiency and public service objectives are met.

The *strategic* model, as described by Mansell, is more pessimistic about the effects of competition and technology. Mansell's strategic model expects economic and political interests built into the network system to prevent network integration because of rivalry in pricing, proprietary standards, and policy intervention. This will create disparities in network access. Contrary to the idealist model, the strategic model described by Mansell will be supply-led with the demand of only a few large privileged users reflected in the development. In the Mansell description, supply and demand forces in the strategic model will provide incentives to design the networks to reestablish power in the marketplace. Technical innovations will not be sufficient to stimulate competition to overcome monopolization. Distortions in the market can occur as a result of imperfect competition, monopolistic competition, oligopolistic rivalry, and monopoly. The ability to mix and match network components will benefit multinational companies (the biggest users) but could create dis-benefits for others in terms of network design and access. The response to regulatory pressures will be to devise new ways to maintain market power. Little progress will be made toward public service objectives. Having described these two models, Mansell believes that, in the United States,

> the potential for a relatively closed oligopolistic system of supply to emerge in the domestic market is strong. The forces of competition have presented themselves in accordance with the tenets of the Strategic model. . . . The present transition in the telecommunication market is not from monopoly to competition, but from monopoly to strategic oligopoly.[28]

ONE WIRE, TWO WIRES

Historically, both telephone and cable businesses have been thought to be *natural monopolies*, where it is more efficient for a single company to provide a service than two.[29] In contemplating competition in broadband fiber integrated networks, the issue is between one wire and two. A single digital, broadband system, where the operator installs many fibers in the distribution plant to meet future demand and save on labor, is already far beyond the capacity needed for existing voice, video, and data services. A second supplier duplicating the distribution plant, also putting in dark fibers, is adding to the overcapacity. In manufacturing, each company has a slight overcapacity to handle cyclical demands, and builds extra capacity as demand increases. In contrast, each communication network must have the capacity to serve 100% of the potential market, because each home passed in the competitive area is a potential subscriber. It is possible that this duplicative capital investment, seemingly unneeded, could be ruinous to the operators and wasteful of materials and labor. Business entry and exit are costly and cannot be accomplished quickly.

To determine the need for rate regulation, the Cable Act of 1992 defined *effective competition* in video program distribution to exist under any one of these three conditions: (a) Fewer than 30% of the households in the franchise area subscribe to cable (with penetration this low, it is assumed that noncable services are adequate); (b) the franchise area has at least two comparable unaffiliated multichannel video programming distributors, each of which offers service to at least 50% of the households, and the distributors, other than the largest, have more than 15% penetration; or (c) the franchise authority operates a video programming service available to at least 50% of the households in the franchise area.[30] Johnson argues that these criteria are not relevant; robust competition could occur at a very low market share and is not assured even at shares above 15%. Further, Johnson notes that the rules could penalize cable operators facing competition: "The more successfully cable operators compete, the longer will be the time required for rivals to attain a 15% market share, and the longer will cable operators be regulated."[31] Other economists note there is little argument "that the exercise of market power by incumbent firms is constrained by the ability of new firms to enter their market."[32] According to this "contestability" theory, a constraint on market power occurs even if the entry never occurs. Others argue that there is no scientific research to support the potential competition-contestability thesis.[33] Whatever the case, the 1996 telecommunications reform bill adds a fourth criterion, deregulating cable rates as soon as a telephone company offers service by any means comparable to the existing cable system.

Even when it occurs, actual competition between two or more wired services does not meet the ideal of the competitive model. The resulting oligopoly may not deliver the benefits anticipated from true competition. Because of the high capital and operating costs, the firms may tacitly agree to prices, and indeed services, that do not undercut each other. Through mutual awareness of their long-term benefit, *and* awareness of the government competition policy, they do not enter into harmful competition in price, service, or technical innovation. It is not necessary for this collaboration to be explicit. The operators would clearly understand the hazards of upsetting the status quo. There is a danger that the firms would sustain "competition" at higher overall cost of service than a single provider.

Why would public policy encourage businesses to enter into potentially ruinous competition that would not even benefit the consumer? First is the public bias against monopoly; one wire is simply not "politically correct." Second, there is naïveté about the benefits of competition in this context. The assumed benefits would follow from perfect competition, which is seldom, if ever, attainable. Even workable competition achieved through antitrust enforcement and structural regulation—with an acceptable level of imperfection—may not be realized.

In defense of the two-wire level of competition, however, we should note that the capital invested in duplicative distribution plants is becoming less and less significant in proportion to the total investment. In advanced broadband networks, a large proportion of the capital cost is on the consumer premises. Also, an increasing proportion of the cost will be in the servers, switches, and other equipment, which tends to be *variable* with usage or number of subscribers.

Importantly, competition expedites the *initiation* of full service networks. Telephone and cable incumbents are moving quickly to establish the foundations for FSNs so that the basic business of each is not preempted by the other. A further benefit of competition is in technical, design, and service innovations that will evolve from attempts to win competitive advantage. Even if head-to-head broadband competition is not feasible, rivalry at this stage is producing research and development in infrastructure and market trials.

Finally, the innovation and development that are stimulated and accelerated by competition in the United States may ultimately be underwritten by worldwide markets for products and services tested in the United States as a laboratory. This suggests that a certain amount of duplicative plant in the United States, testing the market and refining service and technology under competitive pressure, is valuable to the participants, who will eventually be able to export the equipment, software, and experience. As we head into the information society, costly competitive development in the United States could be written off against opportunities on an international scale.

OPEN ACCESS

To assure competition in content, at a minimum, programmers and information providers must have a fair chance at access to the network; the FSN cannot be a bottleneck. A program, a program network, or data source should be able to compete for shelf space on digital broadband networks entirely on the merits of the service. Price discrimination for anticompetitive purposes by a programmer violates the Communications Act. If price discrimination demonstrably harms a competitor, it may violate antitrust law.

As long as the full service network is not considered a common carrier, its *editorial* judgment in making content choices as a First Amendment speaker cannot be questioned. Only choices that clearly represent a biased, economic self-interest are at issue. For consumers in one community, with only one broadband network—one wire—confidence must be placed in the efficacy of the rules of access. A second provider would better assure that programs and information would be accessible in that community. Even if access to menus for on-demand programs and information is open to all suppliers, promotion of items on the menu is critical. Two broadband networks are likely to have different priorities in promotion, thereby exposing the community as a whole to a broader menu.

Sports programming is an essential television resource that is scarce—generally one major team to a community. Some sports have migrated from "free" television to pay television. Popular programs are also scarce, resulting from a fortuitous combination of talents assembled by good managers with access to financial resources. The windfall revenue from the major hits is referred to as a *scarcity rent*. Large organizations can attempt to corner some of the talent and other resources to get a share of the scarcity rents and reduce risk. They do so by becoming dominant buyers of programming, by horizontal concentration of retail distributors, or by vertical integration of production and distribution.

Horizontal concentration has already been experienced in the cable industry and is expected in the development of integrated broadband wired networks where the major contenders are cable companies and large telephone companies. We have described the importance of volume purchases of programming rights in Chapter 8. The strategy of the operator is to use the size of the aggregated subscribers as leverage for negotiating a low license fee or high split. In negotiating license fees, the threat by a very large operator of *not* carrying the network or program is persuasive.

Horizontal concentration is also possible in the program production area. A very few powerful producers could dominate the creation of program materials. Key partnerships are forming in Hollywood and Silicon Valley representing the entertainment and software elements, respectively, for the development of interactive television. The industry has amused itself with stories of the failure of the minds to meet—the stereotypical big spending, flamboyant Hollywood type who "does lunch" in smart restaurants, and the bespectacled, computer nerd who does lunch from a brown bag—but these groups are already beginning to join in one way or another.

Owning programming is an important competitive strategy for a distribution network. Except in circumstances where program exclusivity is prohibited, if you have a program, your competitor does not—or she acquires it on your terms. Owning programming as electronic communication approaches full service integrated networks is akin to hoarding scarce resources. The cable industry already owns much of its programming. Cable operators bought into programming at first to have a product to differentiate themselves from broadcasting, and later as a hedge against competition, assuming that programming would be a key resource. There is some belief within the telephone and cable industries that, in an integrated broadband network, the distribution network itself is only a minor factor in the business. The provider of the network will earn a modest income for supplying and maintaining the network, but the major revenues, *and revenue growth*, will be derived from the programming and enhanced services. Program ownership may also provide an entrée into international markets.

Hollywood studios are courting broadcast networks, which would vertically combine production and distribution capabilities. A similar combination is seen in the business alignments of all of the RBOCs with Hollywood: Disney with Ameritech, BellSouth, and SBC; Creative Artists Agency with Bell Atlantic, NYNEX, and Pacific Telesis; Time Warner with U S West. These particular groupings have been threatened by other alliances, but soon telephone company based organizations will begin producing programming, which can be sold to outside video distributors and used in-region by their own video affiliates. The vertical integration of producer and retail video distributor secures a distribution base and promotional attention for the programming. The retailer has a firm commitment to the programming. There is no argument about the split. Vertical integration permits control of the process.

Much has been said about *synergy* in the media and distribution conglomerates. In theory, a conglomerate can use all of its products and outlets to advantage, one unit of the company helping another, so that the whole is greater than the sum of the parts. Synergy has often been used as a justification for acquisition or merger but the benefits are not always obvious. A good result in a merger may have more to do with the market power of the conglomerate than synergy.

Full service network operators will make the Internet available as well as a number of freestanding information sources. Online information packagers will need to have some service differential in either (a) ease of use or (b) exclusive information. As intermediaries between integrated broadband networks and original information sources or the Internet, however, they may be bypassed.

The FSN Industry Structure

There are seven basic structural models that can emerge in integrated service networks, all of which we will probably see: (a) a head-to-head competition of FSNs (two wires), (b) FSN versus cable, (c) FSN versus telephone, (d) condominium, (e) an FSN alone, (f) a combined ownership of parallel nonintegrated broadband and narrowband services, and (g) marginal increments in existing networks.

FSN VERSUS FSN

Long prior to the Telecommmunications Act opening competition, in the courts, telephone companies had been pursuing free opportunity to provide video, and had begun planning video services in presenting applications to the FCC for common carrier video dialtone services. Cable companies had likewise anticipated federal authority to offer telephone services, but were also seeking, and in some cases winning, legislation in states that would remove barriers to residential telephone service. These concurrent actions by telephone and cable companies are discussed in the next chapter.

There is no hard evidence on the feasibility of competition between full service networks in the same service area. An assumption is that in high-population, high-density areas, two companies combining telephone and video services *and* adding several unique services beyond the traditional, plain old telephone service (POTS) and traditional cable services might both thrive. As we have discussed throughout this book, it is widely believed that if there are two broadband providers, they will originate separately from the cable and telephone customer base. Market tests will provide some information about the demand for integrated services, but because of test limitations, and the *evolving* nature of the services to be provided, full-scale service over a relatively long period will be necessary.

Now that the barriers to integrated service are removed from the telephone and cable companies, and one is not allowed to buy out the other, except in small towns, how would full service network competitors behave? A variety of strategies have already emerged or can be deployed as soon as competition seriously threatens.

As noted, the conventional wisdom expects price competition. Federally mandated duopoly in cellular telephone did not, however, succeed in keeping prices down. Aggressive price competition between integrated broadband networks is also a poor prospect where cross subsidization is not permitted. Each integrated network will have heavy capital investments to recoup and high operating costs in marketing and customer service caused by the competition. Competitors may still differ in price. One operator will package programming differently than another as a marketing strategy. The consumer could find the most agreeable price and package with a particular operator.

We can expect some *cross subsidization* and *predatory pricing* (where service is priced below cost to compete unfairly) despite efforts to prevent it. In fact, many concerned about both insist that it is not possible to prevent by regulatory scrutiny. In the FSN versus FSN situation, there is the potential for cross subsidy *within* the market by both cable and telephone companies, which would disadvantage consumers of plain old telephone service or plain old cable service. There is also concern about cross-subsidizing the FSN with funds from *outside* the competitive market to support predatory pricing over a long time, disadvantaging consumers outside the FSNs who do not even have an opportunity to subscribe to integrated network services. A telephone company starting with nearly 100% of the market for an essential service has a greater opportunity to subsidize than cable starting with only two-thirds of the market for a nonessential service.

Still, with the two FSNs competing in the same market, it would be difficult to conceal costs. Each provider would have a good idea of each other's costs so that predatory pricing would be immediately protested. And the instinct for self-preservation would prevent obvious predatory practices, given that government has established a competition policy. If both companies price below cost to establish the market, with neither protesting, the consumer enjoys at least short-term benefit. But consumers in the noncompetitive locations for both companies may be paying for development in the competitive market.

Price competition, to the extent possible, may be used mainly by a new service provider to establish a foothold in the market. That is, a cable-based integrated network would try to cut telephone prices to attract new subscribers, while the telephone-based network offers low introductory prices in video for the same purpose. Both will have different pricing and packaging schemes. Here, the full service operator must have done sufficient research to be confident of consumer response. The consumers in one company must be comfortable enough with the pricing and packaging not to be persuaded by alternate plans offered by the other. Because almost everything will be relatively new, and the competitive environment full of contradictory promotional messages, consumer satisfaction may be difficult to achieve.

The integrated broadband systems competing in television will begin with similar programming. A competitor from cable origins will evolve from the cable programming as we know it now—basic, expanded basic, à la carte, pay per view—with the addition of video-on-demand and interactive video services to be expanded as the market dictates. A competitor originating as a telephone company will use cable networks and other program packages, perhaps giving greater attention to video on demand because it has been so heavily promoted by telephone companies as the future of television. But because cable has already defined multichannel video service for most of the people who are interested, there are practical limits on the ability of the telephone companies to be innovative in video competition.

Assuming that all multichannel television providers will eventually be vertically integrated, the rules against program exclusivity in vertically integrated companies would limit program competition. Most programming would be in this category. Where a telephone-based full service network might have the resources to develop unique programming, as have the cable operators, that programming would also be available to competitors. Competition in programming would occur in the *makeup* of basic packages, but even so the channels left out of one provider's basic packages would be available à la carte. Competing broadband systems could differentiate in local programming, which would be exclusive.

Full service broadband networks serving the same area have an opportunity to differentiate in communication services. The degree of integration of computer, telephone, television, printers, audio, and video recorders and other devices, the initial installations, customer preparation for use, and, finally, the navigation system will each reflect some differences and, however minor, be heavily promoted as more convenient or effective. This is a particularly sensitive area. The ordinary consumers, beyond the first wave of high-tech innovators, will have some trepidations about a full service network and may be easily overwhelmed. If one competitor were to be perceived to have a consumer-friendly edge, the other could be in jeopardy.

Customer service will most certainly be a strategic factor in competition. A first response to competition would be to tighten the standards for customer service in the knowledge that the customers unhappy with service would quickly desert. A telephone-based FSN has an opportunity to promote its traditional reputation for service against a cable-based FSN. Cable companies may align themselves with long-distance or other companies that have a reputation for excellent service, such as Time Warner/AT&T, to the overcome the negative image of cable.

In Chapter 5, we discussed the principal technologies for full service networks. At present, it appears they are the hybrid fiber to the feeder or curb and coaxial cable to the home. Much of the rest is developing along predictable lines although there is some hope of design breakthroughs that could lead to a cost advantage to one competitor over another. The cable industry research group, Cable Labs, is funding a research effort to develop new technology for cable telephone services, and the RBOCs have Bellcore research to draw on. A number of companies are working on servers to store and distribute video and data from the headend or other locations, and still more are developing the home hardware and software. Because both home terminal and headend costs are major factors, the strategic alliances that have developed between manufacturers, software designers, and network operators would produce at least temporary technical advantage for one competitor unless all equipment is standardized from the beginning. There have been informal agreements, at least within the cable industry, to share or cross-license technology.

The telephone industry has a strategic advantage over the cable industry in its relatively greater size and cohesion. The local exchange carriers have annual revenues of about $83 billion[34] compared with about $26 billion for cable.[35] The RBOCs with most of the local telephone business have pooled their resources for research and development in Bellcore. But the future ownership of Bellcore is uncertain as competition among the RBOCs increases.

We commented earlier on the different capital resources of the telephone and cable industries. Telephone companies have greater cash reserves and better credit ratings (cable, BB; telephone, AA).[36] This would mean that a telephone-based broadband network would have greater resources to cover the operating losses in a competitive environment, where it takes a long time for the market for services to develop.

Almost all participants in the competition have developed alliances designed to capitalize on independently acquired expertise. This is a response to the complexity of integrated network development and the need for expeditious advancement in the face of competition. Some of the alliances will be more successful than others because of factors such as interpersonal relationships, commitment, financial resources, creativity, and cross-fertilization. There is great variation in creativity and experience among cable companies in futuristic services. Some cable partners would bring more to joint ventures than others. The first alliance of a major cable MSO and a regional telephone operating company occurred almost immediately after the passage of the 1996 telecommunications bill. U S West announced its intent to acquire Continental Cablevision. Because such a merger of expertise gives the corporation an advantage in competition among integrated broadband networks, others can be expected. Computer hardware and software company alliances with telecommunication companies could also be critical.

An important strategy for FSNs will be to concentrate ownership of local systems. For cable operators growing into full service networks, it is necessary to regionally concentrate systems. For both cable- and telephone-based FSNs, size is important in acquiring capital and in negotiating the rights to content. Cable operators aggregating subscribers over many systems enjoy volume discounts in network affiliation and have an opportunity to acquire equity in program networks in exchange for carriage, as described in Chapter 7. Also, there are the traditional scale efficiencies in operations and purchasing of capital goods. Many cable companies, at a size disadvantage against the Regional Bell Operating Companies, are currently acquiring more systems both to improve regional concentration (clustering) and to increase the overall scale of their business in preparation for competition. Independent telephone companies have the same scale problems of nonclustered cable companies but are less likely to be in the larger cities where competition occurs.

Scope economies could also be significant in competition. The company that can offer more services from the same platform and the same administrative structure has an advantage.

Cable and telephone independents and smaller MSOs are debating future survival in a competitive FSN environment. Some believe that they could thrive, just as small independent telephone companies have thrived. Joint service agreements would provide whatever services the small operator could not provide alone. Government competition policy, implementing the 1996 Telecommunications Act, will probably protect the independents from predatory behavior by bigger, clustered operators requiring interconnection, but many cable independents and smaller MSOs are selling to larger ones.

CONDOMINIUM

In a *condominium* approach to competition, two or more service providers share the same facilities, avoiding duplication. There could be different owners of parts of the network. Others would complete a network by leasing the parts they do not own, relying on open access at fair prices. Or two or more companies could share ownership of the whole network. Whatever the ownership and leasing arrangements, the important element of the condominium approach is nonduplication of facilities, reducing capital costs for service competitors. Such arrangements may be necessary if competition is to occur in some markets. The condominium could be necessary in all markets if revenue potential does not justify two wires or a decision is made to forgo oligopolistic rivalry in favor of regulated distribution systems.

FSN VERSUS CABLE, FSN VERSUS TELEPHONE

There will be communities where either a telephone company or a cable company, *but not both*, chooses to build an FSN. With limited capital resources and uncertainty about the short-term potential, the builders of integrated networks will select their markets carefully. Once one has committed, the other may choose to compete only with its traditional service, riding that horse until it dies. This suggests an advantage to the *first mover* in integrated broadband services development; the first company to make the investment may effectively deter others.

Competing against an FSN, a traditional cable or telephone service would position itself as an affordable, no-frills, alternative. The price competition would probably be effective against a full service network, which would have a greater capital investment and be prevented from predatory pricing. The traditional cable or telephone systems offer close substitutes for major parts of the full service network product. In the short term, the traditional service provider may be able to capitalize on skepticism about an integrated network: "too complicated," "too expensive," "unreliable."

A freestanding telephone or cable system with low debt service could compete with an FSN for several years until the integrated services become so much a part of the lifestyle that they seem essential. Although the intransigent traditional service risks obsolescence before the physical plant has been fully depreciated, it may still be a prudent business strategy if over the term it has repaid the owner's investment and been profitable. The greater risk could be to build a full service network and be obligated to develop new markets against such a competitor.

In this context, the case of a cable system competing with an FSN is somewhat different than the telephone system. The cable operator can choose to play out the string as suggested above, with minimal additional investments, or assess demand by observing the FSN in the local market and make modest upgrades in the areas of greatest promise. A cable operator who sees a service demand has the advantage of making incremental investments dictated by demand. For example, the cable operator who observes a demand for VOD can take fiber far enough into the feeder to accommodate a peak demand for major movie releases. This could be only a small additional investment. On the contrary, the telephone company must make a major initial investment.

The conventional cable system competing with an integrated full service provider has a handicap, however, in that it can no longer promote its programming without also promoting the competitor, who has essentially the same programming. The prior investment in creating an image, "brand," for the network, and identifying it with a local system, is mostly lost. And sooner or later, the scope efficiencies of the full service system, packaging all services, will underprice the stand-alone telephone or cable service.

FSN ALONE

An integrated full service network alone is the potential outcome of the technological imperative toward integrated services generally feared by consumers and public policy makers. This is a monopoly with potentially greater impact on the consumer than the independent monopolies of cable and telephone. The federal ban on buyouts in one's own market—cable buying telephone or telephone buying cable—does not extend to the smallest cities lest those cities thereby be excluded from the possibility of advanced systems. Therefore, a full service broadband system with no competition in its market could occur by acquisition. And, of course, it is the outcome of the scenario described above in which a traditional telephone or cable company eventually capitulates to an FSN after competing for a transitional period.

The unlimited channel capacity of the single system still provides an incentive to offer every possible service. To do otherwise would waste opportunity. Competition among content and service providers accessing the network could keep prices down and the consumer would suffer only to the extent that the system is inefficiently run and valuing the physical distribution network contribution too highly. Where the integrated network itself is the owner of programming, or discriminates against services competing with those in which it has an ownership interest, regulation might be necessary.

There is also the expectation that terrestrial broadcasting and other technologies, such as DBS, MMDS and PCS would share the market for at least some of the services of the integrated network and, therefore, restrain its market power.

PARALLEL NONINTEGRATED BROADBAND AND NARROWBAND SYSTEMS

A means for a telephone company to compete in multichannel television would be to build a broadband network in the hybrid fiber coaxial cable architecture just for the video service. Some telephone companies, such as Ameritech in the north central area and SNET in Connecticut, are obtaining cable franchises for this purpose. The plan would allow the company to upgrade the broadband network incrementally in response to demand, just as a cable operator would do, thus spreading the investment over many more years while acquiring immediate experience in the video market. Telephone customers would continue to be served by the twisted pair. The integration of voice, data, and video in this dual broadband-narrowband system would be awkward, but still possible.

Cable response to this development would be to make investments in the distribution plant to match the new telephone-based state-of-the-art video service. Having made these investments and the commitment, the next step for both companies would be to install the modems for telephone service as well. The danger for two such competitors in this circumstance is that they are entering into rivalry for each other's business, after making major capital investments, without increasing the total business—two companies dipping into the same revenue pool without expanding its size. Nonetheless, the investment in these networks is less than would be required for a fully integrated broadband system with all of the anticipated services.

MARGINAL INCREMENTS IN CAPACITY

It may be feasible for cable to increase its capacity by digital compression, meeting the DBS competition and preparing for later competition with other potential video providers, adding services that are closely related to its core business. The telephone companies would solve the immediate need for high-speed data communication for computers with ISDN. Telephone companies could test markets for video and gain experience by investments in MMDS (as some have done). Cable and telephone companies compete in home shopping, a relatively promising area. Ultimately, telephone companies have broadband networks because all new plant is HFC fiber to the feeder or fiber to the curb. Cable companies add telephony on their residential networks and through their ownership of CAPS. When both have full service networks, it will be because the new services have generated the revenue to support them and existing facilities are depreciated.

The Consequences of Competition

Competition may not work for a number of reasons. Demand may not support sufficient volume in the new integrated services to cover capital and operating costs. But, although it is not a certainty that competition policy can be made to work effectively, having taken that direction, and depending on it to create the national information infrastructure, it is necessary now to implement public policy in a way that does not inhibit the development. At worst, in the long term under these policies, the monopolies will only erode slowly, and even this has benefits. We address the public policy issues in the next chapter.

Notes

1. "Cable Television Developments" (Washington, DC: National Cable Television Association, April 1994).

2. Fred Dawson, "In-Home Broadband Cost Tabbed at $800-$900," *Multichannel News*, 22 August 1994, 26.

3. Thomas W. Hazlett, "The Policy of Exclusive Franchising in Cable Television," *Journal of Broadcasting and Electronic Media* 31, no. 1 (1987): 8.

4. *Preferred Communications v. City of Los Angeles*, 754 F. 2d 1396 (9th Cir. 1985).

5. 47 U.S.C. 541 (a)(1).

6. For a full discussion of overbuilds and an example of a municipal overbuild, see Marianne Barrett, "Direct Competition in Cable Television Delivery: The Montgomery, Alabama and Paragould Arkansas Examples" (Ph.D. diss., Michigan State University, 1993).

7. 47 U.S.C. 541.

8. Leland Johnson, *Toward Competition in Cable Television* (Cambridge: MIT Press, 1994), 33.

9. Implementation of Sections of the Cable Television Consumer Protection and Competition Act of 1992, Rate Regulation, MM Docket No. 9266, 8 FCC Rcd. 5631, 5977 Article 561 (1993). The comparison excludes systems with penetration below 30%.

10. "Cable Television Developments" (Washington, DC: National Cable Television Association, April 1994), 1-A.

11. DIRECTV plans 30% to 40% penetration of 6 million urban homes within the first three years (Vincente Pasdeloup, "DBS: Don't Be Scared," *Cable World*, 17 August 1992, 18). USSB expects 1.2 million subscribers from cable franchised areas in the first 18 months (Carl Weinshenk, "DirecTv, USSB Map Their Game Plans as April Launches Near," *Cable World*, 14 February 1994, 4).

12. Marianne Barrett and Thomas F. Baldwin, "Cable Television in Local News: Capital Budgeting Models" (paper presented at the annual meeting of the Broadcast Education Association, Las Vegas, Nev., May 1992).

13. Thomas F. Baldwin, Marianne Barrett, and Benjamin Bates, "Impact of Cable on Television Journalism Audiences," *Journalism Quarterly* 69, no. 3 (1992): 651-658.

14. Pasdeloup, "DBS: Don't Be Scared," 18.

15. Christopher Stern, "DirecTv Aims for Cable Viewers," *Broadcasting & Cable*, 6 December 1993, 42.

16. K. C. Neel, "Going Wireless," *Cable World*, 16 May 1994, 16.

17. Bishop Cheen, Paul Kagan Seminars Inc., quoted in Joel A. Strasser, "Wireless Markets Take-Off," *Private Cable/Wireless Cable*, June 1994, 53.

18. Lowell Hussey (panel presentation at the National Cable Television Association Convention, New Orleans, La., May 1994).

19. K. C. Neel, "Going Wireless," 16.

20. Rick Mendosa, "Private Cable Grows Up," *International Cable*, November 1994, 16.

21. Raymond Smith quoted in Harry A. Jessel, "Superhighway Open to Broadcasters," *Broadcasting & Cable*, 28 March 1994, 19.

22. Steve McClellan, "The News Is Good in the New Business," *Broadcasting & Cable*, 10 October 1994, 50.

23. For a discussion of potential broadcaster-provided services, see Richard V. Ducey, "Broadcasting in a Converging World," in *Convergence: Transition to the Electronic Superhighway*, ed. Marcia L. De Sonne (Washington, DC: National Association of Broadcasters, 1994), 23953.

24. George Reed-Dellinger, "TeleMedia: Collision of Industries," *Convergence: Transition*, ed. De Sonne, 17208.

25. William J. Baumol and J. Gregory Sidak, *Toward Competition in Local Telephony* (Cambridge: MIT Press, 1994).

26. Baumol and Sidak, *Toward Competition*.

27. Robin Mansell, *The New Telecommunications: A Political Economy of Network Evolution* (Newbury Park, Calif.: Sage, 1993), 7-9.

28. Mansell, *New Telecommunications,* 18, 65.

29. Natural monopolies occur when single-firm production of a product or service is always more efficient than multifirm production regardless of the level of output. As Noam notes, this occurs when the marginal cost of providing a service (i.e., the cost of adding each new subscriber) declines with the size of the network. Thus, the larger network will always be able to offer services at a lower cost, and will eventually win out over smaller networks. See Eli Noam, *Telecommunications in Europe* (New York: Oxford University Press, 1992).

30. 47 U.S.C. 541, 623.

31. Johnson, *Competition in Cable,* 150.

32. John J. McGowan, "Mergers for Power or Progress?" in *Antitrust and Regulation: Essays in Memory of John J. McGowan,* ed. Franklin M. Fisher (Cambridge: MIT Press, 1985), 3-4.

33. William G. Shepherd, "Potential Competition v. Actual Competition," *Administrative Law Review,* Winter 1990, 5-34.

34. George Reed-Dellinger, "Collision of Industries," in *Convergence: Transition,* ed. De Sonne, 172.

35. "Cable Television Developments" (Washington, DC: National Cable Television Association, Fall 1994). (This figure combines $23 billion in subscription revenue, including local advertising, with $2.7 billion in national cable network advertising revenue for 1993.)

36. Reed-Dellinger, "Collision of Industries," 172.

11

Communication Policy

overnment is deeply involved in telecommunication and media, making general policy and day-to-day regulation. A major part of communication law serves administrative purposes, allocating and assigning frequencies in the electromagnetic spectrum, protecting copyrights while making information as widely available as possible, encouraging innovation, assuring critical government communication functions for public safety and rate regulation, and, now, promoting competition. An important part of government policy is designed to keep the communication free of government influences on content. Federal, state, and local government agencies have recognized the imperatives toward convergence, but development has moved so fast that policy has lagged. This chapter will provide the contemporary context for communication policy and describe current law and the mechanisms for monitoring the communications industries.

U.S. communication policy is made at the federal level by Congress using its power to regulate interstate commerce. Legislation originates with the Subcommittee on Telecommunications, Consumer Protection, and Finance of the House of Representatives' Commerce

Committee and the Subcommittee on Communications of the Senate Committee on Commerce, Science and Transportation. Details of regulating communication industries are left to the Federal Communications Commission (FCC), an independent regulatory agency established and overseen by Congress. The president nominates the five members of the FCC and names the chairperson, subject to the approval of the Senate. The executive branch has its own communications advisory agency, the National Telecommunications and Information Administration in the Department of Commerce.

The FCC has three Bureaus that deal with matters of interest here: the Cable Bureau, the Mass Media Bureau, and the Common Carrier Bureau. The Cable Bureau was formed only recently, in 1994, to meet the demands placed on the agency by the Cable Act of 1992. The Cable Bureau Consumer Protection Division is concerned with rate regulation, must-carry, retransmission consent, customer service, technical standards, and equipment compatibility. The Competition Division of the Cable Bureau monitors ownership and program access regulation and other competitive issues, such as mergers, sales, and horizontal and vertical integration. The bureau's Policy and Rules Division drafts rules, reports on industry trends, and analyzes the effectiveness of regulations. The Mass Media Bureau is responsible for licensing broadcast stations. The Common Carrier Bureau is concerned with telephone and data communication. That convergence is not reflected in the FCC organizational structure causes some coordination problems.

States and local governments also have a role in communication policy, which must be coordinated with national policy. Convergence creates new jurisdictional problems because the locus of regulation for each of the traditional services is at a different government level.

Policy Goals

The contemporary national communication policy goals are relatively straightforward and generally accepted in government and by the interested public. Broadly, the goal is to have an efficient, universally accessible, "advanced telecommunications infrastructure,"[1] which implies the *building of integrated broadband networks*. The Clinton administration, led by Vice President Gore, made the national information infrastructure a priority. In addition to improving the information infrastructure through private investment and having it widely accessible, the government seeks to promote technological innovation and applications both in the private and public sectors. A matching grant program for this purpose was funded for $25 million in 1994 and $100 million in 1995. Through this development, the government hopes to ensure privacy and reliability, protect copyrights, facilitate dissemination of government information, coordinate state and local jurisdictions, and represent the United States internationally.

The principles of the new Republican majority, stated in the "discussion draft" of the Senate's "Telecommunications Competition and Deregulation Act of 1995" are similar but attempt to set a minimalist regulatory tone: create a national policy framework with open and full competition, open and equal access, and equal opportunity but not equal outcome; preserve and revise universal service; promote federalism; minimize, remove, and reform regulations; introduce no new entitlement or protectionism; and maintain competitive neutrality.[2]

Implicit in the making of overall communication policy, and explicit in administration goals, is the intent to reestablish the traditional international role of the United States. As Douglas has suggested, "... America acquired power ... by colonizing the future, defining, monopolizing and selling at steep rates the modernization process itself."[3] Leadership in telecommunication not only gives the U.S. economy a competitive edge but positions U.S. industry to become a major supplier of equipment and management expertise to world markets. The United States, having lost its commanding international position in manufacturing, has been searching for the next plateau. Advanced communication systems usher in a new information age in which the United States has major assets.

That integrated networks must be built is not often debated. It is justification enough that it is possible. The social and economic benefits of high-speed communication in the computer age seem self-evident. Universal access has been a fundamental concept in the development of telephone service and has been a historical goal of public policy. Equality in access to information is central to democratic principles. It has guided federal policy in both education and communication.

While these broad policy goals have widespread acceptance, there is much less agreement on the means of achieving them. Even where there is agreement in principle, there is conflict over the details, as reflected in the long struggle to pass telecommunication reform legislation. Bringing the vision to reality is a public policy challenge and continues beyond the passage of the 1996 act to its implementation by federal, state, and local authorities.

There was a time when the building of a national-global telecommunication infrastructure appeared so complex, involving so many competing private interests, that public ownership and development was considered. This notion failed on two critical points. The first is the massive funding required. Increasing the deficit to build the infrastructure is not politically practical. The second reason is that it would have required a government commitment to a system architecture at an evolutionary stage. Private builders will innovate for competitive advantage at least in the nuances of system design.

Expecting private entrepreneurs to build the national information infrastructure led to the competition policy discussed in the previous chapter. Implementing a competition policy would be easily accomplished if the government could simply remove any barriers to telecommunications industry entry and then stand out of the way. But the changeover to competition is made difficult by the old structure established for the independent elements of the industry now converging, a structure that has served its purposes quite well. The media are strong, relatively free of government control, and extremely popular. Voice communication is efficient, reliable, and nearly universal. Any change in communication policy must first do no harm. Venturing into a new structure, where the old has been successful, carries political risk.

Congress attempted to remove barriers to competition in cable television in 1992, prohibiting the award of exclusive franchises, making most cable program networks available to distributors outside the traditional cable industry, providing for leased commercial access, and regulating rates only as long as there is no effective competition. The FCC took video dialtone applications from telephone companies and permitted telephone companies to provide a variety of information services.

In 1994, Congress attempted to repeal the cross-ownership legislation. A bill in the House of Representatives removed the cross-ownership restriction from both cable and telephone companies, passing by an overwhelming margin of 423 to 4. A similar bill in the Senate failed to come to a vote, although it was reported out of the Senate Commerce Committee by an 18 to 2 vote. The regional Bell Operating Companies (RBOCs) had effectively withdrawn support by seeking to add amendments that were untenable to the committee. In 1995, both the Senate and the House presented new bills. The two bills went to a conference committee in the fall. After some late squabbling over broadcasting issues, a bill was passed and signed into law in February 1996. Senate Majority Leader, Robert Dole, delayed passage by questioning the provisions giving broadcasters additional spectrum for advanced television. He preferred an auction of the spectrum, which could produce many billions of dollars for the federal treasury. The senator's objections were withdrawn after he extracted a promise from the FCC and members of Congress that no licenses would be granted to broadcasters for additional spectrum until the matter had been reconsidered in the Congress. Thus, the bill finally became law. Its major provisions are referenced below along with other pertinent law and the historical antecedents.

Cross Ownership

Historically, regulated carriers were not permitted to compete in unregulated markets for fear that they would abuse their monopoly position in the regulated services.[4] Remember also that AT&T had signed a Consent Decree in 1956 promising to stay out of unregulated businesses and focus only on *basic* regulated telephone services. As the demand for data communications services grew, there was pressure on the FCC to define the conditions under which AT&T and other regulated common carriers could provide these services. A crucial question was whether data communications services were more like basic regulated telecommunication, or if they were *enhanced*, and, therefore, unregulated services.

For more than 20 years, the FCC struggled to specify the conditions under which regulated common carriers could provide unregulated or enhanced services. These efforts were mostly centered in a series of investigations known as the Computer Inquiries.[5] In Computer Inquiry I, the FCC decided to analyze, on a case-by-case basis, whether a service provided by a carrier under its jurisdiction was more like communications or more like data processing. Those that were considered to be data processing could be offered only under strict separation from regulated, tariffed services. This regime soon became unwieldy, however, and in Computer Inquiry II, the FCC attempted to define two classes of services—basic transport, in which the content was not modified in any way, and enhanced services, in which some processing of the content did occur. The FCC ruled that AT&T could offer only enhanced services through a structurally separate subsidiary. Packet switching was not considered a basic service but, rather, an enhanced service because there was processing of content associated with transmission. When coupled with the previously mentioned rules that permitted (1) attachment of non-Bell devices to AT&T's network (essentially creating a competitive equipment market) and (2) resale of bulk capacity purchased from AT&T, independent, value-added network providers such as Telenet and Tymnet were able to flourish. Thus, the United States developed many competing public and private packet-switched networks.

Distinguishing an enhanced service from a basic service has proven to be more formidable in the age of digital networks, so yet a third Computer Inquiry was held. In this final inquiry, the FCC decided to eliminate the structural safeguard approach and substitute a new set of safeguards built on accounting and access controls. Initially, the principle of *comparably efficient interconnection* was proposed, which would require AT&T (and now the RBOCs) to offer the same type of network access to competing service providers as it provides to its own services. Additionally, the *open network architecture* (ONA) principle was proposed, which requires carriers to *unbundle* their network services—that is, to offer all services separately rather than folded into a package—and offer *basic service elements* to enhanced service providers on a *tariffed* basis, by which prices and specific services are filed with a regulatory commission.[6] Although this approach has been challenged in the courts over the years, the basic principle remains the FCC's preferred approach to opening up access to the local telephone monopoly in advance of true network-based competition. It was hoped that ONA would also ensure fair interconnection arrangements with other network-based service providers.

Telephone companies were also prevented from cross ownership of cable systems by FCC rules and federal statute as discussed in Chapter 1. The intention was to allow cable to develop as a separate industry. There was also the fear that the telephone company monopoly would be egregious if it included all communication to and from the home. Under this policy, cable did develop into a strong industry independent of the telephone companies. Now, with the technology leading toward integrated broadband networks and with *growth* in both telephone and cable services dependent on such networks, the telephone industry has insisted that the video service cross-ownership ban be dropped. The cable industry has acceded, with the stipulation that cable be permitted to enter the telephone business and that both industries operate under similar rules. The cable industry expected that federal legislation would preempt laws, in all but a few of the states, that prevented cable telephone service to residences. In 1995, nine states allowed some local telephony competition: Connecticut, Illinois, Iowa, Maryland, Massachusetts, Michigan, New York, Oregon, and Washington. Six others leaning toward a more liberal position have been targeted by the National Cable Television Association to overturn the prohibitions: Florida, Georgia, North Carolina, Ohio, Texas, and Virginia.[7]

FEDERAL COURTS AND CROSS OWNERSHIP

Most of RBOCs and some of the independent telephone companies have won federal district court decisions in their respective areas against the cross-ownership legislation. The district courts have agreed that the cross-ownership prohibition on telephone company video service violates the First Amendment rights of the telephone companies. (See First Amendment section below.) Furthermore, the courts disagreed that the cross-ownership ban actually served the procompetitive objectives of the government. The FCC itself, a defendant in the case, is quoted in one decision as recommending the amendment of the 1984 Cable Act to permit local telephone companies to provide video programming directly to their telephone areas, *subject to appropriate safeguards*, which would *promote* competition.[8] The decision also quotes the Department of Justice, another defendant: "The Department believes that LEC provision of video programming will have procompetitive benefits that outweigh any anticompetitive risks involved." Still another federal agency, the National Telecommunications and Information Administration (NTIA) of the Department of Commerce, is cited: "Well-developed safeguards can address two of the 'traditional' concerns regarding cross-subsidization and also discrimination, as evidenced by the history of pole attachment access and rates."[10] These court decisions, assuming they would stand appeal, would have given telephone companies the right to own and distribute video programs in their service areas subject to "safeguards" designed by the FCC, the Department of Justice, and the courts *without* overarching statutory policy guidance. This was a major impetus for passage of the telecommunications reform bill. We discuss the business and management advantages of program service ownership, which are considered critical by the telephone companies, in Chapters 7 and 10.

VIDEO DIALTONE

Since 1987, the FCC has been attempting to permit telephone companies to offer video in their own service areas through *video dialtone* authorization of "an enriched version of video common carriage under which LECs will offer various nonprogramming services in addition to underlying video transport."[11] Telephone company ownership of the video programming would have been limited. The common carrier customer-programmers would have paid the telephone company a non-discriminatory price to use the wire. The customer-programmer would set the consumer price, make bundling and tiering decisions, and if an advertiser-supported channel, control all advertising spots. The telephone company would not have served any video subscribers directly. The FCC limited the proportion of channels a single video dialtone programmer could lease on a common carrier system. Neither the telephone company common carrier nor the customer-programmer would have had to obtain a franchise from the city for the video dialtone service because it was not defined as "cable service." This FCC exemption of video dialtone from obtaining franchises was strongly contested by the cities and cable operators but was sustained by a federal court.[12] The claims and counterclaims in these actions were based primarily on the issue of cross subsidy. What proportion of the cost of the network is appropriate to the video service? The FCC was vague on cross subsidy. On applying for authorization, the telephone company had to show how the incremental costs of providing video would be recovered through video-only revenues. The video dialtone concept ends, with the Telecommunications Act of 1996, although some of its principles are reflected in the options for telephone company entry described below and will be pertinent to FCC implementation of the bill.

NEW OPTIONS FOR TELEPHONE-VIDEO CROSS OWNERSHIP

The 1996 telecommunications reform bill recognizes several options for telephone companies to offer video in their own service areas. They may use "radio communication"—for example, multichannel, multipoint distribution service (MMDS)—be regulated as such, but not regulated as a cable system. The telephone company may also provide video entirely as a common carrier and thereby be regulated as a common carrier. They may become cable franchisees, offering a video in the same territory as the telephone service under the same rules as a traditional cable system.

Another option is created by the bill—the *open video system*, which is a combination of the original video dialtone service and a cable system. The open video system is not to be regulated as a common carrier and not to have as many regulatory burdens as a cable system. It could conform to a telephone company service area without requiring a franchise in each community. Special fees could be collected in recompense for the use of rights-of-way instead of the franchise fees permitted under cable regulation. The state could impose assessments instead of the franchise authorities. Any such fees could not exceed the fees paid by cable operators in the corresponding service areas. Similar to cable franchise fees, these fees could be itemized on the customer's bill.

The open video system provider can control—have a substantial ownership interest in—a maximum of one-third of the channels in circumstances in which demand for the channels exceeds channel capacity. Presumably, if the number of channels, through digital compression or activation of dark fibers, always exceeded demand by unaffiliated programmers, the provider could own more than one third of the channels. This problem is addressed only in the case in which video service evolves into a switched digital video system—the type of system we would eventually expect in a full service network. In the switched video case, the channel capacity would no longer be meaningful, and the FCC is charged with the responsibility of considering whether unaffiliated video providers are having difficulty getting access.

The open video service provider will have to observe the must-carry retransmission consent, syndicated exclusivity, network non-duplication, and program access rules as well as the public, educational, and governmental access rules. Leased access channel rules will not apply. The open video system provider is not able to discriminate among programmers in determining carriage, although if two or more programmers offered the same channel, the system would only have to carry one. The open video system operator is prevented from discriminating in program navigational services and in supplying information (including advertising) for subscriber program selection. The open system is required to allow unaffiliated programmers to identify themselves. Since the *unaffiliated* programmers of an open video service are expected to keep a check on the prices of the *affiliated* services, there is no rate regulation.

Details of this open video system alternative structure are to be developed by the FCC over a relatively short time now that the bill has become law. After establishing the rules, the FCC will certify that the provider is in conformance.

Interestingly, franchised cable operations, which have begun to offer telephone service, may opt to become open video system providers, thereby avoiding the local cable franchise and some of its obligations. The practicality of the open video system option for telephone or cable systems will be in the details of the FCC rules and the costs of right of way. But the plan could represent a convenience for telephone companies serving large areas and cable systems as they geographically cluster systems. An open video system is also an escape from more direct regulation by local authorities.

CROSS OWNERSHIP BY CABLE OPERATORS

The reform bill exempts a cable company from obtaining an additional franchise agreement to enter the telephone business.

By the same token, the bill does not permit local authorities to require cable companies to offer telecommunications services, other than intergovernmental services, as a condition of an original franchise or renewal. The bill specifically exempts any nonvideo telecommunications services over a cable system from being included in the assessment of a franchise fee.

BUYOUTS

It is possible that telephone and cable companies would avoid competition by one's buying out the other in the same market, creating a powerful, integrated operator with a large customer base in both video and voice. This would undoubtably foreclose competition in a wired service. Outside companies would not directly assail this fortress.

Under the 1996 legislation that opens competition, neither cable nor telephone companies can own more than a 10% interest in the other within their service areas. Nor can they enter into joint ventures in the same market. Cable or telephone companies are allowed to buy each other out, in markets of less than 35,000 subscribers that are outside urban areas, although buyouts in these smaller rural areas cannot exceed in aggregate more than 10% of the households in the telephone service area. Under some special conditions there may be waivers of these buyout rules.

CROSS OWNERSHIP BY LONG DISTANCE COMPANIES

AT&T and other long-distance carriers may wish to become full service networks, offering local telephone and cable services, as well as interactive and information services. There does not appear to be any legislative or modified final judgment-related restriction on either AT&T or any of the other interexchange carriers for such a move. Theoretically, these companies could seek licenses from state public service commissions and/or franchises from local municipalities controlling public rights-of-way to build their own local infrastructure. Or they could attempt to acquire existing local telephone or cable companies, obviously excluding an AT&T acquisition of a divested Bell Operating Company. In the past, state public service commissions, which have jurisdiction over all intrastate telecommunications services (both intra and interLATA), had historically not granted licenses to competitors for local, residential switched telephone services for fear of undermining the ability of the incumbents to keep local telephone rates down.

SPECIAL PROVISIONS FOR RBOCS

Under the telecommunication reform bill, RBOCs will have to be certified on a "competitive checklist" before going into long-distance service. The FCC will determine on a case-by-case basis whether it is in the public interest for any telephone company to be in the long-distance business. An RBOC could not offer long-distance service until it faced competition in local business and residential service.

The new bill generally requires that there be a facilities-based competitor in an RBOC's service area before it can enter long-distance markets in its own region. Competitors who provide only interexchange access service (such as a CAP), resale, or cellular telephone service do not qualify. RBOCs will be able to offer out-of-region interLATA services immediately.

Other provisions bar RBOCs from jointly marketing local and long-distance service and, in general, require that the RBOCs enter new competitive services, such as long distance, telemessaging, and electronic publishing through separate subsidiaries with no cross subsidization. Restrictions on manufacturing would be lifted from the RBOCs once requirements for offering long distance are met.

CONSENT DECREES AND COURT ORDERS

In many ways, the new bill supersedes the various consent decrees entered into by telephone companies, including the MFJ agreement. It treats the consent decrees as "continuing injunctions" and holds that all activities that were subject to these injunctions must now follow the new bill. Hence, the MFJ's restrictions on RBOC entry into long distance, manufacturing, and electronic publishing are revised as noted above. Similarly, any of the restrictions on GTE's entry in long-distance areas where it has local service will now be subject to the requirements of the bill. The bill does not interfere with the Justice Department's authority on antitrust.

PUBLIC UTILITIES

Public utilities (e.g., gas, electric, water, and steam) under the new telecommunications bill, may engage in telecommunications and information services. Protections against cross subsidy are put in place, and jurisdictional issues and conflicting law affecting the FCC, Federal Energy Regulatory Commission, Securities and Exchange Commission, and the states are addressed. These issues are similar to those discussed for communication companies that could come to have a mix of regulated and unregulated services.

CROSS OWNERSHIP BY BROADCASTERS

The new bill permits ownership of a broadcast television *station* and a cable system in the same television market. The FCC is required to make rules necessary to ensure carriage, channel positioning, and nondiscriminatory treatment of the competing broadcast stations in the market. Station license terms are to be extended to eight years.

Impediments to broadcast *network* and cable system cross owner-ship are removed by the reform bill. Again, provisions are to be made to prohibit discrimination against other network affiliates in the cross-owned market.

The bill eliminates any ownership limits on radio stations and limits on the number of owned television stations. A limit on the aggregate reach of television stations under single ownership is set at 35% of the U.S. television households. Mergers and acquisitions of broadcast networks are restricted if one of the parties is a member of the big four networks: ABC, CBS, FOX, or NBC.

CABLE-MMDS CROSS OWNERSHIP

The restriction on cable cross ownership with MMDS is lifted by the new bill if there are two or more unaffiliated wireline video services in the area.

Regulating Competition

Structuring the communications industry to remove barriers to competition is not sufficient. It is necessary to take steps to make the competitive structure *workable*—a significant burden under the telecommunications reform legislation. Those businesses that might wish to enter a market must have a fair opportunity. This condition is popularly referred to as a "level playing field." If players do not secretly desire a playing field that is tilted in their favor, they certainly have a biased concept of "level." Whatever the case, it is incumbent on each of the communication industries to fight aggressively for favorable policy and in the end do no worse than achieve a competitively neutral policy. Lamenting the conflicting self-interests of the parties, an FCC chief economist, Michael Katz, notes:

> TV broadcasters say, " We want free markets, but we don't believe that the government should use markets to sell us spectrum." TV broadcasters have their own definition of a free market—"Give it to us free and we'll market it." Radio broadcasters say they favor free markets, but they ask the commission to block competition from entrepreneurs who want to use satellites to deliver radio services. The local telephone companies say, "Get out of our way and let us into the video-dial-tone

business." Then you say to them, "How about letting the electrical utilities into telecommunications?" They say, "Don't let them in!" The cable companies say, "Don't let either of them in; they'll use their captive-monopoly rate bases to compete unfairly." Yet they want no pricing regulation for themselves. The long-distance telephone companies say we should let them into the local telephone business, but they don't want the local companies in the long-distance business. So all industries say, "Get out of our way—but regulate our rivals."[13]

Between 1984 and 1993, communication companies made the following political action committee (PAC) contributions to Congress: local telephone, $13.5 million; long-distance telephone, $7.5 million; cable, $4.4 million; entertainment, $2.8 million; computer, $2.8 million; satellite, $2.5 million; broadcasting, $1.6 million; newspaper/ electronic publishing, $0.9 million. The figures are considerably higher if soft money contributed by industry executives is included. John Dingell and Ernest Hollings, recent chairmen of the House and Senate Commerce Committees each received $336,640 and $329,411 respectively in PAC money from the listed industries, 1984-1993.[14] This does not include the millions budgeted for lobbyists by the respective industries. The telephone industry is notorious for its armies of lobbyists in Washington and state capitals.

If one element of the converging industries should actually obtain a steeply favorable tilt, it could doom the others. Legislation, regulation, and the courts must mediate among all interests, always in a present context of shifting technology, business conditions, and consumer appetites, compounded by the political realities of imbalances in the relative power of the players. In a circumstance where several industries are converging, one or the other may gain a temporary or long-term advantage. *Ideally, public policy would prevent these outcomes without micromanaging competition.*

A word should be said about the issues that concern the business relationships of competitors. From the public policy perspective, these are consumer issues. While policy protects one business from another and seeks to provide an environment that encourages business entry for efficient and innovative companies, these are only intermediate objectives. The ultimate goal of effective competition policy is consumer welfare. We should bear in mind, however, that the policies developed to govern competition are a series of compromises worked out among the key businesses with government as a mediator. The compromises may not necessarily reflect consumer interests. This said, we turn to the measures designed to make integrated broadband networks competitive.

COMPETITION AMONG TELECOMMUNICATIONS CARRIERS

To ensure competition, *interconnection* is essential between the end users of one common carrier and the end users of another, at a reasonable cost and without unreasonable conditions or restrictions. To facilitate interconnection, the new legislation would require access to unbundled network functions and a carrier's telecommunications network, which includes the switching software. The price and quality of interconnection must be equal to what the carrier would provide to itself. To do so, utilities are required to allow access to poles, ducts, and conduits they control.

The new bill also mandates *telephone number portability* so that users can retain existing numbers across telecommunications carriers and have *dialing parity* from one carrier to another using the same number of digits. Users must have prompt access to directory listings and directory assistance. The law requires integration of carriers' switches and fair reciprocal compensation arrangements for the origination and termination of telecommunications. Arrangements for interconnection must be made within a fixed time period so that one party cannot unduly delay interconnection.

TELEPHONE RATE REGULATION

Although much of the regulatory oversight of local telephone exchange carriers (LECs) occurs at the state level, the FCC does preempt state commission action in a number of areas, including some types of rate regulation as well as rules regarding the conditions under which LECs make their networks available to other service providers. Because LECs do serve as the entry and exit points for most interstate calls, fees charged to long-distance carriers for traffic coming from or going to an out-of-state location are regulated.

Beginning in 1991, LEC prices under FCC jurisdiction were regulated using a *price cap* formula.[15] Under price caps, a ceiling is placed on prices of various *baskets* of services, where a basket represents a set of similar services. Each year, the prices are allowed to fluctuate with the rate of inflation, minus some sort of productivity factor. This type of regulation is generally thought of as *incentive based*, since it encourages carriers to be more productive. That is, carriers that are more productive can earn more profits, since the gap between costs and earning will be greater. Under the old regime, *rate of return* regulation, telephone companies enumerated all costs of doing business and were permitted to adjust their prices so as to earn a certain (e.g., 12%) return on investment in a given year. Excess profits had to be refunded back to subscribers, so there was no incentive to be more productive and to lower costs. Each method may have its strengths and weaknesses. For example, although there are few incentives to be more efficient with a rate of return method, it theoretically does encourage more investment in infrastructure, improving reliability and quality. On the other hand, price caps may encourage more efficiency but may also result in lower infrastructure investment and lower quality.

Of crucial interest for the growth of integrated broadband networks are the conditions under which other companies may access LEC services and interconnect with LEC networks. These issues have also been addressed at the federal level, mainly by the FCC. In terms of access to LEC services, mainly stemming from ONA deliberations (see Chapter 3), the basic philosophy is that LECs will have to *unbundle* and separately price their services, so that other carriers are able to buy only what they need at competitive prices. For example, suppose a cable company wanted to use its own distribution network for the telephone access lines but use the LEC switch to route calls to a long-distance carrier. It should be able to buy this service and not have to pay *retail* rates for each call. Other types of services that should be unbundled include billing and SS7 switching.

In addition to the rates charged for use of LEC facilities, the physical interconnection to LEC networks has also received attention. Companies licensed to offer competitive access services (e.g., CAPs, see Chapter 3) now have the right to *collocate* their equipment on the LEC exchange office premises, lowering the cost and improving the quality of interconnection.

Consumer rates for telephone service will be monitored under policies set by a federal-state joint board to ensure "just, reasonable, and affordable rates" (see Universal Service below).

CABLE RATE REGULATION

Rates for services on cable are regulated by the FCC, the state, and the franchising authority. Rates for "noncable services" provided by a cable operator (e.g., voice and data) may be regulated by state utility commissions. Monthly fees for the basic cable tier, which includes broadcast stations, are regulated by the franchising authority under FCC guidelines. The franchise authority also regulates the rates for lease of household equipment, such as remote tuners and converters. The 1996 telecommunications law allows cable operators to average the cost of equipment in its pricing. Therefore, a system could offer powerful digital converters and average that high cost in with the lower cost existing converters, raising their price slightly, to make the introduction of the new converters more palatable to consumers.

The rates for the broadcast tier and the expanded basic tier with the satellite services were capped by the FCC in 1994 using benchmarks varying from system to system according to size, total number of channels, number of satellite channels, population density, and average household income. The rates are permitted to be increased annually by a modest percentage to reflect inflation. Only these tiers are rate regulated. There is no rate regulation of à la carte services. If a cable system experiences effective competition, as defined in Chapter 10, rate regulation is discontinued. The benchmark rate regulation plan permitted only negligible rate increases for new channels. The rules were modified in late 1994 for the express purpose of "going forward" with additional channels in the lower tiers at a maximum additional price to subscribers.[16]

In accordance with the new telecommunications bill, cable companies will continue to have the upper-tier basic rates (e.g., the satellite tier, likely to contain cable networks such as MTV, ESPN, USA, TNT) regulated only until March 31, 1999—unless, of course, they faced effective competition at an earlier date. The effective competition standards are expanded by the new bill to include any level of video competition

competition by a phone company or by MMDS or LMDS—any type of video service, that is, except direct-to-home satellite, which is already available in every cable service area. As noted earlier, the cable operator would also escape rate regulation if it were to become an open video service.

Absent "effective competition," the broadcast basic tier of a cable system would remain regulated beyond 1999. An individual subscriber could no longer initiate a rate review of the upper tier by the FCC. Only the local franchising authority, a city official, or a state regulator could initiate a review based on a complaint.

Small cable companies, under 50,000 subscribers and not owned by a company with gross annual revenues exceeding $250 million, are rate deregulated for the upper tier under the reform bill. The bill would allow consumers the option of buying the set-top boxes in retail stores. The operator could continue to lease the boxes to customers but could not subsidize the cost with subscription fees.

COMPETITION AS A MEANS OF PRICE REGULATION

If it existed in a pure form, competition between integrated broadband networks would regulate prices. In the absence of ideal competition, we have price regulation in both local telephone service and cable service. Brenner suggests that in choosing between the marketplace and regulation, "The question is whether imperfect market forces or imperfect regulation perform better."[17] As discussed in Chapter 10, there will be a modicum of price competition between integrated broadband networks, particularly through differences in packaging. If universal service comes to mean access to integrated broadband networks at reasonable rates, then at least the entry-level services of plain old telephone and the basic broadcast tier of video could be rate regulated even in competitive circumstances.

CROSS SUBSIDY

The issue of cross subsidization is discussed in Chapter 10. Two principal means of safeguarding against cross subsidy of new services with regulated telephone services are (1) accounting separation and (2) structural separation. The 1996 telecommunications reform bill requires a structural separation but also mandates accounting practices for the Bell operating companies that would clearly identify all transactions between the separate affiliate and the parent. The transactions would have to be priced at the same level as to a nonaffiliate. The subsidiaries would keep separate accounts and have separate officers, directors, and employees from the parent. The parent could not back any loans of the subsidiary.

Either plan is an awkward arrangement for fully integrated broadband networks. Separate accounting for so many different products using joint facilities and shared employees could be difficult. In the past, attempting to assess costs for rate-making purposes has had limited success, but at least in the new competitive environment, the government can rely on competitors to alert authorities of suspected cross subsidization. A competitor will also be able to provide a reality check on costs, whereas in the past there was only a single company experiencing the costs.

ADVANCED TELEVISION

Under the reform legislation, broadcasters are allowed to offer ancillary and supplementary (flexible) services, if they indeed provide the advanced television program service. Public interest obligations apply to the new licenses, meaning that the broadcasters on the new frequencies have to continue to operate in a fiduciary relationship to the public. The FCC is to assess fees for the portion of the additional spectrum that is used for the ancillary and supplementary services, thus recovering some or all of the funds that might have been collected in an auction of the spectrum. The original broadcast spectrum assignments might have to be given up at the point when consumers had replaced almost all National Television System Commitee (NTSC) standard television receivers. These provisions may be revisited by Congress as promised by Senator Dole.

OLIGOPOLY/DUOPOLY

The government interest in maintaining competition might serve as a powerful deterrent to flat-out aggressive business behavior that could drive one's competitors out of business. Such behavior would probably invite government policy to change the playing field. If two or more companies remain in a lethargic, inefficient rivalry, however, new public policy may be needed to regulate the oligopoly—a very difficult prospect because of the likely absence of direct evidence of a conspiracy and unique local conditions that would make comparison to other systems difficult. It is also possible that an oligopoly, where each company associated with a huge corporation, would form an industry-political alliance that attempts to keep other technologies from threatening any part of the business—for example, wireless communication services.

In the worst-case duopoly-oligopoly circumstances, competition policy has not gained much. Perhaps the best hope for competition policy in this case is that the integrated services business is dynamic enough for two competitors to keep finding new markets and new ways to reach the next plateau. In the interim, until competing broadband networks are fully established, competition will be preserved in a duopoly by each party's fighting intensely to replace revenues lost from its previous monopoly—cable companies fighting for the video business, telephone companies fighting for the telephone business.

VERTICAL INTEGRATION

Another important policy area for a functionally competitive industry is keeping the integrated networks open to suppliers. The society might better tolerate oligopoly in wired networks if the networks are not a bottleneck. Theoretically, the high capacity of fiber broadband networks would maximize the available services and content. But as we have pointed out earlier, the capacity will not be unlimited, and there could be a higher return on selective promotion of one's own programming.

One method of keeping the networks open to all information providers is to limit vertical integration. The assumption is that the vertically integrated company will favor its owned sources and discriminate against other sources or that a system will seek equity in return for carriage. Congress sought to prevent this in the 1992 Cable Act:

It shall be unlawful for a cable operator, a satellite cable programming vendor in which a cable operator has an attributable interest, or a satellite broadcast programming vendor to engage in unfair methods of competition or unfair or deceptive acts or practices, the purpose or effect of which is to hinder significantly or to prevent any multichannel video programming distributor from providing satellite cable programming or satellite broadcast programming to subscribers or consumers.[18]

The 1992 Cable Act itself, and the FCC regulations implementing the act, limits ownership to 40% of the channels (in the first 75 channels, unlimited thereafter) and requires economic justification for any price discrimination favoring the vertically integrated systems and programmers.

It has been argued over the years that vertical integration in programming and distribution actually encourages diversity. Desperate to have programming to attract urban subscribers, the larger cable multiple system operators (MSOs) invested in programmers such as the Discovery Channel, Turner Broadcasting (CNN, CNN Headline, TNT, WTBS, Cartoon, a sports channel, Turner Classic Movies), USA, MTV, Nickelodeon, and many others. Telephone companies are also developing programming in the alliances with Disney, Creative Artists Agency, and others.[19]

PROGRAM ACCESS

Vertically integrated cable companies, with programming and distribution system holdings, are prevented by the 1992 Cable Act from keeping their programming exclusive. The telecommunications reform bill expanded "cable companies" to include common carriers providing video programming. Banning exclusive contracts, in these circumstances, is procompetitive in the sense that it provides *program access* to other video providers—cable overbuilders, direct broadcast satellite (DBS), MMDS, LMDS, satellite master antenna television (SMATV). The ban may be waived if the FCC determines a waiver to be in the public interest. The FCC has already ruled on several program exclusivity cases. In one case, the Court TV channel had been denied to a New York City wireless system because of an exclusive contract with

Time Warner cable, an owner of Court TV. The commission determined that the exclusive arrangement was not in the public interest. In another case, New England Cable News, a 24-hour regional news channel was permitted to make exclusive contracts to foster financial investment in the new service.[20] The point here is that the FCC may allow some exclusive programming agreements to stimulate new networks. If a new programmer can get carriage only by offering exclusive access, diversity would be served if it were allowed.

At this point, only vertically integrated cable companies are precluded from exclusive programming contracts. Broadcast networks and syndicators have exclusive contracts, and it is possible for DBS to make exclusive contracts.

Where there are two integrated broadband networks competing in the same community the prohibition of program exclusivity might be dysfunctional. Program exclusivity would be useful in differentiating services. Assuming that consumers could have low-cost access to both services and there were vigorous competition to sell on-demand programming, the resulting program innovation could benefit consumers.

HORIZONTAL CONCENTRATION

Another major means of keeping networks open to a diversity of programming is to limit horizontal concentration. If concentration were unlimited and an operator controlled a large percentage of subscribers, then a refusal of that operator to carry the programming service could be fatal. The limit for cable operators is now 30% of subscribers nationally. Therefore, even if a programmer is denied the entire subscriber base of an owner with this level of concentration, 70% of the market remains. Johnson believes the limit should be lowered to 20% because *niche channels* might need carriage by almost *all* systems be able to aggregate enough subscribers to survive.[21]

Horizontal concentration limits would likely be applied to telephone companies becoming integrated broadband networks. Any one of the RBOCs could acquire 20% or 30% of the national subscribers through within-region or out-of-region systems.

Horizontal concentration limits, if low enough, protect the programmer in the context of the national market, *but not the consumer within the concentration,* where there is only one full service network available. The consumer living within the concentration has nowhere to go if there is just one wire. Wireless services might be an option for some programming but probably not for interactive television.

The telecommunications reform bill makes special provisions for small businesses developing telecommunications applications through low-interest loans and financial guarantees. The fund will come from deposit monies in spectrum auctions.

WIRELESS COMPETITION

Another set of policies is necessary to keep integrated broadband networks honest and other communication technologies viable. If other distribution methods are available to provide the same or similar services, the full service broadband networks will be challenged to continue innovation and keep prices reasonable. These policies could include flexible use of broadcast spectrum and licensing of new spectrum applications, such as local multipoint distribution service and personal communication service. Wireless competition should reduce the market power of the wired networks.

Of course, the *must carry* rule assures broadcasting a place in the wired world. Network affiliates, at least for now, are vital to wired video service and a competitive advantage against direct-to-home services that cannot carry the broadcast network programming.

In the new telecommunications bill, the FCC preempts all authority over direct-to-home satellites. Local authorities cannot tax the satellite services although they might tax equipment. Cities cannot write zoning ordinances or otherwise inhibit a household's ability to receive video from direct-to-home satellites, MMDS, or broadcast stations.

LEASED ACCESS

A safety valve to ensure the availability of a diversity of information to a community is to mandate access to integrated broadband systems by outside providers—to have channels or space reserved so that any programmer may pay for access. Certain channels are treated as common carriers. Federal law requires a cable system to reserve a portion of the active channels so that any business, individual, or institution could buy time or lease a channel. These are called leased access or commercial use channels. The Cable Act of 1992 gave the FCC authority to monitor the lease rates. Open video systems, an alternative to a franchised cable system under the new telecommunications reform act, also allow outside providers access to the system on a nondiscriminatory basis. However, very few programmers have attempted to lease cable channels. Furthermore, the telephone companies had difficulty in finding programmers interested in the planned video dialtone services. This experience suggests that these requirements of the law may not function as intended.

Public, education, and government access channels also add diversity to programming. Some cable franchises require such channels. In the new telecommunications bill, a similar set-aside is required of telephone company-based video services.

REGULATORY SYMMETRY/PARITY

Even in a competitive environment, universal service and the preservation of workable competition require regulation, generating a debate about how to integrate the legislation so that there is a *regulatory symmetry* or *parity* across all participating industries. Or indeed, since each industry is starting from a different point under different conditions, there is a question whether symmetry is desirable or necessary. Symmetry suggests the often-invoked level playing field but only when the players have equal opportunities to begin with. Furthermore, there are long-established regulatory precedents, different for each industry, that would be difficult to retract. Symmetry might demand radical surgery—a complete deregulation of all of the relevant industries. Another concern is that the potential competitors are of unequal strength. Some think that if there is to be competition, particular parties need to be nurtured by favorable policy until they are competent to stand alone. Finally, certain functions of a full service network could be regulated while other functions are not regulated. The latter is relatively novel in utility regulation and not well understood.

One way of dealing with the regularity dissimilarities among the converging industries is to try to counterbalance requirements. Since this is an attempt to offset apples against oranges, it is bound to be called unfair by one or more parties. It may be politically necessary, however. A case in point is the issue of franchise fees. Cities will not willingly give up the 5% of cable gross revenues that most are now receiving. Newcomers will be reluctant to pay franchise fees. The open video system option of the telecommunications reform bill does not require providers to pay a franchise fee, but communities may assess a fee for use of rights-of-way not to exceed the cable fee. However assessed, the fees could fall below the cable fees. Should, or could, they be made exactly equivalent? Do state fees and universal service obligations of telephone companies offering video as common carriers or open video systems balance franchise fees and PEG access channel requirements of cable systems? It may depend on the circumstances. Does government scrutinize these services on a case-by-case basis to achieve a better balance, or does it try to achieve a minimal regulatory scheme that applies equally to all providers?

UNIVERSAL SERVICE

Universal service becomes an issue in competition because regulatory parity requires competitors to be equal or nearly equal in their obligations to provide universal service. In areas where scale and scope do not justify competition as established in advance by law or where circumstances prove competition not to be feasible, universal service would be required of the monopoly provider. A goal of telecommunications reform is to ensure that all Americans, including those in rural and high-cost areas, have advanced telecommunication and information services. Services in rural areas should be "reasonably comparable" to those in urban areas. Advanced telecommunications services should be available to elementary and secondary schools and classrooms, health care providers, and libraries.

Public policy will attempt to prevent "cream skimming"—coming into a market and taking only the biggest and best potential customers. If one company has a universal service obligation and another takes only the better parts of the market, the first company is disadvantaged and may not be able to compete in price and service. Prices inflated to accommodate universal service are easy targets for competitors.

To develop a system ensuring (1) universal service in remaining monopoly situations and (2) preventing competition from subverting universal service when competition occurs, a coordinated federal-state joint board would be convened by the FCC under order of the telecommunications reform statute. Every interstate telecommunications carrier would be called on to contribute to universal service through mechanisms that are specific and predictable. In actuality, the contributions would be providing the service or, if not, paid into a fund that offsets the cost of the provider. In some cases, it may be necessary for the government to designate a provider from among those supplying services in an area—choosing one from a number of applicants or identifying one when no provider comes forward.

Universal service would also mean no *redlining*—that is, discriminating against any subscriber or class of subscribers (e.g., excluding low-income neighborhoods or having unfairly discriminatory credit policies). Individual franchise provisions often attempt to prevent redlining. It is usually required that rates for services be the same to all consumers. The telecommunication reform bill permits cable systems to offer bulk rates to residents of multiple-dwelling units, netting lower charges to individual households.

ON-PREMISES EQUIPMENT

Traditionally in the cable industry, the operator owns the remote tuner and the converter. After the Carterphone decision, telephone companies could no longer be the sole source of customer premises equipment.[22] For integrated broadband networks, which tradition is to be followed? The new bill instructs the FCC to study what standardization is appropriate to prevent consumers from being forced to buy or lease proprietary equipment, such as set-top boxes or converters, that will not interface with other equipment or networks.

Questions about property ownership rights and service access arise for multiple-dwelling units. Will all providers of communications services have access to the buildings, and in turn, will the residents have access to competing services? The telephone company has access to the buildings as a public utility. In some states, access by cable operators is mandatory—that is, the apartment building cannot deny the cable operator access. In other states, there is no access law. Multiple-dwelling units can exclude cable and offer their own SMATV service if they wish. Where traditional telephone and cable are integrated in broadband networks, is the apartment owner obligated to admit every provider in the interest of furthering competition or to supply building wiring capable of accommodating all services?

POLE ATTACHMENT

One competitive issue as old as telephone and CATV is pole access rights. Utility poles and conduit are usually owned by an electric company or telephone company. In the earliest days of CATV, some telephone companies—foreseeing the circumstances they face today—discriminated against cable companies and their subscribers in fees for pole (conduit) rights and make ready (preparing the facility for another user). Now, so that the pole owner does not discriminate against cable operators or cable subscribers, pole attachment fees are regulated either by the states or, if not by the states, by the FCC.[23] The law, however, only regulates the fees, it does not mandate access. The telecommunications reform bill and FCC rulings in its support will attempt to make access available. But even with the mandated cooperation of the pole owner, required clearances limit the number of wires on a pole, and aesthetics limits the height of a pole.

ANTITRUST

Legislative and regulatory guidelines for competition are complemented by enforcement of existing antitrust law. The first legislation in the United States was the Sherman Antitrust Act of 1890, which has two key provisions. The first:

> Every contract, combination in the form of trust or otherwise, or conspiracy, in restraint of trade or commerce among the several States, or with foreign nations, is hereby declared to be illegal.

The provision is concerned with restrictive actions by two or more parties. The second provision relates to market power by an individual business:

> Every person who shall monopolize, or attempt to monopolize, or combine or conspire with any other person or persons, to monopolize any part of trade or commerce among the States, or with foreign nations, shall be guilty of a felony.

The goal is to eliminate *restraint of trade* from manipulating industry structure, as is the concern in the first provision, or aggregation of market power, at issue in the second. Behavior in restraint of trade became a crime punishable by fine or imprisonment.

The Clayton Act of 1914 attempted to provide guidance beyond the "rule of reason" used to adjudicate behavior under the Sherman Act, specifically restricting price discrimination, tying and exclusive dealing, acquisitions of competing companies, and interlocking directorates. The communications industries, as common carriers, regulated licensees, or franchisees, were exempted from much of the antitrust law. The natural monopoly status of long-distance telephone carriers was ended in *U.S. v. American Telephone and Telegraph Company*[24] in 1982. Exclusive cable franchises became questionable in *Preferred v. Los Angeles*[25] in 1985 and were essentially ended by statute in the Cable Act of 1992. Exclusive program contracts between vertically integrated programmers and multichannel television systems were also prevented. As cable and telephone companies enter each other's traditional business lines, antitrust law and principles will play a major role in governing conduct, because it is impossible to prescribe by legislation and rules, in advance of experience with competition, a complete set of competition safeguards. The Chief of the Antitrust Division of the Department of Justice, Ann Bingaman, believes her role is to ensure that the "opportunity for greater local telecommunications competition" is not lost to private restraints, existing market power, or unnecessary government restrictions.[26]

Because of the subtlety of antitrust violations and political differences in enforcement philosophy, the antitrust remedy to competition problems is distrusted. Some federal administrations are thought to be lax in enforcement and others more rigorous. A further problem is the relative strength of parties in antitrust litigation. The larger companies that are most likely to be defending against antitrust charges have the resources to exhaust the government and smaller business plaintiffs in litigation. Actions initiated by the government have to involve egregious problems.

REVIEW AND FORBEARANCE

The telecommunications reform bill introduces a periodic *review*, in odd-numbered years, by the FCC of all its regulations applying to telecommunications services, to determine if competition had rendered them unnecessary. The bill also gives the FCC discretion to *forbear* application of any of its provisions if the commission determines enforcement is not necessary to keep competition fair or to protect consumers and the public interest. The forbearance could apply to any class of telecommunications carriers or services or to specific geographic markets.

Other Public Policy Issues

While the most hotly contested public policies are associated with competition, a number of other areas not directly associated with competition are very important to integrated broadband communication services. These include copyright, piracy, some of the First Amendment issues, and privacy.

COPYRIGHT

The general purpose of copyright law is to maximize the availability of creative works to the public. To do so, the Copyright Act grants monopoly property rights in the production and publication of literary, musical, artistic, and dramatic works so that the copyright owner gets a fair return for the effort. But the law also recognizes the roles of media, technology, capital investment, cost, and risk in opening markets for creative expression. The Copyright Act attempts to balance the interests of the public, the creator (owner), and the disseminator of copyrighted materials.

Integrated broadband systems enhance opportunities for all of these parties if the balance is maintained. Precedent indicates that competition in the form of exclusive dissemination of copyrighted materials will be permitted only if it can be demonstrated that it actually widens public access to the content—for example, in a situation where the content might not have a market at all unless it is protected by exclusivity.

Cable systems must pay copyright royalties for carriage of *distant, non-network broadcast stations*. Only distant signals are covered because the copyright owner has already been compensated for local audiences in the broadcast license fee. Only non-network programs are covered because the network broadcasters pay for rights to national audiences. Fees for the distant, non-network signal usage are collected by the Copyright Office and distributed to the copyright owners. The cable operators hold a *compulsory license* that permits them to pay the blanket fee. The compulsory license has been extended to wireless cable and MMDS; the license also applies to SMATV because it meets the definition of a cable service. The license is functional because (1) it compensates copyright owners and (2) at the same time relieves the video distributor from negotiating individually with distant stations or the owners of copyrighted programs carried by the stations, a process generally considered to be too cumbersome. On the other hand, copyright owners generally favor negotiated fees that would represent a "fair market value" of the work as opposed to the arbitrary valuations of the Copyright Office.

Copy protection technology (e.g., Copy Guard which prevents video copies) may reassure providers of intellectual property to full service networks, but professional hackers sell equipment capable of defeating it.

Copyright issues also come up in the use of copyrighted materials to make television programs and create databases—for example, use of pictures, video clips, electronic data and text, recorded music, and voices. In the media world before integrated networks, few providers were familiar with the law and relatively few outlets made detection of violations reasonable. PEG access channels and online services, with novice users, sometimes violate copyrights. With a great many more providers on digital broadband networks, having substantially more outlets through the various menus and programming options, detection and enforcement of violations is much more difficult.

SIGNAL THEFT

The consumer cost of any information and programming on integrated broadband networks will be higher if there is substantial theft. The difficulty in protecting content is cost: the better the protection, the greater the cost. The Cable Act of 1984 makes it a federal crime to steal scrambled and unscrambled cable signals. Unauthorized reception of satellite signals, even those not scrambled, for other than private viewing, is a violation. Most federal enforcement, usually as a result of investigation by the FBI, is aimed at eliminating the manufacture and sale of devices designed for theft of signals. The violator may be fined and jailed. Violations by individuals are generally prosecuted at the state level under similar state laws. In most cases when an individual is detected stealing signals from coaxial cable, the operator attempts to sell the service to the illegal user. This failing, the service is terminated without prosecution.

Signal piracy from a full service network would raise the same issues. It took some time to create a general public recognition that there could be proprietary rights in video material transmitted via wire or directly from satellites to television receivers. That threshold has now been crossed, but it will probably be necessary to do so again as more widespread text and audio services are available independently and integrated with video through the full service networks.

FIRST AMENDMENT SPEAKERS

The First Amendment (Congress shall make no law . . . abridging the freedom of speech, or of the press.") applies to cable. Cole summarizes the litigation:

The Supreme Court has laid down an unambiguous, well-lit path of precedent leading to the conclusion that cable television operators, when performing "communicative" functions, engage in "speech" and constitute a "part of the press" entitled to that constitutional protection traditionally afforded publishers, editors, and distributors operating in the other media of communication.[27]

The First Amendment has been invoked in several ways by both telephone and cable industries to advance business interests. Telephone companies have used the First Amendment as a means of shedding cross-ownership restrictions. The cable industry has used the First Amendment against "must carry" rules to free up choices when there were more programmers than channel shelf space.

In deciding these and other cases in which a regulation intended to advance a public interest is seen to conflict with First Amendment rights, the courts have asserted that the law is constitutional if it is "*content neutral*" and imposes only an "*incidental burden*" on speech.[28] *U.S. v. O'Brien* has determined content neutral to mean regulation that (1) "furthers an important governmental interest," (2) where that "interest is unrelated to the suppression of free expression," and (3) "the incidental restriction on the alleged First Amendment freedoms is no greater than is essential to furtherance of that interest."[29] It is not necessary that the regulation be the "least speech-restrictive," only that it be "narrowly tailored" not to "burden substantially more speech than is necessary to further the government's legitimate interests."[30]

One may wonder whether telephone or cable companies, given rights as First Amendment speakers, will be careful guardians of the First Amendment. The concern is clearly illustrated in the case of audiotex services offered by telephone companies. Local telephone companies, faced with increasing criticism from the public over adult-oriented "976" services, eventually engaged in a form of "self-regulation" (actually a form of censorship). Initially, and with prompting from regulators, they first offered various methods of blocking access to all 976 services. However, soon both local and long-distance companies stopped providing the billing and collection services so necessary for the profitability of these services, if an information service provider was deemed inappropriate.[31]

"TAXATION" AND THE FIRST AMENDMENT

Other principles derived from the First Amendment are important to the development of integrated broadband networks. Governments cannot impose a tax that singles out media as opposed to all businesses or one medium over another.[32] In general, this area of law may be used to assert nondiscriminatory treatment of media (e.g., full service network vs. a telephone company or cable company, or full service network vs. wireless systems). The concept may also be raised in contemplating payments such as franchise fees or fees to be pooled for universal service. If the fees are placed into general funds and not used to cover the cost of regulation or universal service or if the fees are more than a fair value for the use of rights of way, they could be considered a discriminatory tax. The new telecommunications bill takes some steps to prevent differential taxation or fee structures.

OBSCENITY

Obscenity is not protected under the First Amendment. A full service network would be responsible, under criminal penalty, for including obscene material. The responsibility would apply to the operator, as well as to the owner, in cases in which the operator is only licensing the material. To protect speakers, obscenity is very narrowly defined. The "Miller test" prescribes the grounds:

> (1) the average person applying contemporary community standards would find the work, taken as a whole, appeals to the prurient interest, (2) the work depicts or describes, in a patently offensive way sexual conduct specifically defined by the applicable state law, and (3) the work, taken as a whole, lacks serious literary, artistic, political or scientific value.[33]

It is important to note that *contemporary community standards* are to be applied, meaning that what is obscene in one community may not be in another. The sexual conduct that is not permitted must be specifically defined by state law. In the telecommunications reform bill, the fine for transmitting obscene language by broadcast or cable is raised from $10,000 to $100,000.

INDECENCY

Broadcasting has had to meet a special standard for programming content. The U.S. Criminal Code prohibits "obscene, indecent, or profane language by means of radio communication"[34] adding "indecent" and "profane" specifically for broadcasting. In *FCC v. the Pacifica Foundation*, the Supreme Court upheld the FCC position that *indecent* language, even if not obscene, may be regulated because broadcasting is "uniquely accessible to children."[35] However, attempts to apply the indecency statute to subscription television have failed. A Miami city ordinance and a state of Utah statute with this purpose have been found in violation of the First Amendment. The courts reasoned that the responsibility is on the viewers and their guardians, not on the cable operator, since cable households must affirmatively subscribe and must make regular additional monthly payments for service.[36] Now, under the 1984 Cable Act, subscribers may choose to lease or purchase lock boxes. The lock box, or a personal identification number (PIN) for ordering, is a "less restrictive alternative" than banning indecent speech.[37] The U.S. Court of Appeals has recently rejected a provision of the 1992 Cable Act that would have required cable operators to censor "indecent" content on PEG and leased access channels.[38] But the telecommunications reform bill allows the cable operator to refuse to transmit public access or leased access programs that contain obscenity, indecency, or nudity.

BLOCKING

The new bill also reinforces previous legislation that allows a cable *customer* to request that the operator "fully scramble or otherwise fully block the audio and video portion" of any channel to which the customer does not subscribe, at no charge. This would not apply to a channel within a package of channels since the customer is subscribing to the *package*. The bill requires the *operator*, whether or not a subscriber makes a request, to fully scramble adult sexually oriented programming.

The telecommunication reform law requires television set manufacturers in the future to install a "V-chip" so that people, if they desire, can electronically block programming from cable or broad-cast channels precoded as having violent, sexual, or indecent content.

LIMITS ON THE FRANCHISING AUTHORITY

One further issue involving the integrated network as a First Amendment speaker is important to discuss at this point. Federal law places limitations on franchising authority involvement in pro-gramming. The franchising authority may not specify, in the request for proposal (RFP) for a new franchise or a renewal, a *program service* or even *broad categories of video programming* or other information services. For example, in the RFP, the city could not ask the system to put the ESPN network, a program service, in the channel lineup or even ask for sports programming, a broad category of program-ming. However, if the cable operator *offered* sports programming, the city could then write the provision of sports programming into the franchise agreement. The cable operator could not offer a specific program service (e.g., ESPN). This reserves programming selection to the operator, preventing government officials from making those choices and putting programming into a political arena. Addressing the problems concerning private businesses exercising their biases in programming choices, at the expense of maximizing citizen access to particular information, is the burden of open access policies and statutes that create common carrier or leased access facilities.

FIRST AMENDMENT ISSUES IN DATA SERVICES

Online database services have had some difficulty determining who has First Amendment rights in electronic messages: the online operator as publisher or the user as publisher. Fixing responsibility is important in determining who is liable for obscenity and libel and in establishing individual freedoms in electronic discussions. Are online service operators accountable when user content is libelous or obscene, reproduces copyrighted material without authorization, or is otherwise criminal (e.g., using the service to plan a crime, making transactions with stolen credit cards, stealing electronic funds)? This raises the question of the extent to which users have a right to privacy in their electronic communications or if system operators have a right or requirement to examine and censor content under their responsibilities as "rebroadcasters." Prodigy has taken responsibility for the content of mail and discussion communications, censoring some users and discontinuing their service. Other online services have given complete freedom to users. The issue went to court in a case involving CompuServe and Don Fitzpatrick Associates, publishers of an electronic newspaper called *Rumorville*. CompuServe claimed that the contract gave total responsibility for the contents to Fitzpatrick. The court found for CompuServe: "A computerized database is the functional equivalent of a more traditional news vendor, and the inconsistent application of a lower standard of liability to an electronic news distributor such as CompuServe than that which is applied to a public library, book store, or newsstand would impose an undue burden on the free flow of information."[39]

While it may be possible for a commercial online service to regulate its content or discipline its members, it would be nearly impossible to exercise such control over the Internet. Now, the new telecommunications bill states that no provider or user of an interactive computer service is to be treated as the publisher or speaker of information provided by another information content source. But the bill protects a provider or user in taking "Good Samaritan" action—that is, efforts taken in "good faith to restrict access to or availability of material that the provider or user considers to be obscene, lewd, lascivious, filthy, excessively violent, harassing, or otherwise objectionable, whether or not such material is constitutionally protected." Making available the technical means to restrict access is also protected. Therefore, according to this bill, although the provider or user is not liable for the content of Internet or other online interactive computer services, if the provider or user voluntarily elects to restrict access, that restriction is within the rights of the provider or user.

The telecommunications reform bill prohibits using any "facility or means of interstate or foreign commerce" that knowingly "persuades, induces, entices, or coerces" a minor into prostitution or any criminal sexual act. It is a violation of provisions in the new bill to present *indecent* material in online display without taking precautions to protects minors from access.

ACCESS TO GOVERNMENT INFORMATION

Integrated broadband networks will most certainly attempt to offer information gathered and stored by local, state, and federal government agencies. Much of the information will be from material identified as a "public record." This does not necessarily mean that records must be offered in machine-readable form.[40] A U.S. District Court has declared that federal government agencies may deliver information in forms they consider "most convenient," which might be computer printouts. [41]

Government agencies with a primary objective of informing the public use the Government Printing Office as the major means of doing so, along with news releases sent to media. According to Branscomb, the government maintains over four hundred computerized databases, many of which are purchased by commercial organizations who buy the databases and market the information to subscribers. Their lobbying group, the Information Industry Association, is opposed to direct online access to government-held data, even though it is collected at taxpayer expense, because it would be a government encroachment on a private industry. At one point, the federal government proposed to prohibit government services from supplying online access to information. PC users defeated the proposal, but the issue remains.[42] Does the government assume the cost of making the databases available directly to consumers, a process facilitated greatly by integrated broadband networks, or wholesale it to private companies who sell it to consumers? Branscomb concludes that "the bottom line is the question of how much the public, as voters, is willing to allocate in taxes to public dissemination of information and how much it is willing to pay as purchasers of information in the information marketplace."[43] These issues may be important to integrated broadband networks as they become a major part of that marketplace.

PRIVACY

Full service networks will have access to and process a great deal of personal information about subscribers, such as entertainment preferences, general interests, exposure to advertising, product purchases, the content of e-mail, banking and credit records, and per-haps even opinions and performance on tests. In aggregate, this information may be quite revealing, requiring guidelines safeguard-ing its use. For video service, guidelines are found in the Communi-cations Act. This would form the platform for privacy regulation that would have to be integrated with regulation of the broader services of a digital broadband network.

Cable operators are required to provide *notice* in the form of a separate, written statement informing subscribers of the following:

1. The nature of personally identifiable information collected on the sub-scriber and the nature of its use
2. The nature, frequency, and purpose of any disclosure that may be made of the information and to whom disclosure is made
3. The period the information is kept
4. The times and place at which the subscriber may have access to such information
5. The right of the subscriber to enforce some limitations on the use of information, including the right to correct errors

The notice must be circulated to subscribers every year as a reminder.

The cable operator may not *collect* personally identifiable informa-tion without first obtaining written or electronic (in the case of a two-way system) permission, except when the information is neces-sary to offer the service (such as pay per view) and to detect un-authorized reception of cable communications. Cable operators may not *disclose* personally identifiable information without prior written or electronic permission except as necessary to conduct the business and provide the service, or under court order. The operator may disclose names and addresses of subscribers to any cable service if the subscriber has had an opportunity to prohibit or limit the disclo-sure. For example, a cable company might give subscriber addresses to the Disney Channel for a direct-mail marketing piece. It is the subscriber's responsibility to exercise the option to limit this form of disclosure after having read the notice.

The cable operator may collect and use *aggregated* data that does not identify particular persons. This privilege is important to operators who may desire to gather aggregated data on program audiences for advertising sales or programming purposes.

There have been several attempts by federal policy makers to define the responsibilities of telephone companies for protection of subscriber policy. In the late 1980s, the FCC held several hearings on the subject of *customer proprietary network information* (CPNI), which includes data collected on the services to which customers subscribe as well as their use of the network. Much of this information may have value to other firms wishing to obtain relevant marketing information on potential customers. Of even greater concern from a privacy perspective is the information that is collected on usage, such as the called numbers (e.g., imagine if a record of calls to an adult-oriented "900" number were made public).[44] According to FCC policy, telephone companies may not release CPNI without the consent of the customer.[45]

A special case of CPNI was brought to the fore during the debates over the privacy implications of Caller-ID and other automatic number identification services. In these services, the called party is informed of the telephone number of the calling party prior to answering the call. Many people objected to this service, including those with unlisted numbers who wished to maintain their privacy.[46] Policy here has mainly been made at the state level, with many states permitting Caller-ID service only in conjunction with another service that enables callers to block the transmission of their telephone number.

E-mail that travels on integrated broadband systems would be protected by the federal Electronic Communications Privacy Act of 1986, which affords most of the same protections of mail and telephone conversations to e-mail. The police and other agencies, such as the FBI, cannot read e-mail without a warrant.

Wireless communication, whether it is independent or an element of a full service broadband network, is viewed as having a lesser expectation of privacy because of the ease with which it can be overheard. Without better protections, privileges such as those afforded attorney and client, clergy and penitent, or husband and wife, as well as the constitutional protection against search and seizure, may be undermined or lost by users of wireless communications systems.

Integrating video, voice, and data privacy protection regulation will be a major task as full service networks evolve. Privacy will require a fresh look because of the much broader body of personally or household-identifiable data that is being transmitted and stored.

State and Local Regulation

The arrival of integrated broadband networks upsets carefully drawn government jurisdictional lines between federal, state, and local authorities. Intrastate telephone service is regulated by state governments; local governments have no role. Under home rule privileges granted by the states, cable service is franchised by local governments; states play a role in regulating pole attachments, theft of service, and a few other areas. This section discusses the function of state and local governments in electronic communication and the jurisdictional conflicts presented by the emerging integrated networks.

CURRENT CABLE REGULATION

In almost all states, cable systems are franchised by a local government—the city grants rights-of-way to go over and under streets and bridges. In return for this privilege, the city collects a franchise fee. Federal law limits the fee to 5% of all revenue, which is the amount most cities charge.

The franchise fee has generated substantial revenue over many years for most cities. For a city of 100,000 population, a franchise fee of 5% generates about half a million dollars annually.[47]

At the time that most cable franchises were granted, local franchising authorities had published an RFP, taken applications for the franchise, selected the single most desirable applicant, rejected the others, and written a franchise agreement for about 15 years with the winner. Under present law, cities must not auction cable franchises and are required to entertain other applicants at any time. Cities usually request that several channels, the PEG channels, be set aside for public service and public use. After a franchise agreement is signed, the city monitors the performance of the cable operator to make sure the system is built according to schedule and technical standards, resolves customer complaints that are not settled with the cable company, and administers the PEG channels. The city plays a role, described earlier, in rate regulation along with the FCC, if "certified" to do so by the FCC.

At renewal time, the city, the operator, or both ascertain cable-related community needs. The operator then makes a proposal for renewal. Renewal is granted if the operator has (1) complied with the existing franchise and the applicable law; (2) past service has been reasonable in the light of community needs; (3) the proposal indicates that the operator has the financial, legal, and technical ability; and (4) the proposal reasonably meets the future cable-related community needs and interests *consistent with practical costs*. Renewal is usually for 7 to 10 years. If the operator has not met all of the above four criteria, renewal could be denied after a formal administrative proceeding. Since denial is a draconian step, the franchisee and the franchising authority usually negotiate the new agreement. In the negotiating process, the cable operator has on its side the track record, the community goodwill it has accumulated, city fear of major legal costs and its promises for the future. The city has on its side the operator fear of bad publicity and legal costs and the ultimate threat of denial. When cable was not facing competition from DBS, MMDS, and telephone company entry, cities were able to get concessions from the cable operator at renewal time. Most recently, the cable operators have been unwilling to make new concessions, lest they be unevenly burdened in future competition.

CURRENT TELEPHONE REGULATION

Historically, LECs have been most heavily regulated by state public service commissions. Traditionally, these commissions have granted exclusive franchises for switched local telephone service. In return, they have exercised great control over the prices that telephone companies can charge. As noted earlier, in the past, the dominant mode of controlling prices was through rate of return regulation. All telephone subscribers were a part of the *rate base*, so when companies used private networks to *bypass* LEC facilities, there was a fear that overall rates for the remaining subscribers would have to go up to maintain the authorized return on investment. Since businesses could afford bypass technologies, while individual subscribers could not, this caused great concern among state policy makers.

More recently, most states have moved away from rate of return regulation to more incentive-based schemes, the most popular of which is the price caps approach discussed above. Other incentive-based approaches include allowing telephone companies to retain a share of earnings in excess of some limit, if the money is used to reinvest in local infrastructure or other specified goals.

The specific means of monitoring prices is through *tariffs*, the prices and conditions of service that have to filed with and approved by public service commissions. These help commissioners ensure that LECs are not engaging in any form of price discrimination, which is not legal under their status as common carriers. LECs complain that the need to file public tariffs well in advance of offering a service limits their flexibility to respond to the marketplace. Moreover, LECs believe that their tariff requirements and, in particular, rules regarding non-discriminatory pricing may place them at a disadvantage if competing firms do not face the same restrictions.

Jurisdictional Problems

As suggested above, aside from the federal government, the states are most important in regulating telephone, and the cities most important in regulating video. Once telephone and video services are integrated, there are three possible means of dividing jurisdiction: (1) leave the three-tiered regulatory structure more or less intact with adaptations to the new circumstances; (2) take the cities out of it, giving the states the present functions of the local governments; or (3) integrate all regulatory functions at the federal level, eliminating state and local roles.

THREE-TIERED REGULATION: LOCAL, STATE, AND FEDERAL

Politically, adapting the three-tier federal, state, and local regulatory structure is most feasible, if also most cumbersome. It is difficult

344 CONVERGENCE

to take authority and revenues away from governments. On the other hand, three-tiered regulation would mean that cable and telephone companies, which already consider themselves heavily regulated, would each be submitting themselves to another layer of regulation—telephone to local authorities, cable to the state.

Nonetheless, it may be feasible to establish clear division of labor over the three government levels. The local governments are perhaps best able to cope with complaints about service—ordering, billing, repair. Consumers would be comfortable raising these issues locally, whereas they might have little faith in the strength of their voices at the state or national level. Service standards could be established at the federal level so that there was no disparity within a service region for any given provider who would span more than one state. Local jurisdictions, too small to adequately deal with telecommunications matters could delegate this responsibility to a regional office. Each community would contribute support to the regional office in proportion to its population. The city or region would have authority to enforce the standards. Service issue conflicts between an operator and the local authority could be appealed to the state or federal government.

Local governments supervise cable construction in rights-of-way and issue permits for telephone company use of rights-of-way. The permit process would work for integrated broadband systems as well and, presumably, would be implied in the new open video systems structure. Not only would this ensure local control over rights-of-way, but it could expedite construction since a higher authority might be slower to respond to construction demands.

All other functions would be preempted by the state or federal government. This removes the local authority from any opportunity to influence the content of full service networks—a critical point, if the integrated networks are to actually function as First Amendment speakers. For example, each major metropolitan area is likely to have 24-hour local news services. Eventually, these services may be quite elaborate, including news on demand and access to electronically stored "morgues" or news item files. If cities have the authority to regulate full service, integrated broadband networks as they now regulate cable, much mischief could be done in violation of the First

Amendment. Public officials offended by rigorous news coverage and investigative reporting could punish the system through rate regulation, rejecting legitimate requests for cost-of-service increases, or rejecting requests for changes in the lease rates for household equipment. Renewals and transfer requests could be held up or denied.

The existence of these potential punishments could cause *self-censorship*. It is almost unthinkable, under the First Amendment traditions of the United States, that a medium would be so intimately involved, through specific regulation, with a government authority. Full service network executives could be quite docile, shying from robust journalism in response to local government intimidation since business goals might be negatively affected. Therefore, the separation from local authorities of any regulatory function that could affect content is indicated. It saves telecommunications companies from themselves and heavy-handed officials.

A problem in giving any authority to local governments over integrated broadband networks is that single companies, even in competitive circumstances, will be large operators spanning major metropolitan areas that could include hundreds of individual jurisdictions. The open video system structure in the 1996 telecommunications law could solve this problem if all of its particulars make it an attractive alternative to separate franchises.

Asymmetry of regulation can arise from jurisdictional differences, particularly if cable-based franchises are not treated the same as common carriers, open service systems, or other video services. The most contentious areas are the fees and public service requirements of cable franchisees.

The franchise fee may be assessed against all cable system revenues—subscriber fees, converter and remote rental, advertising sales, shopping channel commissions, and so on. It is capped by federal law at 5%. The fee covers regulatory expense and the value of the rights-of-way. While much of a broadband network would be built using public easements on private property, the rights-of-way across streets, bridges, and other public property, owned entirely by the city, are essential. As potential users of rights-of-way increase, the value may increase. If a city gives up the rights-of-way, without charge, to a private profit-making company, it could be argued that the city is not acting in the best interests of the citizens or even that the city has violated the doctrine that asserts that public rights-of-way may not be used for private enterprise, only for the public convenience. Therefore, the city might extract the maximum fee, taking advantage of its control of the essential rights-of-way. On the other hand, because communication facilities are essential to the livelihood and well-being of the community, the city might waive the "value" of the rights-of-way to encourage development. Of course, some compromise may be made between these extremes. The telecommunications reform bill makes it clear that a franchise fee may be assessed only against cable-type revenues and not other telecommunications services even if provided by a cable operator.

Whatever the fee, it can be passed on directly to the users of the services. In effect, the users of the video service are paying the whole community for the rights-of-way that belong to the whole community. As suggested, however, this could be shortsighted if the communication facilities represent a general benefit to the community. At least the community should be aware of these issues and not mistakenly believe that the city is producing revenue from the *telecommunications provider* instead of from the *consumers and businesses* within the community.

One of the most pressing problems for local authorities is the likely uneven geographic transition to full service, integrated broadband networks. Construction will proceed in locations selected by the providers based on economic parameters or on the anticipation of competition. For example, Ameritech, serving Wisconsin, Illinois, Indiana, Michigan, and Ohio, at one point designated five cities (Chicago, Columbus, Cleveland, Detroit, and Indianapolis) for development of broadband networks. This will no doubt stimulate competitive response by cable operators in those areas. The other cities in the Ameritech region (e.g., Ft. Wayne, Grand Rapids, Toledo) are likely to lag behind, experiencing some comparative economic and lifestyle deficits as a result. To add to the insult, these lagging cities will probably subsidize telecommunications development in the designated cities. This situation may lead some cities to actively seek full service network builders, hoping to *force* development ahead of other cities. The city of Seattle issued an RFP seeking an investor/developer . . . to build and operate a broadband telecommunication network, or information highway, in the city. The City envisions a telecommunications network that would provide two-way voice, data, video and multi-media communication capabilities to *all* residents, businesses and institutions within the City of Seattle.

The city goal was to "achieve real competition," to ensure "diverse, cost effective services."[48] To this end, the city of Seattle was willing to defer collection of fees and be "flexible" in other ways. The city of East Lansing, Michigan, passed an ordinance that assesses no fees against revenues for operation of advanced telecommunications services, beyond cable, well ahead of the similar state and federal laws. The result was almost immediate development of new services in the community.

The aggressive seeking by cities of full service, broadband builders may cause some problems for general competition policy. The city could make so many concessions in the attempt to lure one telecommunications investor, that potential competitors are disadvantaged. Or the city may ask for so much of the first full service provider, in the way of dedicated public facilities, that a second builder, being obligated to match the first, would be discouraged.

Whatever the city policy, there is a danger that the first movers in telecommunications services preempt others. Space on poles and in critical conduits across rights-of-way is limited. Perhaps these problems can be resolved in advance by ordinances that require the sharing of space and the building of overcapacity in key locations. Again, cable and telephone companies, and perhaps electric utilities, have an advantage in circumstances in which space is scarce. There may be similar problems with access to the home. If access to the home is not shared by all providers, the householder does not have the choice intended by competition policies.

State governments, in the three-tiered structure, might best fulfill the function of ensuring interconnection. The states already regulate access of long-distance carriers to LECs. The interconnection of all of the networks that become the national information infrastructure could be supervised by the states. Conflicts over access between networks and services within a state, which would include pricing, could best be resolved by the state's applying national standards for interconnection.

If the anticipated competition occurs, governments will be minimally concerned with rate regulation in the larger markets. In the smaller markets where competition does not emerge, states could regulate rates. States are presently staffed to do rate regulation. The task would overwhelm the federal government and require too much special expertise for smaller local governments.

Enforcement of theft-of-service statutes is also an appropriate function of the state. Although this responsibility would be shared with the federal government in big interstate and mail order cases, intrastate sales of illegal equipment and individual subscriber theft is most effectively handled by the state. Since major thefts are possible from an integrated service that includes video on demand and long distance telephone service, enforcement will be important. Prevention of theft of data for criminal purposes and invasion of privacy will also be significant state functions.

In the three-tiered regulatory scheme, the federal government would set policy guidelines and enforce some of them—safeguarding competition, enforcing equal employment opportunity, setting a maximum for fees charged to operators by states or local authorities, protecting content choices by operators, attempting to maximize diversity, and establishing universal access (at low rates).[49]

TWO-TIERED REGULATION: STATE AND FEDERAL

It is possible to eliminate local regulation for integrated networks entirely. In such a system, the state would assume all of the responsibilities of the local authorities described above. This would solve the problems caused by the discrepancy between community political boundaries and the broader, economically determined boundaries of integrated broadband networks. Supervision of construction in rights-of-way could be delegated to the city engineers, allowing them to make decisions consistent with city codes except where they would be unreasonable in the context of telecommunications services and at odds with the goal of full development of compatible telecommunications systems within the state.

The state would be more consistent in handling consumer complaints. This would aid the network developers in building uniform policy within the organization instead of a patchwork plan catering to varying policies and decisions across hundreds of communities. However, as noted above, having the complaint resolution process one step removed from the local community could discourage the complainant.

FEDERAL PREEMPTION OF REGULATION

A case can be made for a single regulatory entity. Several states will be spanned by the network operators. Rate regulation schemes, in which books must be kept separating video and telephone service in these interstate companies, would be more complicated if further subdivided by state. Other policies would perhaps be more easily made and monitored by one authority.

Federal policy might be more concerned with development of service pertinent to consumers and businesses than state and local authorities who may be more interested in revenue and authority. The federal government better understands First Amendment freedoms and is more insulated from consumer pressures that would seek to curtail such freedoms.

The most serious objection to vesting the entire authority in the federal government is the scale of the task. The federal government would be closely involved in business operations, enforcement, and policy development across a vast geographic area involving citizens and businesses in thousands of communities. Communication companies are likely to have much greater impact at this level than individual citizens or user businesses.

Notes

1. Telephone Company-Cable Television Rules, Sections 63.54-63.58, *Second Report and Order, Recommendation to Congress, and Second Further Notice of Proposed Rulemaking*, CC Dkt. No, 87-266, 7 FCC Rd. 5781m 5783 2 (1992).

2. "Telecommunications Competition and Deregulation Act of 1995" (Discussion Draft), U.S. Senate, 31 January, 1995.

3. Ann Douglas, *Terrible Honesty* (New York: Farrar Strauss, 1995), 185.

4. The basic problems are broadly grouped into two types: cross subsidization and discrimination. In the former case, AT&T could overcharge telephone subscribers in order to subsidize competitive services. Hence, they could undercut the prices of any competitors, driving them from the market. In the latter case, because any competitor needed to use AT&T's basic transmission services, the fear was that they would be given lower-quality and higher-priced connections, making competing services less desirable.

5. See F. Matos, "Information Services," in *NTIA Telecom 2000 Report* (Washington, DC: NTIA, 1988).

6. Matos, "Information Services."

7. Dianne Hammer, "Cable Lobbying Changes Gears," *Cable World*, 28 November, 1994, 38.

8. *Video Dialtone Order*, 7 FCC Rcd at 5847, para. 135.

9. *DOJ Cross-Ownership Rules Reply*, supra, at 44.

10. *The NTIA Infrastructure Report*, at 233 (October 1991).

11. *First Report and Order*, 7 FCC Rcd 300 at 306, para. 10. Telephone Company-Cable Television Rules, Sections 63. 54-63.58, *Second Report and Order, Recommendation to Congress, and Second Further Notice of Proposed Rulemaking*, CC Dkt. No, 87-266, 7 F.C.C.,cd. 5781, 5783 2 (1992).

12. *NCTA v. FCC (1994)*, 33 F.3d 66.

13. Quoted by Ken Auletta, "Selling the Air," *New Yorker*, 13 February, 1995, 37.

14. Kim McAvoy, "Industry Funnels $50 Million to Congress," *Broadcasting & Cable*, 2 May, 1994, 47 (Source: Common Cause).

15. FCC CC Docket 87-313, *Second Report and Order*, 4 October, 1990, Recon, 17 April, 1991.

16. The going-forward rules permit new channels to be added to the previous total in the cable programming service tiers at 20 cents per channel charge to subscribers up to a maximum of six channels and $1.20. The operators could then add up to 30 cents in aggregate in subscriber charges to cover license fees for the programming. More expensive channels could be introduced if the total package did not exceed the overall caps. In January 1997, the $1.20 maximum channel fee goes up to $1.40 and license fees can be recovered in full, should they exceed the original 30-cent limit. The going-forward rules end in January 1998.

17. Steven Brenner, *Competition Policy and a Changing Broadcast Industry* (Paris: Organisation for Economic Co-operation and Development, 1993), 175.

18. 47 U.S.C. 628b.

19. A study of the effects of vertical integration on program diversity is provided in Hoekyun Ahn, "Vertical Integration and Consumer Welfare in the Cable Industry," (unpublished paper, Department of Telecommunication, Michigan State University, 1995).

20. Vincente Pasdeloup, "FCC Rules on Program Access: No exclusive Deals for Court TV," *Cable World*, 6 June, 1994, 1.

21. Leland L. Johnson, *Toward Competition in Cable Television* (Cambridge, MA: MIT Press, 1994).

22. In the matter of use of the Carterfone device in message toll telephone service (1968). FCC Docket Nos. 16942, 17073; Decision and order, 13 FCC 2d 240.

23. 47 U.S.C. 224(d)(1).

24. *United States v. AT&T*, 522 F. Supp. 131 at 140.

25. *Preferred Communications Inc. v. City of Los Angeles*, 754 F 2d1396 (9th Cir. 1985).

26. Jeannine Aversa, "Antitrust Chief Lays Out Highway Markers," *Multichannel News*, 17 January, 1994, 24.

27. John P. Cole, Jr., "The Cable Television 'Press' and the Protection of the First Amendment—A Not So 'Vexing Question,'" *California Western Law Review* 28, no. 2 (1991-1992): 350.

28. *Turner Broadcasting System, Inc. v. F.C.C.*, 114 S.Ct. 2445 (1994).

29. *United States v. O'Brien*, 391 U.S. 367 88 S.Ct. 1679, 20 L.Ed.2d 672 (1968).

30. *Ward v. Rock Against Racism*, 491 U.S. 799, 109 S.Ct. 2758 105 L.Ed.2d 661 (1989).

31. C. Steinfield and R. Kramer, "US: Dialing for Diversity," in *Cash Lines: Audiotex Developments in Europe and the United States*, ed. M. Latzer and G. Thomas (Amsterdam: Het Spinhuis), pp. 227-255.

32. *Minneapolis Star & Tribune v. Minnesota Commissioner of Revenue*, 9 Med.L.Rptr. 1369, 460 KU.S. 575 (1983) and *City of Alameda v. Premier Communications Network, Inc.*, 202 Cal.Rptr. 684 (Cal.App. 1984).

33. *Miller v. State of California*, 413 U.S. 15 (1973).

34. 18 U.S.C.A. 1464.

35. *FCC v. Pacifica Foundation*, 438 U.S. 726 (1978).

36. *Cruz v. Ferre*, 755 F2d 1415 (11th Cir. 1985) and *Community Television of Utah, Inc. v. Wilkinson*, 611 F. Supp. 1099 (D. Utah, 1985) and *HBO v. Wilkinson*, 531 F. Supp. 987 (D. Utah, 1982) and *Community Television of Utah v. Roy city*, 555 F.Supp. 1164 (D. Utah, 1982). See Howard M. Kleinman, "Indecent Programming on Cable Television: Legal and Social Dimensions," *Journal of Broadcasting and Electronic Media* 30, no. 3 (1986): 275-294.

37. *Carlin Communications, Inc. v. FCC*, No. 84-4086 (November 2, 1984).

38. 47 U.S.C. 532.

39. *Cubby, Inc. v. CompuServe, Inc.*, 776 F. Supp. 135, 1991 U.S. Dist., LEXIS 15545; 19 Media L. Rep. 1525 (1991).

40. A review of the computer complication in accessing records is provided in Sigman L. Splichal and Bill F. Chamberlin, "The Fight for Access to Government Records Round Two: Enter the Computer," *Journalism Quarterly* 71, no. 3 (1994): 550-560.

41. *Dismukes v. Department of Interior*, 603 F.Supp. 760 (D.C. 1984).

42. Anne Wells Branscomb, *Who Owns Information?* (New York, NY: Basic Books, 1994).

43. Ibid., 173.

44. See J. Katz, "US Telecommunications Privacy Policy," *Telecommunications Policy*, December 1988, 353-368.

45. Ibid.

46. James Katz, "Caller ID, Privacy and Social Processes," *Telecommunications Policy*, 14, no. 5 (1990): 372-411.

47. 100,000/2.6 members per household × .63% of cable subscription × \$35 month subscription fee × .05% franchise fee × 12 months = \$508,846.

48. Draft #6a(2), "Request for Proposals for an Information Highway," City of Seattle, 8 August, 1994.

49. A regulatory structure similar to this one is proposed by Michael A. McGregor, "Toward a Unifying Regulatory Structure for the Delivery of Broadband Telecommunications Services," *Journal of Broadcasting & Electronic Media* 38, no. 2 (1994): 125-143.

12

Multinational Full Service Networks

Joseph D. Straubhaar
Joonho Do

This chapter addresses the potential for a global information infrastructure that would include individual residences.

Existing Conditions

In many countries, the systems that may converge to form full service networks are still quite separate. Outside the industrialized nations of Europe and Japan, and the rapidly industrializing nations of East Asia, most countries are still struggling to consolidate and expand broadcasting, construct separate telephone systems, and figure out how to deal with the beginnings of satellite and cable television.

TABLE 12.1 Per Capita Income and Telephone, Television, Cable, and Satellite Penetration

	GNP per Capita	Telephones per 100	Televisions per 100	Cable/Satellite/ Pay TV Receivers per 100
Brazil	$2,680	8	35	less than 1
France	$19,490	50	40	2
Indonesia	$730	3	10	less than 1
Taiwan	$10,500	38	45	10
OECD average (industrialized countries)		44	55	32

SOURCE: Data from "Perspectives des Communications" (Paris: Organisation for Economic Co-operation and Development, 1993); *World Development Report* (Washington, DC, 1994); *ITU Regional Reports* (International Telecommunications Union, 1993-1994); *Europa Yearbook* (1994); GIS Taiwan (1993); S. T. Davies, "Indonesia's TV Jungle" (*Multichannel News International*, March 1995, 6A, 30A-31A); L. G. Duarte, *Television Segmentation* (M.A. thesis, Michigan State University, Department of Telecommunication, 1992).

A quick look at some of the basic indicators about these industries in a few countries makes it clear that the infrastructures for networks are still quite nascent in many countries.

In most countries, both governments and private industry operators still tend to see the construction of separate industries and technical infrastructures in telephony, data communication, and cable as most feasible. Several factors may lead this thinking to change, however. One is the possibility of technological leapfrogging. It is beginning to occur to people in many countries that if they are laying down new wired infrastructure for telephony, it might make more sense to start with broadband capacity. Another is the desire of the existing successful industries to expand and diversify. Most telephone companies in the world are beginning to offer other interactive services, at least to a limited degree, and a number have begun to contemplate entering cable-type services. A third factor is the increasing privatization of communication industries, which opens them up both to expansion-minded national entrepreneurs and to foreign investors who may be contemplating an infrastructure that lends itself to worldwide full service networks.

All multichannel and integrated broadband network scenarios in developing countries, including much of the former Soviet Union, are limited, however, by low income and poor income distribution, which put a ceiling on potential audiences for cable. The users of full service networks would be a fraction of the population corresponding to the middle class or even upper-middle class, often under 5%. For example, Indonesia has a population of 176,000,000 but a "middle class" of only 3% of that figure capable of affording air-conditioning or cable or satellite television. Only 18% of urban homes have a telephone, far fewer in rural areas. Average income is $730 per year, while the sign-up cost for existing satellite services is $1,045. Furthermore, of the audience for existing satellite services (between 750,000 and 1,300,000), only 20% watch any of the foreign programming, because less than 10% of the population speak English.[1]

TELEPHONE SYSTEMS

As most developing nations still have fewer than 10 telephones per 100 people, most discussion focuses on how to grow telephone most quickly. New telephone systems, however, often incorporate digital switching, optical fiber transmission, and other modernizations that might eventually facilitate full service networks. Where telephone systems have not been extensively built up yet, or where they need major technical overhaul or rapid expansion, both public and private planners are increasingly contemplating trying to jump to newer technologies. The main current example is not wired full service networks but leapfrogging basic wired telephone service to a cellular or other mobile telephone technology. This option is widespread in Eastern Europe and parts of Asia and Latin America, where wired networks cannot meet rapidly growing business and residential demand. If countries move to digital mobile services, one might see those become limited bandwidth, multiservice networks.

In more advanced industrial economies in Europe, North America, and Asia, and in rapidly developing countries such as Hong Kong, Singapore, and South Korea, telephone systems show some promise of moving relatively quickly toward full service networks. In countries such as France, government-owned telephone monopolies (PTTs) have been moving aggressively into information services, starting with videotex. In some other countries, full service networks seem likely to develop in competition between telephone-based companies and cable-based operations. This seems likely in the United Kingdom and in Hong Kong and Singapore.

BROADCAST, CABLE, AND SATELLITE TELEVISION

Countries and private companies are also trying to expand the reach of their broadcast television networks. Most often this involves using satellites to distribute television signals to remote parts of the countries, where they are then rebroadcast. For example, India innovated in sending television to village satellite dishes, while Brazil has thousands of small receiving dishes coupled to retransmitters bringing television to remote parts of the country. These satellites also begin to provide a platform for telephone, data, and other two-way services.

Satellites are beginning to feed television to dishes for direct home reception and to cable television systems. Direct dish reception is still relatively rare and limited to the wealthy outside the industrialized countries, due to cost. Cable and satellite master antenna (SMATV) systems within apartment buildings, however, are beginning to become more common in middle-class areas of cities around the world. At this moment, typical monthly cable fees in most countries keep lower-middle-class, working-class, and poor people from access to cable. For instance, in most Latin American countries, monthly cable fees range from $15 to $30, and in many countries, median monthly income is under $100.

Integrated Systems

FROM CABLE TO FULL SERVICE NETWORKS?

Because interest in cable is growing, at least in middle- and upper-middle-class areas around the world, this may open the door to full service networks from the cable base, expanding to interactive television and telephone services. In rapidly developing industrializing cities, there are areas demonstrating extensive demand for both cable and telephone service. In several middle-class suburbs of São Paulo, Brazil, private companies have proposed building local networks integrating the two services. Most of these systems have not proposed to add interactive services much beyond basic telephony yet, but a switched broadband infrastructure would be built that could be upgraded to accommodate additional services.

Some of the highly industrialized countries, such as Japan and the United Kingdom, originally saw cable as a potential infrastructure base on which to build up full service networks.[2] The United Kingdom provided incentives for potential cable operators to build interactive systems, assuming demand would follow,[3] but the initial systems constructed required pricing that exceeded the willingness to pay, and subscription rates were too low. (See p. 363.)

More recently, several countries in both Europe and Asia have considered whether to create competition within telephone-based services by encouraging the development of interactive cable television that would compete with telephone companies that are currently monopolies. For example, the government of Hong Kong wants to create competition for Hong Kong Telecom (the telephone monopoly largely owned by British Cable and Wireless) by encouraging Wharf Cable to build an interactive infrastructure, capable of offering telephone and other telecommunication services. Both HK Telecom and Wharf are among the first in developing countries to conduct interactive and on-demand service trials.

Most of the experiments with integrated broadband networks currently under way are in North America (where both telephone and cable system operators are involved), Europe (where a slightly broader spectrum of telephone companies, broadcasters, other companies, and a few cable operators are trying out various approaches), and the Pacific and Asia (where a mixture of telephone companies and cable system operators are experimenting, mostly in industrialized countries). Companies primarily are looking at video on demand, telephony over cable, and pay per view or pay per channel. A few are looking at interactive games, home shopping, banking, education, and multimedia. Table 12.2 shows the trials under way or planned as of March 1995.

CONSTRAINTS ON DOMESTIC DEVELOPMENT

Only a few countries will be able to generate enough resources domestically for investment in the creation and expansion of full

TABLE 12.2 On-Demand and Interactivity Trials Outside the United States

Country	Company	Site	Homes	Time	Services*
Chile	CTC	Santiago	200-400	1995	PPV, VOD
Mexico	Condumex Cidec	Mexico City	1,000	1995	TP over CATV
Austria	CPTV	N/A	N/A	1995	VOD
Belgium	Electrabel	N/A	20	1995	VOD
Belgium	Belgacom, DEC, Alcatel	N/A	50	1995	VOD
Finland	HPU	Helsinki	30	1995	VOD
France	French Telecom	N/A	1,000	1996	VOD, super Minitel TP
France	Lyonnaise Comm.	N/A	N/A	N/A	VOD, cable, modem
Germany	DBP-Telekom Alcatel SEL	Berlin	50	1995	PPC, PPV, PR NVOD, HS
		Hamburg	1,000		same
		Köln/Bonn	100		same
		Stuttgart	4,000		same
		Leipzig	100		same
		Nürnberg	1,000		PPV, NVOD, VOD, games
Germany	Beynischer Rund. or TK	Munich	4,000	1995	VOD
Germany	Herdelskammer	Hamburg	1,000	1995	VOD, banking, HS
Italy	SIP	Rome	20-70	1994	VOD
		Milan, Rome	500 each	1995	VOD
Netherlands	Enertel	N/A	N/A	1996	VOD, TP over cable
Norway	Norwegian Telecom	N/A	300	1995	VOD
Sweden	Svenska Kabel, DEC, Telia	Jaraberg	500	1995	VOD
Switzerland	Swiss PTT	Nyon	400	1995	VOD
		Zurich	N/A	N/A	VOD, TP over cable
		Grenchen	300-400	1995	VOD
Switzerland	Rediffusion	St. Moritz	N/A	N/A	VOD
United Kingdom	British Telecom	Kesgrave	70**	1994	VOD, HS, E
		Ipswich, Colchester	2,500	1995	VOD, HS, E
		N/A	25,000	N/A	VOD, HS, E
United Kingdom	Cambridge Cable	Cambridge	10	1994	VOD
			200+	1995	VOD
United Arab Emirates	Emirates Telecom	2 places	60	1995	VOD, TP over cable

(continued)

TABLE 12.2 Continued

Country	Company	Site	Homes	Time	Services*
Australia	Telstra	Sydney	20	1994	VOD, TP over cable
Australia	Access Syst.	Melbourne	100	1995	VOD
China	Nynex	Beijing	N/A	1995	TP over cable
Hong Kong	Hong Kong TK	Hong Kong	50	1994	VOD
		HK/Lantau	400	1995	VOD
Hong Kong	Wharf Cable	Hong Kong	N/A	N/A	VOD
Japan	Yokkaichi	Tokyo	50	1995	TP over cable
Japan	Yokohama TV	N/A	N/A	1994	VOD, TP, multimedia
Korea	Korea Telecom	Seoul	100	1994	VOD***
New Zealand	New Zealand TC	N/A	N/A	N/A	VOD
Singapore	Telecom, H-P, Philips, Fujitsu	Singapore	300	1995	VOD
Singapore	Singapore Cablevision	Singapore	N/A	1995	VOD
Taiwan	forming MSO	N/A	N/A	1995	VOD, TP over cable
Thailand	UTV	Bangkok	N/A	1995	VOD

SOURCE: Data from *Multichannel News International* (March 1995 Supplement), 20A-21A; used by permission.
*TP = telephony, PPC = pay per channel, PR = pay radio, HS = home shopping, E = educator.
**Employees.
***This information was not reported in *Multichannel News*. The source was Korea Telecom.

service networks. These are probably limited to the major industrialized nations and some of the more rapidly developing economies of East Asia.

As of 1995, almost all countries have been attracting resources into the expansion of television. In many cases, that represents primarily the expansion by regular broadcast television to cover more of the population, because in many countries only urban populations are effectively served by television currently. Many countries are using satellite services to distribute channels for rebroadcast, which also leads to a certain amount of television-receive only (TVRO) dish diffusion in rural areas where those who can afford to pay want a better signal. In terms of expanding television, some countries, such as Brazil, are looking to use more broadcast channels by opening up

UHF services, including some pay services.[4] Many investors, both foreign and local, consider expansion of broadcasting to have better potential payoff than cable or satellite services. For example, MTV in Brazil is distributed by satellite but also carried by new UHF stations in several major cities, which accounts for most of its audience.[5] Such projects are drawing foreign investment, where it is allowed. Many countries do not allow foreign investment in regular broadcast television or radio.[6]

It is a concern that multichannel television, with more channels and imported content to fill the channels, could undermine the markets for domestic broadcasting and television production industries. On the other hand, assuming a demand develops for more culturally relevant programming, there is some prospect that the infusion of new money into television through subscription fees would stimulate greater domestic television production.

Most countries are expanding investments in telephony. Nearly all countries operated telephony via state-owned *postal, telephone, and telegraph* companies or administrations (PTTs) until the last decade when they began privatizing these companies, usually to acquire new resources for expansion of services, pay off debt, or increase administrative efficiency.[7] In telephony, far more than broadcasting, cable, or satellite services, governments have recognized that national needs for infrastructure have often outstripped their ability to generate domestic savings or attract loans. Although the World Bank and others have increased lending in telephony, recognizing it as a development need, demand outstrips availability dramatically.[8] Only a few industrialized countries, such as Japan, and even fewer developing countries, such as South Korea, have decided to privatize telephone companies but limit private investors to national citizens.

INVESTMENT LEADERSHIP

A number of countries are working hard to generate domestic investment. Both telephony and broadcasting attract domestic investment capital in many of the larger economies in both industrialized and developing nations. In some larger or more advanced economies, such as North American, Europe, East Asia, and some Latin American countries such as Brazil, Mexico, and Venezuela, national entrepreneurs are also pursuing the development of large cable and satellite systems. In almost every country, some entrepreneurs are building small, local cable and SMATV systems. National regulations in many countries also require potential foreign investors in telephony or cable or satellite operations to have a local partner, who is often required to have a majority interest.

Several international firms are leading in investments in telephone systems. The U.S. regional Bell Operating Companies (RBOCs), particularly BellSouth and SBC, have invested in Western and Eastern Europe, Latin America, and some parts of Asia.[9] Cable & Wireless of the United Kingdom has invested heavily in the United States, the Caribbean, the Mideast, and Hong Kong as well as in laying undersea fiber optic networks. France Telecom and Telefonica of Spain have also invested, particularly in Latin America.[10] Although these companies are primarily investing in conventional or cellular telephony to meet local market demands, some of the U.S. RBOCs are intending to pursue full service network trials in the United Kingdom through the cable companies in which they have invested.

Several North American cable system operators and programmers are also investing in cable and satellite services abroad. Turner Networks and HBO, MTV, and CNBC are adapting those services to the distinct audience demands, and in the case of Europe the regulatory demands, of regional markets. At one time, Rogers Cable of Canada had invested in cable systems in the United States and TCI had discussed investing in Mexico, perhaps even in a venture to compete with telephone company services. Many others have invested in systems in Europe and other continents.

CROSS OWNERSHIP OF NETWORKS AND PROGRAMMING

It seems likely that there will be more extensive cross ownership of networks and programming in other countries than in the United States. Elsewhere, broadcasting and telephony networks have more often than not been owned and operated by governments. In most countries, broadcasters have provided more of their own content than in the United States, where FCC financial-syndication rules until recently forced a separation between production or ownership of programming and the broadcast use of it.

In a number of countries, it looks as though governments will promote expansion by PTTs, or government telephone companies, into cable and full service networks. In these cases, the operator will try to supply some of the programming channels or other content but will probably also have to consider programming from a variety of other sources. An example of how this might work is provided by the French videotex system, Minitel, owned by the PTT, France Telecom. It offers a couple of basic services, such as an electronic telephone number database or basic e-mail, but then serves as a gateway and provides a common billing system for other commercial services, which use the France Telecom infrastructure.

REGULATORY FRAMEWORK
IN BUILDING FULL SERVICE NETWORKS

Regulatory tradition and framework play an important role in how a full service communication system evolves in a nation. Regulation of the telecommunication industry has been justified by the incapability of the marketplace to deal with structural problems. Due to rapid technological and economic changes, however, deregulation of the telecommunication industry is occurring in many countries. The degree of deregulation varies with differences in the history and institutional structure. At one extreme are countries where government builds and operates the whole telecommunication infrastructure. At the other extreme, the private sector builds the infrastructure without government intervention. Most countries fall somewhere between. Korea and the United Kingdom are discussed here to represent regulatory philosophies different than those in the United States.

In South Korea, as a developing country, the degree of government intervention in building an integrated broadband network is relatively strong. The Korean government adopted a unique regulatory approach to achieve an advanced system. Cable, which began operation in 1995, is expected to play an important role. As a late mover in implementing cable, compared with developed countries, the Korean government can take advantage of the opportunity to build toward an integrated network in a coordinated way.

The regulatory model in Korea can be considered a "separation of functions" approach. The government separates the cable industry into three functions—network provider, program provider, and system operator. No single entity is allowed to get involved in more than one area. In each area, competition is encouraged so as to have multiple providers. Network providers such as Korea Telecom and Korea Electric Power Corporation will build most of the broadband networks for system operators.

The United Kingdom has implemented a more liberal regulatory approach toward achieving integrated networks. The government allowed cable operators to provide alternative telephony services in their service areas but restricted British Telecom from offering video services on their network. The idea was to open existing networks to competitive providers and speed infrastructure development. By July 1995, one million telephone lines had been installed by cable companies.[11] The rapid growth of cable penetration in the last three years is mainly due to the successful operation of telephony by cable companies, who at the outset integrated the marketing of services but maintained parallel broadband and narrowband lines. Telephony generates more revenue for new operators than does cable. As the number of subscribers grows, cable operators are implementing their own switching facilities. Large MSOs are installing fiber optic rings within the franchise areas that can handle broadband multimedia applications.

The member states of the European Union have recognized that the many separate national regulatory approaches have resulted in a European telecommunications market that is fragmented. This in turn harms European equipment and service providers, since they are unable to enjoy the same economies of scale as their counterparts on the other side of the Atlantic. Hence, in 1987, the European Commission issued the now famous Green Paper on Telecommunications, which laid out a blueprint for the progressive introduction of competition in this sector.[12] The Commission proceeded with a series of legislative initiatives that had the effect of removing barriers to entry, first in provision of equipment and in value added services—which could be broadly defined to include video services.[13] The policy of competitively provided services was reaffirmed in 1993, with issuance of the Bangemann Report, which argued that competition was the best route to move Europe into the *Information Society*.[14] The European Council set a timetable to open up even basic telephone service to competition throughout the European Union by January 1, 1998, with special arrangements given to countries with poorly developed infrastructures so that they could ready themselves for the coming competition.[15] The most recent Green Paper issued by the Commission has potentially the greatest impact on the development of FSNs in telecommunications and cable television infrastructures.[16] This document clearly indicates that Europe will attempt to encourage the development of FSNs in a competitive environment, with the elimination of longstanding prohibitions on any entity other than the state Post, Telephone, and Telegraph monopoly to lay infrastructure.

INTERCONNECTION AND INTERNATIONAL STANDARDS

As full service networks develop in each country under their own structures, they will eventually be connected to each other, creating a Global Information Infrastructure (GII) through which vast quantities of information can move not only within a country but also across borders. In March 1994, U.S. Vice President Gore advanced the concept of a Global Information Infrastructure in a speech to the ITU World Telecommunication Development Conference in Buenos Aires, Argentina. The United States suggested five fundamental principles in the Commerce Department document "Global Information Infrastructure: Agenda for Cooperation":

- encourage private investment
- promote competition
- create a flexible regulatory framework to keep pace with technological and market changes
- provide open access to the network for all network providers
- ensure universal service[17]

This particular U.S. vision of the GII is dependent on free trade arrangements, open access, and interoperability among the component parts, including networks, devices, and information sources for all countries. The private sector is engaged in an effort to address standards and interoperability issues that are critical to a smooth GII evolution, especially in the context of changes in technology and the convergence of previously disparate fields. It will be a difficult task at this early developmental stage as technology and operating systems are in infancy and individual countries and companies will be competing for leadership roles. Although the principles above were incorporated in the Buenos Aires Declaration at the conclusion of the conference, the world is not of one mind on these issues.

Connecting networks developed under different country-by-country designs will demand some common standards. Open access and interoperability are essential to establishing a Global Information Infrastructure. Network standards and transmission codes that facilitate interconnection and interoperation between networks have to ensure the privacy of users and the security of the information carried. Without standards, moving information from one country to another would be quite costly in the necessary transformations.

The time it takes to develop standards can slow the introduction of new technologies. And standards can be used to protect national sovereignty by keeping out foreign products and services or, conversely, to advance particular systems in the self-interest of private industry.

At the plenipotentiary conference in Nice in 1989, the ITU passed a special resolution on the issue of "the changing telecommunications environment." In the many clauses and subclauses of this resolution, ITU members are invited to take action in response to factors such as technological convergence, globalization, competition, product and service innovation, and the widening telecommunication gap between developed and developing countries.

As well as passing this general resolution, the Nice plenipotentiary also decided to set up a high-level committee to examine how the structure and functions of the ITU could be adapted to the changing telecommunication environment. On the basis of 96 recommendations for reform issued by the high-level committee, member states met at a plenipotentiary conference to decide on the scope and timing of structural changes and associated functioning and modify the ITU Constitution and convention accordingly.

As the global information infrastructure develops and grows, its progress should not be slowed by the imposition of standards that limit flexibility to incorporate new technologies. The world marketplace theoretically should select the best standard for each portion of the GII. In this context, for the global interoperability of integrated broadband networks, firms should cooperate to prevent incompatibility. By developing the standards ahead of market competition, corporations reduce risk because the standard is in place early. It is likely, however, that a few dominant firms in highly developed countries will seek a significant market share before standardization, making their products de facto standards.

ORGANIZATION

If the private sector plays a major role in constructing and operating the GII, the national government may need to create a flexible legal environment to allow structural efficiency to develop naturally in response to consumer demand. Some governments may promote technological innovation and new applications through research, tax, and other incentives. To facilitate development, it will be necessary to ensure information security and minimum standards for network reliability. The government may itself become an innovator in the supply of information to the broadband networks. And, finally, as we have suggested in an earlier chapter, in recognizing that there is a social benefit to wide citizen use of broadband networks, governments should take some responsibility for educating people to take advantage of the available services either at home or in public institutions.

OPERATION

The operation of various applications and services on the GII basically would be similar to that within a nation but not constrained by national borders. People can search for and order simple text information or full motion video entertainment stored on the other side of the earth. The geographic distances are irrelevant except for the transmission cost.

The subscriber to services in an integrated broadband network in an information-poor country would theoretically have the same access to information as the subscriber in an information-rich country if governments do not block access in fear of weakening political control. Theoretically, subscribers, institutions, and businesses in the less developed country can present material for access by the rest of the world, again assuming no governmental gatekeeping. In reality, there are many obvious economic and social reasons this may not occur aside from any government constraints.

Due to the global development, operation of the GII would be closely related to international marketing efforts for products by private corporations. Promoting specific products on the GII in foreign countries will be important to the successful operation of information providers. Established program providers such as major movie studios and cable programming networks in the United States would have an initial advantage in international marketing. Informing consumers of specific products on the GII will be a difficult task in the international markets.

Providing a proper pricing and billing method for a product is a key to smooth operation of the GII. Deciding how much a user is charged for the service is a crucial marketing decision. Like information products and services generally, most GII applications will have high initial development costs and low replication or usage costs.

Given that many applications, or information, are available only upon payment, a convenient billing process is an important element in operation of the GII. Credit cards accepted throughout the world are the most likely means of facilitating international transactions. Another option is for international information providers to have national brokers who resell information and programming through licensing agreements in other countries.

Intellectual property rights are also essential elements of the infrastructure of the information superhighway. They must be an integral part of the rules of the road. Neither networks nor content will develop unless there are financial incentives for individuals and businesses to create and distribute material. Although international law recognizes property rights in creative work, difficulty has been experienced in enforcement. When copyrighted material is imported, there is little interest in copyright enforcement because it would increase public expense or deny public access. To the extent that integrated broadband systems as they develop depend on imported copyrighted materials, however, royalty payments are difficult to avoid. These payments, adding to the back-end revenues of the producer, make the producer stronger and better able to continue serving the market. This is another piece of the problem facing smaller countries with economic limits on production capability. It could result in a widening gap between information-producing countries and information-receiving countries. The General Agreement on Tariffs and Trade finally approved the Final Act of the Uruguay Round, which ended the seven-and-a-half year Uruguay Round of multilateral trade negotiations in Marrakech, Morocco, on April 1994 and opened the door to a new world trade order. On intellectual property, the rules for protecting brands, trademarks, and copyright and prohibiting forgery have for the first time been included in a GATT agreement.

The most important offspring from the Uruguay Round, the new World Trade Organization, marks a new era in world economic cooperation, as stressed in the Marrakech Declaration, showing a general desire to operate in a fairer and more open multilateral trading system, to the benefit and the prosperity of the population of the GATT member countries. The World Trade Organization will be a formal international organization, whereas GATT was merely a provisional agreement. The World Trade Organization will become responsible for the next steps in opening up world trade, and also for supervising the resolution of conflicts in intellectual property via more efficient, binding mechanisms.

Asymmetrical Flow of Media and Information

Within the study of world media flow, a number of scholars are worried that cable, satellite television channels, and full service networks will lead to a renewed U.S. domination of television in the world, a renewed media imperialism. In 1972, a UNESCO study found that most of the world's countries imported over half of their television programming, mostly entertainment, mostly from the United States.[18] That domination of world television sales declined somewhat as more countries produced for themselves or imported from regional producers. The current prominence of U.S. channels in the global satellite and cable television markets, however, would seem to support the idea that the United States is renewing its dominance via new media.

There is a continuing economic logic to transmitting cultural and information services over a distance and between countries. To lower costs, many countries have imported television and more recently information products, such as computer software. The United States and a few other longtime producers of film, television, computer programs, and information services have already established the economies of scale to produce these relatively cheaply. Particularly in film and television, they also have enormous stockpiles of programming, which fuel new cable and satellite channels as well as traditional program exports. The established media and information services, such as CNN and MTV, have considerable advantages, including brand names that either are known or are becoming known worldwide. As Collins observes: "Although new communication technologies have reduced the costs of transmitting and distributing information over distance (space binding—according to the definition of Innis), distinct information markets remain; here the most important differentiating factors are those of language and culture."[19] Collins goes on to argue that what does make international information producers of one country successful versus another is the size of the language community within which the work is produced. That argument may not explain why English-language producers sell more in the world market than those from Hindi- or Chinese-speaking regions, but it does begin to explain why producers in all three of those languages have an advantage over someone producing in Icelandic, Italian, Punjabi, or Afrikaans.

U.S. domination may be more apparent than real. Although the United States does tend to dominate the English-language market and the global level of both television trade and the new global satellite and cable channels, things change when viewed at regional and national levels. There are at least four layers of world television, all of which are relevant to the development of full service networks. Currently, many people are focusing on the global level, where U.S. programming still dominates world television trade and U.S.-based channels such as CNN and MTV seem to dominate the new channels of cable and satellite television. U.S. exporters and channels, however, are suddenly faced with enormous competition by major producers within the language and cultural groups that dominate various regions, such as Spanish, Arabic, and Chinese. At the national level, many countries are increasing the amount of television they produce for themselves, although many import much from both global and regional producers. Finally, within some larger countries, major institutions, localities, and subnational regions are beginning to produce more television as well.

This is not the classic situation of U.S. domination that media imperialism and cultural dependence theories might have predicted. Better perhaps might be the term *asymmetrical interdependence* to refer to the variety of possible relationships in which countries find themselves to be unequal but possessing various degrees of power and initiative in politics, economics, and culture. This builds on the concept of dependent development in which dependency may direct or limit national growth, but growth or development can take place.[20] It particularly allows for the possibility that, although the United States may dominate global television trade and truly globalized channels, other countries and non-U.S. companies may amass a considerable role in the regional, national, and local levels.

Of particular interest in satellite and cable television, and integrated broadband networks, is the idea that regional-level markets and producers will become increasingly important. These markets are often seen as based in regions—Asia, Europe, Latin America, or the Mideast. The European experience in trying to use regional-level policy to create a common market in television, based on the "Television Without Frontiers" initiative, however, shows the problems of thinking in terms of geographic regions. So far, audiences seem resistant to attempts either to create multilingual productions for export or showing throughout Europe or to define English as an acceptable regional language for television.[21] French audiences seem open to U.S.-imported programs, particularly when dubbed or subtitled, but resistant to English or German programs, and vice versa.[22]

Audiences within Europe do not seem to seek, or even accept, "European" television. It is a geographic and political construct that does not necessarily match up with audiences' identities or interests as applied to television. Two recent analyses seem to explain this. Hoskins et al.[23] argue that audiences apply a cultural discount against programming that is in the wrong language or not culturally relevant to them. Straubhaar[24] applies similar logic, arguing that audiences seek and are attracted to programming that is culturally similar or proximate to them. Applying these concepts to the development of cable, satellite, and full service network channels at global and regional levels helps explain some trends.

GLOBAL MARKETS

At the global level, U.S., European, and Japanese channels are finding some level of acceptance among external middle-class and upper-middle-class audiences, who are more likely to be globalized in their interests, travel outside their countries, speak English or other world languages, and have the economic capital to afford access to the new networks. From early audience figures in such places as Brazil[25] and Indonesia,[26] it seems as though the audiences for global television channels, particularly those such as CNN that require language competence, are restricted to this global English-speaking elite. Audiences for channels in which language matters less, such as MTV, may be broader.

The channels with broadest global reach at this point are probably MTV and CNN. MTV currently has regional versions in the United States, Europe, Brazil, Spanish-speaking Latin America, and Asia. Until 1994, it had an Asian service, based with Star TV in Hong Kong, and intended to launch its own Asian service in 1995. MTV's world audience in March 1995 was 117,300,000 households, including 59,000,000 in the United States.[27] MTV is also the channel that has adapted most extensively to each region in which it operates, using local videos and announcers and, in some cases, local business partners.

CNN is carried on cable channels in parts of Europe, Asia, and Latin America. Its audience is harder to determine because it includes a number of travelers in hotels. CNN has resisted regional adaptation more than MTV. CNN's model for the future is to avoid engineering a complete overhaul, which would force the service to translate broadcasts into a variety of languages. Instead, it hopes to cultivate partnerships similar to ones it forged with the German-language news network, NTV. NTV and CNN share footage, pooling their resources to broaden the focus of their coverage.[28] In terms of global news, CNN's main competition is the BBC, although regional news services are growing in Europe and Asia and are likely in Latin America. HBO, Turner Network Television, the Cartoon Channel, and Discovery are all expanding channel offerings to a more global basis, although they are also tending toward language versions and other regional adaptations, to reach a larger audience.

English-speaking elite audiences or users will be those most likely to be interested in new interactive services. English is clearly the dominant language of the Internet, as of 1995, and is predicted to remain so in the foreseeable future. This has raised considerable discussion on Internet forums, such as CPSR (Computer Scientists for Social Responsibility)—Global, where several correspondents have observed that the large majority of the world's population, who do not function fluently in English, will find themselves excluded and only a small globalized elite will be able to use the new medium well, even among the middle class that could conceivably afford it—a *language gap.*

REGIONAL MARKETS

A number of global channel or content providers are finding they have to adapt regionally to language and differences. Conceptually, instead of geographic regions, it seems that program or content channels are focusing on geo- or cultural-linguistic regions. Language defines certain groups of countries as having a common base, a potential for sharing cultural products such as television. Within Asia, the group of Chinese-speaking countries clearly shares a potential television market related to a potential common market in other products. Chen[29] speaks of a Chinese Productivity Triangle of China, Hong Kong, Singapore, and Taiwan in which shared or cross-border television production and distribution may be an example of a growing geolinguistic market. Beyond language, per se, shared cultural elements also help reinforce a potential common market for programming. Certain elements of historically shared culture, such as between China and Korea, may help define a less intense or more diffuse geocultural market.

The main regional or geolinguistic markets in 1995 are Latin America, Asia, the Mideast, North America, and Europe. Latin America is served primarily by Mexico, Brazil, Venezuela, and Hispanic producers in the United States and Puerto Rico in television exports. In terms of channels for cable or satellite, Latin America is targeted by Mexican (Televisa), Mexican-owned Hispanic (Univision and Galavision), Brazilian (TV Globo-GloboSat and TV Abril-TVA), and U.S. channels, such as HBO Olé, MTV Brasil, and MTV Latino, CNN (in

English and Spanish translation), TNT, the Cartoon Channel, Discovery, and others. Brazil serves as an example of geocultural versus geolinguistic marketing. Although Brazilian program exports are dubbed into Spanish, all the other cultural cues are close enough to please audiences, and Brazilian channels are directly received by a number of Spanish speakers who can understand much of what is said in Portuguese.

In Asia, the dominant service in 1995 is Star TV, which originally carried BBC news, MTV Asia, two Chinese-language channels, and movie and entertainment channels. Star TV has regionalized further, dropping BBC out of deference to mainland Chinese political demands, creating its own music video channel, and offering channels in more languages, such as Hindi.[30] Star's primary competitor in Chinese-language programming is the Galaxy consortium, which includes Time Warner, other U.S. channels, and TVB, owned by Hong Kong film producer Run Run Shaw and Robert Kuok (an entrepreneur from Malaysia), which began broadcasting Chinese-language programs throughout the region in 1993. Already TVB dominates the Cantonese Chinese-language market with entertainment and Chinese news.[31] Japan also operates a DBS service, which has direct reception and cable audiences in Taiwan and some direct reception audience in South Korea, where a number of older people remember Japanese. Doordarshan, the government television network in India, has been thinking of expanding regional coverage, and there is potential for an Indian film channel, which would have regional and geolinguistic regional appeal.

Europe is complicated by being a geographic rather than geocultural or geolinguistic market. Some English-language cable and satellite television channels, with largely U.S. content, are reaching audiences across the region. Those include CNN, TNT/Cartoon Channel, MTV, Nickelodeon, Discovery, VH-1, and Country Music Television as well as British channels Sky One, Sky Movies, Sky Sports, U.K. Gold, and Sky News. Most audiences, however, are clearly focused on national channels or, to a lesser degree, on geolinguistic channels, such as the French TV-5 or several German channels, which reach audiences in Germany, Austria, Switzerland, and German or French minorities elsewhere. Turkish and Saudi channels target Turkish guest workers as well as Arabic-speaking immigrants and visitors in Europe.

To date, new interactive services to the household are also largely based in national systems and audiences. The largest system, the French videotex system Minitel, is available outside France but is much more widely used by French residential customers, French businesses, and others working in France. The European Community has a goal, however, of fostering an EEC-wide market in information services, as in television and advertising. It seems more likely that regional business systems will grow before residential services, which are much more likely to remain national in scope in much the same way television has.

NATIONAL MARKETS

Both television and information services seem to be strongly concentrated at the national level in most countries. This seems to be a function of cultural proximity, the tendency for audiences to prefer programming and services within a familiar language, with familiar cultural/historical references, and with familiar cultural styles and symbols.[32] Smaller countries in both Europe and in developing nations, however, are more likely to accept cross-border services. Cross-border television, on cable in particular, has developed much larger audiences in the smaller European countries, such as the Scandinavian countries, Belgium, Holland, and Austria, than in larger nations, such as Germany, France, or Great Britain.[33] Although the cross-border information service market is new, this situation seems likely to hold for information services as well. In both cases, limited economies of scale do not permit small country national suppliers to meet the demands for diversity of services.

Smaller countries in the Caribbean, Mideast, Africa, and Latin America likewise seem to import more television programs. They are more open to large-scale video and cable/satellite channel importation as well. Some of the smallest in the Caribbean, for instance, developed broadcast television after the diffusion of satellite and cable television using U.S. channels.[34] Importation by small countries also tends to work within geolinguistic areas, however. While the Spanish-speaking Dominican Republic imports much of its programming from other Latin American countries,[35] the neighboring English-speaking island of Jamaica imports much more of its programming from the United States.[36]

BARRIERS TO IMPORTATION

The most important barrier to importation is language, followed by less obvious aspects of culture.[37] The analysis above indicates how language tends to encourage trade in culture and services within geolinguistic regions. The experience of the EU in trying to form a regional market across linguistic and cultural groups indicates that these present strong barriers.[38]

Other major barriers include national or regional government efforts to protect national markets for services. A number of countries, including European nations, such as the United Kingdom, and developing nations, such as Taiwan and South Korea, have historically limited the importation of cultural products, like television programs. Other countries, such as France, have claimed a right to subsidize national information products, such as films or television. Countries such as Sweden and Brazil have attempted to regulate or restrict cross-border information services, under the rubric of the regulation of transborder data flows.[39] Most countries have protected certain industries from foreign investment, particularly telephony and broadcasting, and some are now considering similar rules against direct foreign investment in cable or satellite channels, cable system operation, or full service networks. In considering Communications Act reform, the United States is discussing elimination of all restrictions on foreign ownership for other countries that offer "equivalent market opportunities" to U.S. firms—a reciprocity arrangement.[40]

Regional action in the European Union has opened some barriers while creating others. The European Commission has forced a series of steps liberalizing competition in information services limiting government's abilities to discriminate between European and non-European suppliers of services (see p. 363). That should enable North American and Asian companies to compete in some of the value-added services, which build on telecommunication and may contribute to the buildup of full service networks. The Commission, under the "Television Without Frontiers" initiative, however, created a series of quotas that required a minimum of 50% European content on both broadcast and satellite/cable channels.[41] Those quotas were not implemented by some countries, such as Spain. In 1994-1995,

however, European Union officials were discussing stricter enforcement. These rules were also being enforced more tightly on U.S. and
other satellite/cable channels. Many of those channels, such as TNT
and the Cartoon Channel, were far from meeting a 50% European
content standard, although some U.S. channels, such as MTV and
Discovery, were within the guidelines.

WORLD LEADERSHIP

We have stated elsewhere in this book that telecommunication
leadership—eventually, the leadership in integrated broadband networks—has become a national goal in the United States. This goal
may also be reflected in economic policies and private investment
goals in governments such as France, the United Kingdom, Germany, and Japan. They are counting on international markets to
recover research and development costs. Other countries, and large
telecommunication businesses within these countries, that do not
have overt ambitions for world leadership are at least taking a
defensive posture to prevent domination by the leader countries.

Notes

1. S. T. Davies, "Indonesia's TV Jungle," *Multichannel News International*, March
1995, 6A, 30A-31A.
2. W. H. Dutton, J. G. Blumler, and K. L. Kraemer, eds., *Wired Cities: Shaping the
Future of Communications* (Boston: G. K. Hall, 1987).
3. J. G. Blumler, "Live and Let Live: The Politics of Cable," in *Wired Cities
Communications*, ed. Dutton, Blumler, and Kraemer.
4. Luiz G. Duarte, *Television Segmentation: Will Brazil Follow the American Model?*
(M.A. thesis, Michigan State University, Department of Telecommunication, 1992).
5. Duarte, *Television Segmentation."*
6. W. H. Read, *America's Mass Media Merchants* (Baltimore, Mass.: Johns Hopkins
University Press, 1976).
7. J. D. Straubhaar, J. Bauer, C. Campbell, and P. McCormick, "Country Case
Studies," in *Telecommunications Politics: Ownership and Control of the Information Highway in Developing Countries*, ed. B. Mody, J. D. Straubhaar, and J. Bauer (Hillsdale, NJ:
Lawrence Erlbaum, 1995).
8. Mody, Straubhaar, and Bauer, eds., *Telecommunications Politics.*
9. S. Bagchi-Sen and P. Das, "Foreign Direct Investment by the U.S. Bells," in
Telecommunications Politics, ed. Mody, Straubhaar, and Baurer.
10. Straubhaar et al., "Country Case Studies."

11. Nial Hickey, talk to Telecommunications in Europe program, Paris, France, 7 July 1995.

12. Commission of the European Communities. COM (87) 290, "Towards a Dynamic European Economy: Green Paper on the Development of the Common Market for Telecommunications Services and Equipment," Brussels, 30 June 1987.

13. For a review of the various legislative actions see Johannes Bauer and Charles Steinfield in *Telecommunications in Transition: Policies, Services, and Technologies in the European Community*, eds. C. Steinfield, J. Bauer, and L. Caby (Thousand Oaks, CA: Sage, 1994): 51-70.

14. Lord Bangemann, "Europe and the Global Information Society: Recommendations to the European Council" (presented to the European Council, Corfu, 24-25 June 1993).

15. European Council, Council Resolution 93/C213/01, 22 July 1993. Review of the situation in the telecommunications sector and the need for further development of the market. Greece, Ireland, Portugal, and Spain were the countries mentioned for possible transitional arrangements.

16. Commission of the European Communities, COM (94) 440, "Green Paper on the Liberalization of Telecommunications Infrastructure and Cable Television Networks," Brussels, 25 October 1994.

17. Al Gore and Ronald H. Brown, "Global Information Infrastructure: Agenda for Cooperation," Information Infrastructure Task Force, U.S. Department of Commerce, February 1995, preface.

18. T. Varis, "Global Traffic in Television," in *Issues in Broadcasting*, ed. T. C. Smythe and G. A. Mastroianni (Fullerton, Calif.: Mayfield, 1974), 372-380.

19. R. Collins, "Trading in Culture: The Role of Language," *Canadian Journal of Communication* 19, no. 1 (1994): 386.

20. R. Salinas and L. Paldan, "Culture in the Process of Dependent Development: Theoretical Perspectives," in *National Sovereignty and International Communications*, ed. K. Nordenstreng and H. I. Schiller (Norwood, NJ: Ablex, 1979).

21. G. Wedell, "Television Without Frontiers?" *Government and Opposition*, 20 (1985): 94-103.

22. G. Chapman, "Towards the Geography of the Tube: TV Flows in Western Europe, *InterMedia*, January 1987, 10-21; K Robins, "Reimagined Communities: European Image Spaces Beyond Fordism," *Cultural Studies* 3, no. 2 (1989): 145-166.

23. C. Hoskins, A. Finn, and S. McFayden, "Television and Film in a Freer International Trade Environment: Why the U.S. Dominates and What Canada Should Do About It," in *Media, Culture and Free Trade: NAFTA's Impact on Cultural Industries in Canada, Mexico and the U.S.*, ed. E. McAnany and K. Wilkinson (Austin: University of Texas Press, forthcoming); C. Hoskins and R. Mirus, "Reasons for the U.S. Dominance of the International Trade in Television Programs," *Media, Culture and Society, 10* (October 1988): 499-515.

24. J. D. Straubhaar, "Class, Genre and the Regionalization of the Television Market in Latin America," *Journal of Communication* 4, no. 1 (1991): 53-69.

25. Duarte, *Television Segmentation*.

26. Davies, "Indonesia's TV Jungle."

27. C. Foster, "MTV's Footprint Around the Globe," *Christian Science Monitor*, 25 March 1995, 1, 8-9.

28. J. Dempsey, "U.S. Cablers Hunger for Global Pie," *Variety*, 6 December 1995, 4, 17.

29. S.-L. Chen, "Creating a Chinese Hollywood?" (unpublished manuscript, Michigan State University, 1993).

30. J. Karp, "Galaxy Builders," *Far Eastern Economic Review*, 9 December 1993, 74.

31. Karp, "Galaxy Builders."

32. Straubhaar, "Television Market in Latin America."

33. J. D. Straubhaar, "A Comparison of Cable TV Systems," in *Cable Communication*, ed. T. Baldwin and S. McEvoy (Englewood, NJ: Prentice Hall, 1988), 302-329.

34. S. Hoover and P. Britto, "Communication, Culture and Development in the Eastern Caribbean: Case Studies in New Technology and Culture Policy" (paper presented at the annual meeting of the International Communication Association, Dublin, Ireland, June 1990).

35. Straubhaar, "Television Market in Latin America."

36. J. Straubhaar, C. Campbell, S.-M. Youn, K. Champagnie, M. Elasmar, and L. Castellon, "The Emergence of a Latin American Market for Television Programs" (paper presented at the annual meeting of the International Communication Association, Miami, Fla., May 1992).

37. R. Collins, "Trading in Culture: The Role of Language," *Canadian Journal of Communication* 19, no. 1 (1994): 377-399; C. Hoskins, R. Mirus, and W. Rozeboom, "U.S. Television Programs in the International Market: Unfair Pricing?" *Journal of Communication* 39, no. 2 (1989): 55-75.

38. Wedell, "Television Without Frontiers?"

39. R. F. Aldrich, "Emerging Issues in Transborder Data Flow," in *Issues in International Telecommunication Policy*, ed. J. Yurow (Washington, DC: George Washington University, Center for Telecommunications Studies, 1983), 137-179.

40. S.652, Telecommunications and Deregulation Act of 1995.

41. P. Presburger and M. R. Tyler, "Television Without Frontiers: Opportunity and Debate Created by the New European Community Directive," *Hastings International and Comparative Law Review* 13 (1990): 495-509.

13

Impacts of Integrated
Broadband Networks

When broadly realized, full service networks could have profound consequences for individual behavior as well as for social structure and the structure of the telecommunication and media industries.

It is not especially difficult to predict some of the outcomes of full service networks. We know what services are possible and, given these services, how lives, institutions, and societies could be affected. It is more difficult to judge the pace at which the development will take place. How long will it take to build the networks? How quickly will people adopt the new services? If the building and diffusion is rapid, the impact will be dramatic. If the networks are slow in developing and consumers slow to change, the impact will be felt by only a few at a time and society as a whole will barely notice.

Although the builders of integrated broadband networks may test the waters slowly, enjoying the current monopolies as long as possible, if a few aggressive companies begin to build, momentum will pick up under competitive pressures. Once the substantial investment has been made in digital broadband networks, the search will begin to find new markets for the expanded potential. We could reach the point where a majority of households and businesses in the United States are passed by integrated networks somewhere around 2005. This would not necessarily mean that a majority of the households would be using the full range of services. But such an estimate, this or any other, is not especially meaningful at this point. Capital availability, technical development, creativity in the design of applications, public policy, and the consumer appetites and other dynamics will all play a role in determining pace.

We will begin the analysis of the potential impacts with individuals and then consider society and social institutions, the communication industries, and, finally, international development.

Individuals

Certainly a key impact of interactive multimedia and communication services will be a change from a relatively passive to a more active consumption.

ACTIVE SELECTION

Program choice studies have found that under imperfect awareness of all the program options, the easy solution to deciding what to watch is to form a channel repertoire, that is, a limited number of channels to be used regularly.[1] Similarly, in a price discrimination system described in Chapter 6, viewers may simplify their lives by settling for a limited repertoire of program types from the menu and a limited repertoire of à la carte channels.[2] The selection may be preprogrammed, so that items come up to satisfy interests already registered by the user.

But the user may also select content on an ad hoc basis from extensive menus or favored channels. The program prices are different based on the cost of the program, the recency of its release to television, and the programmer's estimates of demand. The viewer judges a program, against the other options, on merit and price, and thus becoming obligated to learn about pertinent categories of programs available, weighing expected satisfaction against price. These television programs acquire a *value* in the viewer perception just like any other commodity or service in the marketplace. With programs having a price, and a value, television is no longer a thing to be consumed casually without forethought—something of no value. There is a burden placed on the viewer; the quality of the viewing experience is not the responsibility of the programmer but a direct result of the discrimination and budget of the individual viewer.[3]

What is different in the new world of television on demand is the *economic incentive* to choose carefully from a larger body of programming offered at a wide range of prices—in other words, to become a discriminating viewer. By contrast, under the conventional "free" television program distribution system, the viewing of television is not different than the uses of other free goods. Television viewing may be controlled in terms of opportunity costs (i.e., the value of time spent on television versus the value of the time spent on other activities), but there are no direct costs. One may gorge on television without spending any money. Because all programs are equally "free," and have not acquired a value through the pricing mechanism, one does not judge a program by its cost relative to other programs. Therefore, the free television system is likely to result in television viewing that is not planned, selective, attentive, or purposeful.

Past television viewership studies support this conclusion. The studies have identified the decision to view television as most important.[4] Many people first decide to watch television and then find a program that is acceptable rather than going to television for a specific program. Uses and gratification studies that have investigated the relationship between audience needs or motivations and actual media uses make a fundamental distinction between content seeking and process seeking.[5] *Content seeking* is message use to gain knowledge, increase or reduce uncertainty in personal and social situations, or support existing predispositions. *Process seeking* means passive television viewing for the sake of viewing regardless of content, the gratification coming mainly from being involved in the process of communication behavior rather than the message content per se. For most people, television viewing is significantly associated with process seeking.[6]

Process gratification and audience inertia in television viewing have long concerned thoughtful people. Kubey and Csikszentmihalyi characterize conventional television as something of an instrument of desperation, turned to by the bored and lonely with "immediate rewards of low intensity."[7]

But, in the price discrimination model of television distribution, the viewer compares programs using the same convenient monetary standard we use for valuing other media products and consumer goods. Over time, this should result in a quantum change in the attitude toward television—as television acquires value, higher order rewards will be expected. The programming offered on demand will be most heavily promoted so as not to easily escape notice. Electronic television guides or navigators will provide a full description of the programming. The consumer may be aided by preselections coded according to interest in genre, performers, topic, and so on.[8]

Unfortunately, the economic incentives for developing discrimination in television only work for individuals with enough income to buy television by the program. Low-income persons are excluded from the opportunity to make many choices. We will discuss this matter further in considering universal access.

ACTIVE VIEWING

In Chapter 6, we expressed some skepticism about the desire for active viewing, suggesting that active participation in choosing plot, camera angles, and so on is inconsistent with the use of television drama for escape. Some people, some of the time, will want to be caught up in the cleverly crafted entertainment of the master television producers and writers, escaping into the hands of the creators, not interacting in any way, suspending disbelief for the moment. This seems most appropriate to adults attempting to relax in prime time after stressful days of work and interpersonal relationships, coping with children, bills, household repairs, and all the rest.

Nor may we desire information at our fingertips. In another era, we marveled at the fabulous information and entertainment resources in public libraries. Why was every chair not filled? Why were people not standing in the aisles between the rows of books reading? Will interactive home systems make information seeking so much more fun and convenient? Other leisure and purposive activities may be more rewarding. We may prefer to spend leisure time in more passive occupations. Limited education for some people may not permit entry into database information at the most satisfying levels. Or we may lack the curiosity to explore the opportunities presented by full service networks.

Nevertheless, some people, some times, may want the challenge of participation, responding to games, testing themselves against others, calling plays during sports events and comparing these with others', giving opinions, and hearing others' ideas. The sense of the rest of the audience (unseen or seen) that is created by such interaction will be rewarding. Speaking out, asserting oneself, could be cathartic. Calling the camera shots may be aesthetically satisfying. Acquiring knowledge for a specific purpose or just to learn a few new things by browsing information is stimulating.

One expects that interaction will be most enthusiastically embraced by younger people and children because they have less entrenched viewing habits and more energy. It is entirely possible that some members of the younger generations will come to prefer interactive television activities to the more placid forms, thus causing a shift of production resources into interactive media. Truly becoming involved in the programming may also come to have greater value as escape. For people accustomed to interactive media, the traditional forms *may not be engaging enough.* Eventually, a new standard for entertainment and information may emerge.

It is safe to say, for now anyway, that full service networks will not replace conventional media. The traditionalists will resist. Interactive formats will be crude; it will take time to perfect this form of programming and information. And there may always be a place for both, depending on the individual viewer's mood and energy level.

Assuming more active use of television suggests that the theories of audience-centered media activity will have a new test. One of the problems in studying uses and gratifications of media has been the limited variability in uses. Full service network subscribers will be (a) confronted by a wider range of utilities, (b) allowing the exercise of much greater selectivity as well as (c) content that is responsive to a greater variety of motivations and (d) permitting avoidance of certain media influences without avoiding media altogether.[9] With greater information resources, a fuller menu, and interactive options, the variability of gratifications will be further expanded.

OVERLOAD

In the old days of television, one easily fell into the habit of viewing at particular times. The television set was turned on and the channel might not have been changed until the set was turned off again, due to inertia. Now we come to full service networks where there are hundreds of channels of television entertainment and information services. Audio services, online information, and chat services are other options. We can take courses, vote, play games, talk back to our political representatives, work on personal matters (balance the electronic checking account), do work related to the job, read and respond to e-mail—any of the things we have talked about thus far as well as others that are now being invented.

Choosing *what* to do becomes a problem. But making a choice among the broad categories of activities is only the beginning. Within the category are still more choices. For the first time, cost must be factored into the decisions. Some of the most desirable activities will carry a price tag; others will have been prepaid, such as an à la carte channel. It is not difficult to imagine being overwhelmed by these options. One response would be to entirely reject the advanced services of integrated broadband networks because of the complexity and revert to plain old telephone and broadcast television. This is a danger that is supposed to be countered by the user-friendly navigational systems.

But even the consumer who accepts full service networks must learn some shortcuts. Preprogramming the navigational software to reflect interests helps to edit material for the individual. Further television channels can be selected, à la carte, to match up with one's interests—an individualized channel repertoire. Everything else, including the menus of on-demand material, can be ignored.

Although we may sometimes condemn media for gatekeeping, that function is extremely valuable. Digital broadband systems may allow us to make up our own newscasts from raw, unedited coverage and unlimited background files, but few will have time for it. Even though there may be errors or bias, a journalist has the skill to immediately cut to the most important aspects and interpretive background, often presented in an appealing style. Too narrow selection or too much reliance on others in this new environment, however, could be dysfunctional. If we narrow our categories of interest, and then set rigid budget limits on our usage, we risk missing items of general interest that fall outside the designated categories or budget. In the midst of plenty, we could become more narrow than we are now. Ideological, class, religious, and race associations might become stronger. Any member of any of these groups might have her or his news edited to present only commentators and sources that agree with personal philosophies. We need to be narrow enough in our selection to fit our information use and entertainment into a schedule while still being open to a regular sampling of information from general geographic and topical areas to establish the community of information that helps to bind us together and broaden perspectives.

There is a role for the educational system to play in preparing people in the skills necessary to systematize the selection process. This would be akin to teaching young people how to use library resources and is in addition to any educational program that might help students become more discriminating judges of "literature" available on the system.

There is indeed a danger of succumbing to the pleasures of this bountiful wire and coming to believe the new resource is a "window on the world" that can now enrich us beyond all previous dreams. McKibben, after immersion in megachannel television, where he viewed on tape the entire 24-hour output of an 80-channel system, offers a few sobering notes in *The Age of Missing Information*:

> I don't fret about TV because it's decadent or shortens your attention span or leads to murder. It worries me because it alters perception. TV, and the culture it anchors, masks and drowns out subtle and vital information contact with the real world once provided [what McKibben calls "fundamental information"].[10]

McKibben asserts that even our much-prized nature films on television are unreal because they eliminate boring reality to cut to the action-packed, close-range, high drama of the chase and kill. Cute and ferocious animals are overexposed. Endangered species are shown so often they seem plentiful. Television is commerce. In nature, we can't buy a thing. The "crackling urgency" of the news in

9.8-second sound bites is "information" but perhaps not "understanding" or "wisdom." "TV makes it so easy to postpone living for another half hour."[11] Even the great moments on television pass into oblivion. There is no time for reflection as "each line of thought is replaced by another." "If you could pick three conditions on earth to change in the next 50 years, would you want "advances"—picturephones, virtual reality, computer shopping—or would you want more quiet, more community, cleaner air?"[12]

ADVERTISING, SHOPPING, AND CONSUMERISM

As discussed in Chapter 9, shopping via television provides an opportunity for the consumer to be nearly perfectly informed, to become a much better consumer without the time investment this would have required in another period. There will be a much broader selection of merchandise for each purpose, and we can compare prices across all sources. The efficiencies of such a system, where the retail display space is replaced by interactive television and goods are shipped directly to consumers from manufacturers' warehouses, should reduce prices. The retailer, with the 100% markups, has been bypassed.

Advertising in the programs we watch and the information we request will more precisely fit our interests, either because the program itself is so narrow that it would attract only the appropriate advertisers, or because advertising is inserted specifically in our program based on our interests or demographic profile—the advertiser has purchased inserts in a particular program, but only for people meeting a specific description. Thus we are much more likely to be subjected to advertising that will be interesting.

But, at the same time, the "wedding of information and desire," as described by Shorris in *The Tyranny of the Market and the Subversion of Culture*, could become detrimental.[13] If we are to be dogged by merchants armed with extensive detail on our habits, interests, and past purchases, registered through all of our use of full service networks, we are in danger of becoming still more materialistic. We may be too weak to resist sales messages so precisely matched to our own behavioral profiles.

Commercial announcements will have to be consistently more intrusive to make an impact in the clutter of the integrated broadband networks. This would mean advertising prior to each program and information item ordered, interruptions at critical points, screens bordered with logos and sales messages, and other obstacles in the way of getting to the desired content. Full channels and menus will be commercial, where we can surrender to our most base materialistic selves fantasizing about what we might have and, when so moved, actually buying with the touch of a button.

It remains to be seen whether this society will give in to ever more commercial messages in exchange for discounts on the cost of the contents of broadband networks. Or will we learn to buy some information and entertainment at its full value without commercials? Our experience would tell us that U.S. society, already inured to commercialism, will continue to allow commerce to subsidize information and entertainment. The increasing cost of the contents of a full service broadband network may make this choice even more persuasive. It will take self-discipline, and money, to avoid excessive exposure to the commercial content.

SOCIAL ISOLATION

One can imagine an extreme case arising from integrated broadband services—the urban hermit, safely in rooms isolated from all physical human contact, electronically buying food, clothing (maybe not needing clothing), other necessities and amusements, working at a computer terminal, with perhaps an occasional video conference. Communities may be formed by such people through selective choice in using materials delivered by a broadband network and in communicating with remote and anonymous persons of like interests. These are valuable communities. Because they are so homogeneous, the relationships can develop great depth. But face-to-face social interaction is actually necessary for one's physical and mental health, and happiness.[14] The introverted, alienated person may use the network to become even more withdrawn. Crime, or fear of crime, disintegration of families, and other social problems might encourage such behavior, constituting an escape from these problems rather than a confrontation, and could exacerbate social pathologies. Cohen imagines:

The vision of the visionaries, I take it, is abandoned malls, boulevards of boarded-up stores, empty movie theaters—a zillion people sitting before a screen, zapping away for this or that service, each and every one of them in his own little world. If this is interactive video, it's a step backward to the time before people gathered in urban centers and exchanged the ideas that produced culture.[15]

The healthy version of the full service broadband environment is the use of the services for more efficiency in distasteful tasks (whatever they may be for an individual—shopping, homework, research, business communication, account balancing, and so on), thereby freeing time for more rewarding tasks (whatever they may be for an individual—watching movies, browsing on the Internet, socializing face-to-face, participating in sports, and so on). As full service communication systems develop, individuals should attempt to assess for themselves whether a positive balance occurs.

RESTRUCTURING OF TIME USAGE

The integrated broadband network, to the extent we can afford its optimal use, liberates time. It is no longer necessary to fit our schedule to the media schedule, except for live events. The freedom could be disorienting. Television, and radio, are used for "bracketing" one's day—brackets we may need for orientation. We set our mental clocks by the occurrence of news and other programs. Bracketing is still possible in the world of integrated broadband networks, but the user must learn to create the brackets.

In the advanced communication services environment, time given to television has a value. We will pay a high price for the best programming; lesser programming may come to be disdained. It could result in the rationing of time for television. Or we can splurge occasionally on big-ticket programs and degenerate into couch potatoes for hours of low-cost programs in between the splurges.

On a pragmatic level, it is possible to use the capabilities of interactive services to more efficiently allocate time to various household routines such as bill paying, shopping, and information seeking (e.g., for schoolwork). Other efficiencies may arise in such areas as travel time to work, which can be saved for telecommuters who engage in work activities from home. There is some evidence to suggest that, in fact, households are experiencing more constraints on their time, making it difficult to manage everyday activities.[16] Economic and demographic shifts have contributed to this problem. Perhaps most important has been the rise in the number of women who have entered the workforce in the past several decades, particularly those with small children. Inflationary pressures and other assaults on the household standard of living have encouraged more dual-career families. Patterns of divorce and remarriage have created new obligations across extended families, which also constrain time. High costs of housing near urban centers have forced many workers into long commutes, extending the average workday and infringing on the time available for household management and entertainment. Even the character of work itself, especially for those in competitive white-collar jobs, appears to require more work-related activities in the evenings and on weekends.

This suggests that for services to be popular, indeed to be used at all, they must help subscribers "find" time rather than simply consume it. Intelligent services that recognize the limited amount of free time that many people have will exploit information about prior usage (e.g., What type of movie did a subscriber last view, or what type of clothing was last purchased?) so as to suggest services. It further suggests that more *asynchronous* communication services will be valued, because the busier people are, the more difficult it will be to link up and converse in *real time* (witness the difficulty reaching someone on the first try with a cold telephone call). Finally, entertainment services normally consumed in longer blocks of time may need to offer people the ability to *chunk* services in more manageable units of time. For example, someone may only be able to view part of a movie ordered from a video-on-demand service in one sitting. They should not be charged a second time when wishing to finish the movie.

Increased work from home will in turn create new kinds of pressures and problems on household interaction. It may be difficult to remain disciplined in the face of all of the distractions, whether from children, entertainment materials, or the refrigerator, although evidence to date suggests the opposite.[17] Tensions among family members will no doubt arise as work pressures invade the private sphere of the home, taking up space for home offices and infringing on family interaction time.

PRIVACY ↵

Some of the benefits of full service networks require that the user sacrifice privacy, at least to the extent of giving information to the provider. As more communication goes from mail, telephone, and personal contact to full service networks, the danger of government or commercial eavesdropping becomes greater. Can we trust the provider and all of the provider's employees? Is the record so valuable to those who might want to sell us something, or do us harm, that temptations are placed before the company personnel that would cause them to breach our trust?

A difficulty is that, if we create worst-case, stringent safeguards, the system is burdened with such high costs that the economic viability of the service is threatened. It may be practical to offer optional security devices for some services, paid for by those who have the greatest concern, because of position or the nature of their transactions, thus preserving a lower-cost system for those who are not especially interested in security. Or people who are well informed about the personally identifiable data being gathered can abstain from certain uses. We must also bear responsibility for what we put into the system. Neither privacy law nor the First Amendment shields us from responsibility for libeling someone, presenting obscene messages in electronic communications, or proposing crimes.

As the value of entertainment and information on integrated broadband networks rises, attempts to defeat encryption and other security systems will increase concomitantly. Assuming that most thieves would buy the service if they couldn't steal it, the dishonest users put an additional cost burden on the paying customers. In addition to theft of services, the subscribers themselves will also be vulnerable to hackers who steal credit and telephone card numbers and other sensitive financial information. Data flowing between subscribers and the various services they use must be secure if any form of electronic commerce is to succeed.

MORAL QUESTIONS IN CYBERSPACE

Heim worries about electronic voyeurs seeking risk-free encounters in make-believe worlds.[18] In cyberspace, when speaking anonymously or misidentifying oneself, the usual ethical and moral values are not enforced. Are we entitled to trust others in cyberspace? Connell suggests that "the real challenge is building communication systems and user groups that function as moral, if not geographic communities." She relates the story of a parent disturbed to discover that a "boy" sharing a friendship on a teenage chat line was actually a 42-year-old pedophile.[19]

ECONOMIC IMPLICATIONS

Whatever the precise capital cost per household for full service communication, it will require increased consumer spending for its redemption. The cost will represent a significant income redistribution for the middle class. The high values of the middle class for education, diversity, technical novelty, and efficiency may make the cost bearable. There is also the possibility that some of the costs will be recovered through efficiency, as noted above.

Lower-income individuals are of greatest concern. It is tolerable to a society that certain individuals cannot afford a new car and a CD player. It is less tolerable that those individuals are denied access to lifeline communication services, educational materials, and vital information. Universal service from integrated broadband networks may be worked out through public policy with the participating industries subsidizing service to remote areas and some neighborhoods and/or contributing to a pool from which low-income households are given cash or "telecommunication vouchers" or "telephone stamps" for a basic level of service.

At the most fundamental level, access may mean only the right to have wired services or wireless substitutes available at reasonable rates. Much more generously, it could be plain old telephone service for every household or, still more generously, plain old telephone and cable's broadcast basic channels. This is probably the outer limit and is far more than we are now providing to people unable to pay the full cost. The National Telecommunications and Information Administration includes the following in universal service: touch-tone telephone, emergency services, equal access to long-distance carriers, and services for the hearing impaired.[20] A more extensive list offered by the California Intelligent Network Task Force includes an intelligent network, meaning access to databases, protocols for conversations between unlike computers, simultaneous voice and data, voice mail software delivery, videotex, audiotex, advanced "976" services, household security, health care monitoring, remote environmental control, and network access for disabled persons and those not fluent in English.[21]

But even at this previously unrealized level of subsidy, *access* to an integrated network, and even to the basic levels of service such as plain telephone and broadcast basic video, is relatively meaningless. People will have to have the dollars to buy programs and special services to fully realize the benefits. There will be serious "gaps" between the haves and the have-nots in the information society.

The first gap of concern is the *information gap*. A part of the society will have access to news and encyclopedic information at great depth and diversity, on demand. Use of such resources will stimulate a desire for even more information and use, and positively affect the earning power of the user while at the same time the technology is "accelerating the obsolescence of the information."[22] Thus, the gap between the best informed and least informed increases over time; an information underclass develops. Vice President Al Gore repre-sents the concern for the developing situation: "We cannot tolerate— nor in the long run can this nation afford—a society in which some children become fully educated and others do not; in which some adults have access to training and lifetime education, and others do not."[23] Less developed countries may suffer the information gap most acutely as they lag behind the "information societies." The language gap (generally meaning the inability to use English) exac-erbates the problem.

Perhaps less important to the well-being of the society, but cer-tainly important to individuals, is an *entertainment* (and *sports*) *gap*. The price discrimination system will siphon the best entertainment and big-time sports from "free" television, leaving an unhappy low-income television user with stale entertainment in the nth rerun and very little sports. We may no longer have *Murphy Brown,* Bill Cosby, ABC news, and Notre Dame football in common as a society. A *social gap* widens between higher-income people and the poor. The ability to communicate from a common base of knowledge across income groups deteriorates.

Perhaps the greatest sacrifice for low-income multichannel or broadcast-only households will be in the lost opportunity to develop a more discriminating use of television; a *gap in TV discrimination capability.* Low-income people may be left as the "couch potatoes," absorbing television leftovers indiscriminately, unlike the more affluent subscribers who are following economic incentives toward recognition of a value for television and more planned, selective viewing. Furthermore, the low-income household is more likely to be exposed to commercial content, because they will not be able to afford as much of the noncommercial, on-demand content of the digital, interactive broadband systems; a *gap in the ability to avoid commercials.*

There are still other gaps. The advanced network subscriber has the capability to become a discriminating shopper, conveniently gathering objective information on features and price. The low-income person, who could profit most from such a service, will have shopping services but probably not the objective product information and product evaluations—thus a *product information gap.*

A *child gap,* which could be of social and educational significance, develops between children in a full service network household and children without access. The non-FSN child has heavier commercial content, more limited programming, little of it age specific, and most designed for adult consumption, and as suggested above, the child does not have the benefit of the household economic forces that lead to learning discrimination in television viewing. The wealthy child has information and educational resources way beyond that available to the less well-to-do FSN child and the non-FSN child. We will create an information elite among children, disadvantaging the others and complicating formal education.

There will be an *urban-rural gap.* Rural households will have multichannel television services at a parity with urban households but will lack the interactive services. If integrated broadband networks do get into rural areas because they have become economically viable, or through a universal service subsidy, it will be late and only one provider will be available. The benefits of competition that could differentiate programming and services will not be available to the rural subscriber; a *freedom of choice gap.*

Specific solutions to the anticipated "gap" problems have been only vaguely suggested. Noam recommended a pooling of funds from all providers to be distributed to those who sign up subsidized subscribers.[24] What rules would be necessary to determine eligibility. What content would be required on the basic levels? Would prices at these levels be regulated?

Another possibility for closing the gaps is to have information kiosks in public places, including libraries and schools, and perhaps subsidize their use. This would assure city people, at least, of access. But a principal value of full service networks is convenience. Information from all sources around the world is available, on demand, at home. Lower-income schoolchildren might be minimally served through the schools, but this does not compare favorably with wealthy children who would have unlimited access at home daily and on weekends. Determining how to subsidize rural and poor households "without creating a cumbersome new entitlement system won't be easy."[25]

In sum, the full service, integrated broadband network subscriber of the future

> is more active in his or her selection of entertainment and information; is more discriminating because of the economic incentives to be aware of the options; comes to value television, that is, is not throwing away time (and money) on television; learns to interact with entertainment and information; prefers more involvement at least some of the time; uses navigational devices to cope with the abundance; risks being too narrowly exposed to information shared with few others; still needs gatekeepers to select the significant elements from the raw records of events; is in some danger of being seduced into thinking that an interactive information and entertainment system is comprehensive, thereby missing the information from other realities; has the opportunity to become an efficient consumer, but at the risk of being more enveloped in materialism, and could be more isolated although less private.

The low income multichannel television subscriber, or the household only accessing broadcast television may *suffer* an information gap, being less informed than those on the FSN; an entertainment and sports gap, if such programming migrates to higher cost distribution systems; a social gap resulting from a denial of video and information services common to the larger society; from a children's programming gap; from a surfeit of commercial content because of the limited option to view noncommercial programming; from less complete consumer information; from a gap in the capability to discriminate in television viewing developed more fully by people with economic incentives to be selective.

A full service network will not be entirely responsive to demand. Subscribers may have to buy through some services to access others. Some desired channels may be embedded in packages, not available à la carte.

As we have suggested earlier, "killer applications" of the interactive television technology probably will not be discovered. The most prominent application is video on demand, which might take a bite of the video store rental business. If video on demand were to get two-thirds of about $130 spent in the video store—$87 per year—it would add $7.25 per month to video revenues (providing VOD does not cannibalize other video revenue). If there are two competitors dividing this business, the revenue per system, per month, per subscriber is $3.63 for each—hardly enough in itself to justify the capital investment.

Competitors will be scratching and scrambling for this $3.63 per month and money from Internet users. Whatever revenues can be generated from games, home shopping, and some other services that might at this point be considered even more marginal. With the initial investment, the tremendous development costs to create these new products to use the network capacity, and after that, huge marketing costs to convince people they want them, the consumer cannot expect much benefit from *price* competition. And, compounding the problem, if competition works to stimulate innovation in service and programming through product differentiation, the consumer will have to pay to access two or more services to take full advantage of all of the products and programs born of competition. The household cost will go up. Lower consumer costs will *not* be a feature of the information superhighway.

Industry capital reserves and borrowing only initiate convergence. We can be certain that most of the costs for convergence will be carried by the full customer bases, of which a small number are using the full capacity of the systems. The circumstances demand cross subsidy, despite efforts to prevent it.

Although the higher-income consumers will eventually enjoy a revolution in home communication services, information, and entertainment, and have a more healthy attitude toward the use of television, in the short run, consumers will pay a heavy price for convergence. If ever, competition will only provide efficient prices over a very long time frame. Consumers will be making a monthly cash contribution now for future services that most of them will be hesitant to use until they overcome fears of technological novelty and their own inertia. There will be a long period of consumer sacrifice before demand catches up to the fully realized plans of integrated networks.

The sacrifice is probably necessary, but we should not be naive enough to expect immediate rewards for the average consumer as a result of integrated broadband system development. The rewards will come later, after considerable up-front investment by *consumers*.

Society 🕉

If individuals do not make a positive adjustment to full service networks, society could deteriorate. For example, a widening gap between the haves and the have-nots could be devastating to communication within the society.

COMMUNITY

Traditional communities, barely experienced in the most urban areas, could be lost to smaller places as well. That is, the human contact, the caring and responsibility for others, might be sacrificed to new loyalties to virtual communities. On the other hand, the new communities one joins electronically, not geographically circumscribed, could be deeply enriching and broadening. Universal service in this context could mean that humankind, across geographic boundaries, is united in new subcultures.

Additionally, there is a loss of community that once resulted from a common television viewing experience. Common viewing of mass appeal television programming has been reduced by multichannel television and will be further diminished by digital megachannel systems and on-demand programming.

MEDIA/JOURNALISM TRADITION

Integrated broadband networks arguably will become our most important First Amendment speakers as the principal gatherers, custodians, and distributors of information. The full service networks will have enormous editorial discretion in television programming and in accumulating and distributing databases. The resources of the systems will not be unlimited, particularly in the supply of *local* information, where one or two operators will be important gatekeepers. Even if there is an economic incentive to maximize the information resource—open the gates to everyone—there will be counterincentives to try to focus subscriber attention on the most profitable information, perhaps from sources owned by the system.

The gatekeeping responsibility for the distribution of information will come into the hands of businesspeople and managers who have only a layperson's exposure to the traditions and ethics of journalism. The fierce independence of journalists antagonistic to the institutions covered, at best, results in a surveillance of the society occasionally exposing malfeasance, incompetence, graft, corruption, and social problems. The aggressive protection of First Amendment rights is a part of the culture of journalism. Although there are other institutions sharing this interest, none attempts to practice free expression daily and is as quick to react to any encroachment. This culture has been developed over many years, supported by journalism societies, journalism schools, and the courts. It is not the culture of common carriers and cable operators. Whereas journalism has historically been the core business for newspapers, magazines, and, to a lesser degree, local broadcasters, it will be only a small part of the business of a full service network. We can expect the owners of the systems to lean toward preserving good relationships with regulatory authorities and away from rigorous reporting of government, economics, and sensitive social issues.

There is also the probability that local broadcast television news services will be reduced. One full service network with a 24-hour local news service could become dominant. One broadcast station might be sufficient to serve the dwindling number of broadcast-only television viewers. If so, there would be a net loss of one local television news source in the middle markets (perhaps markets 10-40)—a serious loss, because each source makes a unique contribution to the community.[26]

As the major means of distributing information, the broadband network to the home is a potential bottleneck in the marketplace of ideas especially given that we are unlikely to have more than two wired broadband systems in urban areas, and in the smaller markets, only one. Because of the potential of a corporate bias in selection, some safeguards to prevent the bottleneck are likely to be put in place. A few of these have already been suggested. One is to make the service a common carrier for at least part of its capacity, as in the cable commercial use (leased access) channels. A second is to set aside public, education, and government access channels as is now required in many cable franchises. A third safeguard is to monitor discriminatory distribution of channels as in the rules for vertically integrated cable operators. The assumption is that these regulations will carry over, in some form, from their use in cable applications to full service networks. Competition policy where it develops may stimulate efforts to present a full, well-rounded budget of information.

PUBLIC, EDUCATION, GOVERNMENT ACCESS

After the federal requirement for public, education, and government channels was vacated by a federal court, the channels remained under franchise agreements in many places. The requirement is now a contentious issue because telephone company providers of video service may not be franchisees although some have "volunteered" to offer the channels.

Are these channels important to the community? Government and education channels can also be useful for internal and external (public) information. It is clear in many places, however, that government and education agencies must make a greater investment to create meaningful channels. Furthermore, in a full service network, government and educational institutions have more to offer than video service. City records, zoning ordinances, building codes, property assessments, and other databases could be available. School courses, assignments, research materials, audiovisual library materials, sample tests, goals and objectives for each grade level and course, announcements, and more could be there in various formats. Will full service network capacity be available for these data, and on what terms?

Proponents would argue that public access channels are vital to community expression in an environment otherwise controlled by the system provider. Creating a *public forum* on a broadband network, video or data, requires recognition that it cannot later be withdrawn to avoid disagreeable content.[27] The concept of free expression is not fully understood, or even condoned, by the public when the content is judged offensive, despite the First Amendment and American traditions. Maintenance of public channels carries an obligation by the community and the broadband networks to educate the public to an understanding of the functions and to disassociate the network provider from the public users.

ECOLOGY

There is also an ecological interest in developing interactive broadband networks. It takes about 27,000 trees to produce the Sunday *New York Times*. Discarded newspapers represent 7% to 10% of municipal solid waste—6% of the total landfill.[28] Although full service networks will not replace newspapers, they may deliver news electronically and only print items of specific importance to the user.

Communication Industries

A profound change is overcoming the communication industries. They are on the verge of an exceptional service to residential and business users, offering potential access to the entire world supply of information interactively in data, voice, and video. As we have outlined in the previous chapters, media, information, and communication industries need to redefine themselves, amass tremendous amounts of capital, engage in substantial construction and reconstruction, and then create markets for new products. New relationships between suppliers, the broadband networks, and the consumers will form.

STRUCTURAL

Several independent industries each have a part of the broad scale of business that will go to full service networks. These companies must now join forces to assimilate the necessary capabilities, hence, the convergence of Silicon Valley, Hollywood, common carriers, cable operators, and broadcasters. They will join not only to share expertise and capital but to share the risk. There will be a clash of disparate corporate cultures. Because the companies joining are all leaders in their independent industries, they will not fit comfortably into a new industry where roles are not well defined.

In particular, the cable industry must concentrate geographically. As we pointed out in Chapter 7, it will be difficult to efficiently manage a metropolitan service area that integrates voice, video, and data when there are a great many individual franchise holders, especially in competition with RBOCs which are already well integrated over several states. The need to cluster systems is now forcing each cable system into a strategic decision: to acquire capital, get bigger, and begin building, or sell out.

It is plausible to envision seven RBOCs and one large independent telephone company, each evolving to an integrated broadband network in its own service area. Then, perhaps a like number of geographically concentrated cable operators, serving areas of similar size. If the resulting 16 are about equal in size, none would control as much as 10% of the market. Nonetheless, even a modest degree of horizontal integration gives a company significant power over television programmers and information services as well as the potential to deny services to subscribers. Some channels serving the narrowest niches will need almost all of the broadband networks nationwide to break even. Advertiser-supported networks would be at a distinct disadvantage in national markets if they did not have full national distribution.

Cable operators are already vertically integrated with programmers. Three RBOCs are attempting to form partnerships in Hollywood. Cable and telephone companies are aligning with software designers and hardware manufacturers. Broadcast networks are "in play," with Hollywood studios, cable MSOs, and telephone companies all mentioned as prospective buyers. Most of the converging companies are also buying into or creating online services, a business strategy useful in its own right and as a stepping stone to integrated broadband networks. We can expect that in the end the new industry will thoroughly integrate the businesses of television and audio production, multimedia production, program distribution, database creation and distribution, and broadband networks to the home.

A vertically integrated network will not be permitted to deny access to competitive programming, deny its products to competitors, or discriminate in the conditions of affiliation or price. But a vertically integrated broadband network can promote its owned content and services heavily, to the neglect of the others. Promotion is critical because of the difficulties a subscriber may have in choosing and finding content in the plethora of options available on a digital broadband system. Of course, any program, network, or information service can buy time for cross promotion, but if the system uses *unsold* advertising availabilities for promotion of its owned content, it has a promotional cost advantage. The full service network could also favor a new owned network by packaging it with another very popular network at a discounted price.

It is also possible that a vertically integrated full service network with substantial market power might deliberately attempt to keep the number and diversity of programs and information services to a minimal level, so that audiences are not too fragmented and the services they own get greater attention. Advertising demand and prices in this limited environment might be high enough to offset revenue losses from nonowned services.

Vertical integration could have the healthy effect of stimulating programming if competing full service networks seek to differentiate content. They may make major investments in programs and information to distinguish their particular network. If there is an aggressive attempt at product differentiation, and more money for product investment, we can look for integrated broadband networks to stimulate program development.

Overall, there is a real possibility of less money for mass appeal programming—the most costly programming—because digital broadband networks offer so much diversity that there are no more mass audiences. The dilution of audiences could cause a deterioration of the quality of television. More likely, however, are lower budget programs of reasonably good quality, with the industry learning, of necessity, how to keep costs down.

AFTERMARKETS

Full service networks will exploit television programming through many windows and price levels, as described in Chapter 6. By the time an integrated broadband network has exhausted all its exhibition opportunities, broadcast syndication may be of only minor significance. If, after full development of digital broadband networks, there are fewer broadcasters, the lower-income households, unable to buy into full service network programming, have even less choice and, at that, among old materials.

In this circumstance, the relative strengths in negotiating rights fees between a program owner and full service system become of interest. Now, programs in syndication are auctioned in the broadcast television markets, where there can be four or more bidders. In the age of full service networks, there will be at most two wireline television bidders for programming when it is still fresh and at its peak in value. These broadband distribution networks may have an advantage in settling on the split for all but the blockbuster films and programs.

OPERATIONAL

We have described elsewhere the operational challenges in creating integrated broadband networks. The coordination and integration of traffic across so many sources and applications present challenges that have already caused delays in the rollout of market tests.

As much as full service networks try to develop user-friendly "customer interfaces," they will *not* be hospitable to some people. The fear of computerlike home services will repel a large body of potential users. Those who do subscribe have to deal with all of the electronic devices for accessing services. These cannot be built into the home terminal or a single remote unit because the uses and users will be so varied. As the devices proliferate, frustration grows.

CULTURE

As we have emphasized here, integrated broadband networks with content ownership become First Amendment speakers assuming journalistic functions. If a broadband network is a communication medium, with life-or-death editorial discretion, and is one of two media or is the only such medium in a community, democracy will require an immediate, not gradual, transition by the network to this novel First Amendment speaker role. In fact, as the central resource for information and entertainment, the full service network eventually will become a medium of far greater influence and power than any yet experienced. System managers will not be able to shy from this role. There will be social pressure for telecommunication executives to assure the openness of the network and look at the overall service for its balance and comprehensiveness.

What happens to other media as full service networks develop? They will, of course, be sources of content for full service networks and wireless competitors. As Daniel Boornstein has said, "New technology forces the old technology into new niches."[29] But newspapers, radio, television, magazines, video stores, and movie theaters can survive entertainment and information delivered by full service broadband networks, more or less intact, because of some of the specific values of these sources, for example, the hard copy and portability of the newspaper, the portability of radio, the high gloss and portability of magazines, the large screen and audience at the movie theater, or the hands-on selection and social occasion of video store rentals. These media sources, with these special characteristics, can all be priced competitively against the full service network products at the same time as being among their suppliers.

Business Structure

The increased use of integrated broadband networks for all forms of transactions, including shopping, banking, and accessing a variety of services, may have profound effects on the structure of industries. One school of thought argues that such use of networks lowers the many types of costs that formerly precluded firms from marketing products directly to end customers (e.g., advertising, promotion, and maintaining local retail outlets that carry sufficient inventories). Proponents here suggest that the primary impact, then, will be the dismantling of traditional *value chains*, the set of organizations and activities through which raw materials flow as they become valuable products that are then marketed and distributed to end customers.[30] Essentially, the traditional *intermediaries*, such as retail stores and various service agencies (e.g., travel agencies), will get bypassed under such a scenario, because their functions can now be subsumed by electronic networks at lower cost to the original suppliers of goods and services.[31]

There is another school of thought, however, that argues for the continued existence of traditional intermediaries, and possibly the evolution of new types of entities serving an intermediate role in the flow of goods and services. Some authors point out the other functions intermediaries fill in addition to holding inventory and displaying products and services. Included here are absorbing risks (e.g., sharing the costs of defective products and taking back returned goods), evaluating alternative offerings for buyers, and persuading or selling (e.g., the familiar, "My, that looks good on you!" heard from every clothing salesperson).[32] Evaluative functions will probably be even more important in electronic commerce, because goods and services may be offered by many distant suppliers who are unfamiliar to local audiences. Someone will need to vouch for quality. Perhaps the full service network itself will become this new intermediary.

Throughout this book, and particularly in Chapter 10, we have detailed the plans to make integrated broadband networks competitive with the market itself, regulating telecommunication prices and services. We have also pointed out the naïveté of expecting competition, in the oligopoly that results, to achieve all the social and economic goals for the information infrastructure. Cross subsidy by telephone companies can occur simply by building hybrid fiber coaxial broadband networks and overestimating the proportion of the usage of the network for nonvideo services. Cross subsidy occurs when cable companies upgrade for telephone service and allocate too much of the cost to video. In these cases, the broad base of existing telephone company subscribers, and the cable operator's video subscribers, will be paying for service that they may not want for themselves. While higher-income consumers enjoy a revolution in home communication services, lower-income households, reluctant or unable to participate initially, may be paying as well. Cities in which full service networks develop first will be subsidized by cities in other areas of the providers' regions.

Integrated broadband network development will be slow-paced because of public policy indecision, delays in technical development, fears about marketability, high capital cost, and the relative comfort of current monopolies. Furthermore, immediate profit opportunities from international investment are siphoning capital and energy from the more advanced and speculative communication services in the United States. Many countries have inadequate and poorly penetrated telephone services that are being privatized. Multichannel television is just beginning to develop in a number of countries, opening investment opportunities in both infrastructure and programming.

Almost all U.S. investment in telecommunication and multichannel television services abroad has been with partners from within the market. The United States will certainly take leadership in designing system architecture and will supply hardware and management systems. The operational role will be reduced fairly rapidly as local expertise develops.

As we indicated in Chapter 12, content on digital broadband systems must be culturally compatible. Successful U.S. television and information services are now being customized to satisfy outside markets. These services still represent the U.S. culture. Perhaps more accurately, they have played a role in creating U.S. *television subcultures* now too diversified to any longer be representative of the general culture. These products will be exported, creating television subcultures in the importing places. The television subcultures, because they are quite narrow, are not likely to have overall cultural impact. The new communities of interest established will be socially beneficial, particularly if the flow of programming is not entirely one way.

That information databases will be diffused internationally through integrated broadband systems as the networks become available, as promised by the Internet experience. In 1994, the Internet was fully available in 75 countries and in simple e-mail in 77 more.[33] Scholars will soon be comparing the proportion of data on the Internet (and other online services) by country of origin to know more about the flow and use of data.

This book has attempted to describe the next plateau of communication services for the home. It will not evolve in every detail as we have presented it here. We have been careful to outline all of the tremendous technical, economic, and public policy challenges in making it work. Also, social inequities inherent in the system must be addressed. Consumers must learn to use the system and place a high enough value on its content and services to pay its price. Although we may not be at the threshold of a communication utopia, if these challenges and issues can be resolved, a new communication system integrating broadband and wireless services will come into common usage. It will be an achievement of major proportion.

Notes

1. Carrie Heeter, "The Choice Process Model," in *Cableviewing*, ed. Carrie Heeter and Bradley S. Greenberg (Norwood, NJ: Ablex, 1988), 11-32; Joey Reagan, "From 'Dependency' to the Repertoire of Information Sources" (paper presented at the annual meeting of the Broadcast Education Association, Las Vegas, Nev., 1993); James Webster, "The Impact of Cable and Pay Cable on Local Station Audiences" (Washington, DC: National Association of Broadcasters, 1982).

2. In the near future, the development of electronic guide technology will enable each member of a household to preprogram his or her preferences so that the available programs in that preference will be called to the screen instantly.

3. Concepts in this section are based on an earlier work: Thomas F. Baldwin and Sug-Min Youn, "The Evolution of Viewer Discrimination in the New World of Television" (paper presented at the annual meeting of the International Association for Mass Communication Research, Seoul, Korea, July 1994).

4. G. Bowman and J. Farley, "TV Viewing: Application of a Formal Choice Model," *Applied Economics* 4 (1972): 245-259; A. Bruno, "The Network Factor in TV Viewing," *Journal of Advertising and Marketing Research* 13, no. 5 (1973): 33-39; R. E. Frank, J. C. Becknell, and J. D. Clokey, "Television Program Types," *Journal of Marketing Research* 8 (March 1971): 204-211; D. Gensch and P. Shaman, "Models of Competitive Television Ratings," *Journal of Marketing Research* 17 (1980): 307-315.

5. E. Katz, J. G. Blumler, and M. Gurevitch, "Utilization of Mass Communication by the Individual," in *The Uses of Mass Communications: Current Perspectives on Gratifications Research*, ed. J. G. Blumler and E. Katz (Beverly Hills, Calif.: Sage, 1974).

6. Walter Gantz, "How Uses and Gratifications Affects Recall of Television News," *Journalism Quarterly* 55 (1978): 664-672, 681.

7. Robert Kubey and Mihaly Csikszentmihalyi, *Television and the Quality of Life* (Hillsdale, NJ: Lawrence Erlbaum, 1990), 174.

8. For example, lists of children's programming will be available by age group and perhaps by prosocial program titles sanctioned by a group such as the Parent Teachers Association (PTA).

9. Based on the meanings for the term *activity*, suggested by J. G. Blumler, "The Role of Theory in Uses and Gratifications Studies," *Communication Research* 6 (1969): 9-36.

10. Bill McKibben, *The Age of Missing Information* (New York: Random House, 1992), 22-23.

11. McKibben, *Age of Missing Information*, 201.

12. McKibben, *Age of Missing Information*, 246.

13. Earl Shorris, *The Tyranny of the Market and the Subversion of Culture* (New York: Norton, 1994).

14. Herbert J. Gans, "The Electronic Shut-Ins: Some Social Flaws of the Information Superhighway," *Media Studies Journal* 8, no. 1 (1994), 125.

15. Richard Cohen, "Visions of Tomorrow," *Media Studies Journal* 8, no. 1 (1994), 116.

16. K. Dudley, C. Steinfield, R. Kraut, and J. Katz, "Rethinking Residential Tele-communications Needs," Bellcore Technical Manuscript (Morristown, NJ: Bellcore, July 1993).

17. Home workers appear to be *more* productive than their traditional counterparts. Remarks prepared for delivery by Vice President Al Gore, Royce Hall, UCLA, Los Angeles, California, 11 January 1994. The complete text of the speech may be found in: gopher://ntiant1.ntia.doc.gov:70/00/papers/speeches/files/gore_telecom_spch011194.txt.

18. Paraphrased from Michael Heim by Joan Connell, "Virtual Reality Check: Cyberethics, Consumerism and the American Soul," *Media Studies Journal* 8, no. 1 (1994), 155.

19. Connell, "Virtual Reality Check," 156.

20. "The NTIA Infrastructure Report: Telecommunications in the Age of Informa-tion," NTIA Special Publication 91-26 (Washington, DC: U.S. Government Informa-tion Service).

21. "Pacific Bell's Response to the Intelligent Network Task Force Report" (San Francisco: Pacific Bell, 1988).

22. Andrew Dixon, "Cable Holds the Key to Lifetime Learning," *Multichannel News*, 27 February 1995, 59.

23. Jack Nilles, *Making Telecommuting Happen: A Guide to Telemanagers and Telecom-muters* (New York: Van Nostrand Reinhold, 1994).

24. Pearl, "Universal Access Rights," A12.

25. Pearl, "Universal Access Rights," A12.

26. Tony Atwater, "Product Differentiation in Local TV News," *Journalism Quar-terly* 61, no. 4 (1984): 757-762. The loss of one assumes that originally there were ABC, CBS, and NBC affiliates in the market offering local news. If this reduces to one, and the full service network adds one, the net loss is one.

27. Michael O. Wirth and Linda Cobb-Reiley, "A First Amendment Critique of the 1984 Cable Act," *Journal of Broadcasting & Electronic Media* 31, no. 4 (1987): 391-407.

28. Ralph L Lowenstein, "The Electronic Newspaper and Journalism Education" (paper presented at the annual meeting of the Association for Education in Journalism and Mass Communication, Atlanta, Ga., August 1994).

29. Daniel Boornstein, Celebrity Lecture Series, Michigan State University, East Lansing, 16 May 1994.

30. For a discussion of the notion of the value chain, see M. Porter, *Competitive Advantage* (New York: Free Press, 1985).

31. R. Wigand and R. Benjamin, "Electronic Markets and Virtual Value Chains on the Information Superhighway," *Sloan Management Review*, Winter 1995, 62-72.

32. M. Sarkar, B. Butler and C. Steinfield, "Intermediaries and Cybermediaries: A Continuing Role for Mediating Players in the Electronic Marketplace," *Journal of Computer Mediated Communication*, 1, no. 3 (Available online at: http: //www.usc.edu/ dept/annenberg/vol 1/issue 3/vol 1 no. 3. html)

33. John W. Verity and Robert D. Hof, "The Internet: How It Will Change the Way You Do Business," *Business Week*, 14 November 1994, 82.

Index

About the Authors

Thomas F. Baldwin is Distinguished Professor in the Telecommunication Department of Michigan State University and was a Visiting Professor at the Chinese University of Hong Kong. His research has been funded by the National Science Foundation, Ford Foundation, and the Corporation for Public Broadcasting. With McVoy, he is author of *Cable Communication* (second edition). He is also author of *Cable Advertising* and numerous book chapters and academic articles.

Joonho Do is a fourth-year doctoral candidate in the Department of Telecommunication at Michigan State University. His research interests focus on the social use and economic impact of new communication technology, with particular attention to the implications for the multichannel industry. His paper, "An Economic Analysis of the Pay-Per-View Industry," coauthored with Barry Litman, won the annual award of Broadcast Education Association/Broadcast Cable Financial Management Association in 1994 and was published in *Broadcast Cable Financial Journal.* His most recent paper, "Assessment of Information Use via Internet," was presented at the 1995 annual convention of International Communication Association.

D. Stevens McVoy, Adjunct Professor at Michigan State University and Ohio State University, is an owner of several cable systems and a competitive access provider telephone service. He holds a number of patents in the communication area and is the author of several technical papers. In the early 1970s, he developed the first commercial two-way, pay-per-view television service. In 1974, he designed and built—with Thomas Baldwin and others at Michigan State and the Rockford, Illinois cable operator—an interactive television system used for training firefighters, teachers' in-service, and hospital applications.

Charles Steinfield is Professor in the Telecommunication Department at Michigan State University. He recently won a Fulbright Research Award in France and the MSU Teacher-Scholar Award. He is editor of the books *Telecommunications in Transition: Policies, Services and Technologies in the European Community* and *Organizations and Communication Technology* as well as several academic articles. He was previously employed by Bellcore's Applied Research Laboratory and was a Visiting Professor at the Institut National des Telecommunications (INT) in Evry, France.

Joseph D. Straubhaar is Professor of Communications and Director of the Communications Research Center, Department of Communications, Brigham Young University. He is on leave as a Professor in the Department of Telecommunication, Michigan State University. He worked as a Foreign Service Officer and research analyst for the U.S. Information Agency. He has published extensively on television in Brazil, regionalization of television markets in Latin America and Asia, *telenovelas,* television and politics in Latin America, new video technologies in the Third World, international spread of VCR and cable TV, television flows between countries, and privatization of telephone systems in the Third World.